administering
and controlling

THE COMPANY
DATA PROCESSING
FUNCTION

administering
and controlling
THE COMPANY
DATA PROCESSING
FUNCTION

Leonard I. Krauss

PRENTICE-HALL, INC.   Englewood Cliffs, N.J.

PRENTICE-HALL INTERNATIONAL, INC., *London*
PRENTICE-HALL OF AUSTRALIA, PTY. LTD., *Sydney*
PRENTICE-HALL OF CANADA, LTD., *Toronto*
PRENTICE-HALL OF INDIA PRIVATE LTD., *New Delhi*
PRENTICE-HALL OF JAPAN, INC., *Tokyo*

LIBRARY OF CONGRESS
CATALOG CARD NUMBER: 69–14439

Eleventh Printing..... March, 1979

PRINTED IN THE UNITED STATES OF AMERICA
B&P

acknowledgments

I wish to express my sincere appreciation to those EDP practitioners who, over the years, have given me the opportunity to share their problems, learn from their experience, and benefit from their wise counsel.

The author is deeply grateful for the painstaking editorial assistance provided by his father, William Krauss. The author is also especially indebted to Bill Kloepfer and Don Miller who critically reviewed the final manuscript and made many helpful and valuable suggestions for its improvement.

A word of thanks is also due to Miss Dolores Neumann and Mrs. Marry André who typed the final manuscript and saw to other details in the preparation of this book.

Last, but not least, I must thank my wife, Sharon, for her enduring patience and also for her assistance in proofreading.

the author

Leonard I. Krauss is a consultant to managements of U. S. and foreign corporations in the area of systems planning and management and is president of the New York based management consulting firm, Leonard I. Krauss Associates. He brings to bear in this book his experience as both a consultant and manager in the computer and information systems field. The author has been directly responsible for numerous financial and industrial information systems projects, covering a range that includes basic data processing, real-time on-line systems, computer-microfilm hybrid applications, and management planning and control systems employing advanced operations research techniques.

A registered professional industrial engineer, Mr. Krauss has earned the CDP (Certification in Data Processing). He is listed in *Who's Who in Computing* and is a popular speaker at international management and systems conferences.

The author has been an officer and director of several companies, a director of management information systems, a project manager, and an applied systems engineer. Earlier in his career, he was associated with Union Carbide and IBM.

Mr. Krauss holds an MBA and a BS in industrial engineering and is the author of another currently popular book, *Computer-Based Management Information Systems*, published by the American Management Association.

the purpose
of this book

This book concerns the management of electronic data processing—its people, its problems, and its potential. A guide for managerial action, its purpose is to show how to act instead of react, and to provide adaptable methods to overcome the "view with alarm" syndrome that prevails today.

To grasp fully the subject matter covered, readers should at least understand EDP basics. The book does not purport to tell the reader all he needs to know. Instead, it supplements information gained by direct experience, offered in other books, presented at industry seminars, and taught in advanced university courses.

Focusing on key administrative issues, this book is written especially for executive and managerial personnel who are responsible for activities at all levels of the EDP function. Its initial assumption is that there are definitive courses of action which can either handicap the EDP effort or make it a planned, cohesive activity in a business enterprise, in government, or any other type of organization. The objective here has been to integrate modern management principles with firsthand experience in a way which suits the unique needs of computer work. To this end, the book examines topics of major importance in an attempt to provide a useful set of principles and guidelines for professional managers in electronic data processing.

Chapter two, for example, offers a unique discussion on EDP organization types. Here, the reader should gain a better understanding of organizational approaches that may be applied to his own company's EDP function.

Chapter four deals with the topic of project management. Many companies are learning that large systems development projects require a new approach. An adaptable approach is described in this chapter, to meet the rapidly growing need to develop and implement major systems.

Chapter eight examines modern data center management problems. The administration of computer operations and the control of data processing activities are areas which have experienced many critical problems resulting from changes in technology together with increased demand for computer service. This chapter attempts to take a new look at some old problems and, in addition, describes how to deal with more recent problems.

Other chapters deal with specific EDP management areas that have proved to be most critical to success.

Readers will note that some of the topics developed in this book begin by discussing what goes wrong. This is intentional: the idea is to pinpoint problem areas where trouble is experienced most often. Having focused on the vulnerable areas, methods to either avoid or correct the problems are explored. The EDP accomplishments glowingly reported in slick magazines usually forget to do this—which may help explain why computer people run into so much trouble.

This book attempts to accomplish more than just educate readers about key EDP problems and how to solve them. It is also intended to stimulate EDP executives and managers into thinking about their own experiences and developing sound management approaches from a workable blend of philosophy and firsthand knowledge. It is hoped that this book will act as both a catalyst and source material in producing such a blend.

An appraisal of the management problem

Beneath the glamour and excitement of computing technology, companies are discovering that they cannot do much with the technology until they learn how to manage its application. Until recent times, top management has let itself be overwhelmed by the continual barrage of glowing claims about computer successes. Having learned that the successful development and use of computing systems demands shrewd, professional management, a number of businessmen are giving technology less emphasis. They are now asking serious questions like "How do we manage the effort of getting from here to there?" rather than issuing directives. Answers are coming, but slowly.

This change in emphasis is occurring because results have not been appearing. Noteworthy actions have been forthcoming as a result. For example, the EDP organization has not only changed hands in many corporations, but it has also changed character. In some, the EDP function has emerged from relative obscurity to become the sole responsibility of a high level, corporate executive. This man's responsibility is to see that the whole company gets the benefits of EDP. With the backing of the president, there is, for the first time, a good chance that this will happen. But, even such an impressive change is only a start. There are many other equally important challenges to be faced.

Underscoring the urgency to get workable answers are such statements as: "*The day may not be far distant when those who analyze annual business failures can add another category to their list of causes—failure to exploit the computer.*"[1] More executives are stating that they are using, and expect to continue to use, the computer to "beat competition." To be able to do this implies being "on top" of the problems involved in managing the computer function. It also implies that top management will know how to exploit computer capabilities. Acquiring this knowledge too late can, of course, dull the competitive edge to the point of business failure—there comes a time when it is too late to catch up. In the opinion of the author, there is already much catching up to be done by many companies, if they are ever to be able to keep pace with competition in management uses of the computer.

Projections show that computer sales will be more than $25 billion by 1975 and that computer users will be spending over $50 billion on computer related activities annually at that time. Growing at the current rate of 20 per cent a year, computer sales are expanding at triple the rate of the automobile industry. At this booming rate, the computer industry ranks first in growth. Considering that EDP personnel costs are roughly equal to EDP equipment costs, many thousands of new jobs are created in the process of this growth. Many new problems and managerial challenges are evolving as well.

One writer, in discussing some of the challenges and problems businessmen have confronted regarding electronic data processing, has aptly said:

> Swept along by the wave of mass media generated enthusiasm, many companies plunged into the significant investment represented by automatic data processing. But to their chagrin they soon discovered that the cost and effort of installing equipment was just the top of the iceberg.[2]

---

[1]Neal J. Dean, "The Computer Comes of Age," *Harvard Business Review*, January–February 1968, p. 91.

[2]William A. Bocchino, *A Simplified Guide to Automatic Data Processing* (Englewood Cliffs, N.J.: Prentice-Hall Inc., 1966), p. 3.

The *iceberg principle* is well known in computing circles. Simply put, it means that the visible problems and expenses are but a small part of the entire picture. Executives and managers have, from time to time, been offered some good advice on these iceberg matters. The following list is representative:

—Demand specifics on anticipated cost-reductions. Be sure to understand the how, when, where, and who aspects. Insist on getting clear explanations.

—Get the "slop" out of current methods. Streamlining here will help put a firm base under new computer operations.

—Beware of proposals which do not offer alternatives. There are always other approaches— demand to see them.

—Make certain that the reasons for putting a job on the computer are valid. Jobs of marginal or doubtful return should not be computerized simply to cut down idle time.

—Require ways and means to measure benefits. Get deadlines, target dates, credible cost estimates and plans.

—Insist on a schedule for development and be sure that it has progress milestones which can be checked. Management controls are "must" items and should be present in the plan.

—Be sure that any major jobs include plans calling for implementation steps or phases— a gradual switchover. Always get realistic answers on recovery procedures in case the new computer job should fail "hard" during start-up.

While the foregoing list is a step in the right direction, it presupposes a capability to penetrate somewhat beyond superficial appearances. One of the things this book is designed to do is to arm its reader with a better grasp of what is involved in tackling points such as those listed.

The editor of *Business Automation* made this comment regarding the management problem:

> . . . Benjamin Franklin once said that "one of the great tragedies of life is the murder of a beautiful theory by a gang of brutal facts." Such a theory is the supposition that business enterprises can take full advantage of modern data processing technology merely by plugging in a computer. The facts are eloquent to the contrary. Be it first, second, third or later generations of computer power, it will benefit the user only to the degree that top management accepts its responsibility for harnessing and monitoring the power.[3]

Another part of the management problem has been due to the fact that computers have been taken out of the scientific laboratory environment and pressed into action for business administration activities. Most scientific computer work has rigorous and highly ordered processing requirements. Business procedures, on the other hand, have not been subject to this level of organization, since they are an admixture of judgment, common sense, word-of-mouth, and even habit. Defining the business problem, therefore, is a task of substantial proportions. It is often difficult because, unlike mathematics and other sciences, so much has been taken for granted. Drawing out and logically representing the assumptions involved is a process subject to many oversimplifications and oversights. Despite these difficulties, there is no other way to computerize. The problem of definition must be solved head-on. Short cuts in this area produce an inevitable result ranging from mediocrity to outright failure.

Other management challenges stem from the fact that the business activity or problem does not often stand still while people eagerly go about solving it. In a sense, it is like shooting at a moving target. A computer solution to a business problem has to be able to track the problem in a dynamic state. Managing change, as in other parts of the business, is another important facet of EDP management.

---

[3]Arnold Keller, "Third Generation," *Business Automation*, January 1967, p. 24.

Because of the factors just described, a proportionately heavier burden for planning, control, and leadership must be assumed by EDP management. Very often, this has not happened. In fact, there is plenty of evidence to suggest that just the opposite has taken place (see Chapter ten). Accompanying this phenomenon are many expensive computerized systems which have been ill-conceived and which can never be justified. As it has turned out, numerous managers have found themselves dealing with so many crises on a day-to-day basis that only a handful have been able to put any meaningful effort into shaping future developments.

How this book is organized

Each chapter in this book corresponds to a major data processing management area. A full range of subject coverage is offered to guide both new and experienced managers. EDP functions of all sizes are addressed. Readers will also find that much of the material is directed toward managing an existing EDP function. However, certain topics are intended especially for an installation about to be organized.

Depending upon the stage of development and size of the EDP function with which the reader is concerned, some management approaches presented require custom tailoring. Some approaches are discussed in the context of a larger organization and may have to be scaled down to accommodate a smaller one. For example, the project management approach covered in Chapter four is oriented to larger installations. However, this does not preclude its adaptation, in modified form, to a smaller installation.

Chapter one, *Planning the EDP Function*, describes how top management must participate in EDP and how to encourage top management sponsorship. It also explains how to decide on application objectives and plan for the development and implementation of computer automated systems. Feasibility studies are explained and tips on how to run and evaluate them are given. Management consultants and pointers on their use are discussed here. Guidelines for high-level management planning and control are also provided in the chapter.

Chapter two, *Organizing EDP Activities*, discusses and illustrates a variety of EDP organization types. Some organizations described are set up on functional lines, others have a project orientation, and still others represent a combination of the two. Trends in EDP organization are discussed, and additional organization charts are provided to show the direction these trends are taking.

Chapter three, *Systems Development and Programming Administration*, covers the management of the effort to produce an application system. Each step in the process is described, with key management points highlighted. A separate section in this chapter is devoted to coordination and controls for systems and programming. Work activity controls, the management of system changes, and documentation types and standards are described and illustrated. This chapter also covers time and cost estimating methods for programming and offers a short discussion on evaluating results.

Chapter four, *Using Project Management in EDP*, is devoted to the management of major systems development projects. It gives criteria for setting up a project, describes the project manager, and shows how to organize multiple projects within the framework of the EDP organization. The 13 steps in the the life of a project are discussed, and management pointers are given for the planning and control of each. The administration of contracts for EDP work done by software firms is also covered.

Chapter five, *Acquiring, Evaluating, and Managing Installation Personnel*, discusses personnel planning and the characteristics required of people in certain EDP positions. Interviewing practices and measurement of aptitude for EDP personnel are explored in this chapter. This chapter also shows how to use various sources for personnel recruitment and examines EDP salary administration. Promotions and career development are discussed here, in addition to a short presentation on professionalism in EDP. Other sections explain how to evaluate, motivate, and get cooperation from EDP personnel.

Chapter six, *Educating and Training Management and EDP Personnel*, discusses requirements for various EDP positions and how to educate top executives. Various methods and means of education and training are described and evaluated. Education in EDP is examined, together with subject and course outlines, as it pertains to managerial personnel, systems analysts, programmers, machine operators and others. Tips on running in-house training programs are provided, as well as a discussion on educational materials and training aids.

Chapter seven, *Considerations for Evaluating and Selecting EDP Equipment*, has been designed as a general management guide in this area. This chapter describes the process of evaluating EDP equipment capabilities and what factors managers should look for and apply in making decisions regarding the acquisition and use of equipment. About thirty equipment evaluation checkpoints, which may be numerically weighted for rating purposes, are presented and described. The criteria which are used in hardware analyses are explained in straightforward terms, so the manager will be able to save time by knowing the appropriate questions to ask. Simulation methods are covered as they pertain to the measurement of computer capabilities in meeting the specific requirements. The use of benchmark problems in the decision-making process is covered. Hardware performance calculations, which are sometimes used to arrive at the relative power value of a computer, are examined. Software decision points are also discussed, and time-sharing services are explored briefly in the final section.

Chapter eight, *Directing and Controlling EDP Operations*, is intended to provide meaningful managerial guidelines for EDP equipment operations and the control of this function. This chapter discusses the operations environment, supervision, and work-flow considerations. Factors which directly control the efficiency level of operations are examined, and a suggested course of action is given for each. Some of these factors are: number and quality of operating personnel, work analysis and scheduling, job priorities and resource allocation, coordination of user requirements, and work specifications. The control aspect of EDP operations is examined in such areas as: documentation, job accounting, audit provisions, data libraries, operating systems, and information transmittal. Other operating considerations are discussed in terms of normal and downtime recovery operations.

Chapter nine, *Cost Estimating, Analysis, and Control for EDP*, is directed at bringing the fundamental concepts of financial planning and control to EDP managers in a form which can be applied. Cost estimating is discussed and the various factors which influence estimates are presented and analyzed. Some of the working information required for financial and economic analysis is discussed in this chapter, along with the use of cost analysis worksheets which have been designed expressly for EDP. The more common methods of economic evaluation are described. Budget preparation and the essentials of budgetary control as applied to EDP are also covered.

Chapter ten, *Management States Its Problem*, delves into the results and conclusions of a number of surveys that have been conducted to determine the effectiveness of EDP and its management. A number of direct quotations from EDP executives and managers appear in this chapter. These eyewitness reports help validate the theme of the book, for it is these executives' problems that the book is concerned with and attempts to solve.

There are also two appendices in the book. Appendix A contains EDP job descriptions for certain management and technical positions. Appendix B contains several management checklists to help plan the pre-installation effort and a fraud control checklist. A short annotated bibliography for EDP management is also included.

Readers are advised to skim familiar subject matter, in favor of directing more attention to topics that are unfamiliar or of special interest. It should also be pointed out that a number of the topics apply to more than just the section or chapter in which they appear. Some overlapping is, therefore, inevitable—this is the nature of the subject matter in certain areas. To eliminate redundancies, the approach taken here has been to give a full discussion only once, and to reference it elsewhere as required.

The term *software*, as used in this book, refers only to one or more generalized programs that facilitate the use of the hardware. Neither application programs nor people are included in the definition.

The term *installation* refers to the physical location that houses the hardware, and quite often, the systems analysts and programmers as well.

Leonard I. Krauss

contents

administering
and controlling

THE COMPANY
DATA PROCESSING
FUNCTION

PLANNING THE EDP FUNCTION

Planning is imperfect work beset with uncertainties of all kinds, yet it is essential to keep the gap between disaster and simple variance wide enough to enable progress to be made in some orderly way. Rewards resulting from planning can have an unusual slant, for it is not what they make happen, but rather what they can prevent from happening that makes them vitally important. This chapter sets forth some of the ground rules for EDP from a planning standpoint, starting with top management's relationship to EDP and going from there to discussions on: (a) the selection of computer applications (b) the framework of the EDP planning process (c) feasibility studies and how management evaluates them (d) pre-installation work plans, scheduling, and controls, and if all this looks like too much work (e) how to get the most out of outside EDP consulting services.

Top management participation from the outset

Management must embody those planning, organizing, and control activities which are necessary to insure that delegated activities are timely and meet specific needs. In relation to the installation and progress of the electronic data processing function, the failure of management at any level can easily result in the failure of the entire EDP effort. It may be possible for certain departments in a business enterprise to operate at an acceptable level without much management participation. However, this is not the case with EDP today, principally because this function cuts across organizational and functional lines and frequently demands the cooperation and work of individuals from various areas of the business. Such individuals participate in the EDP effort with a broad range of understanding, ability, and attitudes; so that the management problem, then, becomes one of tying together and giving direction to these diverse interests and talents.

To date, the best way known to insure the success of EDP in the business enterprise is to engage the support and participation of top management at the outset. According to several surveys, the chances of success without top management approval and support are slim indeed. Following are selected excerpts from these surveys.

According to recent studies, approximately one-third of the computer installations are significantly successful, one-third are relative or outright failures. The key to computer application success is: competent computer personnel; top management support; middle and operative management participation and cooperation.[1]

Other data processing specialists and professional managers have repeatedly admonished the business world against setting up an EDP organization in the absence of top management involvement. One article discussing the "condition factors" in successful installations states:

... without meaningful top-management support and the discipline of proper planning, the contribution of the whole data processing program may be nullified.[2]

A number of individuals and EDP management studies have strongly suggested that the company president become closely associated with the EDP effort. In writing about the EDP function in the organization structure, George J. Fleming has said:

... the data processing function must also seek to obtain the sponsorship of the chief executive of the organization or enterprise. No other can provide the assurance of a stabilized budget, an environment that encourages expansion, and a process of evaluation and justification ...[3]

Depending upon the size of the enterprise, someone close to the president should have the direct responsibility for the EDP effort. In increasing numbers, businesses have taken this advice and have been setting up computer departments reporting to top-level management.

Even the best EDP manager has his hands tied if he cannot get interdepartmental cooperation and money to run the department properly. As a rule, support and approval from top management open the channels to both money and cooperation. A project authorized and approved by top management will get the money required to accomplish the desired objectives. Also, any effort supported by top management usually gets the cooperation of any department involved in that particular effort, regardless of personal attitudes which may otherwise retard progress.

If top management wants the EDP effort to be successful, it must give its approval and support in meaningful ways. Furthermore, if the EDP effort is to continue to function properly and expand, it must have their continuing approval and support. If top management does not intend to both approve and support the EDP effort, then it is strongly advised that no attempt be made to set up the EDP organization. A poor alternative is the mediocre performance which usually attends the lack of enthusiastic sponsorship, especially where EDP is seen as a management tool, not just a faster accounting method.

GETTING TOP MANAGEMENT SUPPORT

To start with, no high level executive is going to vigorously support something about which he knows very little. The first order of business, it would seem, is to prime executive interest with some education. Bringing this about, however, can be more difficult than it may appear. Executives sometimes display an astute willingness not to get involved with things that do not seem absolutely essential. Operating on a "need-to-know" basis, chances are that top managers may feel imposed upon if a direct and obvious approach is taken to gain their involvement. Salesmanship and the use of various incentives, on the other hand, have produced some gratifying

[1] Jay Mettler, "Profile: Computer Personnel Characteristics—1964," *Business Automation*, March 1964, p. 31.

[2] Frank Roodman, "Helping Management Manage," *Journal of Data Management*, August 1965, p. 21.

[3] George J. Fleming, "EDP's Organization Function Within the Corporate Structure," *Journal of Data Management*, February 1965, p. 45.

results. Putting one's imagination to work on such schemes is a must. There are several approaches described below which have proved to be quite successful.

EDP equipment manufacturers run special orientation courses which are planned exclusively for top executives. Some of these even reach a point where the executive can try his hand at programming. Enrollment is sometimes limited to specific executive positions for a particular industry. For example, computer concept courses are conducted for board chairmen and presidents in banking, or for manufacturing vice-presidents. Knowing that the other members of the group are likely to share the same interests and problems, the potential executive student will probably be more receptive to the idea of attending.

Executive courses can be run in-house as well. Often, however, there are too many distractions, and sometimes "homemade pitches" fall on deaf ears. Short demonstrations of EDP equipment in action may produce better results.

At least one company has managed to get a sizable group of its executives acquainted with EDP through the use of business management games (simulators) employing computers. These evening sessions were conducted by the computer department once every few weeks with eight or more different executives each time. Without exception, the executives reported that the experience was both stimulating and enjoyable. Through their participation in the games, the executives were also exposed to modern computer concepts. As a result of these management games, the computer department was able to get many of these same executives interested in taking short after-hours courses in computer and data processing fundamentals. Outside reading of popular business magazines, such as *Harvard Business Review* and publications of the American Management Association, is also advised to supplement classroom instruction.

A basic understanding, achieved by any means, paves the way to gaining top management sponsorship. When ideas and propositions are presented to top executives who have some understanding, much more attention can be concentrated upon the real issues. With prior knowledge of EDP concepts, the executive will be in a better position to grasp the essence of new ideas without having to worry about filling in all of the background details.

As in all things, "a little bit of knowledge can be dangerous." From time to time, EDP practitioners have expressed dismay at the circumstance in which an executive has managed to get an overview that was much too oversimplified. The fact that an executive has written one easy FORTRAN program in some course sometimes gives him peculiar notions as to what programming is all about. Should this appear to have taken place, the EDP managers must take steps to rectify the problem by showing what the realities are.

KEEPING MANAGEMENT INFORMED

Any EDP effort that is underway with the approval and support of top management has the responsibility to report to that management any significant problems encountered, as well as the progress made toward reaching pre-established goals. Only through a timely exchange of information can management ascertain whether schedules are being met and whether the EDP organization is properly interpreting the needs of the business and taking appropriate action to reach the goals which had been set. Later in this chapter a number of formalized reporting methods are illustrated and discussed.

It is clear that many top executives appreciate having certain practices followed in reporting. Some prefer more details than others, but not many like to pore over heavily detailed reports. By far, the greater number prefer summary information. Flip-chart presentations, supplemented by a report of modest length issued prior to the presentation, are popular among many executives. Computer managers will have to do some detective work to learn what procedure is most effective. Some rules of thumb that occur to the author are:

1. Always introduce the subject . . . assume that the problem requires re-explaining.
2. Get to the heart of the matter immediately.
3. Make points that are tuned to a businessman's ear . . . cut the jargon to absolute essentials.
4. Be prepared to offer supporting material . . . real-life examples are effective.
5. Summarize major points periodically.

TEN GROUND RULES FOR TOP EXECUTIVES

As previously emphasized, the support and participation of top management in EDP is of paramount importance. To enhance this relationship, it has been pointed out that the acquisition of a certain amount of education (from business seminars, equipment manufacturers' special courses, educational literature, trade publications, etc.) on the part of the executives involved will be of considerable value. Beyond acquiring education and supporting the computer activities, top executives must take on the responsibility for shaping the destiny of EDP in the company.

Jesse H. Martin has set down the following ten points aimed at describing part of the role top management must play in bearing the responsibility for the EDP effort:

1. Know the capabilities and limitations of your installation.
2. Have a staff capable of keeping the command current concerning new concepts and equipment.
3. Know what managerial, organizational and technical experts are available to advise you on matters concerning electronic data processing policies and procedures.
4. Conduct periodic reviews of your organization to determine if new areas can be automated.
5. Obtain from your data processing manager only the amount of detailed information necessary for decision making.
6. Insure that you don't develop a stereotyped approach to all data processing problems.
7. Realize that electronic data processing is not the cure-all for all organizational problems.
8. Recognize that feasibility studies which reveal that adoption of electronic data processing is not practical, may also reveal where improvements in the existing system can be made.
9. Remember that it is seldom possible to include new areas in EDP without having a consequent effect on other organizational elements.
10. Never try to use computers for jobs which people can do better, and never become disillusioned with EDP when occasional failures occur.[4]

In the remainder of this book, the implementation of some of Mr. Martin's ten points are explored in detail, in the context of the various chapters.

Deciding on application objectives

Most business enterprises will have a number of possible candidates for computer application, such as: accounts payable; accounts receivable; payroll; inventory control; labor distribution; equipment depreciation accounting; sales analysis; engineering analysis; statistical and operations research applications; capital investment analysis; cost accounting; general ledger accounting; stockholder record processing; and many more, depending upon the specific industry represented.

---

[4]Jesse H. Martin, "The EDP Ten Commandments for Executives," *Data Processing*, September 1962, p. 46.

For reasons of economy, it is usually impractical to computerize all of the obvious functions concurrently. The cost of equipping and manning the computer department, plus other complicating factors, generally dictate that the conversion to computer automation be done in stages based upon an order of priorities. The priority of applications may be determined both by cost reduction factors and by benefits to management. However, it is essential to have some overall concept of integration (such as a management information system) to guide development work.

Objectives for an individual application as well as integrated information systems can be set forth intelligently only after the various company functions are well understood. Systems planning and the setting of objectives and goals, if done in a vacuum, can prove to be costly not only in terms of money, but may also leave the business far behind in its computerization effort. This is likely to be a serious matter in a competitive environment.

In determining which operations should be converted to computer processing, applications analysis is necessary to compare the potential benefits. Points for consideration in this analysis include:

1. Which applications will reduce business operating costs, clerical costs, and overhead expense?
2. What costs can be avoided in the future, considering business growth?
3. Which areas of the business have work to do which is repetitive and might better be done by the computer?
4. Do some departments of the business have chronic problems which can be alleviated by adopting EDP?
5. What are the information needs of management, and which of these are crucial in terms of timeliness and accuracy?
6. What key problems are associated with the applications (such as data gathering and file buildup) as factors in determining the best area to tackle first?

Once a tentative decision has been made to implement a specific application, definite objectives should be established. The next step is a more comprehensive feasibility study of the application to determine whether the desired results will be justified. The feasibility study will be discussed later in this chapter.

INTRODUCTORY APPLICATIONS

An installation in its beginning stages would be well advised to start with fairly uncomplicated applications in order to gain experience. One example of such an application is payroll. It is probable that significant payoffs will not be realized immediately in starting small, but the risks and costs are also relatively small. In banking, for example, demand deposit accounting is often one of the first applications to be automated. The payoffs realized from these early systems are almost entirely due to saving in clerical help. Occasionally these payoffs are substantial, depending on specific circumstances.

Insurance, banking, brokerage and some other industries have high volumes of routine paperwork processing which can be computerized without great difficulty. However, after achieving a good return on investment resulting from clerical savings in the first few applications, there are generally no others which can be computerized as readily to get similar payoffs. In some cases, even the clerical savings cannot be demonstrated. One case involved a credit bureau that was investigating the possibility of putting its credit reporting data on an information retrieval type of system. Upon making a few rough calculations, it was learned that the cost to simply get the data onto computer storage media would be around $300,000. The business in this particular case, which had gross receipts of around $250,000, would have required a computer system to handle the job with a recurring cost almost equal to its total income.

LOGISTICS AND STRATEGIC PLANNING SYSTEMS

Truly big payoffs, particularly on a continuing basis, are not realized through systems that save only clerical labor. On the contrary, they come from systems that deal with the problems of managing the business. Manufacturers are not in the accounts receivable or payroll business; chemical and petroleum companies are not in the general ledger or depreciation accounting business; banks are not in the demand deposit business; insurance companies are not in the premium and claim accounting business; and retailers are not in the invoicing business. There is only a limited return obtainable through automating these kinds of applications, and it is relatively small.

Consider, however, a computer application such as inventory management which makes it possible to release millions of dollars in capital for other uses in a manufacturing company. Or, contemplate a distribution analysis application which cuts freight costs by 5 per cent for a chemical or petroleum company. Perhaps a bond analysis application will bring about an added 1/10 of 1 per cent yield on a billion dollar bank or insurance company portfolio. A market study on consumer products might show a retailer how he can substantially improve sales. Many other examples can be cited for specific businesses, such as competitive bidding analysis applications for various types of contractors, fleet optimization studies for transporters, and production management systems to keep assembly lines and raw material processing operating near optimum efficiency.

Logistics and strategic planning systems such as those outlined, while promising large payoffs, do deserve a rather cautious approach for reasons that include the following:

1. Development costs tend to be, but are not always, high.
2. More careful planning is required for these systems as compared with automated accounting functions.
3. Expensive and scarce personnel talents are required to develop the system. Data processors who can get routine jobs up and running, frequently cannot cope with these vastly more complex systems.
4. Organizational changes are often needed to get these systems properly implemented. The people involved in the organization changes are not clerks. Instead, they are likely to be middle managers, technical professionals, and even high level executives.
5. Obtaining confidence and acceptance of the new system can be a long-term and difficult process.
6. A greater amount of inventiveness and experimentation is required than with other systems. Risks, in terms of failure as well as cost and schedule overruns, are higher.
7. Benefits can and should be measured. However, in many cases, it costs more and takes longer to do so than with other systems.

Some argument can be advanced for the case that "easy systems equate to low potential return, whereas difficult systems equate to high potential return." It should be remembered, however, that logistics and strategic planning systems can offer the advantage of being able to account for business change, competitive situations, economic fluctuations, and so forth. So, a high return, even under changing conditions, can be obtained on a repetitive basis. By comparison, typical accounting systems are usually one-time affairs . . . such systems remain rather stable over time with respect to basic functions.

It is recommended that overall objectives for computer development work include some provision for undertaking more advanced applications. Talent should be developed along these lines even as just a hedge against the future. Once experience has been gained with routine computerization, EDP management should actively pursue some of these more exotic, high payoff applications.

The planning process

There is no question but that EDP systems work requires careful, intelligent and educated planning. There exists no magic which will take over and somehow compensate for shortcomings resulting from poor planning. Revising a system on which programming has progressed to any extent can be extremely costly. Depending upon the scope of the work, these costs can run into the tens and even hundreds of thousands of dollars, not to mention the loss of time and waste of scarce talent.

If a very tight schedule has been established, there seems to be a natural inclination to cut down on the time devoted to planning because the product is not readily apparent. Quite obviously, this could be a serious mistake. If the managers are parsimonious with expenditures and time for the planning effort, it is likely to cost the company more in the end and might even cost such managers their jobs. There are a number of cases in which great expenditures of time, money and effort were made only to fail, in the end, simply because the planning phase was taken too lightly. Many of these cases reflect disregard for the need to look ahead, to identify future problems and to establish adequate controls on the progress of the work.

In order to undertake the pre-installation planning, a somewhat formalized approach ought to be taken. A project or task force may be set up to handle the job, or the planning workshop, about to be described, may be used as an approach.

The concept of a workshop carries with it a definite implication that the group comprising the workshop is meeting to get some work done. Its leader is expected to set forth the objectives of the workshop and to coordinate the efforts of the other members of the group, with certain key individuals taking responsibility for the ultimate decisions.

In some EDP workshops, the key individuals will be those engaged in the actual data processing effort on a full time basis. Included in the group will be knowledgeable representatives of the areas of the business for which the computer installation is likely to perform some services. The entire group will meet only in the first few sessions for the purpose of education and orientation, and to learn what contribution will be expected from each member. From then on, only the key data processing individuals and the representative from one or two of the specialty areas will meet at various times as the planning progresses. In certain types of business organizations, the workshop might be composed of the individuals listed below. (The list might differ slightly for specific industries, such as transportation, banking, etc., but the concept remains unchanged by this fact.)

Data Processing Manager
Systems Analysts
Computer Manufacturer's Systems Engineer
An Independent EDP Consultant
Supervisor of Accounting and Bookkeeping
Inventory Control Specialist
Representative of Personnel Department
Sales Representative
Production Representative
Industrial Engineering Representative
Research & Development Representative

At the workshop, a coordinated interaction takes place between the group members who finally agree upon the objectives and general requirements of the computer applications under consideration. The using department representatives will be expected to outline the requirements of a particular function in their department, while the EDP department members guide this effort and make suggestions for the development of the computerized system under discussion.

It is of the greatest importance to carefully review and plan those interfaces where two or more distinct applications have points of meeting, particularly when it is not intended to implement all of the applications at the same time. For example, accounts receivable processing ties in with sales analysis as well as with inventory control, and even production control. Unless adequate planning is done to insure that these applications mesh smoothly, the implementation of any one of them at a future time might require extensive revision of the entire existing system. To help avoid or minimize this, many planning groups draw up *five year plans* on a continuing basis.

After a review of each of the candidates for automation, priorities must be established for the next formal step, discussed later in this chapter, called the feasibility study. Every possibility cannot even be studied properly, much less developed and implemented.

Care must be exercised during the planning phase, to insure that the group does not become preoccupied with computer hardware considerations and its maximum utilization at the outset. Emphasis must continually be directed toward high priority business needs, otherwise too many systems will be attempted which will give rise to crash development programs. Such systems are usually poorly done, cost much more than they should, and will require extensive rework or complete replacement by a redesigned system in a short time.

After some knowledge has been gained about the various applications under consideration, it is a good idea to take a look at what others have done in similar areas, if possible, prior to pouring too much money into even the study. Hardware manufacturers' application literature, as well as outside technical publications, should be reviewed. In addition, it is usually productive to visit other installations to learn from eyewitnesses.

VISITING OTHER INSTALLATIONS

It has been the author's experience that many important considerations and pointers which had been initially overlooked were brought to light as a result of studying the work of others who had already accomplished what the newly established computer group was trying to do for the first time. Such benefits are almost always realized from visits to other computer installations. A few hours spent reviewing the procedures at another installation can often save months of work.

As part of planning for such a trip, the group should outline definite objectives to be achieved from the visit. For example, they might decide to seek information on:

1. Key problems related to a particular application.
2. Identification of difficult areas of the work and how to cope with them.
3. The amount of money, personnel and time needed for a particular project.
4. The cost reduction and other criteria to be considered when converting to computerized processing.
5. How specific kinds of processing are accomplished.

The host installation should be notified, informally, as to what the visiting group hopes to learn from the trip. In this manner, the hosts can prepare the needed information in advance and, perhaps, have a designated specialist on hand.

The size of the visiting group should be limited to not more than five people, and should include the data processing manager, the systems analysis manager, and representatives of the departments having candidates for computer automation which are to be specifically discussed on the visit. For example, if accounts receivable and sales analysis are under consideration, the visiting group might include the EDP manager, the manager of system analysis, a representative of the accounts receivable department and the sales manager.

EVALUATING APPLICATION PACKAGES

Nothing is so disquieting and demoralizing as finding out that much time, money and effort had been spent by the EDP staff in developing a computer application which was available from an industry source at little or no cost. Needless to say, such duplication of effort is wasteful and should be avoided. Yet, there are numerous instances of this sort which have come to the attention of the author, where very little effort had been made to seek out ready-made application programs, often called application packages.

In computer group discussions, it is often heard that application packages are more trouble to adapt and use than they are worth. To a certain extent this may be true, but it clearly cannot be advanced as reason for rejecting all application packages. Of course, investigation and analysis are required to determine whether the ready-made program is suitable for the job at hand or whether it can be easily modified to meet the requirements.

Application packages are available from a variety of sources. EDP equipment manufacturers (notably IBM) have been providing these packages to customers "free-of-charge," although recent anti-trust suits have forced separate pricing of some packages. A number of installations have developed application programs that can be used by others. They are sometimes willing to trade them for other application programs or sell them outright. Independent programming companies have a variety of applications systems for sale, and for a price, some will do custom alterations to meet the buyer's needs. There are also program brokers whose business it is to get buyers and sellers together, for a fee. Some of the trade associations have taken an interest in program exchanges. And there is at least one catalog service available for an annual subscription fee, which lists programs for sale.[5] Any company wishing to offer programs for sale may advertise in this catalog . . . it is possible that a little extra money can be made for the business in this way.

The feasibility study

The feasibility study follows the preliminary survey effort described previously as the planning workshop. A primary objective of the feasibility study is to arrive at a conclusion as to whether a new project should, or should not, be undertaken. In the majority of cases, the conclusions are based on economic considerations and an analysis of other possible tangible benefits to be gained. However, intangibles must also be considered. To one organization, improved delivery schedules would be an important benefit; in another business, it might be more timely management information or, perhaps, the reduction of out-of-stock situations. In still another business, the computer application may yield a combination of benefits. Whatever the benefits, the ultimate goal is to improve business efficiency and, in turn, increase profits.

A feasibility study is not an original research study, differing in the sense that it is usually assumed that the application project under consideration can be accomplished. The purpose of the study is to explore one or more ways in which the project's goal can be achieved. Knowing that the goal is attainable and some of the ways it can be reached, the study team must determine if the project is worthwhile. Conceivably, they might conclude that a certain project is not profitable at the present time but should be scheduled for reconsideration at a specific time in the future. Very often, such studies lead the team to suggest ways for improving existing methods instead of implementing the major changes that may have been originally contemplated.

It must be remembered that the feasibility study can, in itself, be a project of some magnitude using company funds and other resources. It must, therefore, be approached carefully lest the cost of the study be more than the savings realized under the new methods it may introduce. On what looks like a $100,000 project, a $5000 feasibility study may be appropriate. For a $20,000 project, a less costly feasibility study would seem practical in most cases.

At this point, it should be noted that an exhaustive feasibility study of a major or complex system could be very expensive and take a considerable time to complete. For this reason, man-

---

[5]For information contact: International Computer Programs, 5704 N. Guilford Avenue, Indianapolis, Indiana 46220. See also, advertisements by brokers in *Computerworld* (news weekly), *Data Systems News*, *Datamation*, and other EDP periodicals.

agers should consider the possibility of limiting the study to an analysis of what might be termed **overriding considerations**. In so doing, a decision can be obtained more quickly and at less expense, leaving the highly detailed and peripheral matters for the full system study. The full system study, to be covered in Chapter three, would be undertaken for any system which has been approved for implementation, regardless of the extent of the feasibility study.

It should also be understood that it makes little sense to conduct a feasibility study if a decision has already been made either to go (or not go) ahead with development work. Where such a decision is expressed or implied, the attitude of those engaged in the study is too often that their task is to justify (or not justify) the proposal. One can hardly expect an objective or honest recommendation on the value of the proposal in the case where management has already made the decision.

PLANNING THE FEASIBILITY STUDY

Like any other activity of importance, there is a need for the system planners to have a feasibility study plan. Plans for setting up the feasibility study may include some or all of the following checkpoints:

1. *Objectives of the Study*—what determinations will be made in this study.
2. *Limits of Scope and Penetration*—by organization boundaries, activities, departmental levels, etc.
3. *Constraints and Assumptions*—those known which preempt or define courses of action, limitations, methods, interfacing systems, etc.
4. *Major Phase Segmentation*—define what is included in each phase and what is to be accomplished.
5. *Statistics and Parameters*—to be used or generated.
6. *Target Completion Dates*—for each major phase.
7. *Manpower Estimate*—with specific or preferred capabilities.
8. *Progress Reporting and Control*—what definable levels of achievement can be measured.
9. *Study Team Leader*—should be appointed and participate in planning the study.
10. *Cost Estimate*—for each major phase.

Satisfying the checkpoints listed should provide the necessary ingredients to prepare a charter for the study, a document which will guide the feasibility analysis effort.

CONDUCTING THE FEASIBILITY STUDY

One orderly way in which to conduct the feasibility study is to separate it into three parts as outlined below. It is important to recall that the information gathered is in general rather than specific detail.

PART 1.   Learn and Understand the Present Methods

- What are the weaknesses and strong points?
- What are the functional tasks and activities involved?
- How are the tasks now performed?
- What time constraints exist?
- Where are the tasks performed?
- What inputs and outputs are involved?

PART 2.   Conceptual Design of the New System

- Determine the present and foreseeable future requirements and objectives.
- Combine the requirements of the old system with new concepts.
- Work out the design concepts of the new system.
- Analyze the design for workability, see if it meets intermediate and longer term requirements, and look for possible alternate approaches.

PART 3. Economic Analysis and Work Plans

- Cost out the new system including costs of personnel, training, overhead, EDP equipment, and supplies. Amortize conversion expenses and costs of study.
- Cost out old system on comparable items. Project for three years or more.
- Use discounted cash flow method for evaluations.
- Set up a schedule for the work to be done, showing costs incurred at the various stages. A general PERT chart of the development events may be useful.

When the study has been completed, the conclusions reached should be presented to management together with varying amounts of the detailed information, depending upon the specific points of emphasis required and management's interests.

MANAGEMENT EVALUATIONS OF FEASIBILITY STUDIES

A word of caution must be interjected with respect to initiating a feasibility study and evaluating its conclusions. Some subtle pitfalls and guidelines include:

1. The study must be run by an individual who can be depended upon for an objective analysis.
2. A high degree of interest in the application under study may produce an inertia which tends to give an affirmative bias to the recommendations.
3. There is often a failure to present an evaluation of all reasonable alternatives.
4. Due to a lack of understanding of the more intricate complexities, some major cost items may be overlooked.
5. Partly as a result of the general nature of the feasibility study, there is frequently over-optimism in setting schedules and a failure to estimate costs with a reasonable degree of accuracy.
6. The real question is not often *can it be done* but rather *can this company do it with its talents, resources, political environment, etc.* at the stated time and cost estimate.
7. A study which has been done properly will offer a realistic discussion of disadvantages as well as advantages. Often, advantages are the only points brought out in the study. It might be beneficial to investigate disagreements among the study team members.
8. Feasibility studies which recommend that the application be implemented often neglect to say when this should be done. Penalties or benefits which are realized by waiting are often not analyzed.
9. Sometimes studies presume, either by design or oversight, too much stability in the application requirements. Growth capabilities must be explored.
10. One of the most critical weaknesses of the vast majority of studies is that they assume highly competent systems and programming people are available, or will be made available. Such assumptions can and do lead to worthless systems, not to mention completely unreliable time and cost estimates.
11. Maintenance costs, associated with the regular operation of the system, are sometimes completely overlooked or underestimated.

Work planning and controls

This section describes formalized work planning and controls which are implemented after a feasibility study has resulted in a management decision to carry out the project. At this point, it is often necessary to retrace some of the ground covered during the feasibility study in order to plan in more detail the systems development effort. Documentation resulting from the feasibility study is used to guide the development of plans and as a source of factual data pertaining to basic requirements.

The plans and controls discussed here are what might be termed broad-gauge, as they relate to all project activities. By way of contrast, they are not concerned with details of specific functions, such as programming, which are discussed elsewhere in this book.

THE PLANNING ACTIVITY

A plan is a plateau from which to launch the EDP systems development effort. To plan is to presuppose that the planner understands what steps are involved in the systems development process of moving from some starting point to some ending point or set of objectives. If the individual who is appointed to be in charge of planning activities does not understand this process, then he must learn what it is that must be done before he can plan for it. If this logic sounds somewhat convoluted, the author can personally attest to the fact that literally millions of dollars have gone down the proverbial drain because this simple concept was ignored. It is not a joking matter; some people do not plan because they do not know how, others because they are not capable, and still others because they are too lazy to do so. Guard against allowing the computer to end up in the hands of people like this. The complexities and intricacies of costly computer work cannot be dealt with successfully in the absence of a plan; being without one guarantees failure.

Even the best laid plans can be upset if a schedule of events has not been established in terms of realistic target dates and based upon the availability of manpower with a specific assortment of talents. Realistic target dates can be established only when the problem has been well defined. In addition, characteristics of the people who are to carry out the plan will have a direct bearing on whether the time and cost estimates are valid. EDP managers, systems analysts, and programmers come in a wide variety of performance capabilities—ranging from highly skilled and fast, to almost useless and slow. These variances, plus the fact that nearly all application systems are one-time, specially tailored jobs, makes EDP planning a judgment-oriented activity. In this and subsequent chapters, guidelines, techniques, and checklists that have proven to be useful are discussed.

Remember that a desired objective or end product does not constitute a work plan . . . research and analysis must be done first. And above all, keep in mind the fact that *a desire is not a time and cost estimate*. A desire will always remain so. Any relationship between it and what an estimate will show must be established or viewed after an estimate is made as a result of an intelligent study. Much panic and frustration can also be avoided if everyone involved accepts these facts.

Another recommendation that is in order, is that the planner should solicit and seek all the advice he can get. Discussing the subject with other EDP managers, analysts, and programmers is always a constructive way to start. Visiting other installations, reviews with EDP equipment manufacturer's systems personnel, getting the help of reputable EDP consultants, and researching EDP literature are all worthwhile in terms of garnering a feel for the problem.

PRE-INSTALLATION PLANNING

Once the commitment is made to buy or rent a computer, it should be realized that the total job of installing the system consists of many distinct phases. By dividing the effort into logical phases, personnel can be assigned to the areas of responsibility, and the sequence of events to be followed can be established. Such scheduling, as an integral part of the pre-installation plan, provides for manpower when and where it is needed. If manpower and other resources should appear on the job too early, money is wasted. If they should arrive too late, the consequences are often more serious.

As indicated earlier, it is impossible to set up a schedule without a predetermined set of specific events and activities. There are a number of tools available to assist planners in defining and scheduling these events. PERT (Program Evaluation and Review Technique), PERT-Cost, and CPM (Critical Path Method) have been found to be useful for laying out the pre-installation program. There are many books on the market which explain these methods. Also, the pre-installation checklists shown in Appendix B can serve as a guide in organizing the effort and planning for the various tasks to be done.

An illustrative CPM diagram, Figure 1.1, shows some of the activities which may occur as part of an EDP pre-installation effort. This network diagram shows that computing equipment is being installed and that application systems are being developed as part of the complete effort. Later chapters in this book cover a number of pre-installation activities including those shown in Figure 1.1.

Depending upon the size and complexity of the work to be undertaken, various planning and scheduling devices can be used advantageously. For example, a small scale development effort might better be displayed in terms of a simple bar chart or scheduling form. A larger scale development effort, on the other hand, is more amenable to the more sophisticated types of planning and scheduling techniques. For example, Figure 1.2 shows a PERT chart for part of a large scale multiple application system development effort. This system covers order processing, inventory control, pricing and invoicing, distribution planning and control, financial reporting, and sales analysis. In addition, this particular system is to be tied into several external systems, which means that the points of interconnection must also be studied and provided. Further, this system will be designed to use telecommunications hardware to handle customer orders and respond to a variety of inquiries. This system is both large (multi-million dollar class) and complex, and the planning for it reflects this in a number of ways.

Notice that the PERT network in Figure 1.2 is divided into four phases: (1) Application Analysis, (2) Functional Specifications, (3) Preliminary Systems Design, and (4) Project Review. Because of the way in which this particular set of events is specified, one might properly conclude that Figure 1.2 illustrates only a partial plan for a very large project. This possibility is substantiated by the fact that the last event shown is *Project Approval*. It is important to recognize that all of the work implied in Figure 1.2 is done in order to arrive at a plan for carrying out the project. It does not show what events exist beyond the point where the EDP system development effort has been approved. This part of the total plan calls for another PERT chart that is prepared in the course of the preliminary systems design phase (it happens to be event number 62). A written report with supporting information is prepared in connection with each of the 67 events shown in Figure 1.2. It should now be evident that a considerable amount of effort and expense can go into studying and defining an EDP system. And, this is just a prelude to developing an implementation plan complete with time and cost estimates. These estimates are made as a check on the feasibility study and are expected to be quite accurate. They are the quantitative expression of a carefully developed plan. A management reevaluation of the project can then be made on the basis of this more refined information.

At this junction, one might well ponder the question of how to estimate how much time and money should be spent to get to the point where there is enough information to enable management to render a decision on whether the development work should actually be carried out. Unfortunately, the author is unable to provide any quantitative guidelines on this matter. There are a couple of approaches that are taken, for practical reasons, which can be mentioned.

Based upon a feeling for the dimensions of the system, a manager could state that he is willing to spend a certain amount of money, say $10,000, in order to have the problem studied. When these funds are exhausted, a report of the findings and preliminary conclusions would be offered to management along with recommendations and estimates for looking into the problem in more detail. Conceivably, at some point, one of the studies will present estimates and problem requirements that can be accepted with a reasonably good level of confidence. A decision can

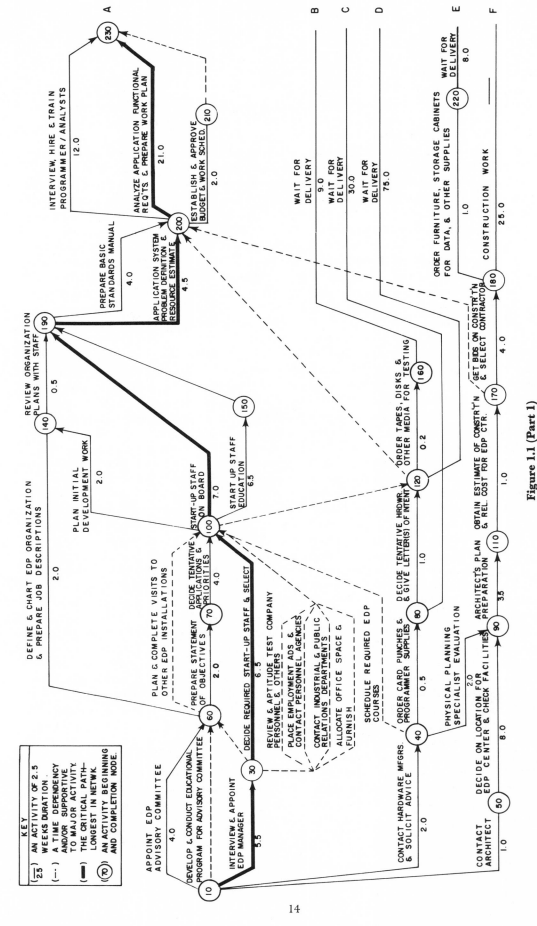

Figure 1.1 (Part 1)

Illustrative Critical Path Network for Pre-Installation Activities

14

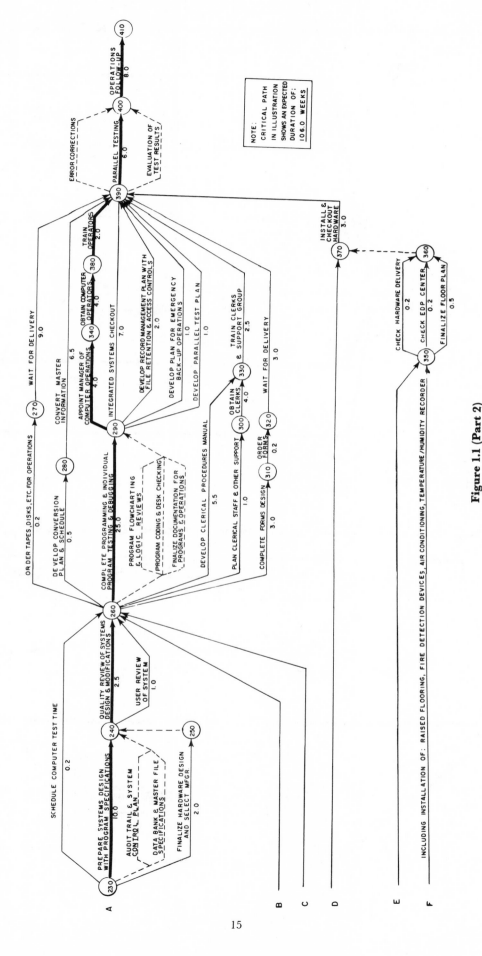

Figure 1.1 (Part 2)
Illustrative Critical Path Network
for Pre-Installation Activities

15

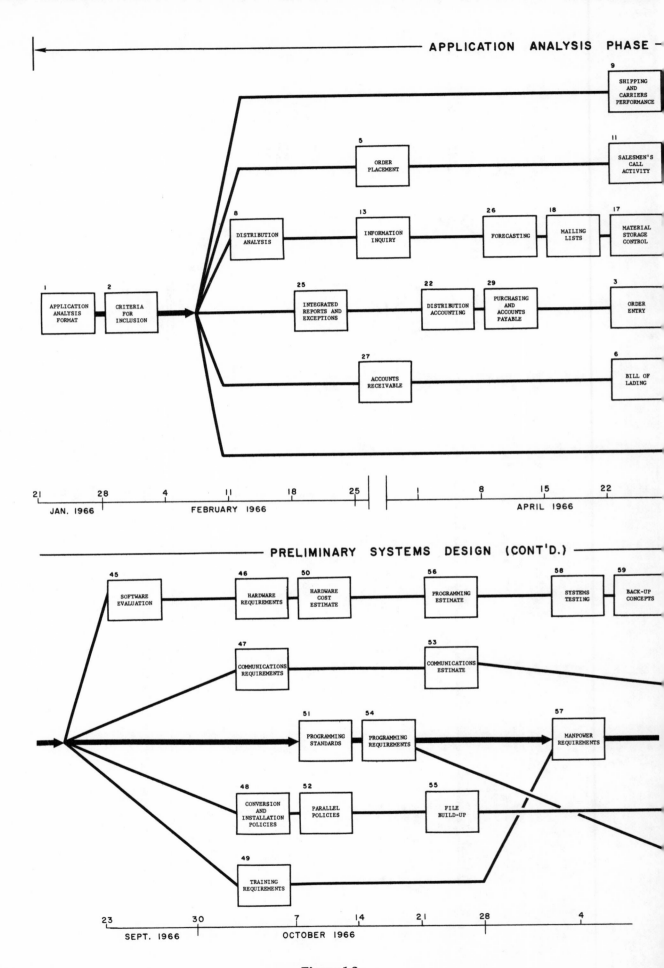

Figure 1.2
Illustrative Pert Network

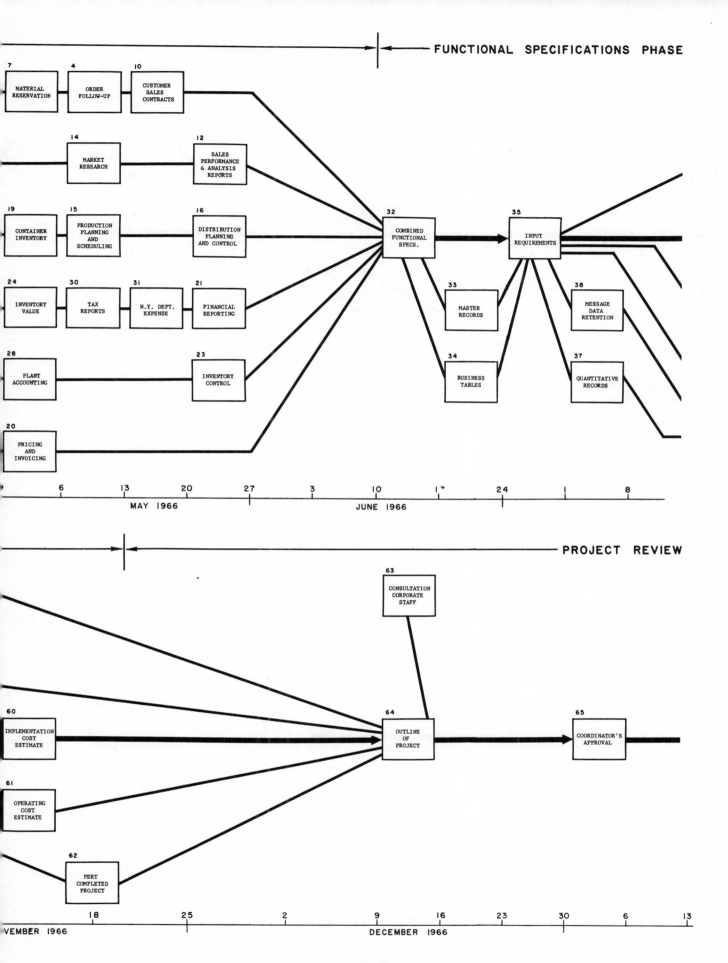

Figure 1.2 (cont.)

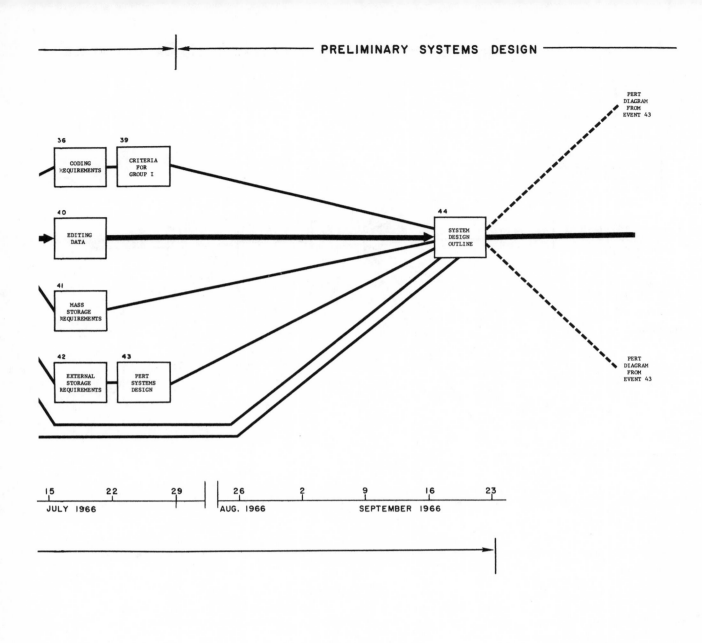

NOTE: HEAVY LINE INDICATES CRITICAL PATH

Figure 1.2 (cont.)

then be reached by management. They, of course, have had to pay for the information that gave them the opportunity to intelligently reflect and decide among alternatives . . . but they have been able to limit the expenditure to a specific amount of money.

WORK PLANS

Developing a Work Plan must necessarily be done following a detailed study of the problem. The PERT charts and other paraphernalia used to display and help control the work can only be as good as the intelligence employed in preparing them. A properly prepared Work Plan serves to bring all of the elements into focus for critical examination. The Work Plan itself, in terms of specific contents, will vary somewhat depending upon the particular work that it covers; however, the items in the following outline should be included in most Work Plans.

1. *Table of Contents*

2. *Introduction*
   - What this plan is used for.
   - What the plan describes—what system.
   - How the plan is used.
   - How the plan is changed or updated.
   - Major assumptions.
   - Application summary.

3. *Background Information*
   - Why this problem is being solved.
   - Who has the problem or need.
   - What are the current conditions.
   - What alternatives had been considered.

4. *Management Summary*
   - How much is it going to cost and how much has already been spent.
   - How long will it take to complete.
   - What other resources and facilities are to be used: men, machines, offices—what are the associated costs.
   - What are the major benefits and advantages.
   - What are the long term features and prospects of the system.
   - Simple graphs or charts to help explain some of the above; for example, a cost-buildup chart by calendar period.

5. *Task Enumeration*
   - State and briefly define each of the tasks.
   - State both the objectives and "non-objectives."[6]

6. *Task Assignments*
   - Who specifically and/or what type of individuals are needed—how many and when.
   - Scheduled starting and ending dates.

7. *Check-Points and Controls*
   - Enumerate and describe what ways and means will be used to monitor progress and quality, to control costs, and to report to management.

8. *Appendices*
   - Organization Chart
   - Description of Responsibilities

---

[6]"Non-objectives" serve to clarify issues by stating what is *not* to be accomplished. This is particularly worthwhile for situations that had been subject to many possibilities.

- PERT and/or other plan documents
- Hardware/Software description and planned usage
- Detailed System Specifications
- Glossary
- Other

CONTROLS

Techniques used in connection with EDP management controls are discussed throughout this book. However, as stated earlier, the controls to be discussed here are those with which higher level EDP management is concerned, meaning that they are more generalized than those of the lower level, to be described in later chapters. They are used to monitor the enactment of the Work Plan previously discussed.

A control of any kind assumes that a result or outcome of some event or action can be subjected to criteria for measurement. It also generally implies that a prediction, forecast or estimate is made for the particular event which has not yet taken place. Management controls for EDP must have these properties plus some others. In EDP work today, one finds that not only are estimates frequently very poor, but also that many management controls suffer this same distinction. A business maxim of sorts might be postulated to the effect that if forecasts are good, controls can be less stringent. Or conversely, if forecasts are bad, controls must be good. Clearly, if the company EDP function is plagued by having both of these done badly for very long, its computer work will end up in chaos. Recently, an EDP professional quipped, ". . . in computer work it is management by smoke." The analogy here is that rather than providing fire detection devices beforehand, the fire is permitted to get out of control before the fire brigade is summoned.

Good controls are ones that:

1. Provide a measurement and an advanced indication of a truly critical situation.
2. Isolate the area where a problem situation exists.
3. Suggest basic remedies.
4. Give indications of outstanding performance.

With this kind of control system, managers can manage by exception, meaning that they can be alerted to specific problem areas instead of everything.

In controlling EDP work, it is imperative to know "who's responsible for what and to whom." Relative to the tasks that have been enumerated in the Work Plan, the assignments matching persons to events will provide this information.

Figure 1.3 shows a simple way in which a manager can keep track of the event assignments. The person assigned to each event is responsible for all of the tasks necessary to complete the particular event. A table such as that shown in Figure 1.3 is used as a reference document in a system of controls. As such, it always contains the latest information at all times but does not reflect any performance measurements.

Figure 1.4 shows a listing of codes that may be used with several of the control documents described in this section. The reason for using these particular codes is that they will help direct management attention to problem areas in a more meaningful way.

A *performance chart* of one type is shown in Figure 1.5. This chart is updated on a regular basis; most often it is revised on a weekly basis. An easy way in which to keep this chart (and others) current, is to make changes to a master copy on which erasures can be made and new information entered. Each week the required number of duplicates of the current master chart can be prepared on an office copier. The positioning of the asterisk (on the top of the chart) shows when the chart was last updated; it moves one block to the right each week. A file of all past charts is maintained for reference, while the current one provides the latest information on progress. Some EDP managers have a chart similar to Figure 1.5 mounted on a large board

Event Number	EVENT NAME	Critical Code	PERSON ASSIGNED	STARTING DATE		MAN – WEEKS		ENDING DATE	
				Estimated	Actual	Estimated	Actual	Estimated	Actual

JOB NO. –   EVENT ASSIGNMENT TABLE   COMPANY I.D.–

Figure 1.3
Event Assignment Table

	CRITICAL CODES	
Code	*Meaning*	
CP	Event is on the critical path. Must be on-time to meet schedule.	
SOA ( )	Schedule Overrun Anticipated ( )—Number of Weeks	
SDA ( )	Starting Delay Anticipated ( )—Number of Weeks	
T	Activity in Trouble. Report Not Issued	
TR	Activity in Trouble. Report Issued.	
S_η	Severity Code. $\eta = 1$ high $\quad\quad\quad\quad\quad \eta = 2$ medium $\quad\quad\quad\quad\quad \eta = 3$ low	

Figure 1.4

Critical Codes

that is hung on the wall of their offices. Often these progress boards will show the person assigned, in addition to other indicative information. Various kinds of progress and scheduling boards are commercially available from office supply firms and EDP accessory dealers.

General status reporting may be done by the means suggested in Figure 1.6. Here the objective is to provide management, particularly at higher levels, with highlights on the total EDP job. The REMARKS section, included in the format shown, is used to briefly describe the major accomplishments and important problem areas. Additional descriptive information, such as plans outlining problem remedies, may be provided by including extra pages, but verbosity is to be avoided.

Detailed status information, broken down by event, may be reported in the manner shown in Figure 1.7. The information entered on this management report corroborates the summary data given in the report shown in Figure 1.6. Reviewing the detailed information helps management isolate the major problem areas so that a priority for action can be assigned as needed. For example, a 100 per cent cost overrun on a $1000 event is not likely to get much attention if an $80,000 event has a projected cost overrun of 50 per cent . . . unless, of course, the $1000 event was causing the $40,000 problem. Such interactions are always a possibility. Through an investigation of the major problem (partly by reviewing lower-level reports to be discussed later in this book), management would quickly discover the dependent relationship, i.e., the $1000 event was causing a much costlier problem for the $80,000 event.

Fancier controls can show these dependent relationships well, particularly if they are computerized. Upon occasion, however, elaborate control methods have been known to confuse the issues rather than help. In a word, *controls should be kept as simple as possible and still work*. The aim is to reveal where the problem is, about how big it is and, perhaps, suggest a remedy. Management action to solve the problem, on the other hand, may very well be quite complex.

Throughout the discussion on controls, the emphasis was on problems as opposed to achievement. Smart EDP managers will also want to know what things are going exceptionally well, and why. In this way, resources can be reallocated to problem areas. Outstanding people and methods can be applied where they will do the most good, and superior performance can be appropriately rewarded.

By now, the vitally important question of how to make these controls accurate must have occurred to the reader. Certainly, they are only as good as the information that is represented on the various reports and charts. There is no single set of answers to solve the accuracy problem. Competent and conscientious EDP personnel and managers comprise better than half the answers; the judgments and data they provide are crucial. Some of the remainder depend on techniques and mechanisms for control, such as those shown here, as well as others to be explored in the following chapters. It is best to set up some mechanics for control first and work on the problems of accuracy afterwards.

A good piece of advice on EDP management control is: Build what it is believed will provide the desired data and relationships . . . try it . . . if it does not work, get rid of it and get something that does work. In any event, the rule on controls for EDP is: *Use them*. They are usually relatively inexpensive to implement and can save plenty of money, time, business resources, headaches and frustration. And by all means, the reporting EDP staff should be told what controls are being used so that they will be able to contribute the information that is needed, when it is needed.

Using an outside consultant in EDP

Consultants are used in EDP for a variety of reasons. The main reason is that they can bring to bear on the EDP function specialized skills and know-how. Very often consultants offer an

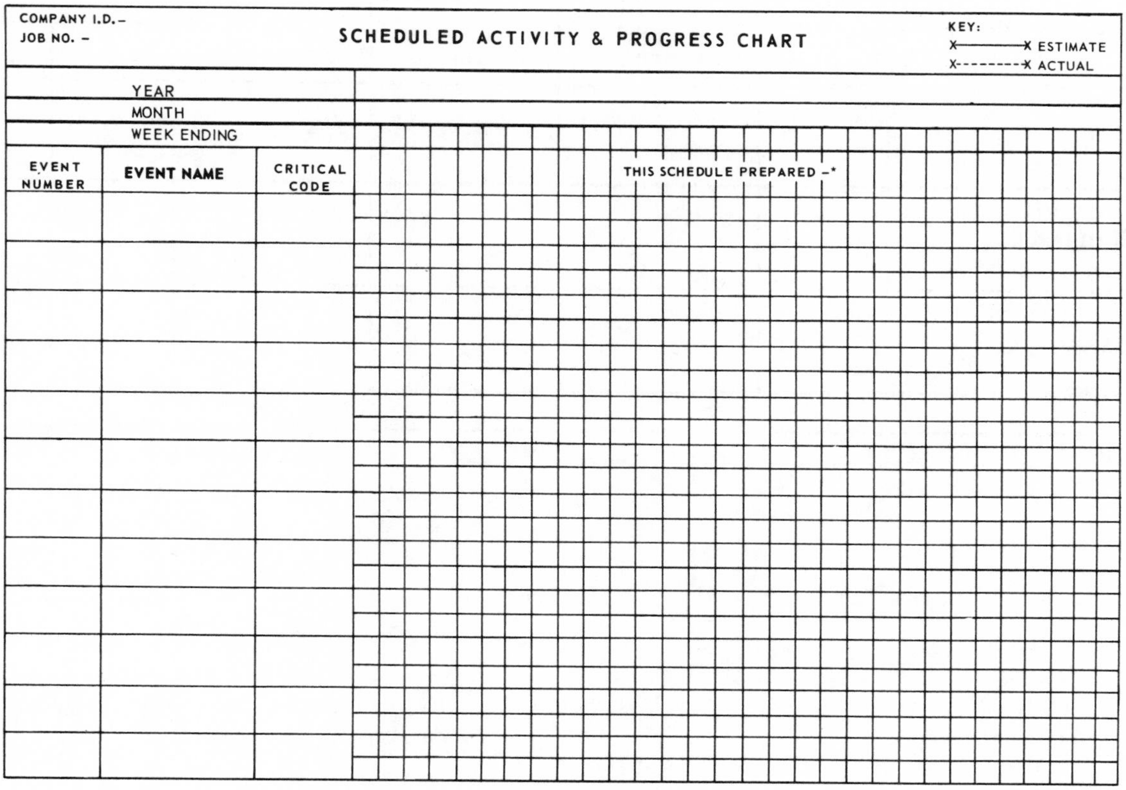

COMPANY I.D. –
JOB NO. –

SCHEDULED ACTIVITY & PROGRESS CHART

KEY:
X———X ESTIMATE
X- - - - - - - -X ACTUAL

YEAR
MONTH
WEEK ENDING

EVENT NUMBER	EVENT NAME	CRITICAL CODE	THIS SCHEDULE PREPARED –*

Figure 1.5
Scheduled Activity & Progress Chart

SUMMARY
MANAGEMENT STATUS REPORT

JOB NO.– START DATE–	PREPARED BY	DATE
JOB NAME –	REVIEWED BY	DATE
COMPANY I.D.–		

Statistics Item	ORIGINAL ESTIMATE	LATEST REVISED	UNDERRUN (OVERRUN)	% DIFFERENCE	LAST CHANGE DATE	LAST CHANGE % DIFFERENCE
COST						
SCHEDULE						
MANPOWER						

REMARKS –

Figure 1.6
Summary Management Status Report

DETAIL
MANAGEMENT STATUS REPORT

JOB NUMBER	START DATE	PREPARED BY	DATE
JOB NAME		REVIEWED BY	DATE
COMPANY I.D.			

Event Number	EVENT NAME	Critical Code	COST			SCHEDULE		
			Original Estimate	% Underrun (Overrun)	Last Change Date %	Original Estimate	% Underrun (Overrun)	Last Change Date %

PAGE _____ OF _____

Figure 1.7
Detail Management Status Report

independent opinion that the client is unable to render because: (1) the special capabilities needed to do so do not exist in the client organization (2) the special skills exist in the client organization, but are not available when needed, or (3) the perspective and/or objectivity needed to make an analysis and evaluation can best be gotten from a qualified person who is free from day-to-day operating pressures and other distractions.

Problems experienced by EDP managers hoping to benefit from a consultant's help arise mostly from two sources . . . the client and the consultant.

On the client side, one finds that some managers do not know what can and cannot be properly expected of a consultant. To put it another way, those who benefit most, know how to use a consultant.

On the consultant side, one sometimes finds that consultants overestimate or overstate their ability to deal with certain EDP mangement problems; hence, the appropriate advice and results may not be realized. Or, to state it differently, it ends up to be a case of the blind leading the blind.

There are fewer problems of this kind today, as a percentage of total consulting engagements in EDP, than in the earlier days of computing. One can attribute this to smarter clients as well as more capable consultants. However, these situations have not disappeared by any means, and when they do occur they are just as serious as they ever were.

TYPES OF CONSULTANTS

There are at least five kinds of enterprises that bill themselves as consultants on EDP activities. In general, each type claims to offer a different or specialized service, although the validity of these claims can easily be challenged. The following list shows the predominant sources for EDP consultants:

1. *General Management Consultants.* Usually called upon for overall EDP planning and organization advice, but not limited to these areas.
2. *Certified Public Accountants.* Engagements may entail management consulting activities, systems analysis, and programming.
3. *EDP Consultants.* (Also *software houses*) Specialize in EDP exclusively and generally concentrate on systems and programming, with limited management consulting activities.
4. *Service Bureaus.* Same as EDP consultants, except that a service bureau can offer an extension, by virtue of the fact that it has hardware to implement and regularly operate application systems.
5. *Free-Lance Consultants.* Usually a one to three man operation concentrating on a few functions or an industry. Some view themselves as general management consultants, others as simply programmers, and some as EDP specialists for a specific industry, e.g., retailing, brokerage, etc.

Aside from the foregoing, a number of other businesses (Lever Brothers, Westinghouse, and others) have entered this field in the course of diversification. Hardware leasing companies have done so, although EDP consultants diversify by going into leasing in some cases. Banks might also be viewed as consultants, in the sense that many now provide EDP services that are quite similar if not identical.[7] Other firms are outgrowths of businesses which are related to EDP hardware manufacturing. Some, of course, just spring up as a result of a company's desire to get "a piece of the action."

SELECTING A CONSULTANT

The inducement to look outside the company for professional consultation on a problem arises out of client management's recognition that the problem may best be attacked by using

---

[7]As this book goes to press a case is on appeal to the U.S. Supreme Court where the plaintiff, an association of EDP service bureaus (ADPSO), is pressing for a decision to limit the activities of banks in EDP services.

independent help. Prior to actually searching for a consultant, however, it is very important to prepare a definition of the problem. This definition should be formulated by the client managers who are directly involved in the problem situation. The result should be an agreed upon definition, explaining the major characteristics of the problem and its scope. The definition may then be used to guide the search for a consultant who is capable of handling the particular assignment.

Most consulting engagements result from referrals of some kind. These can be obtained from a variety of sources: recommendations from contacts in other companies; past experience of the client company's management; colleagues in professional societies; and from trade associations such as Association of Consulting Management Engineers (ACME). Besides referrals, most EDP consulting companies (as opposed to general management consultants and CPA firms) advertise their services in trade journals and by way of direct mail. Some of these consultants emphasize certain EDP capabilities in their promotional literature.

As a general rule, the size of the consulting firm is a good gauge for determining the size of job for which they are best suited. But, of course, this is neither always true nor is it the only criterion for selection. It is often helpful to obtain literature about various consultants (either from them directly or from a business library) that gives an indication of what the firm emphasizes as its specialties. Depending on the definition of the problem, some consultants can be eliminated as being too small (or too large). Others can be eliminated based on the skills they emphasize. Hopefully this narrowing down, together with some kind of referral information, will limit the choices to a reasonable number (five at most, preferably fewer).

After having assembled a short list of names of consulting firms that are likely to be able to handle the assignment, the next logical step is to invite each firm's representative to discuss the problem.

The selection process should be one in which the potential client holds an upper-hand and is, therefore, able to properly direct the interviews with consultants. This not only serves to keep the discussion on the right track but also inhibits the consultant from moving off the problem area into too many generalities about EDP problems.

Some representatives may turn out to be the "pushy" or hard-sell type; others may take a casual attitude, relying on their firm's reputation as the selling point. Still others may display a "know-it-all" air. Each of these types is to be avoided in making the final selection.

On the positive side, potential clients should look for the consultant's interest and depth of his understanding of the problem. Professional consultants can also be expected to probe into the problem, ask intelligent questions, and offer meaningful discussions.[8] They will rarely have answers at the first meeting, but they should express ideas or approaches that make sense to client management. A sincere desire to serve the client in solving the problem must be the impression left by the consultant finally chosen—if the feeling is that the service was "sold," there is reason to be suspect. A potential client should feel no embarrassment in seeking outside help. Nor should he be concerned that penetrating questions put to the consultant might reflect his lack of understanding.

On some jobs it may be appropriate to ask the consultant for references to contact to learn more about his capabilities. Two references are usually sufficient, and it is a good idea to check them in person, if possible. Here, the client-to-be can discuss the consultant's work with one or more individuals with whom the consultant has dealt. It is particularly useful to find out what specific people were engaged in the consulting assignment and if real benefits were obtained as a result of the consultant's work.

---

[8]The consultant may take exception to the proposed definition of the problem. Hear him out, probe his reasons . . . he may be right, and it serves client interests if he is.

Buying consulting services is similar to buying most other things, in that the buyer must be able to apply a value judgment to that which is being purchased, if the proper decision is to be made.

At the conclusion of interviewing and reference checking, the field should be narrowed-down to the two (three at most) most likely prospects, whereupon serious negotiations can begin which will lead to a *preliminary survey* and finally a *proposal*. Most consulting proposals take the form of a lengthy letter outlining the Work Plan, range of fees,[9] and other information pertaining to the service to be rendered. If the client authorizes the work, the proposal constitutes the agreement (or arrangement) which governs the relationship between the two parties. It should not be viewed as a contract in the formal sense. Contractual type agreements are used in what is sometimes termed "EDP consulting," but they usually cover systems and programming work. Further information and guidelines on this are offered in Chapter four, in the section *Contracting for EDP Development Work.*

TIPS ON WORKING WITH CONSULTANTS

Client management will benefit most from consultants by recognizing that it has to make the decisions and take the action. A consultant is not in a good position to do this. Instead, he provides the insights and recommendations as to what decisions should be made and what action should be taken. The affected part of the client organization must take directions from its management, not from the consultant. Misunderstandings and confusion about the consultant's role, in this regard, are a major cause of problem consulting engagements in EDP.

Other tips and pointers for EDP managers, include:

1. If the problem is vague to the client it will be vague to the consultant. Make a sincere attempt to determine its validity and by all means prepare a definition.
2. Investigate possible consultants using referrals, by interviewing the consultant, by discussing him with past clients, and by checking with trade associations.
3. Understand what the proposal means, what work will be done, and what the end product will be.
4. A consulting engagement is a partnership in a sense that client should back up what he has authorized. To get the most out of a consultant, be sure he gets meaningful support. The right doors have to be opened and the stage has to be set by the client.
5. If the client agrees with the consultant's recommendations, he should take action to realize the benefits implied. Otherwise, the client company is wasting its time and its money. There is no need for a consultant if the company is not dedicated to solving the problem.
6. Plan carefully the strategies involved in introducing a consultant into a politically hot company situation. Timing as well as approach are keys to a successful outcome.

---

[9]Fees estimated in the proposal are based upon the billing rates of the consulting personnel to be assigned. Billing rates for junior consultants are typically in the $150 to $250 a day range. Senior consultants and partners are generally over $250, ranging up to $500 per day. Travel and other expense items are not, as a rule, included in the billing rate but are charged to the client directly.

ORGANIZING EDP ACTIVITIES

The aims of this chapter are to: (1) provide general management pointers on organizing the EDP function and (2) illustrate a variety of specific organizational approaches which may be adapted to meet various requirements. Information provided here applies to the reorganization of an existing EDP function as well as setting up one that is entirely new.

Organization considerations

Data processing organization structures vary depending upon business type and size, management philosophy, and the level of systems development and implementation activity. Additionally, there is the need to custom-tailor the organization to satisfy unique requirements, local conditions, and to properly utilize particular talents.

Some of the basic steps in organizing the EDP function are outlined below.

1. Identify and understand the data processing objectives and goals as they apply to the company and relate to its policies, long-range plans, etc.
2. Decide where to place the EDP organization in the context of the company's total organization structure. This decision will depend upon the intended scope of EDP and may include centralization vs. decentralization considerations for larger companies.
3. Determine what impact the EDP organization may have on the company's existing structure and current practices. Study the information flow in the business.
4. Decide as precisely as possible, the responsibilities, accountability, and authority which will be assigned to the EDP function.
5. For each activity within the EDP organization, determine clearly what work each is supposed to perform, what responsibilities each has, and describe the authority that each will exercise.
6. Prepare job descriptions for each position.
7. Document the organization structure and provide descriptions . . . be sure that all affected parties understand what new relationships will exist.

For a large company, carrying out these steps is likely to be a formidable undertaking. This is particularly true where an existing EDP organization must undergo radical changes.

ORGANIZING AROUND PEOPLE

As is true in any field, consideration must be given to more than just the technical aspects of organizing the department. Personal characteristics of the staff members may dictate that certain individuals be assigned somewhat different duties than might normally be associated with their titles or positions in the company EDP function.

Regardless of the size or complexity of the EDP function, current or anticipated, the astute businessman will always want to account for the informal or human organization in a very serious way. At all times, the key objective must be to maximize benefits to the company, and since it is almost impossible to please everyone, management must make certain that the action taken exploits the resources of the company to attain the fullest measure of benefits. In some cases, the enactment of this idea calls for building parts of the organization around individuals who have demonstrated outstanding capabilities . . . the object being to capture and put to work as many of these unusual talents and skills as possible.

After the organization has been set up, its structure should not be thought of as "cast in concrete." If, as a result of new developments or better ideas, it makes sense to modify the organization . . . do so! The fact that new talent will appear on the scene over time dictates that the organization should be subject to regular review for improvement. This is an absolute must, where jobs have been designed for specific individuals.

Many of the talents and skills needed in EDP are truly difficult to find. As a result, the organization should be flexible enough to allow itself to take on styles that draw out the best its people have to offer. Trying to hammer individuals, particularly the creative EDP types, into some pre-ordained pattern is often costly and unproductive. Naturally, the leadership of the organization must be such that the efforts of talented employees are directed toward specific business objectives.

CENTRALIZED VERSUS DECENTRALIZED EDP

Very large businesses with decentralized EDP that decide to centralize will find the going a bit difficult, to say the least. There is bound to be resistance and, sometimes, overt protest. Going the other way, from centralization to decentralization, presents problems of a different nature, but the transition is not likely to be as traumatic.

Decentralized EDP in major companies is fast becoming a bygone phenomenon. This means that all the divisions or groups in a company that formerly had their own computers and systems development staffs are now turning to a "central" EDP organization for the same services. Central, in this context, means that all EDP in the company is the responsibility of a corporate level officer whose job it is to: (1) provide data processing services to the entire corporation, and (2) see to it that the corporation, as a whole, reaps the maximum benefits from EDP. The actual computer center facilities, including the operations and systems staffs may, however, be at a number of different physical locations.

Few cogent arguments can be advanced in favor of decentralized EDP on any long-term basis. The fact that decentralization occurred at all was, in part, due to upper management's failure to recognize the importance of EDP earlier in its development. Those who still favor decentralized EDP, do so on the grounds that they have special problems that need localized treatment by a staff reporting directly to them. Often, the fact of the matter is that they find giving up their little empires a bit distasteful. Also, they may fear that a centralized organization will examine the needs more closely and assess them in the light of the company's best interests and may not be swayed by purely provincial desires.

It is, nevertheless, true that a decentralized group is likely to get a job completed faster and with less formality. Under local autonomy, service may be more responsive and even more efficient because the EDP systems problems may be better understood. In this type of operation, the boss gives an order to the systems staff to produce a system or even just another report, and "presto" it is done. However, it is probable that no evaluation of the system or report will have been made, much less a review of how such work benefits the corporation as a whole.

A number of companies have taken a "half-way" approach to centralization wherein all EDP activities, *except* systems analysis, report to central EDP management. This author has personal knowledge of just one rather large company doing this and in this one case it has been declared a failure by upper management. Coordination was among the major half-dozen problems in this situation.

Some of the major advantages of centralized EDP include:

1. *Lower hardware costs.* By consolidating computer time demands, management can justify larger systems. A larger system may be capable of doing a given job at one-third of the cost of a smaller one. Putting it another way . . . spending twice as much for a computer often yields much greater than twice the performance of the cheaper one.
2. *Lower development costs.* As an example, if a company has five divisions, chances are that five payroll systems or five accounts receivable systems are not really needed. Perhaps one comprehensive version of each application will do the job . . . and will cost much less to build.
3. *Improved control of EDP costs.* Expenditures are in one budget and are controlled by one department.
4. *Standard approaches and methods.* Management information systems, particularly those intended for use by corporate management, depend upon standards. Such company-wide standards could involve names and definitions given to data elements, compatible hardware/software/applications documentation, and many others.
5. *Better utilization of professional skills.* The best talent in the company can be recognized and put to work in a more optimal fashion.
6. *Technical staff obtains diverse experience.*
7. *Improved possibilities for career growth and advancement.*

There are other desirable features of centralization that could be discussed here, but there are also bureaucratic complaints, problems and environmental adjustments to be considered.

1. *Communications.* If the computers, application systems, and people will be talking to each other for the first time, methods and procedures must be established to accomplish the integration.
2. *Continuity of present systems.* Since systems are currently in operation and others planned or being developed, conversion to the centralized organization is quite likely to take a number of months or even years (unless special funding is secured to bring it about faster).
3. *Development of common systems.* A system to serve multiple functional requirements is considerably more difficult to produce than one serving a singular set of requirements. In some cases, larger, more expensive systems will be required. They are not only expensive but are more difficult to develop and harder to manage. New problems must be solved, such as how to coordinate six dozen creative people working on the same system . . . it was a challenge when there were only six or eight people.

It is probably safe to say that some patience will be one of many attributes that managers and their men will need in order to switch to centralized EDP. Some companies have initiated their move to centralization by simply having the decentralized EDP groups start reporting to a corporate level officer in charge of all data processing. In this way, hardware/software purchasing is able to get corporate level treatment right away. Anyone who understands the real problems involved, however, will hastily acknowledge that this tactic is just a bare beginning.

PROJECT VERSUS FUNCTIONAL ORGANIZATIONAL STRUCTURES

Large and medium scale EDP organization structures have undergone a number of interesting changes over the years. At first, systems development work tended to be project oriented, so that for a given application (or application category) all planning work, analysis, and programming was done under the direction of a project leader who carried the total responsibility for the effort. Later, the planning and analysis tended to be separated from the programming activities, with both areas set up as separate functional departments within the EDP organization.

In recent times, there is a growing trend toward the renewal of the project oriented approach. A number of reasons could be advanced as to why this is happening. Rather than explore the cause and effect relationships, it might be worthwhile to outline briefly certain pros and cons in considering the effectiveness of the project organization versus the functional. Figure 2.1 indicates some of the significant qualitative characteristics for various features of both types of organizations. Each type, it should be noted, is subject to different pressures.

Feature	Project	Functional
Management Attention and Control	Tends to be strong	Sometimes weak, poorly defined
Risk of Failure	Lower than functional	Higher than project
Technical Proficiency	Tends to be average due to multiple functions	Frequently strong and highly polished
Development of Personnel	Substantial opportunities for job enlargement and broader development	Attention is toward high competence in narrow field of activities
Cost to Complete Entire Job	About the same as functional	About the same as project
System Operational Efficiency	Lower than functional	Higher than project due to technical expertise
Level of Knowledge about the Application	Higher than functional	Lower than project
Overall Technical Coordination	Lower than functional	Better than project
Overall Flexibility in Making Personnel Assignments	Somewhat rigid	Usually good within specialty area
Group Morale and Interest in End Product	Higher than functional	Lower than project

Figure 2.1
**Comparative Characteristics of Project
and Functional Organization Structures**

Field results and factors shown in Figure 2.1 indicate that the project organization is better suited for carrying out major systems development work. Since many installations are becoming more and more involved with large, integrated information systems (often with multiple applications), it was felt that the topic of project management deserved broader treatment. In Chapter four, *Using Project Management in EDP*, the reader will find criteria which help him to determine when and where to use a project approach. Also, the organization and management of projects are discussed in detail.

Organization structures

A variety of organization structures are included in this section to show some of the possible ways in which EDP organizations may be set up. Some of the charts show strictly functional organizations, others are project oriented, and still others represent a combination of the two. As was stated earlier, EDP organizations that work best are those custom-tailored to the needs of the particular company. Therefore, the organization charts selected for discussion here are meant to stimulate ideas rather than to be lifted out and used intact.

Job titles used in the various organizations about to be discussed are not necessarily consistent, either in nomenclature or duties and responsibilities, from one chart to the next. However, such inconsistencies are common in EDP, and it is useful to become familiar with various different usages of titles, particularly where positions are being created or titles are being changed. Appendix A provides a number of job descriptions for the more common titles in use.

SMALL AND MEDIUM-SCALE EDP ORGANIZATIONS

The small-scale EDP organization chart shown in Figure 2.2 depicts an organization which would not usually be comprised of more than twenty people. In the case of most small organizations, staff members quite often perform multiple functions. For example, an individual may do programming, be a computer operator on a regular basis, and may sometimes act in the capacity of a control clerk. This is typical of the sort of flexibility that makes it difficult to describe the small organization by a chart which does not accurately illustrate what is really happening. Because of the flexibility inherent in the smaller organization, such as that shown in Figure 2.2, problems concerning interdepartmental jurisdiction tend to be minimal. However, it is common to find the small EDP organization functioning as a captive group within some department whose main interest is not EDP, e.g., controller's department, treasurer's department. If past experience can be used as indicator, the captive EDP group is generally not able to serve company-wide information processing needs. Many more advantages can be realized by the company as a whole if the EDP department is under a computer executive who is responsible directly to the company president.

Early in Chapter one, the need for EDP to get into the main stream of business activities was emphasized. By placing the EDP department near the top of the organization, there is a substantially greater opportunity for developing more profitable and rigorously justified systems. Conversely, when the EDP function is a captive group, these opportunities often get lost in the "paperwork shuffle."

Figure 2.3 is an EDP organization chart for a medium-scale installation. Except in those companies that have an exceptionally large clerical staff within the EDP department, this organization typically has less than sixty people. The functional structure of the programming and systems activity in Figure 2.3 indicates that there are no formally established project-type organizations within the staff. The manager of data processing here, as is desirable in any size EDP installation, reports to a high-level executive so that company-wide needs can be properly satisfied. Figure 2.3 also shows an executive subcommittee for data processing. This may be a subcommittee of a working board of directors or a selected group of other top executives. One

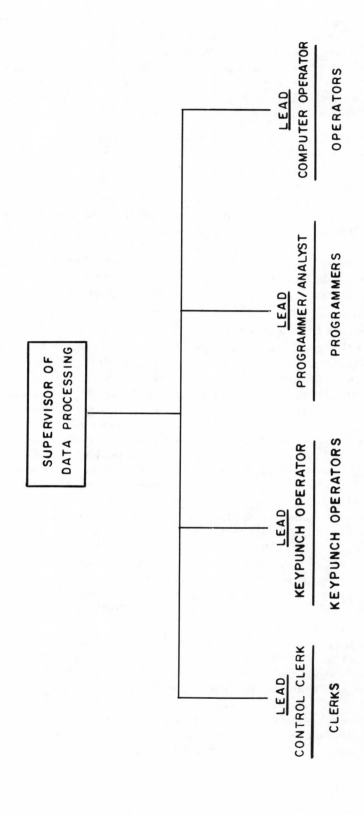

Figure 2.2
Small-Scale EDP Organization Chart

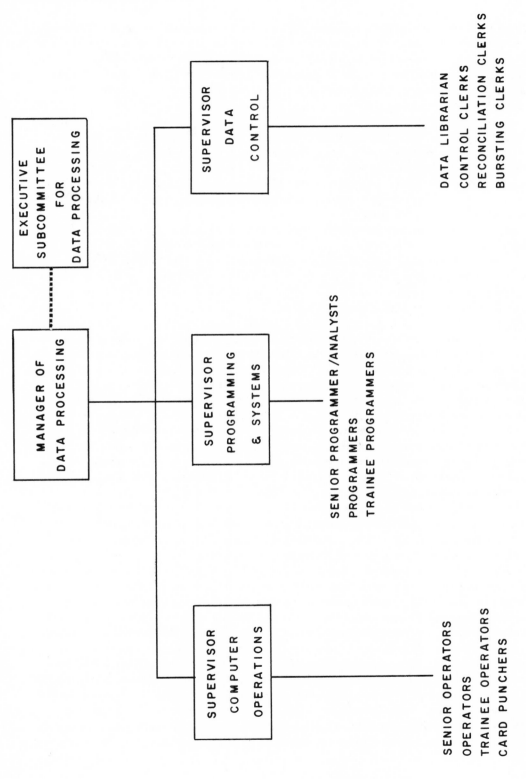

Figure 2.3
Medium-Scale EDP Organization Chart
Functional Structure

35

reason for having such a committee is to insure that, through a timely exchange of information, the gradual education of key executives about EDP will take place. Another purpose of this kind of committee is to formulate policy regarding the company's computer activities. Major decisions, such as ordering new computer equipment or developing high-cost applications, are always made with the advice and consent of this group. Besides acting as a decision-making body, this committee is expected to present the company's goals in terms which are meaningful to the EDP organization and to which it can respond.

Figure 2.3, it will be noted, shows data control activities as being distinct from computer operations. This arrangement is analogous to an ordinary production facility in which quality control is a function separate from production. Some EDP organizations have this feature, while others have data control activities within computer operations. Financial institutions, in particular, prefer that the two activities be separate and distinct because tighter internal and audit controls can be enforced on this basis.

A project oriented structure for systems development work is shown in Figure 2.4 for a medium-scale EDP organization. In this organization there are individuals who hold the position of project leader, each having a team of programmer/analysts reporting to him. The operating characteristic of a project group is that all work to be done in order to bring a project from inception to completion is carried out exclusively by the specifically designated project group. In some installations, a project team may be responsible for several smaller projects. A multiple project team may take on certain functional organization characteristics.

Aside from the project feature of the organization shown in Figure 2.4, there is one group shown that warrants some discussion. It is the Information System Technology group. This kind of group has not had as much significance in the past as it does with today's rapidly changing computer technology. The reason for this group's existence can best be explained in terms of modern hardware and software performance characteristics. While it is true that computing equipment is much more economical today than in the past, with respect to speed vs. hardware costs, it requires that considerably more attention be given to the software that supports its operation. Such software includes operating systems and the multitude of functions that they carry out, compilers, and other standardized programs which are common to many applications. Programs which sort data are just one example of such standardized programs. With the greatly improved versatility of today's EDP equipment and the software required to make it run, it is necessary for medium size and larger companies to have a technology group. This group must constantly keep abreast of the new developments in the computer field, as they have the responsibility for evaluating, specifying, supporting, and developing standards for equipment and software. In subsequent chapters of this book, coverage will be given to each of these activities.

Figure 2.5 illustrates one possibility for organizing an EDP department that serves internal computing needs of the company and, in addition, markets services outside the company. The distinguishing property of this organization is that the external services are marketed and provided by a completely independent department. As can be seen from the chart, the computer operations and technical services departments serve the needs of both the internal and external systems groups. Where services are sold outside the company, a structure such as that in Figure 2.4 is advisable because it is designed to reduce the conflict that otherwise would be present between internal and external demands for systems and programming personnel. Pooling all resources into one group may look practical from a theoretical viewpoint, but it has not worked well where it has been tried. Banks that offer computer services and other similar companies with internal and external services would be well advised to segregate the development activities of the two systems. Within each group, however, either a functional or project approach may be taken.

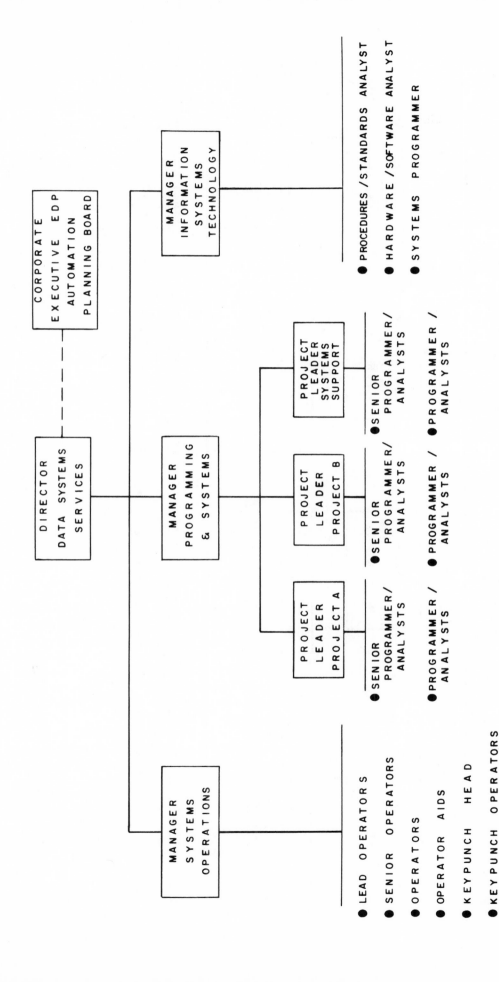

Figure 2.4
Medium-Scale EDP Organization Chart
Project Oriented Structure

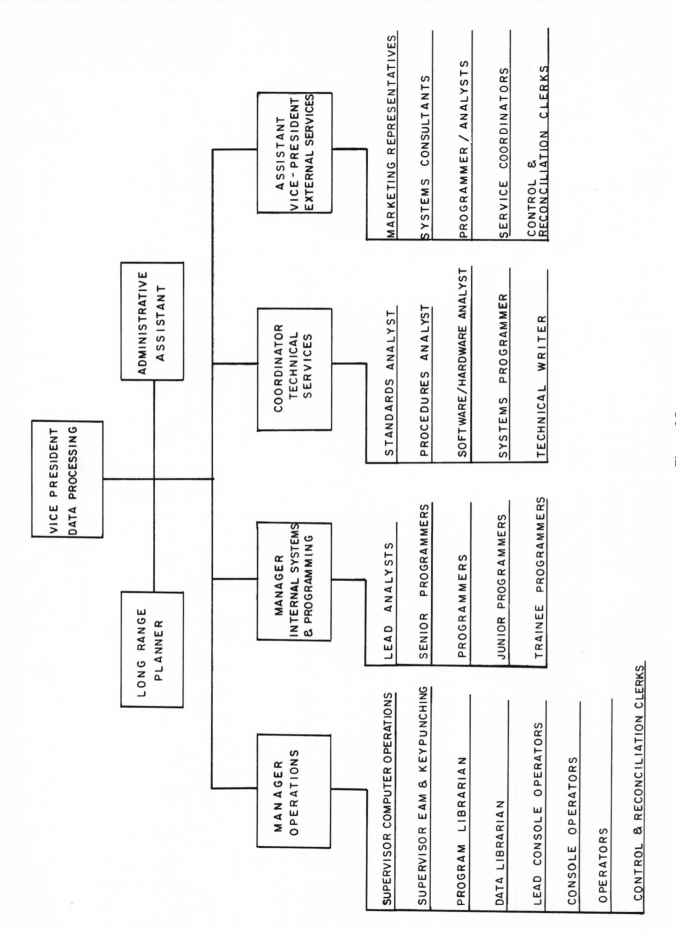

Figure 2.5
Medium-Scale EDP Organization Chart
Functional Structure with External Services

If the company intends to go into the computing services business full-scale, a subsidiary company should be established for this purpose.

A project management approach with a "floating" technical staff arrangement is shown in Figure 2.6. In this organization, project assignments are made as required, drawing individuals from the pool of technical talent available. The assignment of a given individual to a specific project in an organization such as this one, can be made in such a way that special skills can be rotated from project to project as needed. This structure has the advantage of flexibility in its management, but the personnel involved may find it difficult to adjust to the unstable nature of the project teams. Also, they might not feel the same sense of loyalty to the project as would their counterparts in another type of EDP organization who are permanent members of the group.

The organizational approach depicted in Figure 2.6 could, it would seem, be used effectively in a software and/or application programming business. Under those circumstances, the individuals involved are likely to be inclined to anticipate fully the transient attributes of this environment and are more likely to enjoy it.

LARGE-SCALE EDP ORGANIZATIONS

The large-scale EDP organization chart in Figure 2.7 shows the functional activities of systems analysis and programming as two distinct departments. In such an organization all systems analysis and design work is done by systems analysts who specialize in this function, and programming is done by individuals who concentrate their full attention on programming activities. The justification for this specialization is the concept that a specialist should be able to perform his job more economically than someone who must spread his efforts over several functions. A number of professionals in the EDP field hold the opinion that EDP has not matured sufficiently to carry on its activities on a specialized basis. Others have said that they avoid certain personnel conflicts and problems by remaining unspecialized. Most programmers, for example, want to do analysis work too; when they are limited, their enthusiasm is lower. In addition, communications problems arise more often between specialty groups that must work in concert. Further, as systems development efforts become larger in scope, there is a serious question whether this functional separation can provide the appropriate continuity of management attention.

Supporters of the functional structure, on the other hand, contend that it has an inherent set of checks and balances which obviate the requirement for constant attention by a single manager. This is by virtue of the fact that formalized specifications pass from systems analysis to programming in all cases. And, more importantly, such specifications ostensibly get a thorough review at two levels. In most cases, the programming group in Figure 2.7 has the option to reject the specification if it fails to meet certain criteria upon which it is evaluated.

There are a number of other affirmative and negative points on the specialization question which seem to cancel each other out, with the possible exception of certain human factors involved. That is, there is a conflict that sometimes takes place between the two groups that can be detrimental rather than constructive. What happens is that the programmers accuse the systems people of designing systems which bear little relationship to the realities of implementation. Conversely, the accusations flow in the other direction, whereupon the programming group is viewed by the analysts as incapable of understanding systems work and ignorant of the real world of the business. As might be expected, these arguments and rebuttals can build up a momentum which is sufficient to seriously impede progress on the job. This lack of cohesiveness is a sometime thing and one should not, therefore, jump to the conclusion that the functional arrangement should be ruled out as an organizational possibility.

The organizational form displayed in Figure 2.8 has a variety of features that are worthy

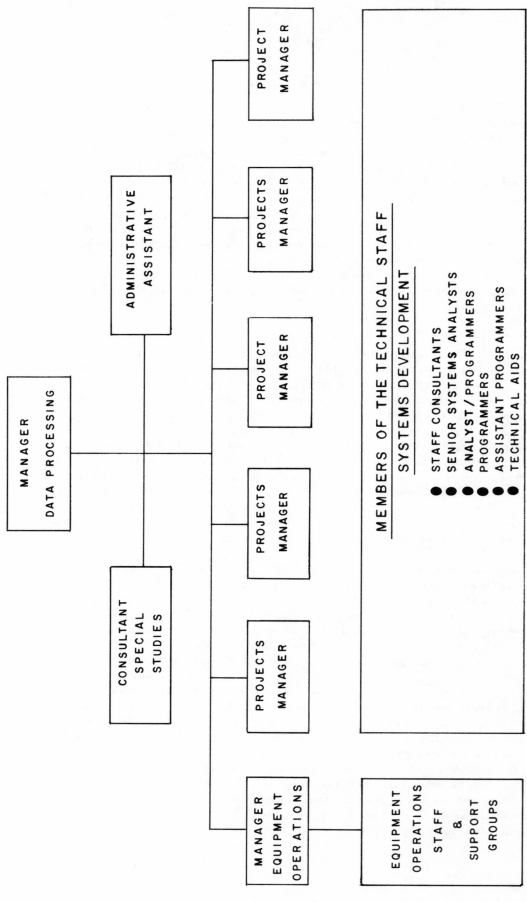

Figure 2.6

Medium- or Large-Scale EDP Organization Chart
Project Team Selected from Mobile Technical Staff

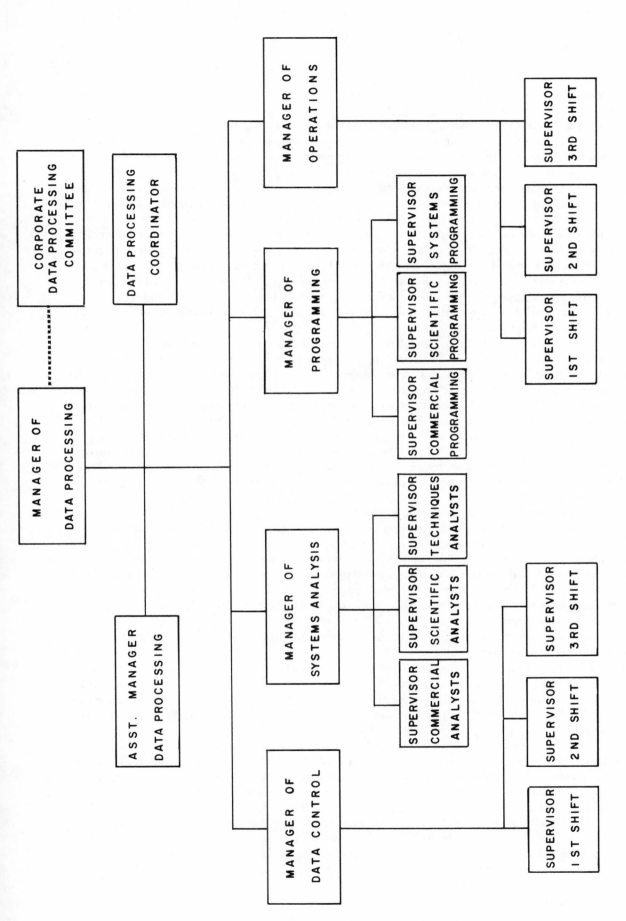

Figure 2.7
Large-Scale EDP Organization Chart
Management in a Functional Structure

of explanation. One key management objective of this arrangement is to recognize and formally deal with the problem of administering and controlling major projects. In this case, there are two independent major projects that demand special treatment; this is accomplished by having them set up as entities reporting directly to the manager of information systems.

The *steering committees* associated with each major project in Figure 2.8 are composed of executives from various parts of the company that have a direct interest in the progress and outcome of the particular project. Members of the steering committees are supposed to exercise their authority to see that business resources and information flow freely to the project group. It is almost always true that at least one member of the steering committee holds the direct responsibility for authorizing the project's existence and is accountable for the results obtained. Within a given project, depending upon the type of computer application it is supposed to produce, a variety of subgroups are often set up. The group leaders shown in Figure 2.8 would have technical personnel reporting to them and are responsible for all activities associated with the particular task that has been assigned to them.

In addition to the two independent major projects, there are two application development groups, each specializing in a different application category. These two groups in Figure 2.8 are functionally organized, and neither would ordinarily have a major project within it. The *systems programming group*, which is separate, works closely with all other departments in the installation in an effort to bring about optimum operating practices and standard techniques. Additionally, this group is responsible for maintaining an ongoing evaluation of hardware and software, so that the installation will be apprised of the newest technology and can take advantage of the most efficient EDP methods. The computer operations department will be discussed in detail in Chapter eight; however, it is interesting and useful to be mindful of the various activities and functions implied by the titles of the operations staff members listed on the organization chart.

It will be noted that the manager of information systems in Figure 2.8 manages the EDP department with the help of an *advisory board* that includes his high level administrators. Also designated is a *control manager* who is in charge of budgetary control and matters pertaining to finance for the installation. *Long range planning* has been made the province of a staff consultant whose responsibility it is to formulate and maintain the overall long range plans and objectives which include the procurement of hardware, people, facilities and funds. (In well managed installations, *five-year plans* are developed on a continuing basis.) One reason for having the long range planning consultant as a separate entity is that it explicitly and formally establishes this activity so that it cannot become neglected under the pressure of short term demands that are placed upon the manager of information systems.

Figure 2.9 illustrates a project management setup wherein each specific application type is handled by a project team that specializes in that category. The way in which the responsibilities are subdivided implies an EDP organization of about 200 individuals. However, the concept of dividing the work among application specialty groups could be applied to EDP organizations having fewer people.

In larger companies, there is frequently the need to set up computer facilities in close proximity to major centers of business activity. A possible top management organization of a large-scale company-wide EDP organization is shown in Figure 2.10. In this centralized organization, multiple computer installations report to the top computer executive in the corporation. As can be seen from the chart, a geographical arrangement of computer centers has been provided to serve regional needs. There is also a computer center that serves the research and engineering center of the corporation. The locations of the various data centers would ordinarily be based upon the distribution pattern of computer demand to be satisfied. Therefore, the traditional

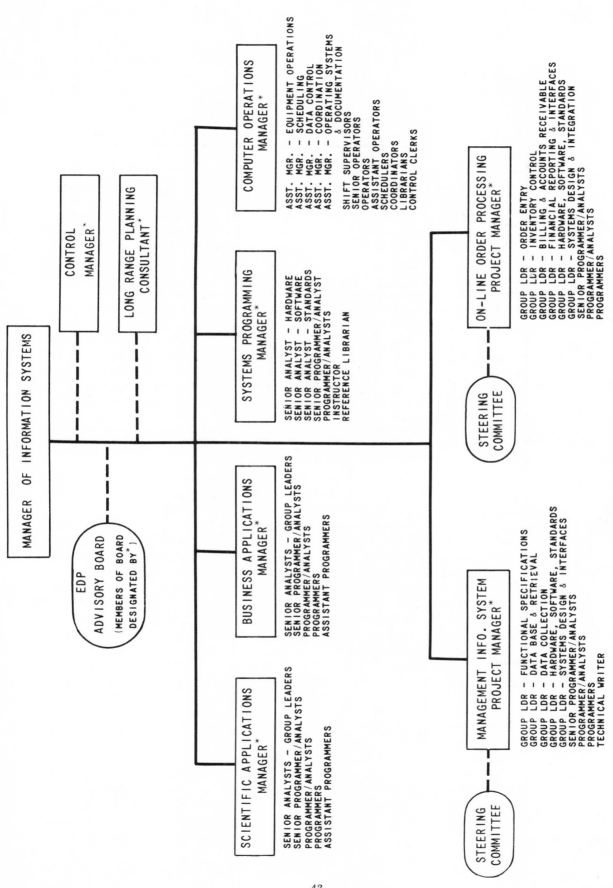

Figure 2.8

Large Scale EDP Organization Chart Functional by Application Category with Independent Major Projects

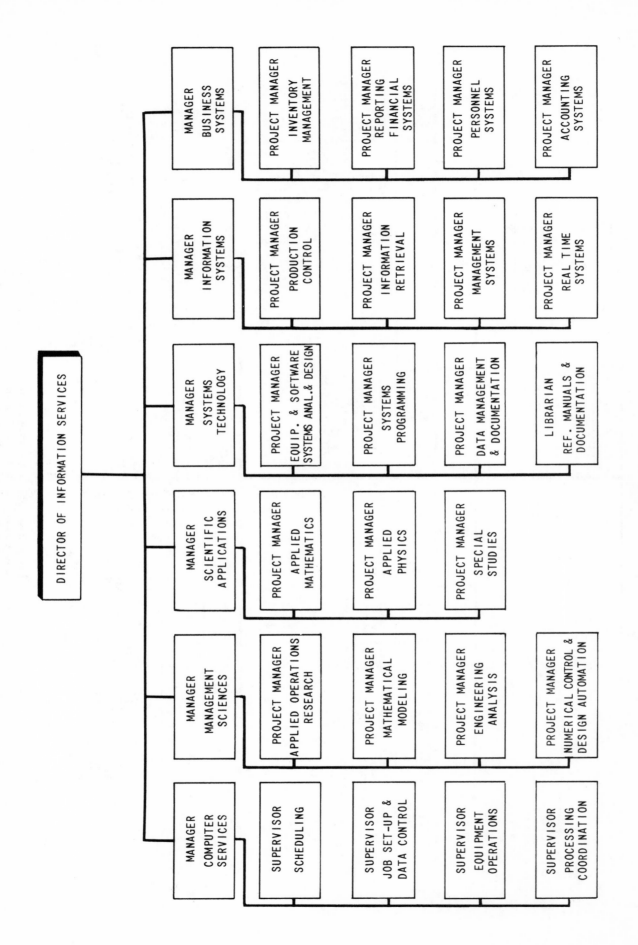

Figure 2.9
Large Scale EDP Organization Chart
Project Oriented Structure by Application Type

geographical breakdown for the nation-wide operations in Figure 2.10 may not hold for a number of companies operating in the United States that have different needs geographically. In practice, all of the installations of the corporation would be tied together via a telecommunications network that would link major computer systems for the purpose of data transmission and distributing demands for computer time.

The manager of information science technology and standards, shown in Figure 2.10, carries the responsibility for seeing that the corporation benefits from the latest developments in hardware, software, and analytical techniques. In addition, he is responsible for establishing the standards used throughout the company's computer centers. Such matters as standard terminology, definitions, and coding structures for corporate data would be within the purview of this manager's group. The remainder of the activities indicated in Figure 2.10 are not discussed, since the title of each is descriptive of the functions.

Figure 2.11 is included to illustrate several possible organizational trends that have been observed. These alterations represent important departures from more common types of EDP organizations. Factors giving rise to the differences are changes in computer technology, rapid growth of computer usage, and a general desire to improve effectiveness.

In this organization the systems programming function and the operations function report to the director of data center services. As previously mentioned, modern hardware technology is very much dependent on software. Combining hardware and software support emphasizes the need for a close working relationship. Since the software is now the interface with which all computer processing must communicate, the organizational approach attempts to reflect the idea of a complete or total entity . . . hardware/software.

Greater emphasis and importance is given to education in the organization shown in Figure 2.11. Elevating this function acknowledges the complexity of modern systems and the very critical need to have informed professionals on the job. Few companies can now afford the hit-and-miss training that was common in the past. Trial and error methods used by programmers and operators on today's complex systems often result in the waste of enormous sums of money. A strong educational program is the logical answer to much of the problem.

Long range planning is another area where management has had to learn many lessons the hard way. Many have paid dearly for their past neglect and are now committed to see that powerful measures are taken to minimize the possibility of repeating the experience. The organizational approach in Figure 2.11 reflects what seems to be an authentic appreciation of the problem.

Figure 2.11 also shows applied systems groups specialized by company division. Each group or division is set up to serve the computer needs of the company's groups or divisions. This idea is an extension of a marketing concept. That is, a business divides itself in order to provide specialty groups that are responsible for dealing with a specific market for a product group or service. Similarly, the divisions in applied systems may correspond directly to those of the business. A given divisional group could be organized on either a functional or project approach. There are many considerations involved in organizing by division, not the least of which is a possible loss of specialized talent that would otherwise be available to work on any division's applications. It seems clear that these problems and others would have to be solved through careful planning.

Epilogue

Organizing the EDP effort along the lines given in any chart is not enough. The right individual must be found for each of the jobs and a suitable professional environment created. These important areas require the attention of key management people. A number of personnel considerations are addressed in Chapter five, *Acquiring, Evaluating and Managing EDP Personnel*.

There are seven areas in which the fine hand of management should be felt:

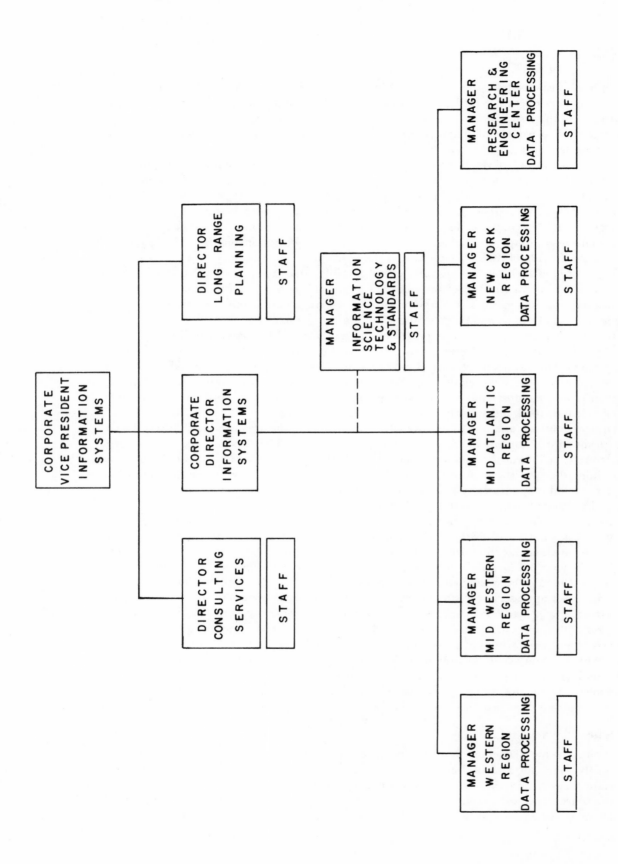

Figure 2.10
Large Scale Centralized EDP Organization
Chart with Multiple Installations

46

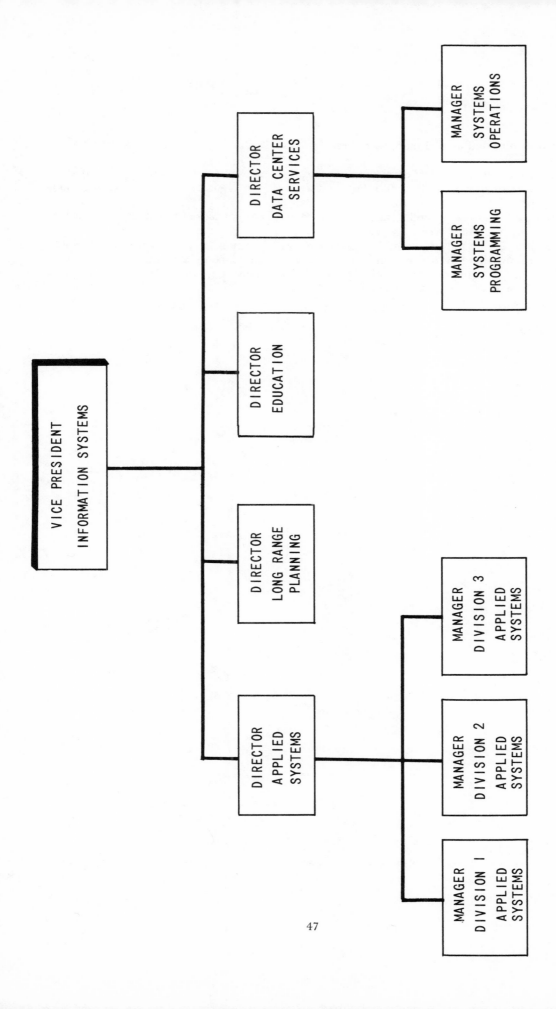

Figure 2.11
EDP Organization Showing Some Observable Trends

1. Ensure that a good man, with a record for successfully achieving change, manages the effort.
2. Ensure that the effort considers all the departments, not just the sponsoring department.
3. Ensure that the effort does not conflict with the organization's over-all long-range plans.
4. Organize flexibly and ensure that the computer is not locked into a department from which it cannot serve the whole company well.
5. Ensure that the effort aims for benefits in basic operations, not just in clerical operations.
6. Ensure that the computer plan is thoroughly prepared, complete, and well documented.
7. Once convinced that the plan is sound, back it by supporting the changes required throughout the organization.[1]

---

[1]S. A. Spencer, "Management's Responsibility to Profitable ADP," *Journal of Data Management*, April 1964, p. 26.

: three : three : three :

SYSTEMS DEVELOPMENT AND PROGRAMMING ADMINISTRATION

This chapter describes the steps involved in managing the effort to develop and implement an application system. It presupposes that the EDP function has been organized using the general guidelines discussed in the previous two chapters. It also assumes that a feasibility study or other preliminary cost evaluation has been completed, and that a decision has been made to carry on further developmental work.

Throughout this discussion it is well to be mindful of the fact that the effort being described is as much creative as it is technical. To view it as though all one needs to do is "turn the crank," and out comes a system, is inviting catastrophic consequences.

Some managers who are not acquainted, or at least do not appear to be, with the realities of systems and programming work have tried to muddle their way through, hoping for a successful outcome. Unhappily, this has rarely happened.

It is in pursuing this detailed and difficult work that the big picture or general concept melts away under the intensity of attempting to translate half-baked ideas into working EDP systems. At the time this work begins, it is advisable to remove the promoters and bystanders from the "playing field," in order to keep the confusion at a minimum.

In this chapter, some of the more formal types of management controls and documentation standards are discussed for systems and programming work. Time and cost estimating is also explored toward the end of this chapter. The first six sections have been designed to give managers a general overview of the basic steps involved in directing the development of an application system. In order of execution, the six steps are as follows:

1. **Systems Analysis.** Studying the problem to define exactly what the system should do . . . a determination of the user's functional requirements.

2. **Systems Design.** Specifying a series of computer programs (which together with non-computer procedures comprise the *system*) that satisfy the requirements as determined by systems analysis.
3. **Programming.** Designing, coding, and testing each program in the system individually.
4. **Pilot or Integrated Testing.** Operating the system with a representative volume of data to determine that all programs work together as a system.
5. **Parallel or Final Testing.** Operating the system with "live data" and comparing and otherwise checking results to an existing system (if one exists) or to especially prepared standards which set forth expected results (for final testing) under various actual operating conditions.
6. **Conversion.** Making ready the computerized data files to be used in the live operation. And also, the activities involved in turning over the new system to user and operating personnel. This may be a continuation of parallel testing up to the point where the old system is completely phased out.

Extrapolating information from several studies that have been done on this process, the distribution of time to each of the steps previously mentioned is as follows:

1. *Systems Analysis.* 25%
2. *Systems Design.* 18%
3. *Programming.* 37%
4. *Pilot or Integrated Testing.* 7%
5. *Parallel or Final Testing.* 8%
6. *Conversion.* 5%

As one would suspect, these percentages are approximate averages and tend to depict an average set of circumstances. At one extreme is the frontier-breaking system wherein the System Analysis would take longer than indicated. On the other extreme, there are systems for which requirements are well known in advance, for example, in reprogramming an existing computerized system for a different computer.

Using a new computer and software for the first time will increase the Programming activity because a learning process is involved—some of it trial and error. Conversely, a great deal of familiarity with these items tends to decrease the time spent.

Conversion time can also be misleading where large masses of data are being computerized for the first time. Recognize, however, that data conversion per se overlaps one or more of the previous steps in many cases.

Again, in the typical situation, one can see from the percentages that between 40 per cent and 50 per cent of the total time is spent in analysis and design before programming commences. Management should be wary of a plan that does not exhibit planning figures that are equal to or higher than these. There may be a legitimate reason for them to be lower, but managers must comprehend and agree with these reasons. What is frequently encountered in EDP is that too little time is devoted to these activities, and the project forges onward to produce a weak system. A weak system requires change upon change after it is implemented, so that the overlooked business requirements are added-on instead of built-in. This adding-on, or maintenance as it is sometimes called, can cost ten times what a given feature would have cost had it been built-in orginally. This could mean that if more than 10 per cent of the system has been overlooked, it may be cheaper to build a new one . . . if the alternative is maintenance. Ergo, it should be clear that it is most prudent to take the study and design steps seriously.

Systems analysis

Systems analysis, in this context, is begun after a feasibility study which results in a decision to develop and implement an application. This in-depth research and analysis of a given application is also known as the *full systems study*. The Work Plan, described in Chapter one, is intended to guide the systems analysis effort, among other things. Additionally, the report issued as a result of the feasibility study, also described in Chapter one, should be used as a reference.

It is the Work Plan that defines the scope and objectives of the system, as well as the schedule and manpower requirements. Logical subdivisions of the application will suggest how personnel should be assigned. Perhaps one of the most difficult problems facing a manager in this area is how to control this work and evaluate progress. Later in this chapter some methods to assist the manager in controlling this activity will be explored.

Systems Analysis is composed of a variety of activities. One of the basic functions is to learn what conditions currently exist. Another is to find out the true business needs, in a detailed manner. Throughout this entire process, the analyst is continually weighing factors and tying in ideas. Eventually he produces a set of requirements.

A superior systems analyst will dig beneath surface requirements for business data to extract and examine the real problems in operating the business. In this way, the analyst attempts to find systems solutions that are both valuable and efficient. At one point he may improve the format for an aged trial balance, at another point he may combine two reports into one that serves multiple requirements. He may suggest new and better ways to provide useful management information, and so on.

INVESTIGATING THE PRESENT METHODS

Narrow, inflexible computerized systems that do not properly satisfy the needs of the user are, in many cases, the result of a lack of understanding of the methods being supplanted.

In order to gain information about the logical basis for the new system, the present methods must be studied in detail. Such an investigation is essential for two important reasons. First, the new system ought to perform at least as well as the present system. Second, a solid knowledge of certain critical factors in the business activity must be gained. These factors include: sequencing of operations, operating time, volume of work, costs, and other information concerning problems inherent in the process itself. A knowledge of these factors should provide the systems analyst with a clear picture of fundamental operations.

Answers to questions, such as those listed in the four categories below, will help to provide the analyst with an understanding of the business requirements:

Management

- What are the past and future objectives?
- What is the general attitude?
- What is the underlying philosophy?
- What organizational changes are planned?
- What are the unfulfilled information needs?
- How receptive is management to new techniques or change?

Procedures

- What work is performed?
- In what sequence does the work take place?
- Who performs the functions?
- How many people are needed?
- When is the function performed?
- What equipment is used?
- Is the function needed?
- What inputs and outputs are involved?
- How much volume is there—average, peaks, growth?
- How much time is required for the functions?

- How often is the work done?
- What controls are required?
- What are the turn-around time requirements?
- What "business rules" apply to each function?

Cost

- How much does the present equipment cost?
- How much is spent on forms and supplies?
- What are the costs for carrying inventory or receivables awaiting collection?
- What are the personnel costs?
- What overhead is charged?

Effectiveness

- Does the current system do what was intended?
- What are the strong points?
- What are the disadvantages?
- What effects would expansion have?
- Is the current output useful?
- How much inefficiency and duplication of effort exists?
- What inter-department relationships exist?

There are various ways in which to go about answering these and other questions. The discussion that follows highlights certain key points in deriving the required information.

OBTAINING INFORMATION

There are three basic fact-gathering techniques which may be used to obtain information about the present system and future needs:

1. Interviewing.
2. Reviewing historical records.
3. Sampling and estimating.

Interviewing is considered to be the most important and productive source of information. Generally, interviewing should begin with top management to obtain broad background information, then with middle and first line management who provide the details, and finally, the individual workers are questioned. Care must be exercised to determine whether an individual's version of what is being done in his area is actually being done, and in the manner stated. Discrepancies which are discovered often put an entirely different light on the operations being investigated. In addition, interviewers must guard against mistaking opinion for fact. While opinions are frequently valuable, they should be identified as such. Interestingly, the lowest graded worker can often point out the imperfections in the present system and will sometimes even suggest worthwhile remedies.

Some basic guidelines for conducting interviews are:

1. Prepare an outline of topics to be discussed.
2. Get authorization for the interviews from the employee's superior.
3. Avoid detailed discourses on day-to-day problems unless they are germane.
4. Be as brief as courtesy permits.
5. Do not offer "on-the-spot" analysis of problems or solutions—the mission is to gather information.
6. Do not ask *why* questions if they can be avoided—interviewee may feel he is being blamed for some condition which exists.
7. Question both those who send and those who receive information from the department under study.

8. Conduct interviews where there is minimal distraction.
9. Remember that the first impression people get about EDP depends on the statesmanship of the interviewer representing it.

It is good practice to have a memorandum authorizing the study sent to the department manager before visiting a department in connection with systems planning and analysis. The memorandum, of course, should originate from higher levels of management. A conference or meeting can also accomplish the same result. In this way the department manager is informed, in advance, that the study team will need his cooperation. In so doing, the department manager should also be asked to make a point of introducing the study team to his staff and arrange for a free flow of information requested by the team.

Depending on the nature of the business and its rate of growth, historical records can sometimes provide useful information. Frequently, the investigator finds that records are out of date or have been poorly kept and can only serve as a coarse measure rather than absolute indicators. Where this situation is evident, the historical records might better be put aside and the balance of the study done in more depth to gain the information needed. Work sampling data can be gathered and representative time studies made with relative ease during the course of the investigation.

It is of the utmost importance to obtain current and accurate data. A specially prepared questionnaire is useful where large numbers of individuals are to be asked to provide information. Because large-scale survey studies give the respondents less opportunity to deal directly with the survey team, considerable skill and effort must be expended in designing the questionnaire. Care must be taken to insure correct interpretation of the questions asked.

Even when many precautions are taken, surveys can still yield a good set of answers . . . to the wrong questions. It is almost impossible to prepare a fixed set of questions which will bring out as many subtle points as can be obtained in a brief interview.

PREPARING FUNCTIONAL REQUIREMENTS

After a good knowledge of current operations has been acquired and the pertinent facts recorded, the analyst is ready to undertake the definition of the aims and functions of the new computerized system. During this phase, the analyst orients himself toward the future objectives of the company and determines the effect of these on the particular application being planned. At this point, the analyst should be able to specify what the system must do, how well the system need perform, and what the system must provide for future growth. All of this analysis should be based upon a detailed definition of the goals of the system, e.g., cost reduction, better customer service, improved and more timely management information, etc.

To provide the system with facilities for future growth and extended capabilities, relevant company plans and policies and their implications must be clearly understood. Management's plans for the near and more distant future must be drawn out in interviews and the various industry indicators studied to determine trends. With this information at hand, the systems analyst:

1. Analyzes future objectives in relation to the new system.
2. Changes existing patterns of the information-flow in the new approach to encompass short and long range plans.
3. Analyzes each element of the system in terms of: the outputs it will produce, inputs it will accept, operations it will perform and resources it utilizes.
4. Determines how well the system need perform.

When the functions of the new system have been completely delineated, the analyst should review his plans with officials of the user organization involved and solicit their suggestions and comments. Not only does this serve to firm up the system function plans, but also gives the user a chance to participate to some extent in the development work. In this way, the new application receives the support from those who will use it, and the total operation is more likely to be successful. In some companies, the user is represented during systems analysis and plays an active role on the study team in gathering information and analyzing procedures. This user participation, if handled properly, can result in much more effective systems. It is recommended that at least one full-time user representative participate in most projects. Large projects should, in general, have more user representatives.

A *Systems Requirements Worksheet,* such as that illustrated in Figure 3.1, has proved to be helpful in getting the systems analyst to organize his presentation of information. Note that there are three categories of detail which may be discussed. The highest level is "Project," next is "Function, "and the lowest is "Task."

SYSTEM REQUIREMENTS WORKSHEET			
Project No. System Name	Prepared By	Date	
Function No. Description	Reviewed By	Date	
Task No. Description	☐ Objective	☐ General Procedures	☐ Special Problems
	☐ Scope	☐ Definitions	☐ Estimates
Version No. Page of	☐ Assumptions	☐ Other	

Figure 3.1
System Requirements Worksheet

Using a payroll application as an example, one would expect to find general descriptive information about the entire application at the Project level. At the Function level, one might find a discussion on taxes in the payroll system. A Task description, within the tax category of the payroll system, could be the explicit methods used to calculate income tax for a specific state.

Note that each presentation level may include information concerning: Objective, Scope, Assumptions, General Procedures, Definitions, Special Problems, Estimates, and other descriptive information. The form in Figure 3.1 shows each of these items to serve as reminders, as well as to give a finer index to the information contained.

Diagrams showing the flow of information in the business activity are sometimes used to display the working relationships in the system. For example, in an order processing system, the *information flow diagram* would show how and where the customer enters the scene and the way in which he interacts with the system. A *customer* can: place an order, cancel an order, receive an order confirmation notice, receive back-order notification, change an order, receive a packing list, inquire as to why his order has not arrived on time, receive an invoice, be sent a payment past due notice, and so forth. The inventory stocking locations in the order processing system would also be depicted in the information flow diagram. A *stocking location* can: receive a shipping order, send an out-of-stock message, issue a shipment notice, receive a hold-shipment request, report inventory receipts, and so forth. The *sales office* can: input sales forecasts, authorize a special discount, receive a weekly recap of sales activity, inquire on inventory levels, and so forth. Of course, the information flow diagram would show many more facets of the system than described here.

It is of the utmost importance to analyze the physical process involved in the system, whether it be order processing, production control, accounts payable, investment analysis, or any other. A system is much more than a set of computer programs . . . it is an integrated activity involving people, computers, and information. A careless study of any of these factors and how they relate to each other is destined to result in a shoddy system, if not worse.

Some companies require a formal and elaborate write-up of the user requirements, which is called an *Application Development Specification* or *Functional Specifications*. The content of the specification generally deals strictly with user-oriented requirements. Whether documentation of this type is required as a result of the systems analysis is sometimes governed by the magnitude of the system under consideration. In a large-scale project (funded at $100,000 or more for systems development), such specifications are usually prepared. Chapter four which covers project management, will discuss Functional Specifications in more detail.

Systems design

Systems design in connection with computer applications consists of laying out the specifications for a series of computer programs, paper forms, clerical procedures, and operating procedures which, together, comprise the system. The function of each program in the system must be outlined in specific terms in the systems design documentation. The step-by-step logic required for the individual programs is not specified, however. A programmer develops the logical series of computer instructions required for each program.

Programming begins with a set of objectives which have been clearly defined in advance by a systems analyst. An analyst (or systems designer) may also be a programmer, or vice versa. The objectives in programming are considerably narrower in scope than objectives of the design of a total system. A problem for systems treatment might be the desire for a company-wide comprehensive financial record-keeping and processing operation. Programming, on the other hand, might only be involved with the task of setting up the computer procedures for printing bank checks for the accounts payable department.

The development of sophisticated, efficient, and original systems demands that the designer have special abilities and aptitudes. Within a given industry, many applications are very similar. Yet, for essentially the same requirements, a system of one design will perform well and efficiently, whereas another might be constantly troublesome, with the cost of operations far in excess of the projected budget.

Persons who have a flair for systems work have the mental capability to deal with a multitude of problem elements simultaneously. These people can be described as parallel thinkers. This is an apt description in the sense that they can visualize the dynamics of a working system as a whole, with its many functions being performed at the same time. At present, systems design is more of an art than a learned technique.

The design and selection of EDP hardware is another activity that is sometimes addressed in connection with specifying and designing the applications system. Sometimes called configuring a system, this activity is not specifically covered in this book for several reasons: (1) numerous highly technical considerations are involved, (2) hardware devices and capabilities across manufacturers' lines are varied and change often, and (3) the hardware configuration is oftentimes pre-established and such hardware is frequently on premise. However, Chapter seven, *Considerations for Evaluating and Selecting EDP Equipment*, should prove to be helpful as a guide to managers in the hardware area.

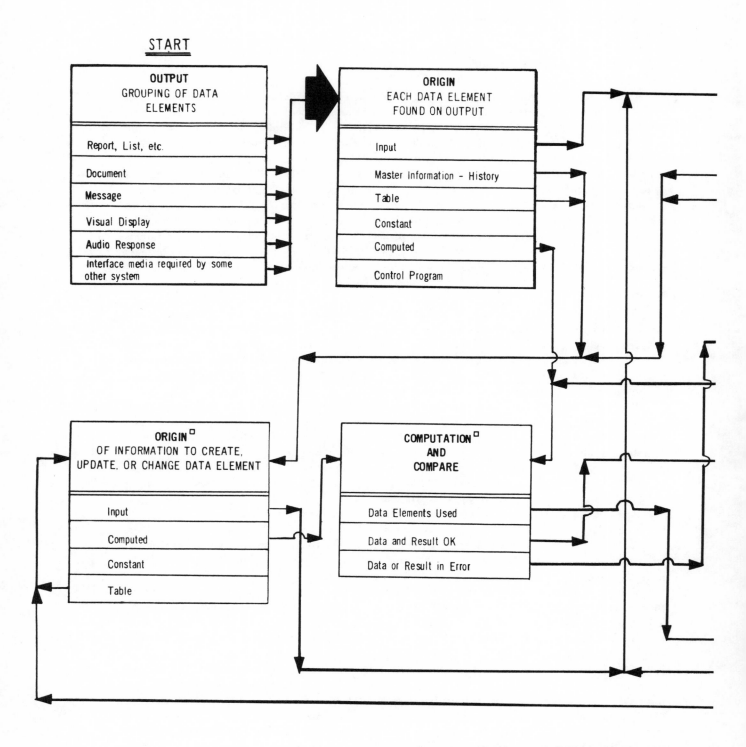

Figure 3.2
System Design Process

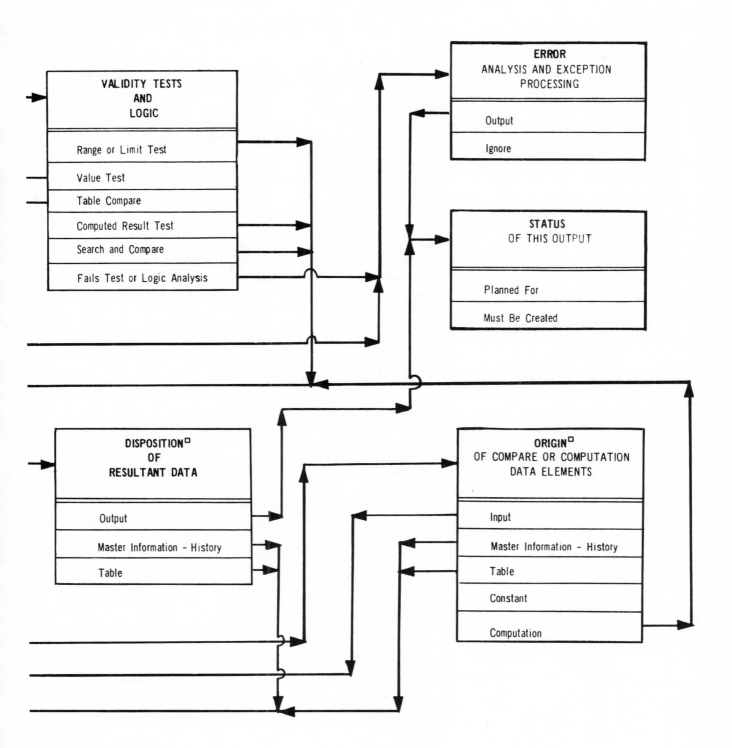

VALIDITY TESTS
AND
LOGIC

Range or Limit Test

Value Test

Table Compare

Computed Result Test

Search and Compare

Fails Test or Logic Analysis

ERROR
ANALYSIS AND EXCEPTION
PROCESSING

Output

Ignore

STATUS
OF THIS OUTPUT

Planned For

Must Be Created

DISPOSITION□
OF
RESULTANT DATA

Output

Master Information – History

Table

ORIGIN□
OF COMPARE OR COMPUTATION
DATA ELEMENTS

Input

Master Information – History

Table

Constant

Computation

applicable items.

Figure 3.2 (cont.)

57

PREREQUISITES FOR SYSTEMS DESIGN

The fundamental requirements of good systems design start with acquiring a working familiarity with the items listed below:

1. Functional requirements for the application.
2. Business environment—current and planned.
3. Programming language and operating system capabilities and features.
4. EDP hardware capabilities.
5. Application design approaches taken elsewhere.
6. Simulation and computer assisted design aids or techniques[1]—especially for large and/or real-time systems.
7. Programming.

Regarding (7) Programming, the question of whether the systems analyst needs to know programming is debated in some circles. The author feels that it is necessary for the analyst to have some knowledge of programming, hopefully in the language to be employed for the system being designed. This does not mean that the analyst must be proficient in programming. It has been the author's experience that better overall systems are produced by analysts who possess a working knowledge of programming.

With a working knowledge of the items just enumerated, the analyst undertakes to draw out, on paper, the flow of computer processing—program by program. Illustrations of various flowcharts are provided later in this chapter under "Documentation Standards."

DESIGN ACTIVITIES

One approach which may be used in system design is what could be described as a *Results Oriented Approach*. It rests upon the premise that the designer knows what the system must produce in terms of output. Essentially, this rather systematic approach consists of examining one output at a time. Each data element which appears in the particular output being analyzed is put through the series of steps shown in Figure 3.2 by the systems designer. The need for a *systems designer* to put each data element through the steps is emphasized, since it is impossible to use the Results Oriented Approach blindly.

This approach leads the designer from known required outputs to a variety of systems requirements to produce those outputs. As the systems designer proceeds through the steps shown in Figure 3.2, he is required to make decisions about the system he is creating. He will have to supply whatever information, processing, and logic he finds missing, anytime he introduces a new data element into the Systems Design Process illustrated in Figure 3.2.

Taking a very simple case, one begins to see the various considerations that are involved in design. Suppose that there is a need to have a computer calculate an annual interest (AI) payment amount and print it on a telecommunication terminal as a message. The inquirer will key in the interest rate (IR) and the loan principal amount (PA). IR is restricted to 1.00 per cent to 10.00 per cent range. PA is restricted to $100 to $10,000 range.

The designer would follow the process in Figure 3.2 and would record his design-decisions in a table such as shown in Figure 3.3. Listed below are the decision points that would arise for this example:

1. The output is a message showing AI, IR, and PA. The origin of AI is *computed*, the origin of IR is *input*, and the origin of PA is *input*.

---

[1]Computer manufactures and some EDP consulting firms have what are called *Computer System Simulators* or *General Purpose Systems Simulators*. These are programs that simulate the system in operation before it is built to learn about hardware and program design requirements. Programs to aid in network design for telecommunications application systems are also in use. IBM has developed a computerized systems analysis and design aid called *Time Automated Grid Technique*, and others, no doubt, exist.

REQUIREMENTS TABLE - Interest Payment Calculation		
CREATE, UPDATE, CHANGES	**CONSTANTS**	**NEW OUTPUTS**
	1.00 and 10.00 for IR 100 and 10000 for PA	Reject Message for IR Reject Message for PA
COMPUTATIONS	**MASTER INFORMATION HISTORY**	**VALIDITY TESTS AND LOGIC**
Method to Calculate AI		Range Test for IR Range Test for PA
INPUTS	**TABLES**	**CONTROL PROGRAM**
IR PA		

Figure 3.3
System Design Requirements Table

2. The *validity* of the inputs, IR and PA, is determined by range tests.
3. The range tests require *constant* data: IR constants (1.00 and 10.00), PA constants (100 and 10000).
4. If either (or both) range tests are not satisfied, an error *message* for each is to be printed.

While the designer is making his way through these steps and rendering decisions, he would have to record, in some way, what he has decided. There are a number of ways to cross-reference items in a requirements table to identify which output each affects. Furthermore, there are time-dependent relationships which the designer must reconcile, i.e., the input required to produce an output exists but not in the time-frame it is needed.

Many experienced systems designers begin by selecting the dominant activity in the system and develop outward from this activity. The dominant activity usually has the master information or data bank associated with it. Another practice that has gained popularity is to establish first a data or information base (data bank) for the system, and then to proceed with program design.

REAL-TIME AND ON-LINE SYSTEMS DESIGN CONSIDERATIONS

Real-time computing procedures have introduced many new and challenging problems for the systems designer and operations control personnel. Real-time refers to the computer processing of transactions or conditions as they occur and often involves a rapid response to these inputs. So, while operating in off-line mode, wherein transactions are generally processed in batches, usually provided an opportunity to readily recover from and correct errors, the on-line or real-time processing requires many more safeguards.

One of the questions which always has to be dealt with is what to do when the computer breaks down on the job. In many instances the requirements of the user are such that a stand-by computer is used if the original system is not operational. In fact, for extremely critical business requirements, and particularly in military applications, several computers may be installed on a stand-by basis. Auxiliary electrical generating equipment which is combustion engine operated, may also be desirable depending on the specific circumstances.

In designing real-time system controls and procedures, the following points should be considered:

1. System restart and recovery procedures.
2. Possible device substitution.
3. Degraded mode of operation.

4.   System checkout procedures prior to each restart.
5.   Periodic status reporting with error statistics.
6.   Duplexing critical devices.

The matter of real-time and on-line systems design and procedures is a vast subject which is only mentioned here for the purpose of recognizing some key items.

AUDIT AND CONTROL PROVISIONS

Some companies make it a practice to have their own internal auditor review the system for controllability and auditability and otherwise comment on accounting methods used in the system design. A good systems designer should know what controls and audit trails are likely to be required and usually builds them into the system without prompting from the user.

The auditor, however, may require special verification programs (some auditors write their own). He may also request that certain control figures be developed in the system for the purpose of verifying the accuracy of the process. Also, the auditor may require that certain security measures be incorporated into the total design in order to prevent the loss of records in case of fire or other disasters, inadvertent errors, or retrieval of confidential information by unauthorized persons. The value of the auditor's contributions to the system will depend upon his understanding of the computer, programming, and computer systems work. Auditor functions are described in more detail in Chapter eight and Appendix B contains a fraud control checklist showing a member of security measures for data processing systems.

EVALUATING PROPOSED DESIGNS

Few designs of any degree of complexity are implemented without frequent consultation between the user and the designer. While the original framework of a good design will probably not be altered appreciably as the work progresses, there are often parts of the system wherein important improvements are made as a result of the consultations.

The manager of systems analysis, project manager, and a review group, composed of technical and managerial personnel, should go over the proposed design in detail. This evaluation board determines whether the proposed system design:

1.   Meets the basic requirements.
2.   Operates within stated constraints.
3.   Is workable.
4.   Is controllable.
5.   Fits into the operating environment of the installation.
6.   Can be improved upon.

During the review, the designer will be called upon to explain and defend his work. From the review session, the designer will take with him the suggested modifications that have been agreed upon.

When the design has been finalized, the work required for each of the programs specified in the system must be outlined for the programming group.

PREPARING THE "PROGRAM PORTFOLIO"[2]

After the system design has undergone the scrutiny of the auditor and evaluation board and is approved and finalized, the programs which make up the system must be assigned to programmers for flow-charting and encoding. At this point, a good set of working documents is needed to guide the programmers in their endeavors.

The systems analyst (or designer) should furnish each programmer with a portfolio of

---

[2]The term "Program Portfolio" is the author's usage.

documents (one for each program) from which to work. Included in the *Program Portfolio* would be the following:

1. Diagrams of the preprinted forms (if required) showing the print format or other display format required for each type of output.
2. Layouts of input and output records for magnetic tapes, disks or other storage media—with all data fields clearly identified.
3. A flow diagram depicting the inputs, the outputs and the I/O equipment to be employed.
4. A brief description or narrative telling how the computer run under discussion fits into the total system. This should include pertinent information about the preceding run and the run following and how the interface is established.
5. A specification, detailing how the various record types are to be treated. Decision tables in matrix form might be included to illustrate the actions to be taken under various conditions.
6. Transaction coding, and the pertinent data to be used should be shown in tabular form with appropriate identification symbols for each item.
7. If applicable, tables to be used for internal cross-referencing, indexes, and data look-up.
8. If needed, details of certain special or complex processes to be used.
9. Miscellaneous information such as that pertaining to run controls, equipment capacities, ready-made program subroutines and operating system standards.

If the Program Portfolio is prepared well, a few short verbal sessions with the programmer should enable him to proceed with the work in a straightforward manner. Illustrations of some of the items in the Program Portfolio are provided later in this chapter under "Documentation Standards."

The computer system planner who does not follow the practice of furnishing the programmer with an adequate set of working documents invariably finds himself involved with the programmer in one clarification session after another. Not only does this take time away from system staff work, but it also introduces errors into the programs due to wrong assumptions made by the programmer when the planner is not available for consultation. A programmer working without clear instruction is like a captain taking his vessel on an ocean voyage and attempting to navigate without charts or compass.

The success of the whole computer installation is impaired when a program becomes operational only to find that certain important phases of "live work" are being processed incorrectly. Losses running into the hundreds of thousands of dollars can result from such a situation.

The systems planner who fails to provide sufficient documentation to cover the writing of even one of the programs may very well be jeopardizing the entire business enterprise. Such a planner is either not sure about what the system is supposed to do, or he is simply careless about communicating the information. In either case, the name of the game is *TROUBLE*, and the stakes can be very high.

Programming

Programming, in a properly managed EDP installation, commences after the Program Portfolio, discussed previously, has been prepared and assembled.

Typically, the programmer's total time to produce a working program is distributed as follows:

1. Designing program logic ....•33%
2. Coding in mnemonic language ....•20%
3. Testing and debugging ....•33%
4. Documenting ....•14%

Management attention to these programming activities must, at the outset, be directed toward seeing that the programmer properly completes Item 1 before proceeding with subsequent steps. One often finds that programmers tend to jump ahead before they have carefully worked out the design details on paper. This introduces at least two problems: (1) A poorly written program that may be both inefficient to operate and inordinately difficult to modify, and (2) Excessive computer time expense because more testing is required.

Documentation, discussed later in this chapter, is an ongoing activity that begins when the program is assigned to a programmer and terminates with a concentrated effort to produce documentation in finalized form.

Coding consists of writing the instructions, according to the design, to accomplish the desired computer processing.

Testing and debugging occurs when the programmer checks his program on the computer and makes whatever corrections or revisions are required. It should be noted that the programmer will change his original coding during this process and often will have to add additional coding. However, little redesign, as such, should be necessary if the person in charge of programming has thoroughly reviewed the design with the programmer.

Assigning Programs

To make the most of individual talent available on the programming staff, the complex programs should ordinarily be assigned to the better, more experienced programmers. Whenever possible, the less experienced programmers should be given the uncomplicated programs to work on. The idea is to present a reasonable challenge. This course of action is suggested not because the newer people cannot handle the difficult work, but because it is uneconomical for them to do so, as it will take them much longer to complete such programs.

In writing complex or lengthy programs, large errors are sometimes inadvertently included. These are often compounded of many "small bugs." An experienced programmer can separate and identify the small individual errors in a reasonable time. When an inexperienced programmer runs into compound errors, he is not as likely to recognize and isolate the component small errors without long, time-consuming study and restudy.

If the newcomer has the appropriate education and background and has acquired some experience, he should be given the opportunity to demonstrate whether he is ready to tackle advanced programs. Consistently picking the most experienced programmers for the difficult assignments denies the newer people the opportunity to develop fully their skills. A manager should avoid, however, training on time sensitive, critical programming work. In practice, the appropriate assignment of programming is a matter of judgment seasoned by experience. Clearly, the work assigned to the less experienced programmers will have to be more carefully monitored and reviewed.

Many managers have found that, during program assignment, better adherence to programming estimates is realized by having the programmer participate in making estimates on the programs he will write. However, some programmers would rather have estimates made for them, while others do not believe in estimates at all. As a rule, programmers tend to be hard on themselves when making their own estimates. This can be either good or bad. It is good if quality is not sacrificed to meet an over-ambitious schedule, and bad if quality suffers.

The estimating methods discussed later in this chapter will provide quantitative measures for time and cost evaluations.

Team Work or Individual Effort

After the time schedules for programming have been outlined, the question of whether one individual should do the work or whether it should be divided among a number of individuals has to be answered. In many cases, it is not simply a question of the amount of work to be done, but rather it becomes a process of evaluating the individual work habits of programming personnel. Some people perform quite well in a team setup, even where a single program is subdivided. Other individuals work better by themselves and seem to find it difficult to work as part of a team.

Programming, by its nature, tends to be more of an individual-oriented job rather than one which lends itself readily to team work. Many programmers work better by themselves. Individual accomplishment and pride in the work are commonly associated with programming.

The selection of personnel for either a team or an individual effort is one of the most important aspects of assigning the programs. Naturally, the programming manager will also consider what abilities, experience, and qualifications are needed for a particular program or project. But the point to be borne in mind is that individual interests, personalities, and work habits may very well determine the efficiency of the effort. Where one person is highly motivated when put on a job alone and excels in such a situation, another individual may feel that such an assignment requires more people and is beyond the scope of his job. More importantly however, the individual may develop psychological problems as a result of worrying about the job in attempting to tie together many tangible and intangible details.

The individual who carries full responsibility for a particular job must be more versatile than a programmer engaged in a team effort. He must also have characteristics which identify him as an individual performer. Quite often people of this kind, in the right atmosphere and on the right job, can produce at a rate which is astonishing. But therein lie a few problems which require careful consideration. Specifically, the individual performer may produce below standard if he is not on a job which suits him or if he is not presented with a sufficient challenge. This person is often considerably more sensitive to managerial meddling than are his fellow programmers. He prefers to be given broad requirements and to be able to use his own ingenuity within this limit.

The individualist sometimes develops resentment during the course of a job because a manager has become too specific or rigid in the requirements. When this happens the individual loses interest. Although most individual performers seem to be open to suggestions, such suggestions must usually come from others whom they respect and, moreover, the suggestions must be of significant value.

PROGRAM TESTING AND DEBUGGING

Program testing and debugging can easily become the most costly step in the entire programming process. Here for the first time in the systems development process, the computer will be used. Overtime and non-prime shift work are frequently required because of computer scheduling demands. If the business does not already have a computer installed or has a different model on order, some traveling expenses are likely to be incurred.

The manager of programming may be able to reduce all costs in this phase of programming by encouraging his programmers to be more careful and accurate in the first place. However, the function of *desk-checking* the program is usually the most significant weakness in testing and debugging. Desk-checking is a step-by-step review in detail, by the programmer, prior to computer testing . . . the programmer plays computer.

Since it is quite natural for the programmer to want to run his program as soon as possible to see what happens, it is not uncommon that programs go into testing and debugging with little or no desk-checking. From the point of view of the programmer, initial computer runs give him something to work with and are the fastest way to get a program operational. The something to work with may be "garbage," however, and in the final analysis there could be a loss of valuable time.

Considering the hourly cost of the computer time against the hourly cost of programmer time, the argument in favor of desk-checking is generally valid from a purely economic standpoint. But, there are other reasons for desk-checking which are equally valid and even more important. Because desk-checking is usually the last detailed review of each functional section of the program, it provides an opportunity to see that all desired processing features have been included, as well as an overall knowledge of the interrelationship between the processing sections of the program.

Several factors have converged in recent times which together present a very strong case for giving each programmer a time-sharing terminal (a typewriter tied into a computer) for the purpose of coding, testing and debugging programs. Where this has been done properly, it has been outstandingly successful. First, because programmers need not wait to have their programs run remotely—which is expensive and annoying. And, second, a higher quality program is produced. Everyone is happier as a result.

MAINTENANCE PROGRAMMING

Improving the performance of existing programs, correcting deficiencies, and making system extensions to comply with new requirements are the primary activities with which maintenance programming is concerned. It involves modifying program logic, testing and debugging, making job control changes for the monitor system, and bringing documentation up to date.

It is a peculiar phenomenon in EDP that the rather delicate and often intricate work involved in this activity is done by junior or apprentice programmers. One might easily and, in the author's opinion, properly conclude that maintenance would best be carried out by an expert. Looking at this activity, the observer would notice that it requires the programmer to comprehend logic which he did not formulate, to understand programming methods which are learned through experience, and to investigate thoroughly how new logic might upset the integrity of an existing program.

Despite these demanding prerequsites, experienced programmers, for the most part, will neither accept nor stay with a position where much maintenance is required of them. This poses a dilemma, which because of the demand for experienced programmers, will not be overcome easily.

Many installations find that maintenance programming has become a major activity, often occupying half of the programmers. Costs for this activity increase each time the installation adds a new system. Further, maintenance work is considerably more expensive than regular programming relative to output of instructions in a given time span. Keeping maintenance costs at a reasonable level calls for EDP management action in a number of areas, including: (1) Seeing that the original systems work is done thoroughly and contains provisions that allow maintenance to be done with less difficulty, (2) Making it difficult to have changes made when such changes are not properly justified, and (3) Respecting programmers engaged in maintenance as important contributors to the well-being of the company EDP function. It is also recommended that maintainence programming assignments be distributed fairly evenly among all junior programmers, unless certain programmers express an interest in doing more than their share . . . some do find it challenging.

SYSTEMS PROGRAMMING

Until about the early 1960's systems programming was found only in the largest installations, although it has been a recognized activity in software development for many years. Software, such as programming language compilers like COBOL, is generally developed by EDP equipment manufacturers or independent firms that specialize in software systems.

What has happened is that modern EDP equipment is separated from the programmer by a software interface. This was not true with most early computing systems wherein the programmer was very often required to understand the hardware, as such.

In order to put modern computers to work effectively, the programmer must communicate with an operating system (sometimes called a monitor or executive program) that controls the allocation of computer resources to the application program that he wishes to have executed.

To communicate with an operating system, in order to "tell" it what to do, requires that a set of instructions be interpreted by it. Instructions to the operating system are given in what is often referred to as a *job control language*. An operating system, which is a collection of specialized programs, will typically perform many functions, all of which are intended to both maximize the efficiency of computer operations and to assist the application programmer by providing features that he would otherwise have to provide himself. It is, in short, the systems programmer's function is to see that all of this happens. A systems programmer will usually spend most of his time at activities that involve an operating system and its myriad functions. A systems programmer will frequently be responsible for evaluating new software features (and sometimes hardware) as they become available and for implementing such features as may be required by the installation. Programming work done by the systems programmer is limited to developing general purpose or utility types of programs and making modifications to software to meet installation needs.

It is of vital importance that the systems programmer be a practical type, well versed in the realities of application work and sensitive to the implications his work has on the effectiveness of computer operations.

Pilot or integrated testing

Sometimes called *continuity testing*, pilot testing is, in fact, a validation of the continuity of the processing in the application system. With all the major programs completed and tested individually, the pilot test serves the purpose of demonstrating that the programs also work as parts of the complete system.

In pilot testing, a small but representative sample of all the various kinds of original input data is processed by the system. Both valid and invalid conditions which the system is supposed to handle are tested. The results and control figures are verified in every respect.

The data records generated within the system must be visually checked and certain manual calculations may have to be made. Checking and verifying the results and preparing special data for the pilot test must be done completely and carefully. There is sometimes a tendency to make assumptions regarding the validity of the results because the manual checking is tedious and boring. Clearly, such assumptions may lead to the failure of the system when it is put into "live" operation. To relieve the burden of some of this manual effort, it is often wise to consider using clerical assistance where it seems appropriate. The programmers who will, in most cases, be conducting the pilot testing should report their findings to their project leader.

One function of the project leader is to make sure the necessary tests are given to the system. Another important facet of his job is suggesting various kinds of tests. Beyond routine types of tests, the value of the suggested additional tests will, of course, depend on the degree of familiarity which the project leader has with the application.

Pilot testing, if done properly, can be of significant importance in determining the success of the system once it gets into operation.

The time allocated to pilot or integrated testing will vary directly with the complexity of the system and conditions it is expected to handle. A pilot test may very well represent the investment of the time and effort of many people, and for this reason it may be relatively costly. Despite this, however, it is one of the foremost ways to correct and prevent the vastly more serious problems which could arise during "live" operations.

As a rule, pilot testing of some kind should always be provided for. It is in those rush situations, where pilot testing is most valuable, that it is sometimes neglected or taken casually. The almost inevitable "headaches" which follow from such action can be substantiated by any manager who has been harassed day and night by problems which continue to arise in "live" operations.

Parallel or final testing

Parallel testing, which is sometimes called *running dual* or *volume testing*, can only be performed when an existing manual, semi-automated, or automated process is to be converted to a new system of programs.

Throughout parallel testing, identical transactions and other data are processed by both the existing system and the new system. Verification of the results is performed wherever it is possible to do so, between the two systems. In those areas where the new system produces results and handles conditions not presently incorporated in the existing system, methods such as those outlined for pilot testing will have to be devised.

Sometimes parallel testing involves running all data in a simultaneous fashion; often a representative, but substantial block of work is run in parallel. Regardless of the amount of work used for the test, the control figures and various output documents must be manually compared for the most part. Parallel testing, as a rule, requires even more of an investment of time, effort, and money than pilot testing. The required clerical help and other additional factors required should be planned far in advance. Otherwise, the parallel test work can fall too far behind the existing system operations.

When program errors are discovered in either parallel or pilot testing, the programmers should be encouraged to make the required changes as quickly and carefully as possible. In order to maintain the testing schedule, these changes are likely to involve varying amounts of overtime effort.

Where the planning and work prior to parallel testing has proved to be very poor, many modifications must be made to the programs or system. Parallel testing may have to be dropped until the errors have been reduced to a point where it is feasible to resume testing.

From a parallel test which has proved the workability of the system, there are two ways in which to accomplish the conversion:

1. Continue running under the new system, gradually adding the remainder of the work and dropping operations under the old system.
2. Drop parallel operations completely and convert all work at one time and operate fully under the new system. The old system is no longer in operation.

Each method has its advantages depending upon the nature of the application in question. There are cases in which the second alternative is impossible because of sheer volume of data. Another consideration is the risk of serious problems vs. cost or practicality of one approach compared to the other.

During the verification and checking of the parallel test data, it should be noted that errors have been discovered in the existing system that make it difficult to prove-out the new system. Such errors, however, must be conclusively identified and appropriate steps taken to reconcile the work of the new system. In at least two cases known to the author, the existing work was shown to have so many errors that management decided to drop testing well ahead of schedule and use the new system. The decision to run under the new system was made on the basis of good parallel test results.

Final testing is done where there is no existing system and is similar to pilot testing except that actual live data is used.

DIRECT CUT-OVER

Direct cut-over carries with it the implication that the full system of programs has not gone through rigorous tests in an integrated environment. Some testing has hopefully been done on the individual programs, but for the most part, they have not been thoroughly tested together as a system.

The danger of this sort of procedure can be quite serious, and it is indeed a rare occasion when such a system has not run into critical problems. However, as long as there continues to be inadequate planning, it is probably safe to assume that direct cut-overs will persist.

Other than rationalizations about tight schedules and pressure to get an application running, there is hardly ever justification for the direct cut-over procedure. In all but a few isolated instances, it is generally possible to conduct either a pilot or parallel test.

If at all possible, the managers responsible for the systems and programming effort should try to include both pilot testing and parallel testing. Parallel testing, as was mentioned, presupposes the existence of another system of processing.

Converting to the new system

The period during which the actual conversion takes place is often remembered as the most hectic phase of the total effort. Usually, a lot of data has to be assembled together to be put on the system. Errors which are indicated as the data enters must be corrected. Controls must be validated. Other information must be checked and verified. Problems turn up in programs which must be corrected immediately. Operating personnel and clerks make mistakes and rework is required. Everyone is anxious to get into full operation; the conversion schedule is tight.

The pressures which can build up during the conversion work sometimes act upon the individuals in a way which could prove to be detrimental. If the elements of judgment become clouded or carelessness is evident, the person in charge may find it extremely difficult to bring about corrections.

To state that the role of planning for the conversion is crucial is to state the obvious. Yet, experience continues to show that for whatever reason, insufficient planning is to blame in the majority of problem conversions. By simply standing at a distance and "zeroing-in" on the manager who is a poor planner, very little is gained. Everyone has been guilty of poor planning at one time or another, and it is generally easy to be critical of others after the fact. The expression that "hindsight is better than foresight" is of value only when some tangible principle can be extracted and learned as a result of the hindsight.

For example, some managers have found it useful to have a carefully prepared schedule for the conversion period. If, for example, the conversion was to be accomplished over a weekend, the functions which are going to take place and the personnel assigned to them are shown for each hour. Such a schedule is easily drawn, but the information it relates contains several key features. First, the fact that activities are shown in time frames generally indicates that the scheduler knows something about the time required to complete various functions. Second, the allocation of manpower has been given some consideration. Third, the time relationship between activities is shown.

Data conversion, of course, would be accomplished in advance of starting up operations under the new system. One of the first functions of the new system will be to bring the previously converted data up to date with transactions that have occurred in the intervening period.

ESTABLISHING RESPONSIBILITIES

It is a good practice to have the programmers for a particular application within reasonable proximity to where their programs are being used for the first time. This helps to facilitate the operations since there may be questions concerning the program. In addition, there may be changes or corrections required to make the program work properly.

A programmer, other than the original programmer, should be able to interpret the work of a colleague. But as a practical matter, during conversion, there is often not enough time to permit it.

Each programmer, therefore, should be informed of his responsibilities during the conversion phase and should be on call for its duration. Especially in medium size and smaller installations, the programmers will play an active part in bringing about the conversion. They will be in close contact with the operations until the application is fully implemented.

ORIENTATION FOR OPERATING AND USER PERSONNEL

The computer operators who will be running the various jobs in the new system once it goes into regular operation should also participate in the conversion. Not only does their work serve to orient them to the nature of the new system and how it operates, but it also gives them useful practice under controlled conditions.

An operator should be able to run a job from the information contained in the *run book*, which specifies the operating instructions. But, it is of great advantage to first teach the operator and then let him use the operating instructions to refresh his memory.

Other individuals who will be engaged in supporting a particular application should also be oriented to the general scheme of the system. Clerks, keypunch operators, and others will need to know their specific function in detail. However, the orientation to the overall operation may prove to be helpful to them and particularly to their supervisors.

Most managers feel that most of their employees desire to perform their work properly. Assuming this to be true, the employees will very definitely have to know what is expected of them. Far too frequently, workers turn in work which is different from what was originally intended, because their managers failed to communicate effectively.

The case for taking the time to adequately orient and teach the workers is a strong one. Aside from the fact that this makes sense in terms of operating efficiency, there is at least one side benefit which can be of major significance. That is, when the employee knows what is supposed to be happening, he will also be in a position to detect variances from the expected results or procedures.

More than one data processing manager has had to regret the fact that he did not take the time and trouble to prepare a good orientation. As a result, and this is the key point, an employee saw conditions which, to him, did not seem to be correct. He, however, failed to notify management because he felt that the unusual condition was supposed to take place under the new system. Had the employee been encouraged to question variances and had he been given more information about the new system, the problem may have been corrected in the early stages of operations.

To employees who have never had contact with computer operations, the "mystery and magic" leave many kinds of impressions—mostly incorrect. It is worthwhile to explain, generally, the fact that it is entirely possible that a program may have errors.

Coordination and control of systems and programming

As in many other managerial situations, once work has been assigned it is necessary to control the effort so that it will yield the intended results. This is a particularly important aspect of systems and programming because it is generally difficult to define levels of accomplishment and, therefore, difficult to take meaningful measurements at each level. The end result of the systems and programming, i.e., a fully documented, operational system is the most positive proof that the original requirements have been properly interpreted and met.

At each step along the way it is often impossible to say that a part of the system or a program will, or will not function, since each subsection is in some way related to all others in the final version. The interaction between these subsections may cause problems, even though each appears to be correct within its own context.

AUDITING SYSTEMS ANALYSIS AND DESIGN WORK

A manager responsible for systems work must attempt to control the effort by continually focusing his attention on two questions: (1) Is the analyst working on the right problem? (2) Is the analyst properly interpreting the business requirements?

Neither of these questions can be properly answered, and control cannot therefore be exercised, if the manager is very far removed from the analysts carrying out this work. To satisfy himself on both questions, a manager should get exposure to the problem by taking occasional field trips to review the problem with the user. He should also participate in meetings of major importance in the systems analysis effort. Doing these things should put the manager in a position of being able to evaluate what his analysts are doing. In this manner, the manager can provide intelligent leadership and keep his men on the right track.

Systems people, some say, will try anything on the computer. That does not mean that they will play games or squander company resources, but rather that they will accept most any challenge thrown out to them. This attribute can be used to advantage, if the systems manager is capable of exercising controls that are based upon business as well as systems rationale.

So, the first rule in auditing analysis and design is that a manager who understands systems work and has a business orientation must do occasional shirt-sleeves investigations.

Another control that the manager can use is to insist on a reasonable degree of formalism in developing systems requirements and describing the design. In other words, get the information written on paper with all pertinent details clearly expressed. Lack of formalism is a major weakness in systems work.

A second rule in auditing systems work might be put this way: If it is not written, or cannot be written, assume that it does not and will not exist. The design is not complete until it is documented.

And, the third rule, very simply is: Get user concurrence. Show the user what are believed to be his requirements . . . encourage his critique of them. During the review with the user, the systems manager should be able to get a good idea as to whether the analysts have properly interpreted the business requirements.

A balance between participation and management must be achieved by the manager in all EDP activites, including controls. One danger in having a "working" manager on an EDP development effort is that he may tend to get too wrapped-up in the minute details of the system. In so doing, chances are that he will lose the essential overview of the business problem as well as the system problem, not to mention being out of touch with his people as their manager. Ideally, a manager should participate when it will contribute to his effectiveness in *managing* the whole effort. Professionals in EDP, it should be remembered, will only stand for so much meddling from the top. Beyond a certain point, they will consider participation to be an intrusion. If the manager respects their capabilities to do their job, they, in turn, will respect the direction that the manager provides. Of course, if a staff member is not capable of doing his job, the long term solution to the problem is to get someone who can . . . the same goes for a manager.

APPLICATION REVIEWS FOR PROGRAMMING

The success of the total programming effort for any given application depends upon the effective timely exchange of information and ideas. One way to accomplish this is by holding regularly scheduled roundtable meetings with programmers. All of the programmers working on a given application (or sub-system) should be present along with their project leaders and managers. In a meeting of this kind there are at least three objectives which can be pursued. Consider the following:

1. Problem areas can be exposed to the team for comment and suggested remedies.
2. Application design changes which affect a number of programs or alter the overall or basic systems approach can be reviewed during the session.
3. Individual programmers may be called upon to explain their particular responsibilities or to present technical information of general interest.

When the occasion seems appropriate, it may be advantageous for the EDP manager and a user management representative to sit in on a couple of roundtable meetings. This may help to clarify the activities of the group and also keeps others abreast of some of the more detailed considerations in the application.

Management is charged with the responsibility for producing an entire system of working programs. Integrating the group of programs required for an application is just one of the managerial functions in the process of preparing a working system. The role which communication plays throughout this process is crucial since the individual programs in a system are almost always interconnected, in that one program accepts information from another and passes information on to others, etc.

The application review roundtable is a technique which helps to tie the pieces of the system together. When programmers have the opportunity to meet with one another in review sessions of this kind, it also gives management an opportunity to more closely examine the application, the points of program interconnection, and certain problem areas.

PROGRAM LOGIC REVIEWS

The *logic review* is one way to help insure that the programmer is on the right track in the early stages of programming. Simply put, the review is a study of the working plans which the programmer has developed, based upon his original information. One piece of documentation, shown later in the chapter, which should be reviewed is the flow chart of the program. Either the programming manager, project leader, or the individual responsible for the programming effort (or perhaps an experienced programmer) should follow the flow of the program in terms of logic and the required processing. Provided that the individual reviewing the program flow chart knows in some detail what the program is expected to do, the logic review provides resonable and adequate control for the initial stages.

A logic review is best done with the programmer present. In this way, there is an opportunity to discuss the program in detail and to, perhaps, develop some ways to improve it. More importantly, a verbal explanation from the programmer is often of value as he can furnish specific details about his intentions. Also, deeper insight into the problem areas of the processing is gained in verbal exchanges.

The logic review gives the reviewer a chance to rethink the various aspects of the original systems design. It is entirely possible that something may have been inadvertently left out in the original planning. At the time of the logic review, it is usually possible to correct such items without disrupting the entire program.

Particularly in the case of newer programmers, one finds instances where a certain amount of the needed logic has been provided by the programmer, but it falls short in terms of good programming practices. To illustrate this point, suppose that the programmer is told that there are only two types of transactions in the input stream: type 1 and type 2. Where the more experienced programmer will generally make positive tests for type 1 and for type 2, the newer programmer may assume that the only alternative to a type 1 is in fact a type 2. In practice, experience shows that it is not impossible that some other transaction type could be incorrectly entered with the input data. Open-ended assumptions, therefore, may very easily destroy the accuracy of the processing.

One point which should be reiterated and may be evident here is that the logic reviewer himself must be familiar with programming practices. If it is otherwise, the system of programs which result will really be no better than abilities of the programmers.

During the logic review, the programmer and the reviewer step through the program flow chart (on paper) block-by-block—varying sets of conditions are assumed each time the process is begun over. In this manner, the competent reviewer will be able to detect errors, non-standard methods, and inefficient procedures in the program. He will, of course, point these out to the programmer. Incidentally, programmers often find that the review solidifies their own understanding of the program and they sometimes catch errors which the reviewer may miss.

Program and System Change Control

Changes are worthy of special mention because they contribute in a significant way to time and cost overruns that have become commonplace in systems development work.

A change, in this context, becomes critical if it is not made at the proper point in the development of the system. Note that changes are a fact of life in EDP and that they must be properly accommodated. However, the point management must act on is concerned with the timing of change. For a simple analogy, consider the man who goes to the local car dealer and orders a red convertible due to be delivered in five weeks. A week before delivery he decides that he really wants a black sedan. Most auto dealers would probably not accommodate this man's desire to change. Yet, computer people will often do so—which is generous—but forget to announce to user management that the change will cost $100,000 additional and will overrun the schedule by four months.

The fact that the penalties associated with changes are often overlooked has been the source of monumental grievances regarding the efficiency and skill with which data processing work is undertaken. The time to alter a system functional requirement is when the analysis work is being done, not during programming, where the specifications should be stabilized. User reviews of the analysis results and of the design are intended to catch oversights early in the development process . . . at which time changes can usually be incorporated with relative ease and low cost.

Changes, poorly timed and otherwise, are, as previously indicated, inevitable. But, non-mandatory change requests, made in the programming phase, should be entered in a "wish log" where they would get consideration *after* the system goes into operation. Management's role is to reduce the penalties associated with change by controlling the development work in such a way that the necessary reviews and evaluations are done, and done properly. Beyond this, it is of importance to the well-being of EDP in the company to have a somewhat formalized change procedure. Such a procedure would call for time and cost estimates for each proposed change and an approval of the change by the management that will pay the bill for having it done. In this way, misunderstandings can be reduced. By having the effects of making changes well documented, company management will be aware of the latest revised time and cost estimate. This kind of change procedure will, in addition, encourage the originators of changes to appraise their desires more carefully, since the accompanying time and expense will be directly attributable to them.

SYSTEMS DOCUMENTATION

A complaint sometimes expressed by the operations personnel, programmers, and others is that the documentation for a particular program is "no good."

If a programmer is involved in changing a program, probably not his own, he means that he cannot readily follow the program logic and processing steps because the original programmer failed to adequately describe the program. By "no good," the operations personnel mean that the documentation left by the programmer for operating procedures is inadequate.

Whether one talks of operating procedures documentation, or program logic and processing documentation, here is one subject where the matter of standards cannot be avoided.

Documentation standards must be followed when it comes to programs and operating procedures. The absence of sufficient documentation is just one problem. Another is the absence of intelligible documentation. Clearly, a great deal of descriptive information which no one can understand is as bad as having insufficient information.

Computerization introduces operating differences which tend to hamper the immediate interpretation and solution of problems. For example, many records involved on the computer are in a form which is not readily available for visual inspection. Prior to computer processing this was not true. It may also be that under the computer approach, source documents may not be readily available. Historical information of various kinds may have been eliminated. The centralization of data processing work tends to concentrate knowledge in one place. Meaningful documentation, therefore, is vital to the continuance of the success of the EDP effort. Fast and accurate solutions to programming problems or data alterations arising in computer operations depend heavily upon good documentation. The efficiency and precision with which computer operations are carried out are often a function of how well the operating procedures have been spelled out.

It is the author's opinion that the "all-purpose" documentation, which is found in many installations, is inadequate. By attempting to serve several needs, such documentation rarely does a good job in filling a particular need. Considering the variety of people involved might help to explain the need for levels and types of documentation.

There are managers, outside of EDP, who want information on the system. There are systems analysts attempting to communicate requirements to programmers. There are non-EDP people who need to know how to interact with the system . . . its users. There are computer operations personnel who must know how to run the system. And there are maintenance programmers who, after the system goes into operation, must be able to understand the work of other programmers.

To meet these requirements, various kinds of documentation are desirable.

1. *General Information Manual*—briefly describes the system and its important features for the layman.
2. *Functional Requirements Manual*—explains what the system must do from a user's viewpoint and also tells the systems designer what he needs to know to design the system.
3. *Systems Specifications*—oriented to the programmer and includes Program Portfolios (described earlier in this chapter).
4. *Program Documentation*—written by a programmer to be used by another programmer. It includes program "listings" and details about the processing logic.
5. *Operations Manual*—for computer operations personnel to tell them how to run the system. Some operations manuals contain system test procedures.
6. *User's Manual*—tells the user what he must do to insure that the system carries out his desires. It should be written by the user with the assistance or guidance of the EDP group.

Permanent documentation, that which is maintained and kept up to date for the life of the operational system, is usually limited to the following:

- Program Documentation
- Operations Manual
- User's Manual

Unless significant changes that alter the features of the system in a major way are made, the General Information Manual will generally remain good enough for its intended audience. The other non-permanent documentation is not needed after the system is operating successfully, since its information is either represented in the permanent types or is no longer of value. For example, all of the Program Portfolios will appear in the Program Documentation in the latest status. So, a substantial part of the non-permanent Systems Specifications does carry through into permanent documentation.

To describe completely the elements in each kind of documentation is beyond the scope of this book. In some of the better managed EDP installations, one can usually find what is called a *Standards Manual* that describes documentation requirements in detail. Some of these are voluminous, running several hundred pages or more. The author has seen them running from the sublime to the ridiculous. Standards, it should be remembered, must be tempered with good sense. The danger is generally in not having enough of the proper standards, although the opposite extreme is not uncommon in large EDP installations.

Some computer programming and consulting firms, for a fee, will come into a company and set up a custom-tailored Standards Manual after making a study of installation requirements. An interesting study of EDP documentation practices and problems that the federal government completed in 1967 shows what kinds of documentation are most critical and gives statistics on the documentation effort.[3]

The *Bibliography* also lists books that may be used to guide the preparation of a Standards Manual. The next section, dealing with documentation standards, will provide a number of illustrations of documentation for the system.

DOCUMENTATION STANDARDS

Since the very nature of data processing implies uniformity of some kind, it is not particularly surprising that certain standards are needed to make the installation efficient, if not workable. From the standpoint of being able to readily understand the work of any programmer in an installation, there must be a commonality of expression within this specialty group. Moreover, the work of this group may have to be interpreted, for various reasons, by someone who may not have an intimate knowledge of programming.

It is important that the exchange of technical information take place in terms which are readily understood by the technician. Similarly, the conveyance for information from the technician to interested parties outside of the field must attempt to give preciseness without being esoteric. Technicians who have prepared information for general consumption will quickly acknowledge the difficulties encountered in explaining "things" in less technical terms.

The failure to formulate and use certain standards has frequently resulted in the inability to follow and comprehend systems and programming work performed by individuals who are no longer working on a project or who have left the company. Even when the same individual who was working on a project returns to it after a period of a few months, he sometimes will be unable to follow his own reasoning because he cannot remember his original ideas.

---

[3]Bernard E. Scott, *et al.*, *Survey of Computer-Program Documentation Practices at Seven Federal Government Agencies* (Paramus, N.J.: Computing Technology Inc., March 1967). Available from: U. S. Dept. of Commerce, Clearinghouse for Federal Scientific and Technical Information, Springfield, Va., Document No. PB175701.

SYSTEM FLOWCHART SYMBOLS

PROCESSING	**INPUT/ OUTPUT**
A major processing function.	Any type of medium or data.
PUNCHED CARD	**PERFORATED TAPE**
All varieties of punched cards including stubs.	Paper or plastic, chad or chadless.
DOCUMENT	**TRANSMITTAL TAPE**
Paper documents and reports of all varieties.	A proof or adding machine tape or similar batch-control information.
MAGNETIC TAPE	**DISK, DRUM, RANDOM ACCESS**
OFFLINE STORAGE	**DISPLAY**
Offline storage of either paper, cards, magnetic or perforated tape.	Information displayed by plotters or video devices.
ONLINE KEYBOARD	**SORTING, COLLATING**
Information supplied to or by a computer utilizing an online device.	An operation on sorting or collating equipment.
CLERICAL OPERATION	**AUXILIARY OPERATION**
A manual offline operation not requiring mechanical aid.	A machine operation supplementing the main processing function.
KEYING OPERATION	**COMMUNICATION LINK**
An operation utilizing a key-driven device.	The automatic transmission of information from one location to another via communication lines.
FLOW ◁ ▷ ▽ △	The direction of processing or data flow.

Figure 3.4
System Flow Chart Symbols

PROGRAM FLOWCHART SYMBOLS

SYMBOL	REPRESENTS
	PROCESSING A group of program instructions which perform a processing function of the program.
	INPUT/OUTPUT Any function of an input/output device (making information available for processing, recording processing information, tape positioning, etc.).
	DECISION The decision function used to document points in the program where a branch to alternate paths is possible based upon variable conditions.
	PROGRAM MODIFICATION An instruction or group of instructions which changes the program.
	PREDEFINED PROCESS A group of operations not detailed in the particular set of flowcharts.
	TERMINAL The beginning, end, or a point of interruption in a program.
	CONNECTOR An entry from, or an exit to, another part of the program flowchart.
	OFFPAGE CONNECTOR A connector used instead of the connector symbol to designate entry to or exit from a page.
◁ ▷ ▽ △	**FLOW DIRECTION** The direction of processing or data flow.

SUPPLEMENTARY SYMBOL FOR SYSTEM AND PROGRAM FLOWCHARTS

	ANNOTATION The addition of descriptive comments or explanatory notes as clarification.

STRIPING

Page reference entered in top section. Description entered in the bottom section.

Figure 3.5
Program Flow Chart Symbols

Reprinted by permission from MANAGEMENT PLANNING GUIDE FOR A MANUAL OF DATA PROCESSING STANDARDS, © by International Business Machines Corporation.

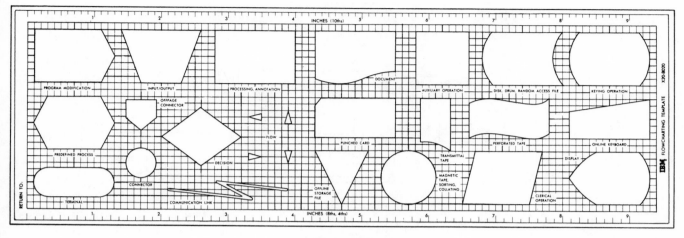

Figure 3.6
Flow Charting Template

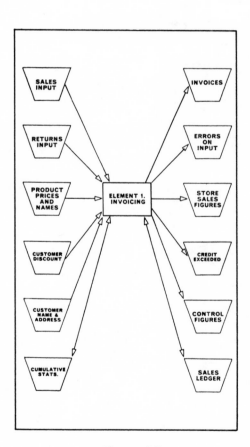

Figure 3.7
System Elements

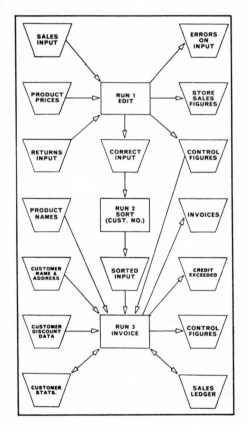

Figure 3.8
Run Segmentation

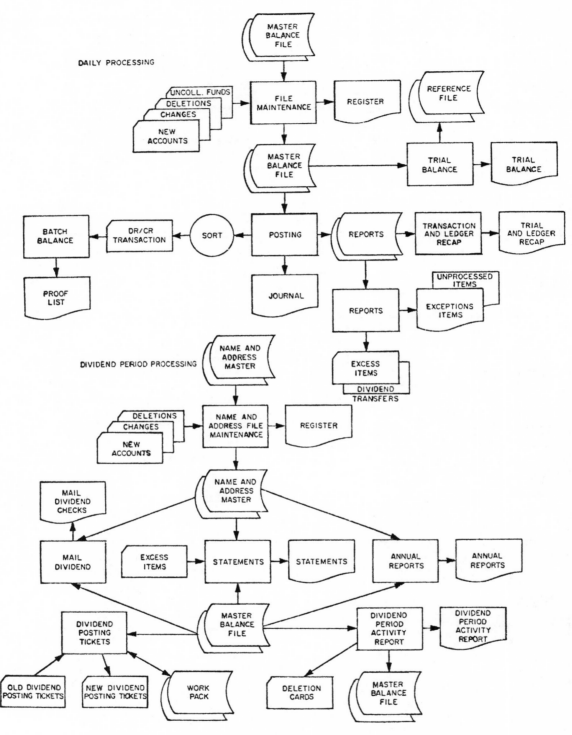

Figure 3.9
Illustrative System Flow Chart

76

Figure 3.4 and 3.5 show standard symbols that are used in system design and programming. A plastic template, such as that shown in Figure 3.6, is used to prepare systems and programming documentation.

Following the Systems Analysis work, the system analyst prepares the Systems Design Specifications mentioned earlier. Developing flow diagrams is one part of this activity.

Figure 3.7 shows a system element *without* regard to specific *programs*. The logical positioning of the computer runs (programs) is shown in Figure 3.8, *without* regard to computer *hardware*. Both figure 3.7 and 3.8 are generalized representations of parts of the system.

Indicating more detail about specific input/output hardware, Figure 3.9 is the *system* flow chart at the program detail level.

The general requirements for a specific *program* in the system are sometimes illustrated as shown in Figure 3.10. This kind of diagram would be part of the Program Portfolio for a specific program.

Also included in the Program Portfolio would be the specifications for the layout of data on input/output media. Figures 3.11 and 3.12 are used to describe punched card data. The record layout sheet in Figure 3.13 would display how data is arranged on magnetic tape, disk, drum or other storage media. Figure 3.14 shows a form that, when completed, would tell the programmer exactly how information should be spaced and formatted for printed output. Additional information about the data records and files is also recorded, sometimes as illustrated in Figure 3.15.

Additional information in the Program Portfolio would include the details of how specific kinds of processing are to be carried out. Decision tables,[4] such as that shown in Figure 3.16, can be used to describe logic requirements to the programmer.

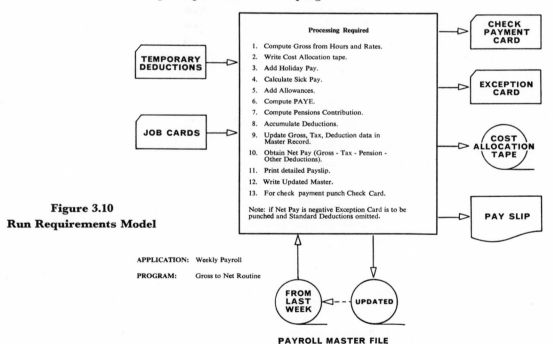

Figure 3.10
Run Requirements Model

Reprinted by permission from MANAGEMENT PLANNING GUIDE FOR A MANUAL OF DATA PROCESSING STANDARDS, © *by* International Business Machines Corporation.

---

[4]Computer programs, sometimes called *Decision Table Processors*, have been written to produce program logic from coded decision table information.

Beyond the basic ingredients in the Program Portfolio just illustrated, there are many others depending on the particular program involved.

With this information the programmer can develop a block diagram, sometimes called a *program flow chart*, such as that shown in Figure 3.17. This block diagram portrays the logic and processing in the program. Most often, it is this document that is used in the Logic Review discussed earlier in this chapter. As can be seen in Figure 3.17, the descriptive information on the block diagram is inside each of the symbols. Although this is still a widely used method, the author and others feel that better documentation can be rendered if the descriptions are not constrained to the physical size of the symbol. What frequently happens is that the programmer writes until he has filled the box and then stops . . . whether or not he has satisfactorily explained the step. A method by which to avoid this is gaining acceptance. It simply consists of drawing the same symbols, of smaller dimensions, and placing the explanations outside the boxes. The lines between symbols are made longer to accomodate longer explanations that run alongside them.

From this point, the programmer can begin to code his program . . . although some installations require a more detailed block diagram that shows each instruction to be used.[5] This gets to be rather tedious work and the instruction-by-instruction block diagram becomes cumbersome to keep updated, as changes are made. Computer automated methods are now used in a number of installations to take over this laborious chore. This automated method is used after the program has been coded and tested. The computer uses the program's *source statements* to draw the detail level diagram. Symbols, as they appear on these printouts are shown in Figure 3.18. Computer manufacturers and independent programming firms have developed *flow chart programs* for various programming languages.

A section of a program listing is presented in Figure 3.19. Of particular importance in this case are the *comments* which the programmer has included to describe what processing is taking place, on nearly every instruction line. These comments in no way affect the program—they are ignored by the computer. So, they may be left out of the program. However, when another programmer has to interpret the program in the future, the comments are almost indispensable if the program is to be understood well.

Figures 3.20 and 3.21 illustrate just one type of operations documentation. In this case, the run specifications shown would provide all but a few of the operating instructions necessary for an operator to run one program on a particular computer type. The forms shown would be part of the *run book* (Operations Manual). In addition, a *message list* would be included to show what action the computer operator should take if a message is typed on the computer's console typewriter.

User type documentation describes the non-computer activities that are an integral part of the total system. Such documentation is bound into a User's Manual and is used for training and reference purpose. Figure 3.22, for example, shows some of the off-line (non-computer) procedures in connection with statement checking for a retail accounts receivable application.

Various forms to be completed by the user are illustrated and explained in the User's Manual. An example of a common type of form is shown in Figure 3.23.

Computer printed outputs would also be displayed and described in the User's Manual. Figures 3.24 and 3.25 are examples of illustrations with key information highlighted.

Sometimes new systems also require explanations to the company's customers. For example, a new statement form might need to be described. Various businesses combine such explanations with promotional features—like, "an exclusive when dealing with us . . . the newest and most accurate billing methods . . ."

---

[5]This is often true of installations that have *coders*—personnel who code computer instructions, but do not design the program.

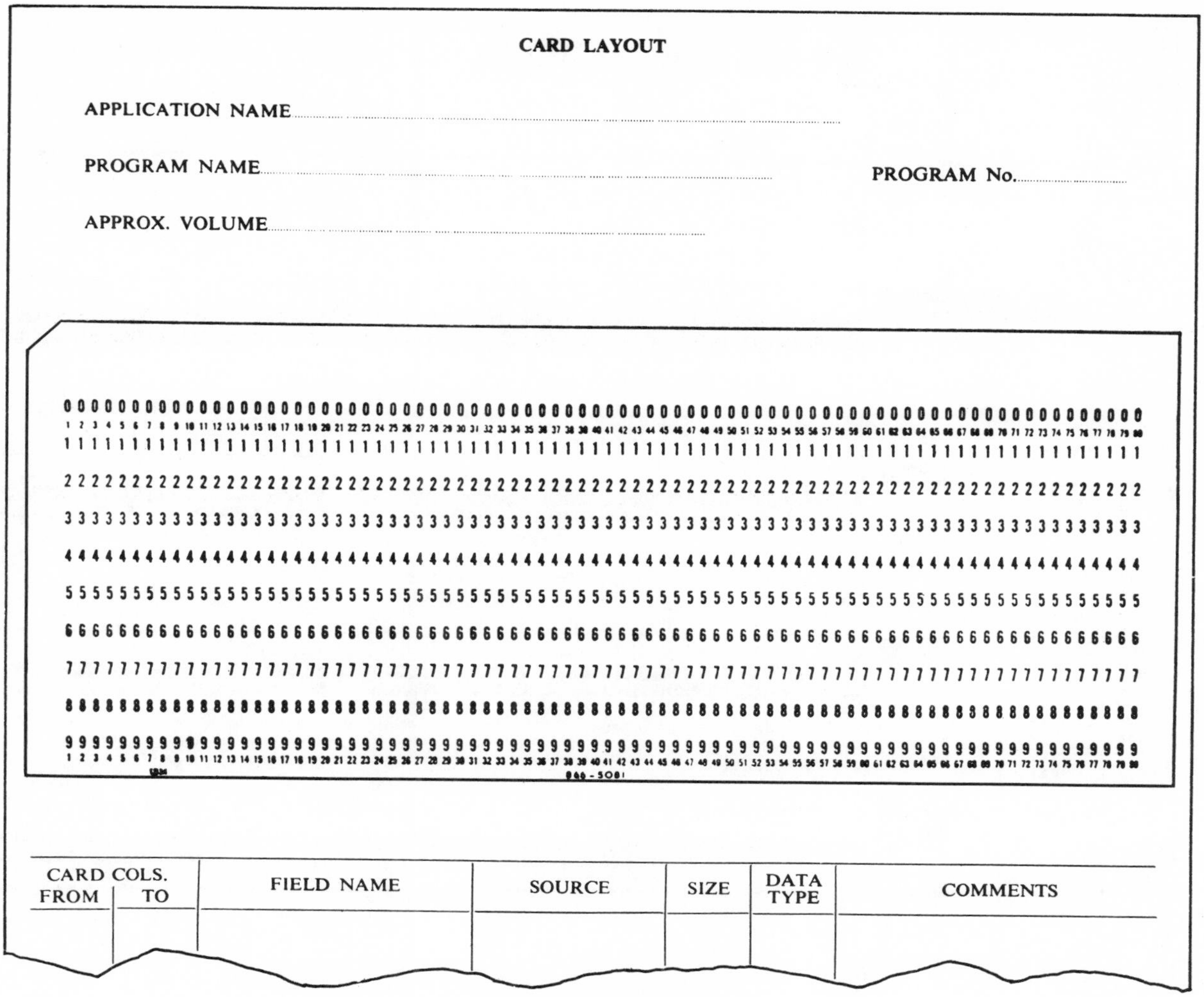
CARD LAYOUT
APPLICATION NAME
PROGRAM NAME
PROGRAM No.
APPROX. VOLUME
CARD COLS.
FROM
TO
FIELD NAME
SOURCE
SIZE
DATA TYPE
COMMENTS

Figure 3.11
Card Layout Sheet

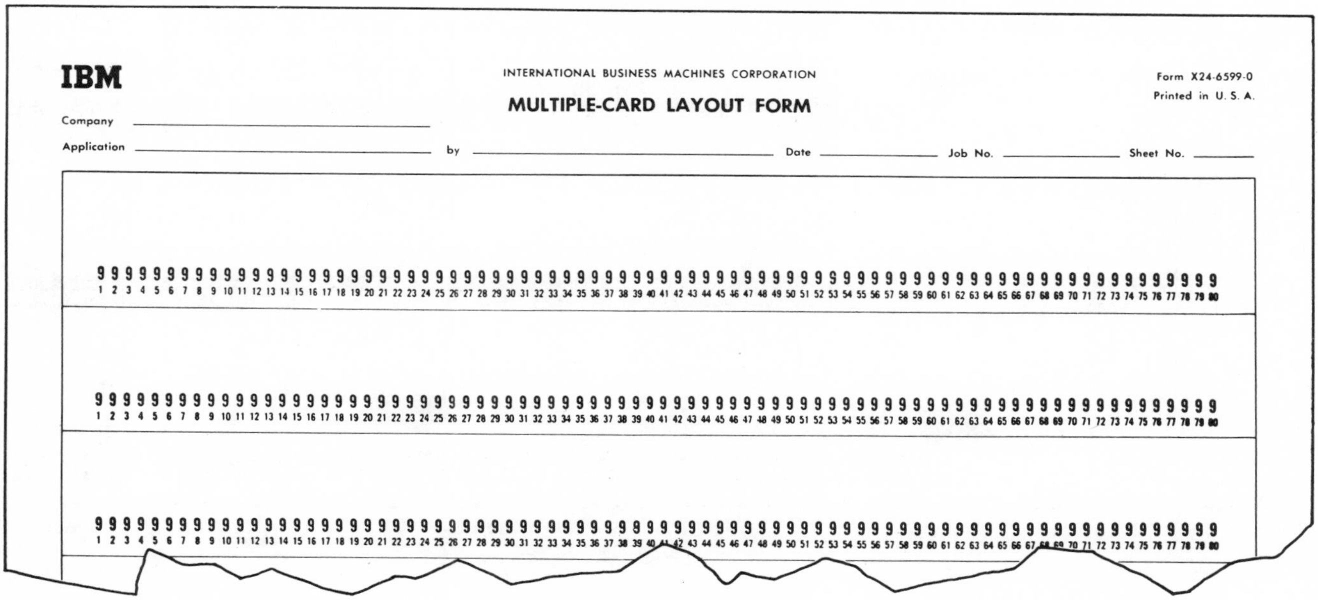
IBM
INTERNATIONAL BUSINESS MACHINES CORPORATION
MULTIPLE-CARD LAYOUT FORM
Form X24-6599-0
Printed in U. S. A.
Company
Application
by
Date
Job No.
Sheet No.

Figure 3.12
Multiple Card Layout Form

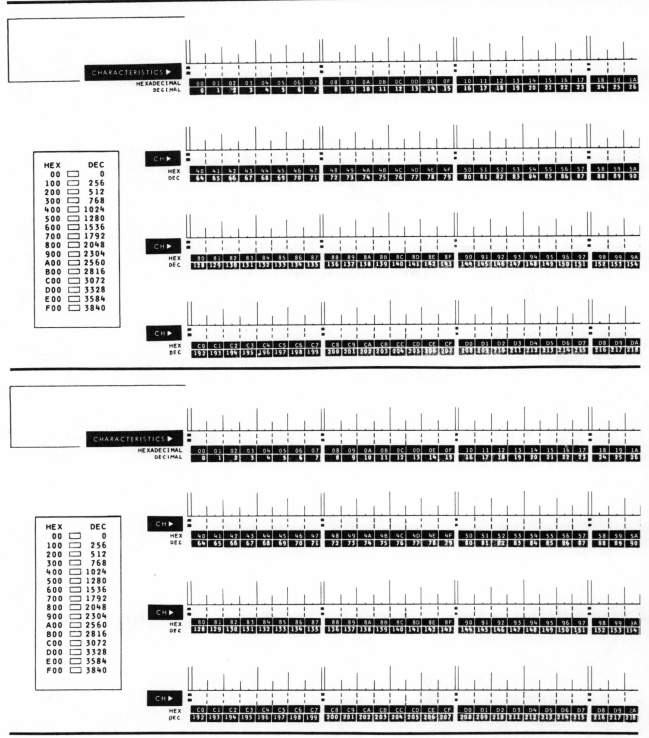

Figure 3.13
Record Layout Worksheet

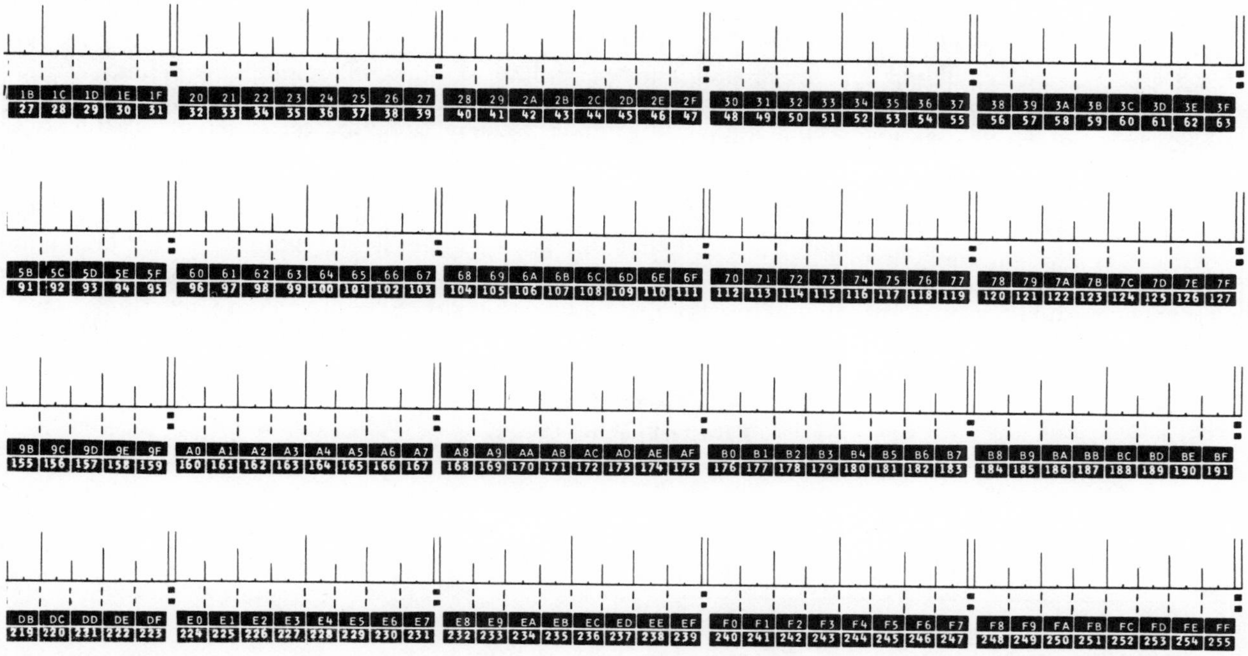

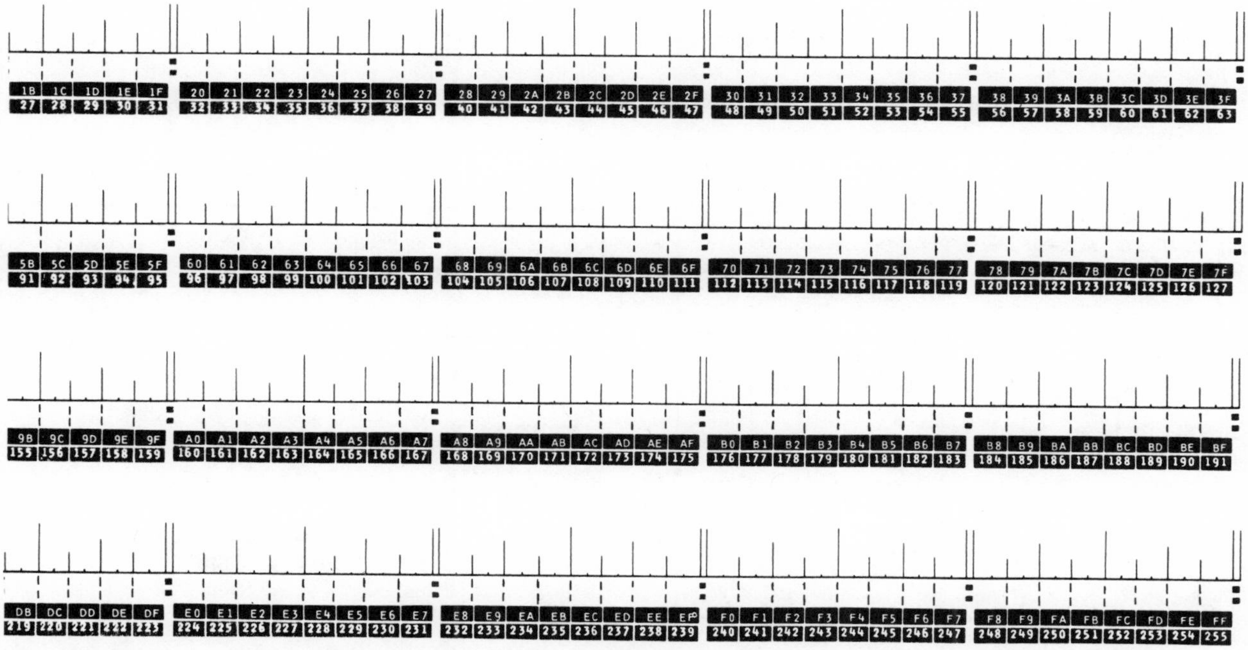

E – floating-point, full word   P – packed decimal   A – address value, full word   V – address, external symbol
D – floating-point, double word   Z – zoned decimal   Y – address value, halfword   S – address, base displacement

Reprinted by permission from MANAGEMENT PLANNING GUIDE FOR A MANUAL OF DATA PROCESSING STANDARDS,
© *by International Business Machines Corporation.*

Figure 3.13 (cont.)

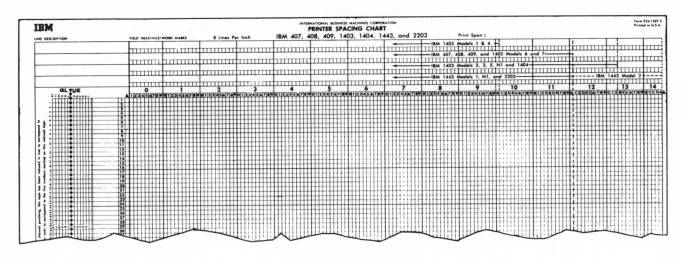

Figure 3.14
Printer Spacing Chart

IBM File Sheet

FILE NAME: COST FILE — FILE NO.: F-4010

LOCATION: QUOTATIONS SECTION — STORAGE MEDIUM: 3X5 TRACK-INDEX ROLLER CABINETS

ACCESS REQUIREMENTS:

SEQUENCED BY: DATE WITHIN BUTODALE PART NUMBER.

CONTENT QUALIFICATIONS:

HOW CURRENT:

RETENTION CHARACTERISTICS: NO CARDS HAVE YET BEEN DISCARDED.

LABELS:

USED IN 001-57X, 001-63 X,

REMARKS: FILE CONTINUES TO GROW, AS NO DISCARD RULES EXIST. OLDEST CARDS ARE AGE OF COMPANY'S RECORDING SYSTEM.

CONTENTS

SEQUENCE NO.	MESSAGE NAME	VOLUME AVG.	VOLUME PEAK	CHARACTERS PER MESSAGE	CHARACTERS PER FILE AVG.	CHARACTERS PER FILE PEAK
	HISTORICAL COST DATA CARDS	1,000 K UPWARDS. FILE INCREASES AT RATE OF 4200 CARDS PER MONTH.				
	(SEE ATTACHED SAMPLE CARD)					

DATE: — ANALYST: R. L. CASEY — SOURCE: QUOTATIONS — PAGE: 1 OF 1

STUDY: BUTODALE

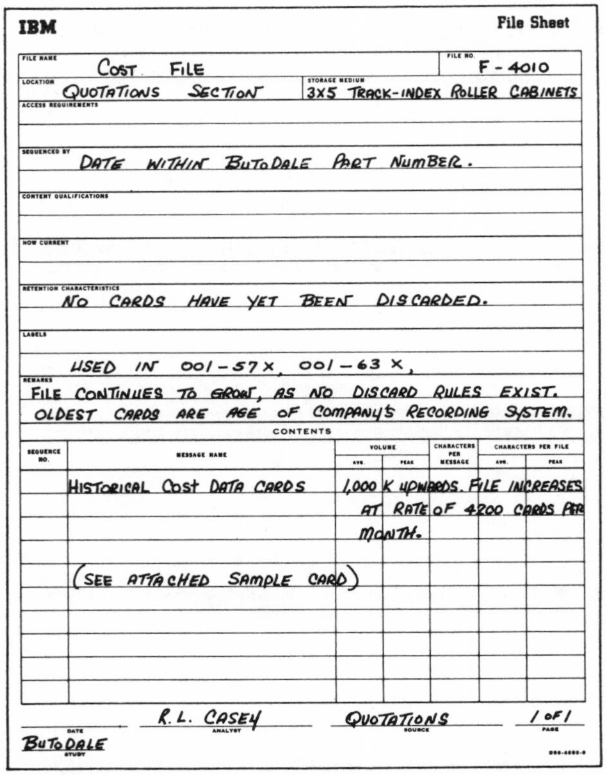

Figure 3.15
File Sheet

RULE No.	1	2	3	4	5	6	7	8
1st Class Request	Y	Y	Y	Y				
Tourist Request					Y	Y	Y	Y
1st Class Open	Y	N	N	N		Y	N	
Tourist Open		Y	N		Y	N	N	N
Alternate Class Acceptable		Y	Y	N		Y	Y	N
Issue 1st Class Ticket	X					X		
Issue Tourist Ticket		X			X			
Subtract 1 from 1st Class Avail	X					X		
Subtract 1 from Tourist Avail		X			X			
Place on Tourist Wait List			X				X	X
Place on 1st Class Wait List			X	X			X	

Figure 3.16
Decision Table

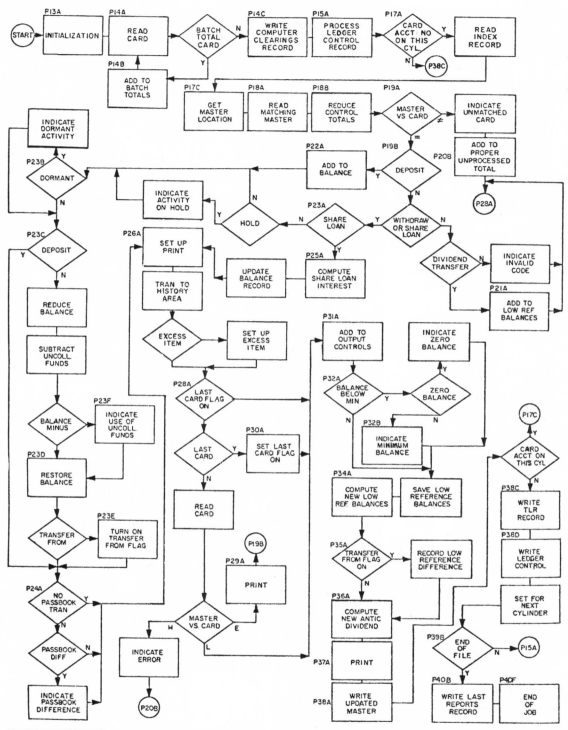

Reprinted by permission from IBM SYSTEM/360 ONLINE TELLER SYSTEMS FOR SAVINGS ACCOUNTING AND OTHER FINANCIAL APPLICATIONS, © *by International Business Machines Corporation.*

Figure 3.17
Illustrative Block Diagram

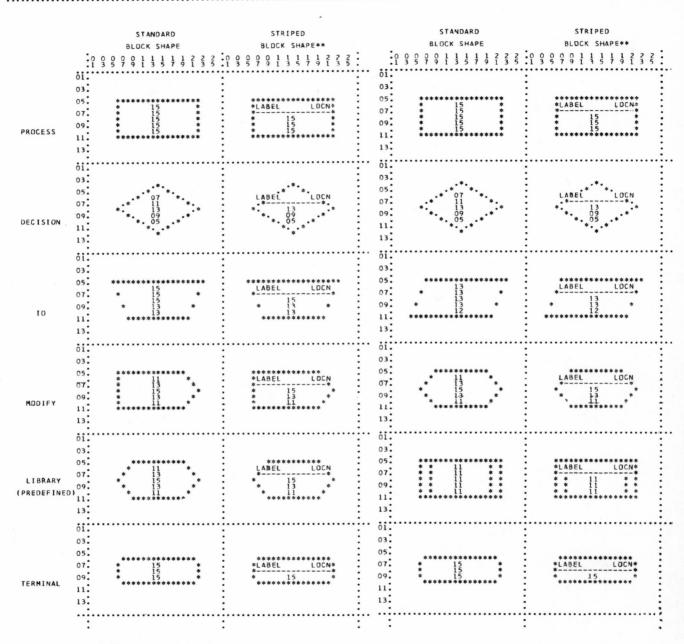

* NUMBERS INSIDE BLOCK SHAPES REPRESENT MAXIMUM TEXT FOR EACH LINE.

** THE STRIPED BLOCK IS GENERATED BY SPECIFYING THE APPROPRIATE BLOCK
   SHAPE OPERATOR AND INCLUDING THE SUBROUTINE LABEL IN PARENTHESES AS
   THE FIRST WORD OF THE OPERAND (TEXT) FIELD.

Reprinted by permission from MANAGEMENT PLANNING GUIDE FOR A MANUAL OF DATA PROCESSING STANDARDS,
© *by International Business Machines Corporation.*

Figure 3.18
Machine-Generated Flow Chart Symbols

ADDR1	ADDR2	STMNT		SOURCE STATEMENT	360P AS 091	V1M7
		0057	*	REGISTERS AND PSW, CHECKS THE EXTERNAL INTERRUPT CODE FOR AN EXTER		
		0058	*	INTERRUPT FROM THE READER SORTER.		
		0059	*	OBJECTIVES OF THIS ROUTINE ARE - TEST THE CONDITIONS SET IN THE		
		0060	*	CSW, EXIT TO A USER DOCUMENT SELECT ROUTINE, POCKET SELECT THE		
		0061	*	DOCUMENT LAST READ AND READ THE NEXT DOCUMENT.		
		0062	SYSSEX	EQU	*	
005FC	C0040	0063		MVC	SPDKD%12¤,64	SAVE CAW CSW
C0098		0064		STM	1,0,SYSCOM+8	STORE REG VALUES
C0090	00018	0065		MVC	SYSCOM%8¤,24	STORE OLD PSW
0001B		0066	SPD21	TM	27,X¤00¤	TEST FOR 1419/1412
0030C		0067		BC	8,SPDMOB	EXIT,NO READER SORTER
006F4		0068		LM	SPDRB,SPDRD,SPDMO2	LOAD PCW, UNIT, BLOCK
		0069	SPDMO5	EQU	*-1	
		0070		USING	SPDMO2,SPDRD	
		0071		USING	SPMPCW,SPDRB	
		C072	*	BRING IN STATUS FROM READER SORTER BY TEST I/O COMMAND.		
00000		0073		TIO	0%SPDRC¤	TEST IO
06622		0074		BC	3,SPDABT-8	
CC044		0075		CLI	68,X¤0C¤	CHECK DEVICE END,CHANNEL END
C032E		0076		BC	7,SPDBA1	BRANCH FOR ERROR CHECK
		0077	*	SET-UP EXIT TO USER		
		0078	SPDAE1	EQU	*	
00724		C079		TM	SPDRDR+4,X¤10¤	BR IF NOT SKIP ON READ
0024A		008C		BC	8,*+16	
006F8		0081		NI	SPDSW,X¤10¤	CLEAR OTHER SWITCHES
006F8		0082		OI	SPDSW,X¤84¤	SET IR WITH BUFFER OVERRUN
002E6		0083		BC	15,SPDAE3	EXIT
00754		0084		L	SPDRL,SPDKC	SET UP SPDRE
00720		C085		L	SPDRS,SPDK1	LOAD UP USER SELECT ADDRESS
00000	00046	0086		MVC	0%2,SPDRS¤,70	MOVE IN COUNT
00002	00620	C087		MVC	2%2,SPDRS¤,SPDSNS	MOVE IN SENSE
00758		0088		LM	SPDR3,SPDRA,SPDRGS	
		C089		BALR	SPDRL,SPDRL	SPDRE TO USER SELECTION
0026D		0090		MVI	SPDAE2,X¤08¤	CLEAR BATCH NUMBER
00222		C091		EX	0,SPDMO5-3	
00708		0092		MVI	SPDPKF,X¤FF¤	
		0093	SPDAE2	EQU	*-3	
00758		0094		STM	3,10,SPDRGS	
00720		0095		LM	SPDR2,SPDR6,SPDK1	COMPUTE
00004		0096		IC	SPDRHD,4%SPDR2¤	SET UP
00700		0097		STC	SPDRHD,SPDNOP	SELECT CODE
00005		0098		STC	SPDRHD,5%SPDR2¤	
		0099		LR	SPDRHD,SPDR2	
0028C		0100		BXLE	SPDR2,SPDR4,*+6	ADDRESS OF
		0101		LR	SPDR2,SPDR6	NEW CELL
00001		0102		LA	SPDR3,1%SPDR3¤	
		0103	*	SET-UP START I/O FOR READER SORTER		
00700		0104	SPDAJ1	LA	SPDRO,SPDNOP	
00048		0105		ST	SPDRO,72	SET UP CAW
		0106	*	NEXT INSTRUCTION TO BE MODIFIED TO GET LENGTH MINUS ONE		
C0000		0107		LA	SPDRO,0%SPDR2,SPDR4¤	
		0108		BCTR	SPDRO,0	COMPUTE READIN ADDRESS
00722		0109		STH	SPDRO,SPDRDR+2	
00000		0110	SPDAB3	SIO	0%SPDRC¤	
002A2		0111		BC	2,*-4	
00720		0112		STM	SPDR2,SPDR3,SPDK1	STORE NEW VALUES

Figure 3.19
Program Listing with Comments

UC 325-241
NYRCC SYSTEM/360
REQUEST FOR MACHINE TIME

Job No.	Run No.	Date	P/D	Request No.	Estimated Run Time
					_____ Hrs. _____ Min.

Programmer Name	Prog. No.	Telephone	Floor	Room	Program System	Mode	Maximum Run Time
						☐ 360 ☐ Comp	_____ Hrs. _____ Min.

Load From (Check one)
- ☐ Cards
- ☐ Tape   IPL _____
- ☐ Disc

System Detail (Check one)
- ☐ Compatibility Mode
- ☐ Basic Operating System
- ☐ Operating System
- ☐ Basic Programming Support

Core Size

Channel
☐ 1   ☐ 2   ☐ Both

TAPE INFORMATION: Must Be Completed In Detail

SYMBOL ADDRESS	UNIT ADDRESS	TRACK		DENSITY				STATUS			REEL NO.	TAPE DESCRIPTION (Not to Exceed 30 Characters)	RETENTION		
		7	9	2	5	8	16	IN	OUT	WORK			MO	DAY	YR

CARD INPUT: ☐ YES ☐ NO

POCKET	DESCRIPTION
R1	
R2	
RP3	

CARD OUTPUT: ☐ YES ☐ NO

POCKET	DESCRIPTION
P1	
P2	
RP3	

DISC INFORMATION: Must Be Completed In Detail

SYMBOL ADDRESS	UNIT ADDRESS	STATUS				DISC LIMIT		DISC PACK NO.	DISC PACK DESCRIPTION	RETENTION		
		IN	OUT	BOTH	WORK	FROM	TO			MO	DAY	YR

PRINTER INFORMATION: Must Be Completed In Detail

NUMBER OF PRINTERS: _____   FEED CLUTCH ☐ 6   ☐ 8   PRINTER CHAIN _____

FORM PART ☐ 1 ☐ 2 ☐ 3 ☐ 4 ☐ 5 ☐ 6   CUSTOM FORM _____   FORM NO. _____
Name

Figure 3.20
Computer Run Sheet
(Courtesy of Union Carbide Corporation)

MESSAGES WAIT STATE:

HALT NO.	ADDRESS	OPERATOR ACTION TO BE TAKEN

SPECIAL OPERATOR INSTRUCTIONS:

OPERATOR COMMENTS:

OPERATOR NO. _____   CHECKED BY _____   DATE & TIME RELEASED _____

Figure 3.20 (cont.)

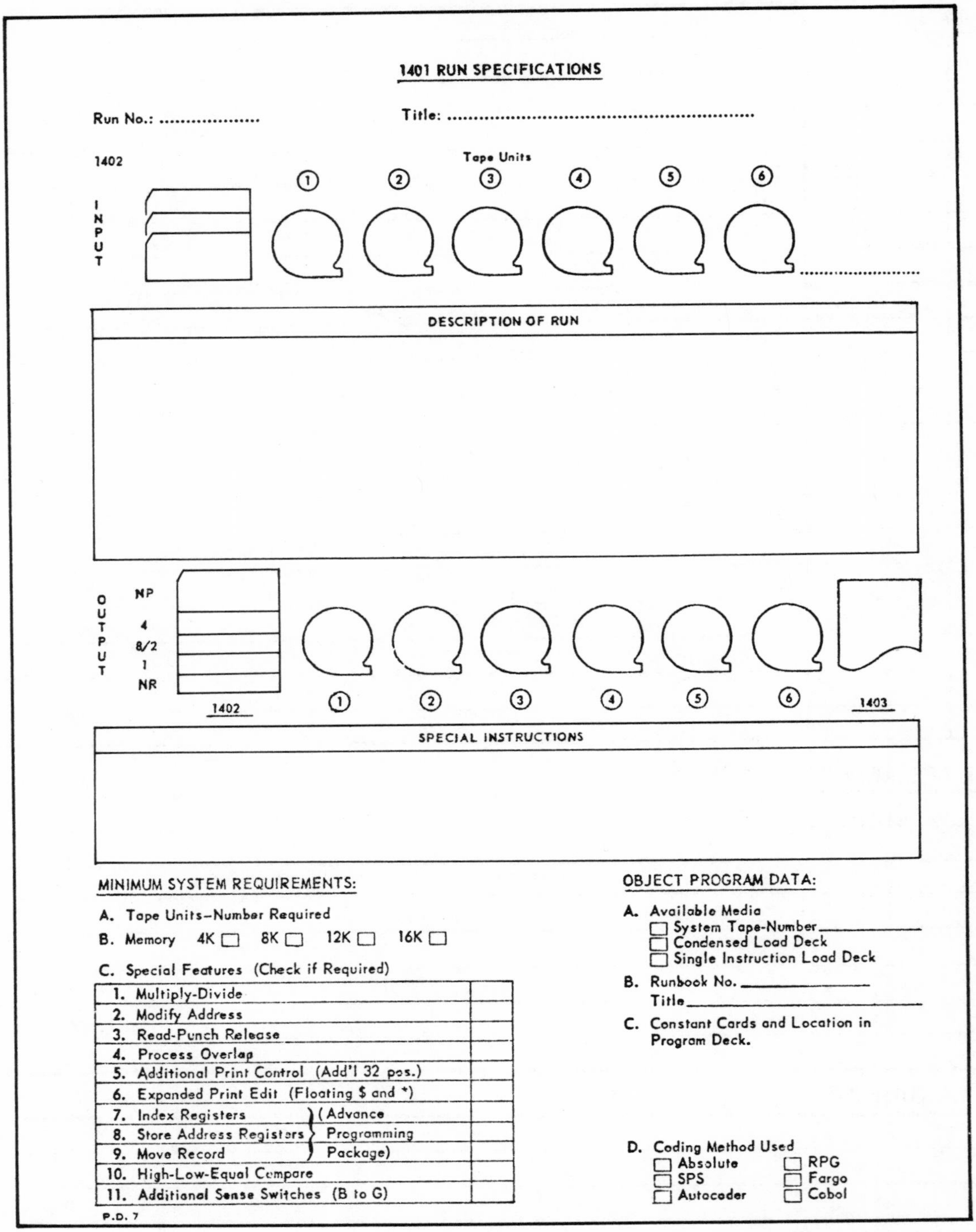

1401 RUN SPECIFICATIONS

Run No.: ....   Title: ....

1402

INPUT

Tape Units
① ② ③ ④ ⑤ ⑥

DESCRIPTION OF RUN

OUTPUT

NP
4
8/2
1
NR

1402   ① ② ③ ④ ⑤ ⑥   1403

SPECIAL INSTRUCTIONS

MINIMUM SYSTEM REQUIREMENTS:

A. Tape Units—Number Required

B. Memory   4K ☐   8K ☐   12K ☐   16K ☐

C. Special Features (Check if Required)

1. Multiply-Divide	
2. Modify Address	
3. Read-Punch Release	
4. Process Overlap	
5. Additional Print Control (Add'l 32 pos.)	
6. Expanded Print Edit (Floating $ and *)	
7. Index Registers (Advance	
8. Store Address Registers Programming	
9. Move Record Package)	
10. High-Low-Equal Compare	
11. Additional Sense Switches (B to G)	

P.D. 7

OBJECT PROGRAM DATA:

A. Available Media
   ☐ System Tape-Number_____
   ☐ Condensed Load Deck
   ☐ Single Instruction Load Deck

B. Runbook No. _____
   Title_____

C. Constant Cards and Location in
   Program Deck.

D. Coding Method Used
   ☐ Absolute   ☐ RPG
   ☐ SPS   ☐ Fargo
   ☐ Autocoder   ☐ Cobol

Figure 3.21
Run Specification Sheet

SYSTEM SET-UP REQUIREMENTS

Run No. .... Job Title ....

TAPE UNIT #	USED AS		DENSITY		FILE RING		FILE DESCRIPTION	FILE SEQUENCE	EST. # REELS	DISPOSITION
	I/P	O/P	LOW	HIGH	IN	OUT				
1										
2										
3										
4										
5										
6										

1402 READ/PUNCH	INPUT	PUNCH SETUP		
		READ SETUP		
		STA-CKER	DESCRIPTION	DISPOSITION
	OUTPUT	N P		
		4		
		8 / 2		
		1		
		N R		

1403 PRINTER	FORM TYPE	# OF COPIES	EST. VOLUME	PRINT CONTROL	PRINT DENSITY					DISPOSITION
					A	B	C	D	E	

1401 CONSOLE	SWITCHES ON	A	B	C	D	E	F	G	I/O

CARRIAGE TAPE# ....

LENGTH ....

Channel 1	Channel 7
Channel 2	Channel 8
Channel 3	Channel 9
Channel 4	Channel 10
Channel 5	Channel 11
Channel 6	Channel 12

NORMAL START SEQUENCE
  1 Place tapes on drives.
  2. Output cards in punch hopper.
  3. Place program cards in read hopper.
  4. Set alteration, switches.
  5. (a) Check Reset, (b) Start Reset, (c) Load

P.O. 8   Program Authorized For Release By_____ Date _____

Figure 3.21 (cont.)

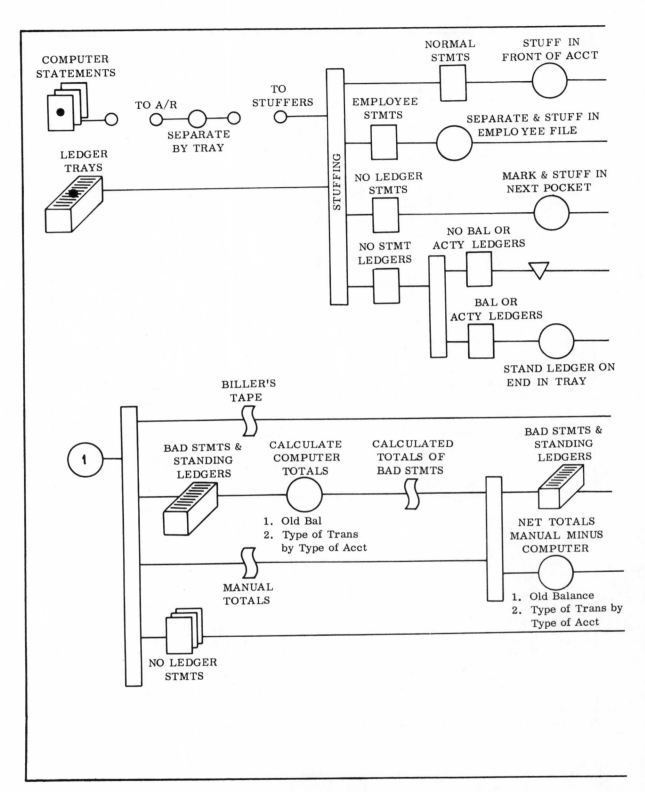

Figure 3.22
User Procedure Diagram
(Courtesy of NCR Corporation)

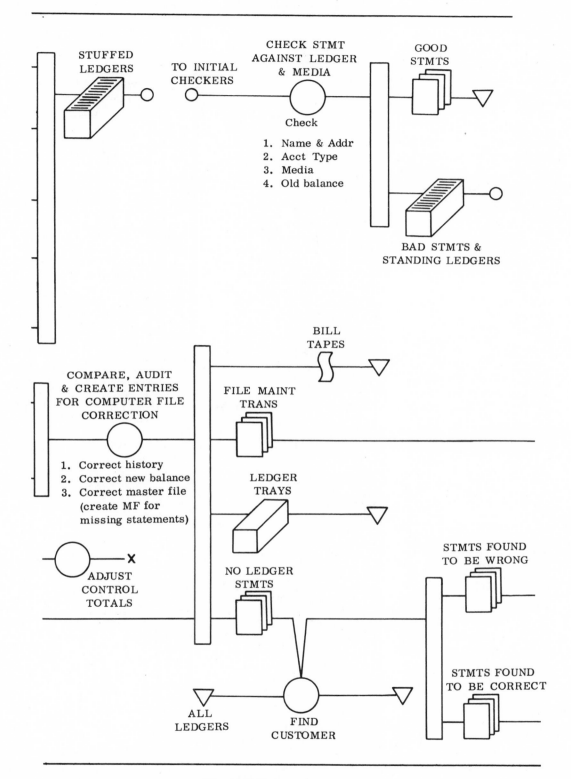

Figure 3.22 (cont.)

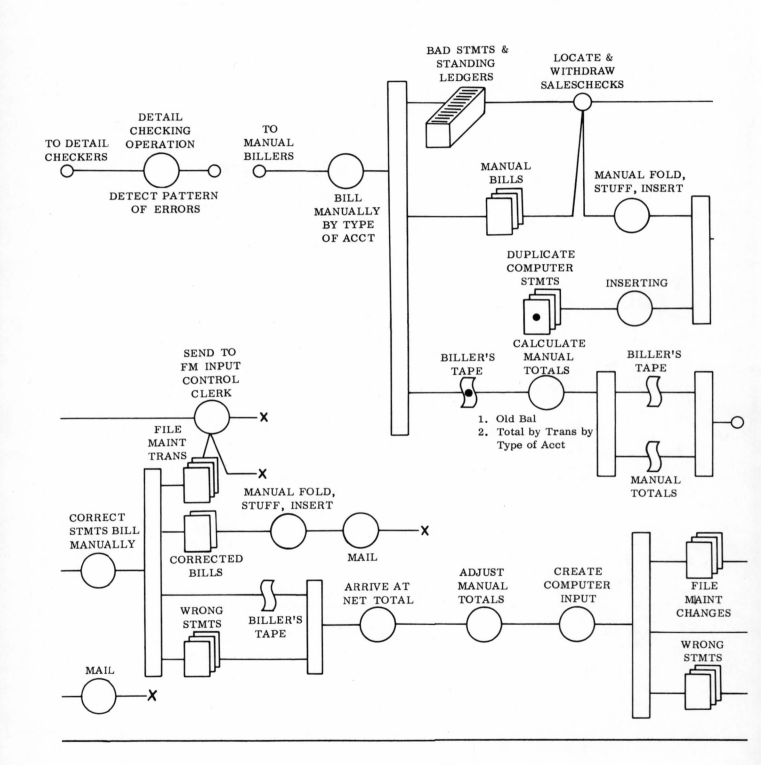

Figure 3.22 (cont.)

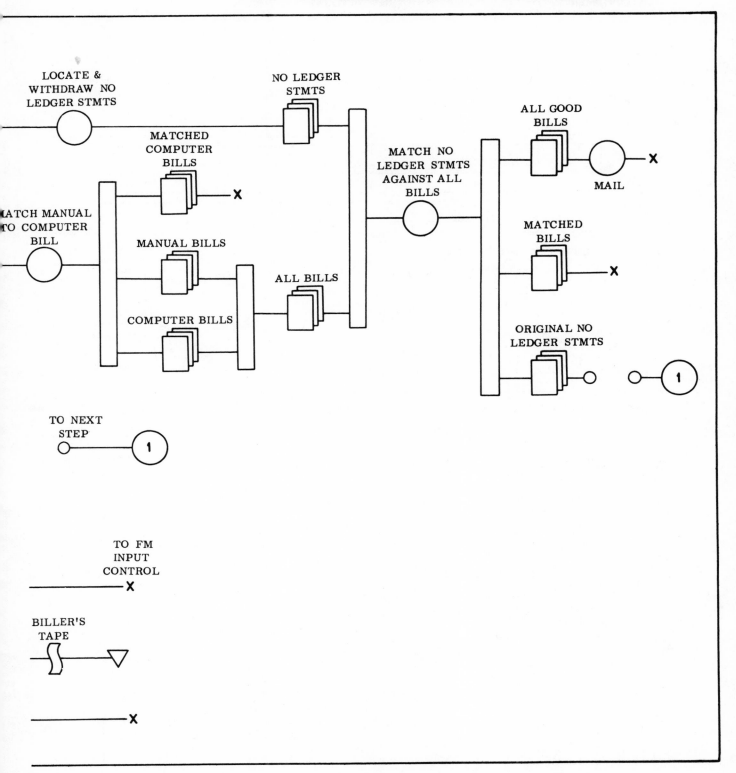

Figure 3.22 (cont.)

FILE MAINTENANCE CHANGE FORM

NEW CUSTOMER

ACCOUNT NUMBER

ACCT. TYPE	TRANS CODE	REFERENCE NUMBER
0 0 0	2 0	

ZIP CODE	0 6		
NAME	0 2		
STREET	0 3		
STREET OR CITY	0 4		
CITY OR BLANK	0 5		

NEW ACCOUNT

ACCOUNT NUMBER

NEW ACCOUNT TYPE	TRANS CODE
	2 4

DATE OPENED | 1 8 - | | | | 90 DAY INDICATOR |

YEAR   MONTH   **90 DAY INDICATOR**

TRANSACTION CODES
20 NEW CUSTOMER
22 CHANGE CUSTOMER
24 NEW ACCOUNT
26 ACCOUNT CHANGE
88 ACCOUNT DELETE
89 CUSTOMER DELETE

ACCOUNT TYPE
30 DAY 010
REV.   020
90 DAY 080
        081
        082
        083

CHANGE OF CUSTOMER INFORMATION

ACCOUNT NUMBER

ACCT. TYPE	TRANS CODE	REFERENCE NUMBER
0 0 0	2 2	

FIELD CODE	8	7	6	5	4	3	2	1		FIELD CODE	8	7	6	5	4	3	2	1

	CUSTOMER FIELD CODES	NO. OF CHARS.
01	ACCOUNT NUMBER	9
06	ZIP CODE	5
08	RESTRICTION CODE	3
09	COLLECTION INDICATOR	1
10	WRITE OFF	1
11	DON'T DUN	1
12	PREFERRED ACCOUNT	1
13	AIR MAIL CODE	1

CHANGE OF ACCOUNT INFORMATION

ACCOUNT NUMBER

ACCT. TYPE	TRANS CODE	REFERENCE NUMBER
	2 6	

FIELD CODE	8	7	6	5	4	3	2	1		FIELD CODE	8	7	6	5	4	3	2	1

	ACCOUNT FIELD CODES	NO. OF CHARS.
01	ACCOUNT TYPE	3
10	CURRENT BALANCE	6
12	STIPULATED PAYMENT	6
13	SERVICE CHG. FACTOR	3
90	ACCOUNT CLOSED IND.	1
91	90 DAY INDICATOR	1
03	LIMIT	6

NAME AND ADDRESS CHANGES

ACCOUNT NUMBER

ACCT. TYPE	TRANS CODE	REFERENCE NUMBER
0 0 0	2 2	

0 6		ZIP CODE

FIELD CODE   INFORMATION

02 — NAME
03 — 2ND LINE
04 — 3RD LINE
05 — 4TH LINE

Figure 3.23

Specimen File Maintenance Form

(Courtesy of NCR Corporation)

STATEMENT

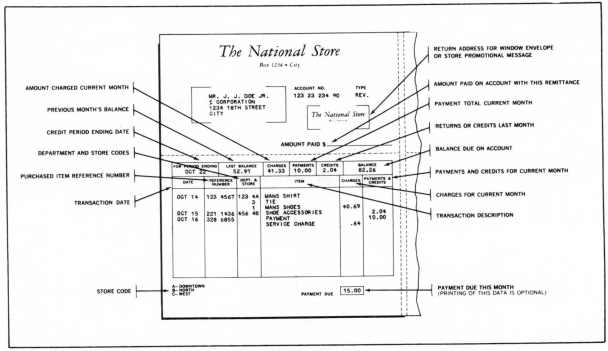

Figure 3.24
Customer Statement with Explanations
(Courtesy of NCR Corporation)

AUTHORIZATION REPORT

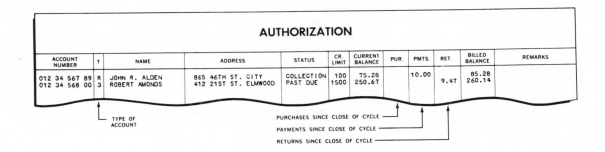

MONTHLY HISTORY LEDGER REPORT

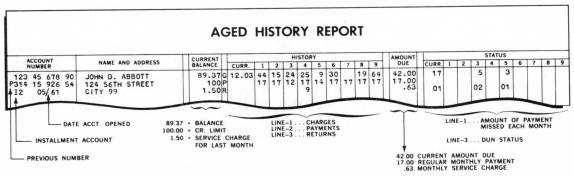

Figure 3.25
Output Reports with Explanations
(Courtesy of NCR Corporation)

In summary, each application will require basic kinds of documentation supplemented with whatever additional information will enhance the effectiveness of the whole system. There are fundamental standard practices that management at each installation must devise and enforce. But, as in all things, standards can be overdone to the point where standards that do not fit are made to fit, and clarity plus other advantages are lost.

Standards which overly inhibit the expression of creative thinking or are simply a nuisance do not, for the sake of uniformity, justify their existence.

When standards appear to be needed in some area of EDP, a decision ought to be made as to whether their presence contributes to the overall effectiveness of the computer effort in a net positive way. In the same regard, existing standards should be reviewed periodically in an attempt to determine whether they have outlived their usefulness in their present form.

ACTIVITY REPORTING AND CONTROL

The Systems & Programming Weekly Activity Report, shown in Figure 3.26, is an example of a form used by a manager to have the activities of his subordinate reported rather formally. With such a document the manager can compare performance against schedules and make adjustments which may be needed. Also, the report gives an indication of where problems may have been encountered and offers the individual an opportunity to express himself on a regular basis.

Naturally, the usefulness of an activity report like the one shown will depend upon how conscientiously it is completed and the degree to which a manager follows-up on it. At least, it gets the programmers and analysts to think about what they have done, what tasks remain, and how long it will take to complete various other tasks which remain.

Managers use the report such as that shown in Figure 3.26 in a number of ways. In most cases, these reports are kept in a loose-leaf binder or file folder. Each person's reports are often grouped together and are in reverse chronological sequence. As the manager reviews the latest report, he can compare it with the one from the past week and if necessary can look back at older reports. Doing this will give him a feeling for problems that are not evident from reading a single form. From this point, the manager may want more information from the person involved. Action on the part of the manager, of course, will depend upon specific circumstances.

Information from the report shown in Figure 3.26 is also used to update a *master progress chart* where each project and program is displayed.

Reports from the systems analysis and programming managers to higher level EDP and user management often will contain selected information that has been extracted from Weekly Activity Reports.

Where there are not too many analysts and programmers, a clerk can compile information from these reports for billing the user for EDP personnel costs. Larger installations usually design the form (as in Figure 3.26) so that information can be keypunched into cards that go into a billing program. More elaborate analyses of activities can be made when this information is recorded on data media.

The historical information that becomes available as a result of using a report such as that shown in Figure 3.26 can be used as a guide for future time and cost estimates. Many other benefits, like personnel reviews and evaluations, are possible when a formalized system exists.

EDP managers should try to keep such forms as easy to complete as possible, consistent with providing needed information only. For example, the reporting of computer time used to test the programs should be a function of the computer operations department, not the programmer. However, a programming manager will, nevertheless, be interested in using such information for controlling and measuring programming efforts. The reporting of computer usages is discussed in Chapter eight, *Directing and Controlling EDP Operations*.

SYSTEMS and PROGRAMMING
Weekly Activity Report

NAME _____

Man Number

Position Code

Week Ending   mo-day-yr

IDENTIFICATION · Project · Application · Other	IDENTIFICATION · Program	PROJECT Number	PROGRAM Number	Activity Code	Regular Days	Overtime Days	Est. Days to Complete	Est. Percent Complete	Est. Completion Date mo-day-yr	Average Turnaround Days
		1 4	5 8	9 11	12 13	14 15	16 18	19 20	21 25	26 27

ACTIVITY CODES

SYSTEMS

	N	MC
Feasibility Study	101	111
Work Planning	102	112
Analysis & Design	103	113
Review Meetings	104	114
Performance Evaluation	105	115
Management Audit	106	116
Forms Design	107	117

PROGRAMMING

Problem Definition	201	211
Review Meetings	202	212
Flowcharting	203	213
Block Diagramming	204	214
Coding	205	215
Desk Checking	206	216
Data Preparation	207	217
Test & Debug	208	218
Documentation	209	219

OPERATIONS

	N	MC
Production Support	301	311
Production Assistance	302	312
Pilot Test	303	313
Parallel Test	304	314
Operations Document'n	305	315

CONSULTING

Systems	401
Programming	402
Operations	403
Instruction	404
Administration	405

EDUCATION

Self Study	501
Attending Class	502
Instructor	503

ADMINISTRATION

Meetings	601
General	602

N — New system work.

M·C — Maintenance and other work on existing system.

— Tenths of days.

yr — Use last digit only

Reviewer's Initials

PLEASE   COMPLETE   BOTH   SIDES

Suggestions to Improve Effectiveness

Plans for Next Week

Significant Accomplishments and Problems During Week

Last Name _____

Figure 3.26
Systems and Programming
Weekly Activity Report

A secretary can be taught to extract information from several sources in order to provide the needed information in one place for a manager, if computer automated procedures are not justified to do this. Again, the manager's time spent on clerical chores must also be minimized if he is to have time to manage.

Time and cost estimating

Estimates, regardless of what they happen to be for, will always reflect the judgment, knowledge, and experience of the person who makes them. A management appraisal of an estimate must of necessity be tempered with an understanding of this fact.

Over-optimism about the initiative and motivation of a programmer can destroy an estimate. Placing a high degree of confidence in being able to get needed test time on the computer wreaks havoc on an estimate, when the practical reality turns out to be the opposite. Many other examples could be given to underscore the notion that estimates are subject to numerous variables which are sometimes difficult to control.

Factors in Estimating

Nearly all of the studies in EDP application development estimating have been unanimous in failing to come up with a method, or even rules of thumb, to estimate the time and cost associated with systems analysis and design work. The author takes some comfort in this fact because he, too, has not been able to develop satisfactory methods for estimating these particular activities. Experience plus an intimate knowledge of the installation, its habits, its people, and its particular problems will help to establish very gross estimates. But these are really educated guesses more than anything else.

Examining the practical attributes of these activities, one can perhaps understand why this area in estimating remains so "unscientific." In the first place, most systems are one-time undertakings, making any reliance on history rather dubious. In the second place, the system analysis activity is intended for the purpose of finding out what the problem is. One has about as much hope in estimating how long this will take or how much it will cost as he does in suddenly asking an architect how much a building will cost. The architect will want to know how many square feet, how many floors, what type of construction, where is it to be located, etc. To answer these questions, one must have analyzed the needs. And so it is with estimating EDP systems analysis and design . . . it depends upon dimensions of the application, which are learned by studying the problem. One can say with more confidence that systems analysis and design is roughly half the total endeavor. But this still does not answer the question in terms of dollars.

Even the most comprehensive study known to exist on estimating EDP development costs has not arrived at an estimating method for analysis and design.[6] To date, this study has only been able to present an estimating technique for programming activities; later in this chapter a technique will be covered for programming. The study just referenced, however, did isolate many factors (variables) which it felt were significant in EDP estimating. Following is a *partial* list of those factors; to the left of each is the factor identifier used in the study.

X1—Vagueness of Design Requirements Definition
X2—Innovation Required
X4—Number of Organizational Users
X5—Number of ADP Centers
X6—Complexity of Program System Interface

---

[6] E. A. Nelson, *Management Handbook for the Estimation of Computer Programming Costs* (Santa Monica, Calif: Systems Development Corporation, March 1967). Available from: U. S. Department of Commerce, Clearinghouse for Federal Scientific and Technical Information, Springfield, Va. Document No. AD648750.

X7—Response Time Requirements
X8—Stability of Design
X9—On-Line Requirements
X13—Total Source Instructions Written
X18—Number of Words in the Data Base
X20—Number of Input Message Types
X21—Number of Output Message Types
X38—Insufficient Memory
X39—Insufficient I/O Capacity
X42—Programming Language
X45—Internal Documentation
X46—External Documentation
X48—Type of Program, such as business, scientific, utility, or other
X52—Average Turnaround Time, the time lag between when a programmer submits a
    program for computer testing and when it is returned to him
X61—Percent Senior Programmers
X62—Average Programmer Experience with Language
X63—Average Programmer Experience with Application
X65—Personnel Continuity
X67—Lack of Management Procedures
X68—Number of Agencies Concurring in Design
X74—Number of Locations for Program Data Point Development
X80—Number of Sources of Systems Information
X82—Degree of System Change Expected During Development
X83—Degree of System Change Expected During Operations
X84—Number of Functions in the System
X87—Percent Senior Analysts
X88—Quality of Resource Documents
X92—Personnel Turnover

It is probably safe to say that few, if any, systems efforts are evaluated quantitatively on each of these factors. However, these factors and others are what should go into a time and cost estimate, in one way or another.

PROGRAMMING ESTIMATION METHODS

Several rules of thumb have been used successfully in estimating programming at a coarse level of accuracy. All of these are intended to give an estimator a rough idea as to what the time and costs might be . . . without getting into specifics.

For example, programming (including everything from program design through final documentation) output is commonly rated at from one to three delivered instructions per programmer-hour. This particular parameter is generally applicable where an assembly-type (one programmer written instruction yields one computer instruction) language is used. Procedure oriented, higher level languages, such as COBOL and FORTRAN, can improve the output, in terms of absolute instructions, by a factor of three to six times.

Cost per delivered computer instruction usually are in the range of $2.00 to $10.00 each, depending on type of program, language, and computer used.

A working programmer typically averages from five to fifteen minutes a day of computer time over the course of developing a working program. A manager can figure that he will need approximately one hour of computer test time a day for every five working programmers.

Charges for a programmer's time, including overhead, are typically in the range from $75 to $125 per pay . . . these are intra-company, non-profit rates. To rent a good programmer from a company engaged in the programming business typically costs $125 to $175 a day. Managers and consultants generally run $200 or more per day.

The per instruction costs have, in general, been coming down only slightly over the past five to ten years, even though technology has brought about much greater efficiencies . . . for the simple reason that salaries and overhead have doubled and even quadrupled in the same period. Better overall estimates can be obtained by making an evaluation of each program comprising the system. Accordingly, the individual performance of a programmer can be measured by having control figures for each program. One way to get an estimate on programming is to have the job estimated by two or three senior programmers and strike an average.

Several formalized techniques for estimating programming time are known to exist; all require an understanding of the program functions. The technique about to be described was developed by the author and has proved to be rather accurate when used as intended; that is, to estimate programming as defined earlier in this chapter. It assumes that a Program Portfolio, discussed earlier in this chapter will have been prepared, as part of the systems design activity, prior to programming. It also presupposes that the programmer will be provided with sufficient computer test time and at reasonable intervals (minimum of once per day—should be two or more).

At the beginning of the discussion of time and cost estimating, the importance of the estimator's judgment and experience was emphasized . . . the adequacy of the method below also depends on these factors.

In order to employ this programming time estimating method, the estimator must be able to ascertain the following five factors:

1. *Size*—estimated number of computer instructions or total storage requirements for absolute code, measured in hardware memory locations.
2. *Complexity*—determined based upon logic and variations in processing required.
3. *Input/Output*—number and kinds of devices to be controlled by the program.
4. *Programming Language*—the programming system in which the program will be coded.
5. *Programmer Know-How*—as measured by his position.

Values for each of these five variables are established as follows:

Estimated Size	*Value Range*
1,000—5,000	1—5
6,000—10,000	6—10
11,000—15,000	11—15
.	.
.	.
.	.
96,000—100,000	96—100
.	.
.	.
.	.

Complexity Rating	*Value Range*
Low difficulty	1—2
Intermediate difficulty	3—6
Average difficulty	7—12
Above average difficulty	13—19
Very high difficulty	20—30
Experimental	31—50

Kind of Input/Output Device	Value
Card Reader	1
Card Punch	2
Printer	4
Console Typewriter	4
Paper Tape	6
Magnetic Tape	8
Disk	10
Data Cell	12
Drum	12
Optical or MICR reader	15
Typewriter Terminal	15
Graphic Terminal	15
Audio Terminal	15
Film Scanner	16

Programming Language	Value
Absolute	2
Assembler	5
COBOL	7
PL/I	7
RPG	9
FORTRAN	10

Programmer Know-How	Allowance Range
Senior Programmer	0.6—1.0
Programmer	0.9—1.4
Associate Programmer	1.2—1.6
Junior Programmer	1.4—1.8
Trainee Programmer	1.7—5.0

Combining the first four variables mathematically, an Unadjusted Estimate can be obtained. The equation shown below is used to develop the unadjusted figure which is in *man-days*.

$$\text{Unadjusted Estimate} = \frac{(\text{Estimated Size Value} \times \text{Complexity Value}) + \text{Input/Output Values}}{\text{Programming Language Value}}$$

The Unadjusted Estimate is what one might term the *standard time*. To account for individual differences, one must apply an allowance, as shown in the following equation.

Adjusted Estimate = Programmer Know-How Allowance × Unadjusted Estimate

As an illustration of how this estimating method is used, consider the following example.

Suppose the program to be developed has been evaluated and was found to have the following parameters:

	Variable	Value
1.	Estimated Size (20,000)	20
2.	Complexity Rating (average)	10
3.	Kind of Input/Output (Printer, Card Reader, Card Punch, 4 Magnetic Tapes, Console Typewriter)	43
4.	Language (COBOL)	7
5.	Programmer Know How Allowance (Programmer)	1.1

The calculation of the Unadjusted Estimate (UE) is:

$$UE = \frac{(20 \times 10) + 43}{7} = 34.7 \text{ man-days}$$

The Adjusted Estimate (AE) calculation to reflect Programmer Know-How, is:

$$AE = 1.1 \times 34.7 = 38 \text{ man-days}$$

Where a program consists of a number of modules written in different programming languages, or by different programmers, or that have different complexities, *each module must be estimated separately.*

The empirically developed estimating method shown here, it should be noted, does not account for time that may be lost or otherwise consumed on nonprogramming work. So, the man-days shown are man-days on the job engaged in programming activities. For scheduling and estimating many programming efforts, where there are more uncertainties, an overall *loss factor* of 20 per cent to 30 per cent should be applied. Such losses occur as a result of: vacations, holidays, administrative duties, personnel turnover, training, company meetings, special assignments, presentations to management, and so forth.

Through some experimentation and an analysis of historical records, a particular EDP installation should be able to get a good start on building an estimating system. The management controls, discussed earlier in this chapter, will assist the installation in developing a base for developing its estimating methods tailored to local conditions.

Evaluating the results

At periodic intervals throughout the pre-installation effort, evaluations should be made in terms of how well schedules are being met, budget performance, and other factors which would be indicative of accomplishment. Where operations are less than satisfactory, corrective action may be called for. Aside from maintaining control, one of the more significant functions and responsibilities of EDP managers is management reporting. Brief, but pertinent reports to top management should outline the progress, to date, on pre-installation efforts.

The same management that authorized the data processing work will also be interested in how well the computer is performing after it has been installed. A formal report, or post-installation review, should provide a comparison of actual to planned results.

FACTORS IN THE POST-INSTALLATION REVIEW

Depending upon the nature, size, and scope of the project undertaken, some factors below may be included in the post-installation performance report:

1. Ratio of actual to anticipated cost reduction.
2. Ratio of actual operating costs to budgeted costs.
3. Revised return on investment figures.
4. Past and present ratios of data processing expense to company bases such as net sales, overhead, assets, etc.
5. Comparative error analysis.
6. Past and present ratios of filled orders to back orders.
7. Improvements in reporting, billing, accounts receivable timings, etc.
8. Comparative records on internal and customer complaints.
9. Machine downtime comparisons.
10. Lost time due to personnel errors.
11. Costs of processing by application, activity, or user.
12. Personnel turnover.
13. Ratio of floor space used, past to present.

The list above shows some of the more common measurement factors, but is certainly not exhaustive. Some installations will want to custom-tailor their comparative reporting to conform with customs in their specific industry. Furthermore, the company itself may have its own "yard-sticks" for performance, such as a company standard discounted cash flow evaluation.

: four : four : four :

USING PROJECT MANAGEMENT IN EDP

Projects are not new. In the world of EDP, any kind of systems and programming work is often loosely referred to as a "project." As used in this chapter, a project is not carried out by a group of people who simply happen to be writing programs for the same system. It is *not* two systems analysts discussing an application over coffee. For the purposes of this chapter, a project is an undertaking by a *formally established entity* within the EDP organization, set up as a "task force" under special management. Project management's mission is definite. Its job is not building systems, but building a specific system . . . all efforts are directed to that end . . . everyone on the project is oriented to that goal. A project manager carries complete responsibility for all that happens on the project— his authority can be likened to that of a general manager.

The aim of this chapter is to describe where to use the project approach, how to organize EDP projects, and to provide guidelines for project management. To get a better grasp of the principles presented in this section, the reader should have an understanding of the concepts presented in the earlier chapters of this book.

As one might expect, many of the functions found in project work, such as system analysis and programming, are identical to those in EDP development work done under less formal organizational patterns. Only the functions and practices unique to the project management concept will be covered here in any detail.

While the main thrust of this chapter is concerned with major EDP projects, i.e., those which are expensive, require long term commitments, and are frequently complex, most of the management techniques described can easily be scaled down for undertaking of smaller magnitude. In the author's opinion, a multi-million dollar development effort certainly needs more controls and checkpoints than a project involving expenditures of $100,000 or so. The author further believes that as the size and scope of an EDP project increases, more rigorous and professional management is required. Administrative mistakes are, of course, vastly more serious on big projects . . . delays which may cost as much as $5000 or more a day make it worthwhile to spend more time and effort on establishing effective management controls.

The discussion in this chapter revolves about an EDP organization within a large business organization. In such an environment, it is the usual practice for the *User organization*, the business function or department that has the need for particular computer application, to call upon the services of this centralized EDP group. Development and other costs are usually charged back to the User. For purposes of discussion, this chapter assumes that the *Systems Development Department*, a part of the EDP organization, is chartered to carry out such projects as are requested.

Why project management?

Today, information systems management is charged with the responsibility for developing and implementing major computer applications requiring capitalization in amounts not dreamed of in earlier days of the computer. To meet the challenge of directing such grand-scale projects requires a new system of management. This new approach is required because the "functional myopia" of the classical data processing organization (system analysis group, programming group, etc.) often precludes its being able to deal effectively with complex capital undertakings. The most striking evidence of this realization has been the gradual emergence of *project management* as a means of coping with these burgeoning, large-scale problems.

Project management has become popular because functional management has, too often, failed to conduct successfully major EDP development efforts, to produce good systems, to meet schedules, and to stay reasonably close to legitimate cost estimates. Failures with smaller, less expensive systems were often forgotten quickly because, in some cases, they were not important enough for anyone to care, and in others because it was hard to find someone to blame. The assignment of responsibility became an exercise in futility because if anyone was at fault, all were at fault. Excuses could always be conjured up and "buck-passing" had become so chronic, that the fact that the bureaucrats in EDP were taking over could no longer be ignored. These facts, together with the need to build high-cost systems, spurred ventures into project management with hopes of finding the right answers. Many have found the right answers, but not immediately—because a project organization is regarded as a "peculiar animal" in many businesses.

As a successor to functional organization, project management needs a little time to learn how to handle its power. A project management system brings with it new practices, procedures, standards, policies, a system of checks and balances, and new organizational schemes. Many of the larger corporations and agencies of the federal government have spent much time and money on establishing EDP project management systems. Such systems afford a number of advantages not realizable under the old functional setups.

Advantages of a project management system

The main advantage to be gained through the use of a project management system is that it provides EDP upper management and User management with a definitive answer to the question, "Who is directly responsible for the total system and its implementation?" With this knowledge, such management can clear administrative roadblocks and release authority to the man who is going to get the job done.

Among other important advantages of project management systems, as compared with the typical functional approach in EDP work, are those listed below:

1. Provides for the preparation of definitive requirements and procedures for financing the project, and for the procurement of systems development and implementation personnel.

2. Insures that a thorough understanding of the desired form and content of the final product to be delivered will be had before work is started.
3. Provides the opportunity to develop realistic plans and schedules.
4. Permits significantly improved control over development and implementation expenditures.
5. Provides documentary control to avoid misinterpretations and poorly defined requirements which result in systems that successfully solve the wrong problems.
6. Through improved means of communication between the User and the systems development group, it minimizes misunderstandings.
7. Through modern management techniques, it assures reduction in redundant effort among system development personnel.
8. Makes provision for the proper definition, description, and control of complex interfaces.
9. Provides an efficient method for managing system and/or configuration changes.
10. Defines complete and proper acceptance tests for checking the integrated elements of the total system.
11. Improves the quality of the system and its programs as measured by the ease of their use, maintenance, and revision.
12. Assures adequate definition of programming tasks.
13. Provides a better opportunity to produce flexible systems and programs which can take advantage of improvements and changes in technology.
14. Assures a process whereby the User can have confidence that the system produced will meet with his approval.
15. Produces standard documentation which makes possible a thorough understanding of the systems and projects under development.

The project management system described later in this chapter will serve to demonstrate one approach to realizing many of the advantages outlined above.

When and where to use a project management type of organization

Application systems development work can be carried out either as an activity within the functional organization or, as a separate entity, in the form of a project. Opportunities for the business can be enhanced, and risks diminished, by selecting the appropriate approach. Even in performing the work, economic benefits can accrue if the proper course is chosen. It is therefore desirable to have certain criteria to help decide when to use the project approach rather than the traditional processes. Attributes of a project include the key points listed below.

A project is:

- *Critical* to the business because of the opportunity for increased returns its completion will yield.
- *Complex* in terms of the interdependence of an involved set of detailed activities. It calls for a combination of personnel with specific abilities and skills, equipment, material, and other resources.
- *Discrete* with respect to having a definite beginning and a distinct end-point. There must be a point at which the project is complete, where the requirements have been met.
- *Unique* to the current organizational activities. It possesses unusual attributes and characteristics which are somewhat foreign to the present environment.
- *One-of-a-Kind*, in the sense that it is generally considered to be non-repetitive for a specific deliverable system.
- *Definable* with respect to having a precise goal or objective.

Frequently, EDP jobs meeting some of the foregoing criteria are established as projects because there is a need to cut "red tape" and bypass existing routines. It should be understood that special management attention must be given to projects in order to arrive at the assigned objective within the defined constraints of money, time, and manpower.

The members of a project team may come from both inside and outside of the business organization. In cases where non-EDP employees join the project team, their current positions in the company would ordinarily not be held open awaiting their return. However, their future beyond the project's completion should be secure. They must be given assurances that a responsible position will be open for them. Such individuals often play key roles in administering the system after it goes into operation and would, therefore, be transferred to the User organization when the project is completed. If this type of provision is not made, these individuals may lose their objectivity about the project and may tend to make a lifetime career of it.

The project manager

Job descriptions for project managers rarely tell much about the kind of man he must be. Instead, they tell what he is supposed to do, what and who he is supposed to do it with, and what he is responsible for.

The author would like to take a little space to discuss "*man*" in the EDP project *man*ager, for, in the last analysis, the ultimate success of any project depends on him.

First he must be the kind of man who is motivated by the accomplishments he brings about through managing. He has special talents for developing people, bringing order out of chaos, and for being an entrepreneur. He feeds on opportunities to improve business through the adoption of better methods; to get ahead by coming up with creative solutions to big problems. He is not afraid of change. He is honest with others and himself, and is comtemptuous of those who are not. He has a statesman-like outlook, but it must serve his purpose. Otherwise, this may not be his inclination.

A project manager stays informed of the latest developments in his field—he reads business and technical literature, always seeking a better way. He understands the functional work that goes on under him, in the sense that he knows the contribution each of the professional people makes to the success of the project. He indulges in sensible risk-taking, and is inclined to share his visibility with his subordinates, to solicit their advice and to give them a chance to participate. He is quick to give credit when it is due.

The project manager is energetic and aware of his effectiveness. He is intensely practical and inspires confidence in others. He is cooperative, but refuses to jeopardize the project just to be agreeable. He is keenly interested in the well-being of the company, but his loyalty rarely blinds his own good judgment. Sentiment does not tie him to people or ideas when the job is not getting done properly. He is inclined to persevere when others have given up and has unalterable notions about fair-play in competitive situations. His zeal is obvious—he works hard and often works long to get to the goal. He has a sales flair and communicates well.

A project manager does not fit in quietly and unobtrusively. His demeanor is not that of a man at rest, content with his environment. He probably is not the best technician, nor the worst. He is not inclined to believe that "things will get better with time." He is not the perpetual compromiser. He is not the man who cannot or will not delegate responsibility. The project manager is not a man who has to be told he is failing, when he is. He is not the political manipulator with ten thousand ready-made excuses for all occasions. He is not the guy who remembers his job at 9 AM and promptly forgets it at 5 PM. He is not a man who dislikes being measured, nor is he a man who has problems—without having cogent answers for most of them.

Impossible to get a project manager who fits this description? Maybe. But one thing is certain—it will not be easy. If such a man is already working elsewhere in the company, he will probably be hard to get. With some luck, a young man who has been developing along these lines may be available. And, of course, the EDP organization could go outside the company for the man.

It is of vital importance to obtain a professional manager for this slot, preferably one having diversified EDP experience in his background. The selection for this post must be done very carefully. (See Chapter five for further information on acquiring personnel.)

Project organization structures

How the project oriented EDP organization is to be structured depends upon a number of factors. Is only one major project to be attacked? Are there several projects worked on concurrently? What kind of project is in the works? No one structure will fit all cases, but the discussion in this section should be helpful in building the organization to fit the jobs to be done.

An Individual Project

Organization structures vary somewhat depending on the specific kind of project and application undertaken. However, looking at the systems development process one finds common activities that are translatable in terms of organizational elements. First, the functional requirements of the system must be studied. Second, there is the computer application design and programming to be considered. Third is the technological side dealing with hardware and software integration. In some organizations, there are other activities that must be specifically recognized and considered.

Figure 4.1 illustrates a three element project organization. It will be noted that the functional part of the organization is set up to ferret out and define User *needs*, that the technology group is concerned with *methods*, and that the systems group *applies* the methods to meet the needs. Nearly all EDP projects have these same attributes, regardless of whether ten or a hundred people are involved in the effort. Sometimes the functional requirements group is not a distinct element as shown in Figure 4.1, but is included in the systems and programming group. When this is the case, it generally indicates that all project work is done by permanent members of the EDP staff. Otherwise, the User has specific individuals on assignment to the project team. These people would ordinarily be selected for their knowledge of particular aspects of the system being computerized.

At the start of a project, the systems staff is the first to be brought in. The User's personnel, who will help define the functional requirements, are brought in next and trained by the systems staff. The systems people work with the functional requirements staff to get a good understanding of the problem, before attempting a *preliminary design*. Shortly before preliminary design work begins, the technology group comes on board. The User's people continue to develop detailed requirements. As these are being prepared and become available, the programmers or programmer/analysts are brought in to participate in the *detailed design* of the system. Following detailed design, the actual programming commences.

Throughout this process, various parts of the organization expand and contract personnelwise. However, the systems group continues to expand until programming is underway, at which time it generally remains fairly constant until it tapers off as the project nears completion. When detailed requirements are completed, the functional requirements staff shifts its emphasis to operational matters, such as field procedures and data collection.

At the conclusion of the project, as mentioned previously, the functional requirements staff members often take over key positions in parts of the User organization which interface with the new operational system. The permanent members of the EDP staff go on to other assignments or projects in the EDP organization.

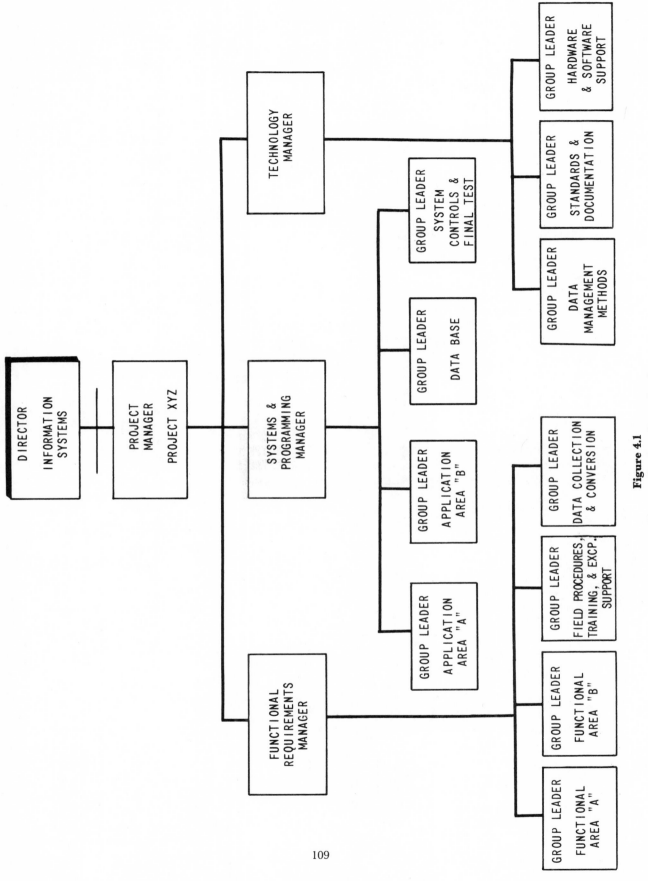

Figure 4.1
Three Element Project Organization

109

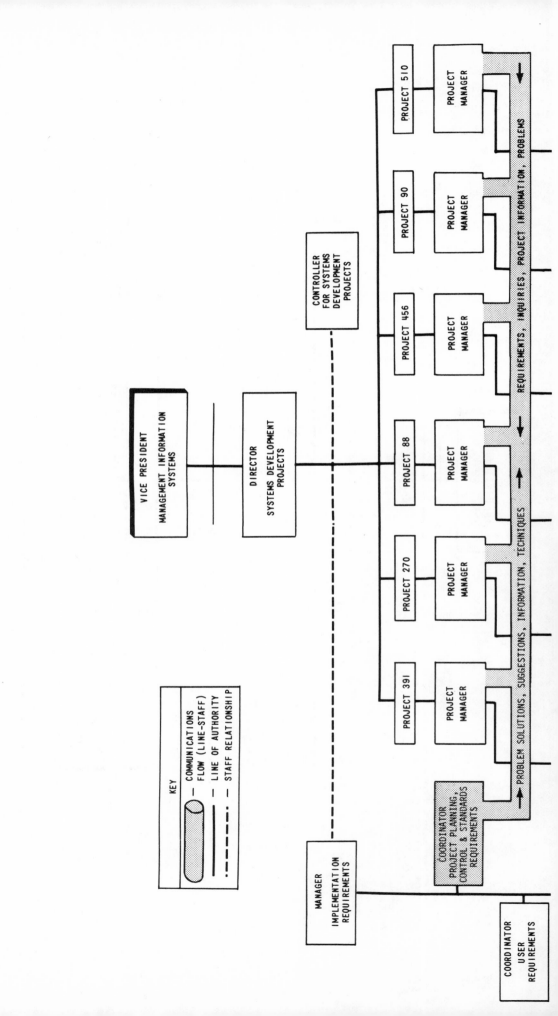

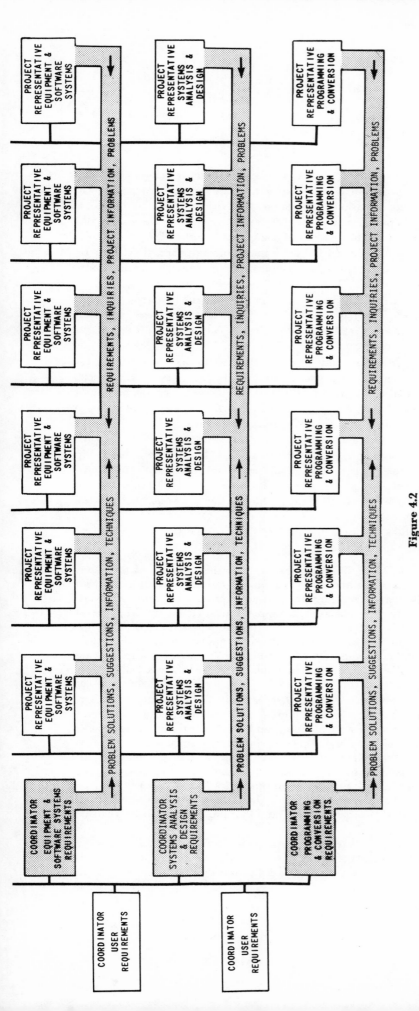

Figure 4.2
Multiple Projects in
the EDP Organization

MULTIPLE PROJECTS

Most EDP installations are likely to have more than one project under development at the same time. Since each project team is set up so as to be almost autonomous and independent of installation-wide considerations, the coordination of all project activities is done by the EDP manager or some other person who is put in charge of overseeing all projects. Hardware and software for the entire installation would be the concern of one group in his staff, and since it is probable that several projects may use the same EDP equipment and software, they must be administered to meet the needs of all. The idea is to keep costs down by centralizing and coordinating hardware selection across all projects. This does not, however, eliminate the need for each project team to work out hardware and software specifications to suit its particular purposes. Similarly, in design and programming, it is wasteful to "re-invent the wheel" for each project. The best known methods need to be related to all of the projects, and this is done by a coordination staff.

The organization shown in Figure 4.2 is made up of individual project teams that, via appointed representatives, bring their needs to a coordinating body that serves all projects. Notice that Figure 4.2 does not show the systems analysts, programmers, User personnel, and other members of each project team. Figure 4.2 requires close examination, as it attempts to show the workings of the organization in addition to the organization itself.

By definition, a project team is set up to make something or do something. Hence, the project effort is not really begun until that something is pretty well defined. The User will need help in defining his needs, and that is the role of the Coordinator-User Requirements. Without providing for this function, ongoing projects would be continually interrupted with requests from other potential Users to take a look at new and different problems, thereby jeopardizing work already in progress.

Below are capsule descriptions that highlight the duties of the people occupying Systems Development Department (SDD) positions shown in Figure 4.2.

1. *Coordinator-User Requirements*—This individual looks out for the interests of the User. His goal is to satisfy the User's wants and needs. In many ways, he is to the User what a sales engineer is to a customer. Expediting, translating requirements, and coordinating User-Systems Development relations are among his duties. He enters the scene at the inception of an idea and follows it through until the project is defined. The new User gets responsive service in this way and the project organization gets the benefit of a buffer, since there should be only limited contact between a new User and working project groups. As a result, other projects can be managed more efficiently and effectively because the working group can concentrate on approved project activities.

2. *Coordinator-Project Planning, Control and Standards Requirements*—As a management consultant and a project status monitor, this individual designs the controls and helps project leaders apply appropriate project planning and control techniques. He works to establish, maintain, and enforce the use of procedural and administrative standards for the Systems Development Department, across all projects. Timely, meaningful, and accurate reporting of project status and financial position are among his interests. He anticipates problems and provides workable means of solution to project leaders. To the extent that this Coordinator is successful, the Manager of Systems Development is assured that policies and procedures are followed, and that project reporting is realistic and meaningful.

3. *Coordinator-Equipment and Software Systems Requirements*—This individual coordinates the equipment and software requirements of the projects with the equipment suppliers and sources of software. He will configure systems and determine how requirements for all

projects can best be met. He provides the formal technical liaison with the Computer Center with regard to equipment and software systems. The dissemination and updating of technical manuals is also his responsibility.

4. *Coordinator-Systems Analysis and Design Requirements*—This person deals mainly with applied systems, and his influence extends into all projects. He provides for maximum integration of activities by bringing to each project techniques and methods to reduce the duplication of effort which might otherwise exist. In reviewing systems designs and suggesting improvements, he attempts to optimize the efforts across all projects. He is concerned with the adherence to standard practices in the systems analysis and design activities.

5. *Coordinator-Programming and Conversion Requirements*—Programming methods, standards, and the problems which arise in programming work are the areas of interest for this person. He brings to all projects the best known methods of programming, and coordinates the solutions to programming system "bugs." This individual is also responsible for reviewing the system conversion plans and for assistance in bringing together the necessary equipment and data for such conversions.

6. *Manager of Implementation Requirements*—This individual is responsible for the work of his staff members in seeing that requirements are coordinated in order that the right results can be achieved in an efficient manner. This manager is responsible for getting the specifications, hardware, software, and management guidance required for all projects. These are the tools which the project groups use in their work. (It should be noted that all coordinators are expected to work very closely with each other on problem solving, particularly in areas which cover more than one coordinator's area of interest.)

7. *Controller for System Development Projects*—An inspector at-large, he is authorized to look into *any* matter which affects the overall performance of SDD. He has the responsibility for recommending courses of action to the Manager of Systems Development for improving operations, correcting problem situations, and for maximizing on opportunities available to SDD. The Controller is responsible for the basic orientation and training programs. He is also responsible for handling all financial affairs of SDD, including: billing for services, expenses, budgeting, adjustments, accounts payable, "make or buy" financial analysis, forecasting, financial reporting, etc. In general he sees that the project gets company resources and services such as: secretarial, graphics, furniture and supplies, office space, equipment, etc. He is generally familiar with all project and personnel activities and may be called upon to act as Manager of SDD in his absence.

The remaining job titles and other features of the organization chart in Figure 4.2 are not explained since they should be self-explanatory from studying the chart and the information above.

Project steps and checkpoints

In the project management system about to be explored, each project is divided into three distinct phases which are, in turn, subdivided into a logical series of functional steps. Each of the steps, thirteen in all, is dependent upon the proper completion of the preceding one.

Figure 4.3 illustrates this approach and the process-flow from one functional step to the next. The three phases are:

    I.   *Definition and Analysis of the Problem and Business Requirements.*
    II. *Designing and Programming the System Solution.*
   III. *Implementing the System Solution.*

Within each phase may be seen the reinforcement each step provides to the next function.

The orderly transition from one step to the next is controlled by a system of formal documen-

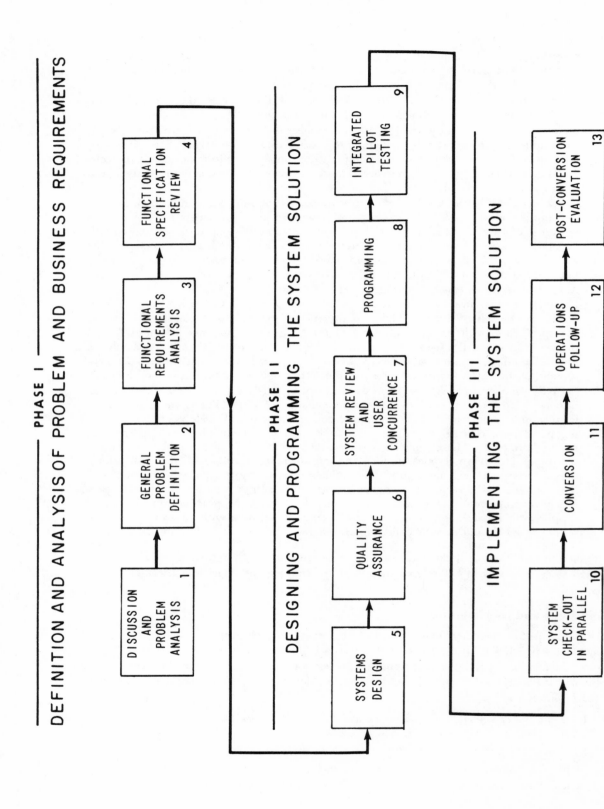

Figure 4.3
Systems Development Phases

114

tation, the evaluation and approval of which determines when each step and phase is completed. In the thirteen sections that follow are outlined the key features and checkpoints for each of the thirteen functional steps required for completing a project. Each section has five parts, titled as follows: Key Activities, Controls and Documentation, Decisions and Administrative Points, Funding, and Checklist.

PHASE I—DEFINITION AND ANALYSIS OF PROBLEM AND BUSINESS REQUIREMENTS

STEP 1—DISCUSSION AND PROBLEM ANALYSIS

KEY ACTIVITIES:

- User has potential requirement for a new system, system change, or makes an inquiry. Or, System Development Department (SDD) has something which may be of interest to User.
- Coordinator from SDD is assigned to discuss problem with User.
- Gross details of problem are analyzed.
- Determination is made whether needs can be met by SDD.
- Existing methods, computer or other, are reviewed for possible use "as is" or modifications required.
- General information exchanged and ways and means discussed.

CONTROLS AND DOCUMENTATION:

- Call Reports from Coordinator on meetings with User.
- Authorization Letter for Step 2 issued by User.
- SDD's Acknowledgement of Step 2 authorization letter.

DECISION AND ADMINISTRATIVE POINTS:

- User decides whether the problem should be explored further.
- Project Number assigned at end of Step 1 if User gives *go-ahead*.

FUNDING:

- Coordinator's services are charged to SDD overhead.

CHECKLIST:

- *Call Reports*

    Prepared by the Coordinator at the time the User and SDD make initial contact and for subsequent contacts. These are to be submitted to Manager of Requirements within one week after each meeting.
    Reports include:

    1. Date and duration of meeting.
    2. Names and affiliations of all persons involved.
    3. Subject(s) covered.
    4. Conclusions reached.
    5. Disposition of inquiry and statement of follow-up action required.
    6. Comments on existence of special or unusual situations.

- *Authorization Letter for Step 2*

    User sends letter to Manager of Implementation Requirements and Director of Systems Development giving:

1. Authorization to be billed for services rendered by SDD in Step 2. (Services will usually include those of the Coordinator and his staff, if any.)
2. User's statement of what is to be accomplished in Step 2.
3. Person appointed as SDD's key contact to be directly responsible for the User's effort in Step 2.
4. Target completion date for Step 2—that is, date when SDD's proposal is required.

•SDD's Acknowledgement of Step 2 Authorization Letter

Director of Systems Development (after conference with Controller and Manager of Implementation Requirements) sends letter to User:

1. Acknowledging receipt of Authorization Letter.
2. Identifying person officially appointed as Coordinator (and members of his staff, if any) and explains his duties and responsibilities in connection with Step 2.
3. States objections and exceptions (if any) to items in Authorization Letter.

STEP 2—GENERAL PROBLEM DEFINITION

KEY ACTIVITIES:

•User prepares, with help of Coordinator, a General Statement of Problem. This is a basic statement of the business requirements and anticipated benefits and the criteria to be considered for justifying the expenditure of capital, time, and effort on the problem.
•SDD prepares Proposal based upon General Statement of Problem. Shows gross estimate of cost, time, and effort. (User may conduct feasibility study using information from SDD Proposal.)

CONTROLS AND DOCUMENTATION:
•General Statement of Problem.
•Request for Proposal.
•Notification of Assignment.
•Proposal.
•Proposal Transmittal.
•Authorization Letter for Step 3.

DECISION AND ADMINISTRATIVE POINTS:
•SDD determines whether Proposal and other documentation are in order.
•SDD decides whether full-scale project or time and materials job is called for.
•User gives go-ahead for Step 3.

FUNDING:
•Billable via Project Number.

CHECKLIST:

•General Statement of Problem

User makes an assessment of the problem, with the guidance and advice of the SDD's Coordinator. This rather formal categorical statement includes:

1. Objectives of the computerized system.
2. Justification, in terms of anticipated benefits from the new or changed system.
3. A description of the business environment in which the system will ultimately operate. Includes business rules, policies, critical requirements.
4. Scope and penetration of the system as defined by organizational boundaries—group, division, department, etc.

5. Plans for organizational changes which would affect the system.
6. Description of the application(s) comprising the system, or application changes, if any.
7. A general *information flow chart* showing key inputs, outputs, volume estimates (average, peak, growth), and time constraints which are critical. Areas of origination, and use for inputs and outputs is shown—department, group, etc. The *information flow chart* depicts field activities and major decision points involved in the process.
8. Interfacing requirements, if any.
9. Concurrent projects which might affect the performance or completion of the new system.
10. Segmentation of the system into sub-systems which are complete and workable on a stand-alone basis, and in order of completion priority, if any.
11. Additional factors which have impact on the system . . . *go–no-go criteria* in terms of time, cost, and other elements.
12. Summary of alternative courses of action and considerations relevant to them.
13. Systems Design constraints—visual display required, real-time operation required, etc.
14. Statement of assumptions.

• *Request for Proposal*

User sends letter to the Director of Systems Development requesting SDD to prepare a proposal. Included with the letter is the General Statement of Problem.

• *Notification of Assignment*

Director of Systems Development notifies the User that:

1. Proposal request has been received and is being studied.
2. Assignment made by SDD is either as full-scale project, or succeeding work to be done on time and materials basis.

• *Proposal*

Proposal preparation is done by the Coordinator (and his proposal team, if any). The proposal team may include some individuals who will eventually be part of the project team. Director of Systems Development, Controller, and Manager of Implementation Requirements review the proposal. The Director of Systems Development must approve it before release.
Proposal includes:

1. Statement of the problem as SDD understands it.
2. Statement of the work to be done in prescribed stages.
3. Statement of assumptions and constraints.
4. Statement of contingent factors.
5. Gross estimate of development costs.
6. Gross estimate of manpower required.
7. Gross estimate of completion date.
8. Explanation of how SDD conducts projects—particularly User concurrence and specification change procedures.
9. Statements concerning User participation and responsibilities in:
   (a) Preparation of Functional Specifications.
   (b) Test and conversion data preparation, editing, and delivery.
   (c) Installation of field procedures and training.

10.   PERT chart (if used) and other schedule monitoring plans.

• *Proposal Transmittal*

SDD Proposal and letter of transmittal sent to User. Letter requests authorization from the User to be billed for Step 3, Functional Requirements Analysis.[1]

• *Authorization Letter for Step 3*

User sends letter to Manager of Implementation Requirements and Director of Systems Development as an:

1.   Acknowledgement of Proposal receipt.
2.   Authorization to be billed for Step 3.

STEP 3—FUNCTIONAL REQUIREMENTS ANALYSIS

KEY ACTIVITIES:

- •Details are gathered by SDD Project Team (with the participation of the User) on what the system must do, key performance features, and what input information it requires and the outputs desired.
- •Project team also acts as adviser and consultant to the User regarding standards for use in the representation of information and for User documentation.

CONTROLS AND DOCUMENTATION:

- •Master Functional Specification and a Functional Specification for each sub-system.

DECISION AND ADMINISTRATIVE POINTS:

- •Project Manager and start-up project team enter at beginning of this step.
- •End result is one or more functional specifications, documents which can be understood and used by the SDD and the User.

FUNDING:

- •Billable via Project Number.

CHECKLIST:

• *Master Functional Specification/Functional Specifications*

Prepared in a joint effort between SDD and the User, to be understood and used by both User and SDD personnel. This is the detailed information about the system's *functional requirements* in a form which is coherent and acceptable for use in Step 5, Systems Design. Where the project at hand is to be developed and/or implemented in segments, the total system must be spelled out in detail. This calls for a complete Functional Specification for each segment which is to be implemented or developed on an individual basis. A priority of implementation is to be stated. Sub-system interfacing requirements must be stated in detail. The project team must prepare both:

a)   A Master Functional Specification which defines the total and final system (but is less detailed than the Functional Specification), and
b)   A Functional Specification for each and every sub-system which is to be developed or integrated separately, as a segment of the total system.

A Functional Specification for an application segment is a complete specification in and of itself, and

---

[1]The User may want to conduct a Feasibility Study at this time, since gross cost and time estimates for development are shown in the Proposal.

it could be used independently of the Master Functional Specification. However, to plan effectively for future systems requirements, this master plan must accompany the specifications for any segment which is to be developed or implemented independently of the total system. *Interfacing requirements* for other systems which are not part of the Master Functional Specification must be spelled out in detail. These include the input and output formats, and the controls required.

The Functional Specification includes:

1. *A revised version of the General Statement of the Problem* which was originally prepared in Step 2. Includes changes which are a result from Step 3 in-depth analysis which have revealed ambiguities or omissions, thus making this revision necessary.

2. *A layout of each type of output* which the system is to produce—printed, displayed, or other. Each output must be referenced in the *information flow chart*, Item 7, in the General Statement of the Problem. This layout shows preprinted information and variable data elements. Each type of variable data element must be identified as to its name, method of calculation, and origin (input, stored history, master information, interfacing system media, etc.).

3. *A layout of each type User input*, showing each data element which appears. Each input must be referenced in the *information flow chart*. The inputs used to create, update or change stored history or master information must be identified, together with the data elements they contain.

4. *A dictionary* defining each type of data element and all other nomenclature which is peculiar to the system.

5. *Decision tables*, showing the specific User oriented logic for taking specific actions under defined conditions. Used as required, with reference to the *information flow chart*.

6. *Processing*—Where the input or output involved requires computation, the details for such computation must be described showing formulas or algorithms to be used. These computational methods must be referenced on the input or output layout. Processing variations are to be delineated.

7. *Accounting type controls* which are required by the User are specified. The controls specified must be referenced in the *information flow chart* or must be specified as data elements of an input or output. A description of how the controls affect the system or processing is to be included.

8. *Volume and Timings*—This section states the volume for each input and output shown on the information flow chart. Average, peak, and growth rate is shown for each input and output. Time dependencies and time sensitive requirements for each output or input-output group are shown. Included would be turnaround time, lead time, and response time requirements—showing desired times and worst cases acceptable.

9. *Pilot and Parallel Testing*—Gives the parameters for test procedures required. The User may be called upon to provide data, in an acceptable form, for such testing.

10. *Preliminary Conversion Plan*—Information on what data the User will provide or make available for conversion. Also defines what methods and steps it is anticipated will be used to accomplish the conversion.

The Functional Specification is the document which, through its statement of requirements, goals, and objectives, is the basic unit of work for one project team. Where multiple Functional Specifications exist, or are to be produced at different times, the Master Functional Specification will be used by the current project team (and those set up in the future to implement sub-system extensions) to define the super-structure into which the sub-system must fit and the interfacing requirements it must satisfy.

STEP 4—FUNCTIONAL SPECIFICATION REVIEW

KEY ACTIVITIES:

- •SDD project team reviews, with User management, the information contained in the Functional Specifications to ascertain whether it is complete and acceptable.
- •User management and SDD negotiate differences, and modifications are incorporated in the Functional Specification per mutual agreement.

CONTROLS AND DOCUMENTATION:

- •Inspection Brief for Functional Specifications.
- •SDD Response to Inspection Brief.
- •User approved Functional Specification.

DECISION AND ADMINISTRATIVE POINTS:

- •User decides on his final requirements.
- •User gives approval on Functional Specifications.

FUNDING:

- •Billable via Project Number.

CHECKLIST:

- *Inspection Brief for Functional Specifications*

The User prepares a *brief*, following his inspection of requirements and information contained in the system or sub-system Functional Specifications, commenting on whether they are:

- •Complete
- •Adequate
- •Comprehensible
- •Accurately and properly stated
- •Consistent and logically sound
- •Realistic and practicable
- •In accord with the General Statement of the Problem

The tone of the Brief is constructive. That is, where objections are raised, the information pertinent to them is explanatory. It is intended to guide the SDD project team in fulfilling specific needs.

- *SDD Response to the Inspection Brief*

SDD project team states whether it agrees to rework the specific points which have been raised in the Inspection Brief. Some negotiation is engaged in, usually on a limited number of points.

- *User Approved Functional Specification*

When each Functional Specification has been revised to the mutual satisfaction of the SDD project team and the User management, the User approves the Functional Specification—signified by the attachment of an Approval Letter, thus completing Phase I.

PHASE II—DESIGNING AND PROGRAMMING THE SYSTEM SOLUTION

STEP 5—SYSTEMS DESIGN

KEY ACTIVITIES:

- •Project team starts to work using the Approved Functional Specifications.

•Project Manager is responsible for system design that includes application programs, hardware, software, and conversion systems.

CONTROLS AND DOCUMENTATION:

•Systems Design Report.

DECISION AND ADMINISTRATIVE POINTS:

•The Systems Design Report includes the General Statement of the Problem, in addition to very detailed systems design information.

FUNDING:

•Billable via Project Number.

CHECKLIST:

•*Systems Design Report*

The Systems Design Report is the end product of this step and it is based upon the information and requirements in the Approved Functional Specifications. Included in the Systems Design Report are:

1. *System Resume*—a narrative description or general overview of the entire system.
2. *Abstract on Sub-Systems*—each sub-system (which is a logical break in the total system) is described in general terms.
3. *Constraints and Assumptions*—which influenced the design approach taken.
4. *System Flow Chart*—showing all programs to be written, inputs and outputs involved, and the source and destination of each. If sub-systems exist, and are planned for in the Master Functional Specification, demarcation of interfaces is shown.
5. *Development and Conversion Costs, Manpower and Time Estimates*—including all costs to completely program and convert system.
6. *Hardware Configuration*—shown in diagram form, with specific devices, features, and price.
7. *Software Requirements*—stating what operating system or executive-monitor will be used and any modifications required. Also shows what utility, sort programs and other software is needed.
8. *Cost, Timing, Volume Analysis*—shown in tabular form for each program (run) on the System Flow Chart.
9. *Record Summary*—shows layout of each type of stored data record used, with reference to the *file* it is stored in, and where it is used. *Data banks* are identified as such. *Retention periods* for each file in use are specified.
10. *Output Summary*—layout of each type of "end item" output, such as reports, messages, visual displays, etc.
11. *Input Summary*—layout of each type of User-prepared input document, message, etc.
12. *Forms Design*—preliminary layout of forms to be preprinted, particularly, key documents in the system.
13. *System Test Specifications*—defines what tests will be given to the system during integrated pilot tests and/or parallel operation. Also defines source of data for such tests. User responsibilities for such tests are also stated.
14. *Conversion Requirements and Plans*—covers the programs and data editing required for conversion, and the procedures involved. User responsibilities are also stated.
15. *Security and Privacy*—techniques and methods to protect information from misuse.
16. *System Controls and Audit Trails*—a description of the ways and means employed for control of system functions.

17. *Program Portfolio*—for each program in the system, the Systems Design Report must contain information needed by the programmer, including:

- Diagrams of the preprinted forms (if required), showing the computer output print or display format required for each.
- Layouts of input and output records for magnetic tapes, disks or other storage media—with all data fields clearly identified.
- A flow diagram depicting the inputs, the outputs and the I/O equipment to be employed.
- A brief description or narrative telling how the computer program under discussion fits into the total system. This should include pertinent information about the preceding run, the run following, and how the interface is established.
- A specification, detailing how the various types of records are to be treated. Decision tables in matrix form might be included to illustrate the actions to be taken under various conditions.
- Transaction coding, and the pertinent data to be used, should be shown in tabular form with appropriate identification symbols for each item.
- If applicable, tables to be used for internal cross-referencing, indexing and data look-up.
- If needed, details of certain special or complex processes to be used.
- Miscellaneous information such as that pertaining to run controls, equipment capacities, ready-made program subroutines and operating system standards.

If the Program Portfolio included in the Systems Design Report has been prepared well, a few short verbal sessions with the programmer should enable him to proceed with the work in a straightforward manner.

18. *Back-Up Methods*—if hardware should fail. Specify stand-by system or list locations of other processing centers to handle work.

STEP 6—QUALITY ASSURANCE

KEY ACTIVITIES:

- SDD reviews and analyzes the information in the Systems Design Report for workability and suggests improvements.
- SDD also checks the Report against the Approved Functional Specification for completeness and accuracy.
- Conversion and systems test plans are analyzed.
- Quality assurance Group *certifies* Systems Design Report when it meets all requirements.

CONTROLS AND DOCUMENTATION:

- Systems Design Appraisal and Certification.
- User Review Request.
- Certified Systems Design Report.

DECISION AND ADMINISTRATIVE POINTS:

- Members of the Quality Assurance Group are not members of the project team.
- Quality Assurance Group may require such rework of the Systems Design Report as it deems necessary.

FUNDING:

- Billable via Project Number.

CHECKLIST:

• *Systems Design Appraisal and Certification*

The Quality Assurance Group, which includes the Vice-President of Management Information Systems, the Controller, Director of Systems Development and the Manager of Implementation Requirements and/or their staff people, examines the Systems Design Report to determine whether it:

- Is complete, in terms of Systems Design Report content requirements.
- Meets the User's requirements as set forth in the Approved Functional Specifications.
- Complies with stated constraints.
- Is workable.
- Is controllable.
- Fits into the operating environment in which is to be implemented.
- Accurately describes the system.
- Qualifies as regards Programmer Portfolios.
- Accurately portrays the estimates of cost, time, and effort which appear in the Systems Design Report.
- Contains acceptable Integrated Pilot Test, Parallel Test, and Conversion Plans.
- Can be improved upon.

During the course of this examination and appraisal, the designers may be called upon to explain and defend their work. In these meetings, the Quality Assurance Group and the designers will come to agreement as to the changes to be incorporated in an updated version of the Systems Design Report.

• *User Review Request*

The User Review Request notifies the User that the Certified Systems Design Report is complete and available for inspection. It also informs the User that SDD is ready to give presentations on the System as it has been designed.

STEP 7—SYSTEM REVIEW AND USER CONCURRENCE

KEY ACTIVITIES:

- At presentations, SDD Project Team reviews system with User.
- Any level of detail may be discussed.
- User's minor modifications are built into the design *on-the-spot*.
- Major revisions are subject to further analysis by the Project Team and *review by the Quality Assurance Group*.

CONTROLS AND DOCUMENTATION:

- User Reviews/Presentations.
- User Concurrence Letter.
- Certified Systems Design Report.
- Change Procedure.

DECISION AND ADMINISTRATIVE POINTS:

- User approval of the system from a functional standpoint.
- Change procedure goes into effect at end of Step 7, after User approval.

FUNDING:

- Billable via Project Number.

CHECKLIST:

• *User Reviews/Presentations*

Project Team presents the Certified Systems Design Report in a non-technical manner giving the User such detailed information as is deemed necessary, understanding that the User may, however, request a discussion at *any level* of detail regarding *any feature* of the system. The User will also be presented with the Certified Systems Design Report. Any User objections are recorded. It is expected that many points would be resolved at the review/presentation meetings . . . remedies could be "hammered-out" on-the-spot, eliminating delays. Problems of a major nature would be subject to further analysis by the project team. As a result of this step, the User gets:

1. Problems remedied and requirements changes designed-in.
2. A revised Certified Design Report with all costs and other information updated to reflect alterations.

When excessive minor changes or any major changes are to be made, the Quality Assurance Group is called up to re-certify the updated Systems Design Report which includes such changes. (Excessive minor changes and any major changes are defined as changes which alter critical cost, time, and/or effort estimates by 10 per cent or more.)

• *User Concurrence Letter*

When the User is satisfied with the final version of the Certified Systems Design Report, he submits letters to the Vice-President–Management Information Systems and Director–Systems Development Projects:

1. Stating his agreement with the estimates as to what the system will cost to build and operate, and specifications as to what it is to produce.
2. Authorizing SDD work on the remaining steps.
3. Acknowledging User's agreement to conform with the Change Procedure which will now be in effect.

• *Approved Design Report*

The User Approved Systems Design Report is the official documentation to be used for all subsequent steps. Changes, which are issued via Specification Change Notices are distributed to holders of the Approved Systems Design Report. These are to be filed in all copies of the Report.

• *Change Procedure*

Goes into effect after User concurrence with the Certified Systems Design Report. All Functional Specification change requests, for whatever reason, must be reviewed by the *Change Control Board* for the project. The board is composed of the Project Manager, Director of Systems Development, and the Manager of Implementation Requirements. *A Specification Change Request* must be submitted to the Change Control Board showing what change is needed, the reason, and problems it may create. The Board decides whether the change requested is a Class I or a Class II change.

• A Class I change is defined as a simple change, which in no way alters costs or target dates or both.
• A Class II change is defined as a change which alters costs or target dates or both. A Class II change requires a "time and materials" cost estimate which the Board submits with the estimated changes in target completion dates to the User.

The User must submit a letter to SDD *authorizing* the additional expenditures and *approving* the slippage in schedule which the change may necessitate. The Change Control Board then issues a *Specification Change Notice* to the appropriate individuals. This document describes what changes are to be made and is an order to make those changes. No change request is honored without a Specification Change Notice. All Specification Change Notices are to be kept in a Specification Change Log which is maintained by the Change Control Board. Each copy of the Approved Systems Design Report is also updated with the changes detailed in the Specification Change Notices.

STEP 8—PROGRAMMING

KEY ACTIVITIES:

- Problem and Logical Analysis
- Block Diagramming and Flow Charting
- Desk-Checking and Logic Reviews
- Coding
- Compilation/Assembly on Computer
- Preparation of Test Data
- Testing and Debugging Programs

CONTROLS AND DOCUMENTATION:

- Programming Procedures
- Program Documentation
- Control of Programming via Logic Reviews and Activity Reporting

DECISION AND ADMINISTRATIVE POINTS:

- Program Logic Check
- Test Results Evaluation
- Project Manager informs Director of Systems Development that Pilot Testing is about to commence.

FUNDING:

- Billable via Project Number

CHECKLIST:

- *Programming Process*

The programming effort begins with a complete understanding by the project programmers of the *Program Portfolio* which was prepared as part of the Systems Design Report. Activities normally associated with the programming effort include:

1. Problem Analysis
2. Logical Analysis
3. Flow Charting
4. Block Diagramming
5. Desk-Checking
6. Logic Review by the Group Leader
7. Coding
8. Compilation/Assembly of programs on the computer
9. Test Data Preparation
10. Testing and Debugging

11. Documentation
12. Pilot Test and Conversion Assistance

• *Program Documentation*

Documentation of the finished product, a working program, would include:

1. The information found in the Program Portfolio.
2. Flow charts
3. Block diagrams.
4. Final compilation/assembly listings.
5. Operating instructions.
6. User instructions.
7. Change sheets—a record of each change made after the program is finalized.

Program documentation should adhere to the standards used in the company's EDP organization as described in an *Approved Standards Manual,* unless otherwise specified for the particular project.

• *Control of Programming*

Methods for managerial controls and scheduling of programming activities are described under "Coordination and Control of Systems and Programming" in Chapter three of this book.

STEP 9—INTEGRATED PILOT TESTING

KEY ACTIVITIES:

• Project Team tests all programs in integrated environment.
• Test parameters and data prepared by both User and Project Team are used.
• Controls are validated and program repairs are made.
• Report on Pilot Test and plans for next two steps (system check-out in parallel and conversion) are prepared and presented to SDD and User management.

CONTROLS AND DOCUMENTATION:

• Pilot Test Report.
• Authorization for Parallel Test or Conversion.
• User Review/Revision of Pilot Test Report and Conversion Plans.

DECISION AND ADMINISTRATIVE POINTS:

• User suggestions, modifications to Conversion Plans.
• User acknowledges responsibilities for participation in Phase III.
• Director of Systems Development authorizes Project Manager to begin Phase III.

FUNDING:

• Billable via Project Number.

CHECKLIST:

• *Pilot Test Report*

This is a report prepared by the Project Manager for the Director of Systems Development which shows:

1. Extent of testing performed.
2. Results and comparison with expected performance.
3. Anticipated problem areas.

4. Plan for next step . . . either Parallel Testing or Conversion. Also details User responsibilities for data, editing, accuracy, field procedures, and training.

• *User Review*

Presentation of Pilot Test Report to User. User comments and suggestions on Conversion Plan are solicited. Revisions are incorporated.

• *Authorization for Parallel Test or Conversion*

A letter presented by the Director of SDD to the Project Manager:

1. Acknowledging receipt of Pilot Test Report.
2. Authorizing entry into Phase III

PHASE III—IMPLEMENTING THE SYSTEM SOLUTION
STEP 10—SYSTEM CHECK-OUT IN PARALLEL

KEY ACTIVITIES:

- Side-by-side operation of existing system (if such exists) with representative volume of work on new system.
- Controls and results compared, checked, validated and reconciled.
- Comparative information is recorded and maintained.

CONTROLS AND DOCUMENTATION:

- Parallel Test Plan.
- Parallel test results are reconciled with the existing system. Differences must be explained.
- Control Sheets showing results of old and new systems are maintained.

DECISION AND ADMINISTRATIVE POINTS:

- After Project Manager and User present alternatives, Director of SDD decides when conversion should start and how it should be accomplished.

FUNDING:

- Billable via Project Number.

CHECKLIST:

• *Parallel Test Plan*

This plan is to be prepared well in advance of this step. It is a more elaborate and up-to-date version of *Systems Test Specifications* which appear in the Systems Design Report produced in Step 5.

• *Parallel Test Results*

The final test of a system of programs is provided by a side-by-side operation with the existing system (if one exists). At the beginning, the existing system is assumed to be correct and serves as a standard for comparison. After the new system is producing acceptable outputs for a certain period of time, the old system is gradually discontinued. Parallel testing usually covers a representative volume of work, rather than all of it. Therefore, a distinct *Conversion* effort (Step 11) is sometimes required.

In parallel testing:

1. Reasons for any differences which are discovered should show that the new system is not at fault. Bugs in the new system are, of course, corrected as required.
2. Dollar and other controls must be 100 per cent accurate or exact explanations for

their being otherwise must be presented. Differences and their reconciliation must be documented.

3. User and SDD efforts are coordinated via the Project Manager.
4. Control Sheets, showing old and new system results, are maintained.

STEP 11—CONVERSION

KEY ACTIVITIES:

- Conversion is the process of initiating operations on the new system and turning it over to User.
- Conversion may be a continuation of Parallel Testing where the old system is phased-out gradually.
- Creation of new files (gather data, edit, interim maintenance).
- User and EDP Operations Training.

CONTROLS AND DOCUMENTATION:

- Conversion Plan.
- Operating Results.
- User Plan for Field Procedures.

DECISION AND ADMINISTRATIVE POINTS:

- Method of Conversion decided by Director of SDD.
- Project Manager coordinates efforts with User.

FUNDING:

- Billable via Project Number.

CHECKLIST:

- *Conversion Plan*

Plan should be prepared well in advance of this Step,[2] to include:

1. Timetable for various conversion activities.
2. Assignment of personnel for specific responsibilities.
3. User's responsibilities, and plan of procedure for installation of system in field.

When proceeding from a parallel test which has proven the workability of the system, there are two ways in which to accomplish the conversion:

1. Continue running under the new system, gradually dropping operations under the old system.
2. Drop parallel operations completely and convert all work at one time and commence to operate fully under the new system. The old system operation is discontinued.

Each method has its advantages and disadvantages, depending upon the nature of the application in question. There are many cases in which the second alternative is impossible because of the volume of data involved. Also, difficulties may be encountered in introducing new field procedures, especially where many people will have to interact with the new system.

---

[2]Data conversion, particularly where non-automated data is to be converted, may begin well ahead of arriving at this step—but it must be completed here. Note that if a great volume of data is converted too early, a significant burden is experienced as a consequence, since *two* sets of data (assuming an old system) have to be kept up to date until cut-over to the new system is accomplished.

STEP 12—OPERATION FOLLOW-UP

KEY ACTIVITIES:

- Project Team assists the User, after Conversion, to smooth out difficulties.
- Project Team updates system documentation to current operating level.
- Project Team gradually turns system over to regular EDP operations group.

CONTROLS AND DOCUMENTATION:

- User Self-Sufficiency Report

DECISION AND ADMINISTRATIVE POINTS:

- Director of SDD determines date for end of Step 12.

FUNDING:

- Billable via Project Number.

CHECKLIST:

- *Follow-up Activities*

After conversion, follow-up is required to smooth out difficulties which arise in the "live" operation of the new system. Such follow-up may include:

1. Clearing-up any misunderstandings regarding documentation or procedures.
2. Providing extra controls, if needed.
3. Repairing programs found to have bugs and correcting program documentation.
4. Bringing all documentation up to the current level.
5. Gradually turning over the system to the regular EDP operations personnel.

- *User Self-Sufficiency Report*

Prepared by Project Manager, report contains:

1. Description of support given to User.
2. Judgment made as to User self-sufficiency.
3. Statement of documentation level.
4. General commentary on the performance of the system.

STEP 13—POST-CONVERSION EVALUATION

KEY ACTIVITIES:

- Project Manager and the User jointly prepare an evaluation of the new system.
- Comparison of planned vs. actual performance is made.
- Project is brought to full completion.

CONTROLS AND DOCUMENTATION:

- Evaluation Report.
- Notice of Project Completion Letter.

DECISION AND ADMINISTRATIVE POINTS:

- Director of SDD determines when project is completed.
- Project is complete when approved system (with approved changes) is fully operational.

FUNDING:

- Billable via Project Number.

CHECKLIST:

• *Evaluation Report*

A brief report on how the system is functioning after operations have settled down to normal. Report covers:

1. *Comparison* of planned vs. actual performance.
2. *Evaluation* of the degree to which the objectives are being realized.
3. Cost, time, and effort *analysis and comparison*—planned to actual.
4. *Suggested improvements* for future consideration.

• *Notice of Project Completion Letter*

Vice-President–Management Information Systems submits letter to User, notifying him that the requirements have been met and that the project is considered to be complete. The Evaluation Report is attached with Notice of Project Completion. This Notice signifies that the User approved design (plus changes via Specification Changes Notices) has been fully developed and is operational.

Project management controls

As previously outlined, there are methods of control for each step and phase in a project. Most are in the form of written evidence that a certain step has been completed and has accomplished something. The validity and completeness of that "something," be it the Systems Design, the Functional Specifications or some other document, is determined *by management* at each step along the way after a complete technical evaluation. Various activity planning and control methods are discussed in Chapter three, and other broad-gauge controls are examined in Chapter one.

The next section deals with a *broad-gauge control* for major information system development projects. Described here is a technique that can be used in conjunction with other selected control methods covered elsewhere in this book. The usefulness of this technique depends upon having a Work Plan for the project, showing what accomplishments are to be made, when they are to be completed, and for how much money.

Management controls imply measurement. Measurement presupposes a Work Plan against which actual performance can be compared . . . *without it, control cannot be exercised*. The control technique presented here can be successfully implemented where management has an earnest desire to measure both performance and planning effectiveness.

Objectives and techniques of control

A number of EDP control techniques have been tried and discarded because they were found to be overly complicated—in the sense that there was much data collected but very little information provided. Another complaint sometimes voiced by managers is that most controls are not quantitative, and those which are, fail to "boil information down to the essentials."

Controls should be simple and easy to use, and should show quantitative and other meaningful information with as little sophistication as possible. Complete control systems should report on existing as well as anticipated problems. Of course, no single control system can cope with all situations, but the technique described below includes some of the desired quantitative features.

CONTROL FACTORS IN THE "COST VS. ACHIEVEMENT" TECHNIQUE

There are three control factors used in this technique:

1. Cost Index

2. Achievement Index
3. Control Status Index

The Cost Index has to do with expenditure of *money;* the Achievement Index has to do with *results;* and the Control Status Index has to do with *both* money and results. Each of the three factors is computed cumulatively over a specific time period, such as each month of the project. The triad could be progressively computed for any other intervals of time if this would be more meaningful for the particular project.

Cost Index

The Cost Index (CI) is the ratio of actual costs to planned costs:

$$CI = \frac{\text{Actual Costs}}{\text{Planned Costs}}$$

Meaning:

•CI greater than 1—Expenditures were greater than planned.
•CI equal to 1—Expenditures were according to plan.
•CI less than 1—Expenditures were less than planned.

Achievement Index

The Achievement Index (AI) is the ratio of actual achievement to planned achievement:

$$AI = \frac{\text{Actual Achievement}}{\text{Planned Achievement}}$$

Meaning:

•AI greater than 1—Achievement was greater than planned.
•AI equal to 1—Achievement was according to plan.
•AI less than 1—Achievement was less than planned.

Control Status Index

The Control Status Index (CSI) is a single measure of effectiveness in planning and performance. It is the ratio of output to input or, to put it another way, it may be viewed as the "rate of return" on expenditures.

$$CSI = \frac{AI}{CI}$$

Meaning:

•CSI greater than 1—Rate of return was better than planned.
•CSI equal to 1—Rate of return was according to plan.
•CSI less than 1—Rate of return was less than planned.

Example:

•*Plan*

Suppose Subtask 88.1 was begun *six weeks ago* and planned expenditures for this period were *$20,000.*

•*Actual*

Six weeks from the initiation of Subtask 88.1, it was learned that the work was *one week behind,* and also that *$10,000* was the actual amount spent.
The calculations would be:

$$\text{COST INDEX (CI)} = \frac{\text{Actual}}{\text{Planned}} = \frac{\$10,000}{\$20,000} = 0.50$$

$$\text{ACHIEVEMENT INDEX (AI)} = \frac{\text{Actual}}{\text{Planned}} = \frac{5 \text{ weeks}}{6 \text{ weeks}} = 0.83$$

$$\text{CONTROL STATUS INDEX} = \frac{\text{AI}}{\text{CI}} = \frac{0.83}{0.50} = 1.66$$

Although it may be apparent, it should be made clear that the use of CSI *by itself* can only show "rate of return" and cannot be relied upon to indicate schedule slippage. The Achievement Index would be referred to for this information.

PROJECT STATUS REPORT

Figure 4.4 illustrates a form upon which these three controls would be formally reported. Report details could vary. For example, the *highest level* of job breakdown summarized might be control factors that apply to a *system function*, and the *lowest level* of job breakdown is for a *single task*. Where there are many projects under surveillance, control factors for an entire project could be the highest level summarized. However, if a given project is unusual or unique in some way, lower levels of summary might be desirable, possibly at the program module level. Specific levels to be selected for reporting control information may also depend upon the level of management that is to use the report.

Figure 4.5 is self-explanatory as to the criticality levels of the Control Status Index (CSI).

PROJECT CONTROL CHARTS

In order to see the trend in project progress and effectiveness, it is important to have the CSI recorded graphically for each time period it is reported.

Figure 4.6 shows how the plots of CSI's on Control Charts A through H can provide management with basic information. The various difficulties indicated by the graphs are listed, along with suggestions for the corrective actions to be taken.

Contracting for EDP development work

Contracting is taken up in this chapter because it is associated more with project type efforts than others. Contracting for systems development work with outside, independent consulting or programming firms came to be a common practice by the mid 1960's. Prior to this time, such work was generally contracted for only by very large private installations and by computer manufacturers. Since then, the use of this outside resource has spread to private and job shop installations of all sizes and is growing rapidly. *Programming houses* or *software houses*, as they are called, have been springing-up at an incredible rate. This segment of the industry is growing faster than computer hardware development, and it is destined to become the single largest area under computer sales.

There are a number of reasons why this industry is booming and why companies that are using little or no outside services should take another look at the advantages, some of which are listed below:

- Avoids having a permanent staff that is larger than is required over the long term.
- Flexibility in meeting widely fluctuating demands . . . better EDP service.
- Services of unique and expensive EDP professional can be used only when and if needed.
- Improved cost control . . . on "fixed-fee" contracts.
- Permanent professional staff at installation can give more attention to User problems, leaving the day-to-day management of programming up to the outside firm.
- It is possible that the outside service, all things considered, could cost less than having the same work performed in-house.

The foregoing advantages should be viewed in light of possible disadvantages of using contract services. These negative factors include these considerations:

PROJECT STATUS REPORT

PROJECT NUMBER	PROJECT MANAGER	DATE THIS REPORT	DATE LAST REPORT	PROJECT START DATE
PROJECT DESCRIPTION		REPORT PERIOD From: To:	REVIEWED BY	DATE

FUNCTION/TASK	DATE STARTED	SCHEDULED COMPLETION DATE	MANPOWER LEVEL	REPORT PERIOD DATA				
				COST Actual/Planned	ACHIEVEMENT Actual/Planned	COST INDEX	ACHIEVEMENT INDEX	CONTROL STATUS INDEX

Figure 4.4
Project Detail Status Report

CONTROL STATUS INDEX (CSI)
CRITICALITY LEVELS

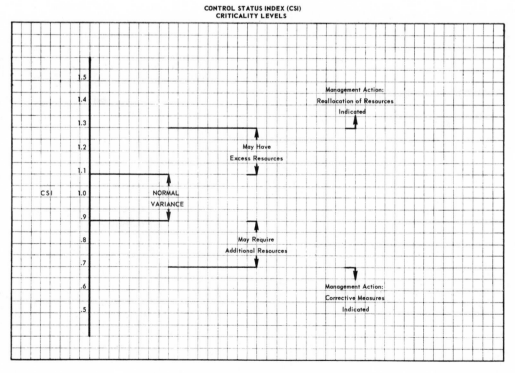

Figure 4.5
Control Status Index
Upper and Lower Bounds

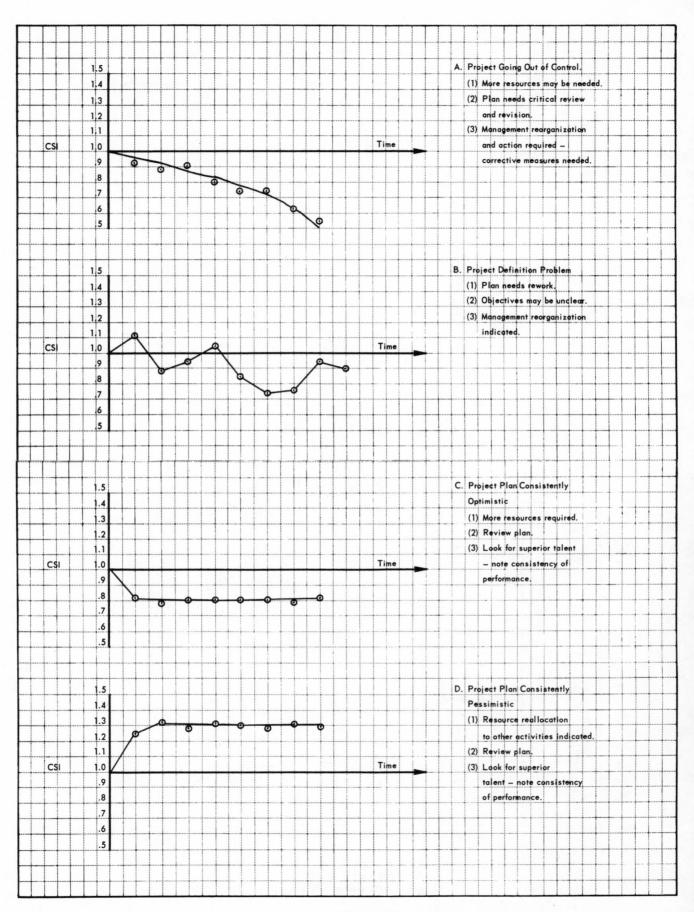

Figure 4.6
Control Status Indexes (CSI)
Used in Performance Forecasting

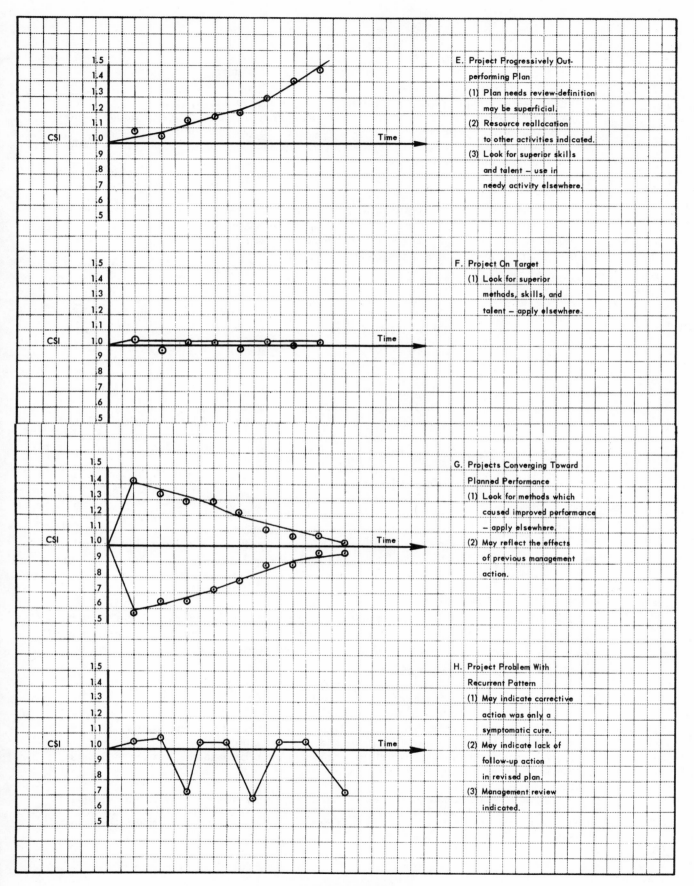

Figure 4.6 (cont.)

- Client's own organization is not gaining the knowledge and experience.
- When the contractor leaves, he often takes with him an understanding that would be most valuable to the client with respect to system maintenance and future revisions.
- Actual (as opposed to claimed) capabilities of contractor's personnel are not usually known at the time work commences.
- A contractor frequently has to learn about a client's problem (mostly at the client's expense), whereas employees of the client may have a high degree of familiarity with it.

A word of warning is in order regarding outside services—the company that expects to use them *must* have its own EDP experts—to assess the contractor's capabilities, evaluate bids, and to administer the contracts. Using software contractors also follows the same general rules as given in Chapter one for using management consultants.

Assessing the Contractor's Capabilities

Due to the sudden appearance of many new programming firms on the scene, it is of utmost importance, before any commitments are made, to ascertain who runs the business and what credits they can present. Often, such an investigation involves talking with technical and management personnel in the firm that proposes to do the work. The size of the programming house does not necessarily reflect capability, unless the firm is much too small for the magnitude of the work under consideration. Its personnel can, however, make or break the firm. Software firms do fail, and the fact that one happens to be in business today does not prove that it will be when the delivery date rolls around. This also goes for the free-lance, one-man operations.

Investigating a contractor involves more than an examination of his credentials. It is also a good idea to find out about the resources behind the sales pitch. It is important to determine if he has people who can comprehend the problems and properly interpret the client's needs. This might be done by briefly exploring specific problems with the firm's staff, to see how well they can identify with particular client needs.

It is well to remember that the best work to let out on contract is that which is well defined . . . a program or a system with well documented specific functional requirements. The client must clearly identify his desires, otherwise, he can incur excessive costs when the analysis is done by outsiders who may not understand his business, and take a considerable amount of time to learn it at the client's expense. Few software houses will contract for a fixed-fee job if the problem has not been properly defined . . . it is too open-ended and risky.

Evaluating Competitive Bids

The previous section ties in very closely with the evaluation of a contractor's bid. So much can be said regarding bids for specific kinds of systems that it is almost impossible to discuss any one and do the subject justice. However, these basic ground rules are *musts*:

1. *Do not* jump at the lowest bid.
2. *Do* contract with the lowest bidder whose credibility is good.[3]
3. *Do* find out whether the job is understood.
4. *Do not* contract unless the delivery date is established.
5. *Do* take notice of the items for which the customer is liable to the contractor.
6. *Do* evaluate the contractor's escape and penalty clauses.
7. *Do* get a fixed-fee price as well as a time and materials estimate, whenever possible.
8. *Do* get legal counsel on the terms of the contract.

---

[3]The author knows of a case where cost estimates were radically different, for the same job. One firm was around $20,000, a second around $250,000, and a third about $400,000. It was determined that the $250,000 bidder was the only one that understood the job really well and that their estimate was, by far, the most credible. The contract was awarded to this firm.

9. *Do* take notice of how long the contract bid is valid.

Contracting for EDP services does not include the traditional safeguards available when contracting for building construction and other kinds of work. Many loopholes exist in EDP contracts; and if the contractor knows his business, they are mostly in his favor. It is imperative that the customer clearly understand the full implication of statements like: (1) The system is guaranteed to operate as specified, . . . with test data *supplied by the customer*, or (2) The customer agrees to supply the estimated computer program test time at the specific time periods shown . . . failure to do so gives *the contractor* the option to invalidate cost estimates, delivery estimates, or both.

ADMINISTRATING CONTRACTS

Assuming that it is the client's project manager who is responsible for administering the contracts for work to be done on the outside, there are a number of things he must do. First, he must understand the terms of the contract and make sure that his company complies, in addition to seeing that the contractor sticks to his part of the bargain. The contractor must know to which individual in the company he is to report . . . it may be the project manager or one of his appointees, but it must be definite.

Once basic business and administrative relationships have been set up, it is particularly desirable to get the contractor to feel that he is part of the project team. Identifying with project goals, the outsider will "pitch-in" a little extra time and effort to see that things are done right. The need for client participation is emphasized in this regard. Everyone benefits from this sort of arrangement, and it is especially important if the contractor's people are working at the customer location.

One way to engender *esprit de corps* is to treat the contractor's on-site personnel as individuals, not just "bodies for hire." Another way is to keep the contractor informed as to how the whole project is going. If he knows in advance about slight adjustments in schedules and so forth, he might be able to accomodate the customer at little or no charge, even if he does not have a contractual obligation to do so. Also, it is a good practice to tell the contractor when his people are performing well. By the same token, the client's representative, sometimes the project manager, must move swiftly if the contractor begins to give unsatisfactory performance. He should advise contractor management of the situation and ask them to quickly resolve the situation.

The project manager must get reports from the contractor which provide him with details of the progress made in specific areas. If poor reporting patterns are experienced, these too must be taken up with contractor management. A project manager also has the responsibility to remove obstacles that prevent the contractor from performing according to the contract. If this is not done promptly and effectively, everyone involved gets annoyed and frustrated . . . besides possibly invalidating the contract and overrunning project time and cost estimates. Simply put, the project manager should be open and frank with his contractor at all times—the same should be expected and required of the contractor.

: five : five : five :

ACQUIRING, EVALUATING, AND MANAGING INSTALLATION PERSONNEL

The computer is of little value without competent individuals to manage, design systems, program, and operate it. As conditioning factors in determining the success and growth of a company in its computer usage, both the quality and quantity of personnel are of prime importance.

In this chapter, a number of key considerations regarding EDP personnel will be explored. Included here are topics related to the special aptitudes and characteristics generally required for certain positions unique to computer work. Discussions pertaining to the assignment of various tasks, the selection and evaluation of personnel, and several other subjects associated with personnel administration are also presented.

Since computer work requires highly skilled and talented individuals in a number of job categories, it is imperative that they be managed accordingly. Otherwise, the computer installation will suffer as a result of low productivity, high turnover, and poor morale. The topics emphasized in this chapter reveal some of the most troublesome areas in managing EDP personnel and offer some ways to avoid or solve the accompanying problems.

Establishing the needs of the installation

To start with, a set of well defined objectives must be formulated before attempting to establish personnel requirements. Once these objectives and forecasts have been developed, and target completion dates have been associated with them, a realistic appraisal of personnel requirements can be initiated.

A somewhat different procedure is followed depending upon whether:

1. Computers are being installed for the first time.

2. Additional computers are being installed.
3. New applications are being added to existing equipment.

Where computers are being installed for the first time, there are generally a variety of personnel requirements. First among them is the acquisition of a data processing manager. He, in turn, may select an assistant and possibly a manager of systems analysis and programming.

Systems analysts, or the individuals responsible for that job, are the first requirement of an installation after the management structure (perhaps in skeleton form) is in place. The number of systems analysts required initially will be a function of the number of start-up applications and their complexity.

As the systems designs start to take shape, the appropriate number of programmers should be brought in when the systems design is ready for programming. If training of any kind is needed, the programmers will have to be given sufficient additional time to acquire the desired skills.

Finally, the operators who will run the computer on a production basis are phased-in near the completion of program testing. Again, sufficient lead time must be provided if special training is necessary.

The addition of computers may require more computer operators and possibly more programmers if a new set of programs is to be written.

Where new applications are to be put on existing equipment, more programmers may be required and possibly more computer operators. The training of computer operators does not take place until shortly before the programs go into production since it may be months or even years before the programs are ready.

PLANNING FOR FUTURE PERSONNEL REQUIREMENTS

It is rarely feasible to convert all candidates for computerization at the same time, and so a plan of action with phases must be developed. A continuing series of *five-year plans for automation development* has proven to be a useful means of getting objectives and timetables down on paper. By projecting into the future, some reasonable decisions can be made as to personnel requirements and work scheduling. If, for example, ten major applications are planned for the five-year period, chances are that ten systems analysts may not be required. Perhaps one or two will be needed. Similarly, if each application requires two programmers, it does not necessarily mean that twenty are required. It could be that only four or five programmers are necessary.

> It would be far better to select a limited number of applications and do these exceedingly well, than to scatter in all directions and come up with many half-baked jobs.[1]

The only logical way to attempt to forecast future requirements is with a plan and set of objectives at hand. Yet, data processing management has to be responsive to unforeseen situations which will develop. Flexibility must be built into the staffing plans in order to accomodate such developments.

Personnel characteristics

Computers are revolutionizing many business practices. However, for those who are not directly involved in the "shirt-sleeves" end of computing, it is easy to lose an appreciation of the demands placed upon EDP personnel. This tendency must be counteracted by management's paying close attention to the personal characteristics and human factors related to particular kinds of EDP work.

---

[1] M. C. Kirkwood, "Problems in Conversion," *Journal of Data Management*, March 1965, p. 16.

Aptitude, skill, experience, creativity, and education are additional variables that enter into the equation determining the quality level of EDP in the company.

Failures in EDP, as well as in all kinds of managerial functions, sometimes occur as a result of shortcomings which are of a personal nature. Listed below are some of the predominate characteristics which detract from the overall effectiveness of managers:

1. Insufficient drive.
2. Lack of ambition.
3. Deficiencies in leadership qualities.
4. Inadequate judgment.
5. Limitations in imagination and resourcefulness.
6. Inadequate analytical ability.
7. Deficiencies in spoken and written communication.
8. Inability to motivate others.

EDP managers have an opportunity to develop data processing into an active tool in the management process, rather than simply a system of reporting past events. In an article concerning management in data processing, it was stated that:

> The EDP manager of the future will not be stretched between the programmer and the executive suite. He will have the necessary tools for bridging that gap; and will be able to turn his attention from the internal affairs of his department to the creative problems of the company-at-large.[2]

Certainly an EDP manager's personal characteristics will play a crucial role in determining how well he manages the internal affairs of his department and even more so in his efforts for the company-at-large. Moreover, he must develop a reliable team of managers under him to look after various EDP activities. The performance of these managers, in turn, depends heavily upon the individuals who support their department's specialty. Where programmers or systems analysts are involved, there have been a number of significant studies on characteristics of individuals engaged in this work.

PROGRAMMER/ANALYST CHARACTERISTICS

One study relates aptitude characteristics between programmers and non-programmers by factors called *predictor variables*. In the following table, the predictor variables shown are mean values of test results for 34 programmers and 30 non-programmers.[3]

Predictor Variables	Programmers	Non-Programmers
Numerical Ability	44.50	32.37
Symbolic Reasoning	13.76	7.93
Numerical Reasoning	12.21	9.23
Tables	74.01	61.63
Memory	12.65	9.30
Visual Speed-Accuracy	101.65	93.33
Verbal Comprehension	20.65	18.73
Coding	120.09	115.10
Verbal Reasoning	15.26	15.10

Another study involved sending questionnaires to 575 firms wherein employers and programmers were asked to rank characteristics of programmers. One of the tables resulting from

---

[2]John W. Field, "A New Breed of Data Processing Manager," *Computers and Data Processing*, September 1964, p. 43.

[3]Herman Roemmich, "Testing Programmer Efficiency," *Journal of Data Management*, December 1963, p. 25.

this study shows the unique characteristics and skills turned up in the study. The following ten are those most often listed, in order of importance:[4]

1. Logical mind.
2. Ability to work with others.
3. Problem definition.
4. Communication ability.
5. Interest and desire.
6. Creativity.
7. Intelligence.
8. Personal initiative.
9. Analytical mind.
10. Inquiring mind.

An article concerning aptitude indications as related to *success on the job* singles out six aptitudes as predictors of achievement:[5]

1. Verbal
2. Numerical
3. Spatial
4. Form
5. Clerical
6. General intelligence

Beyond the aptitude factors already mentioned, there are characteristics of a more personal nature which must be considered. Certainly a job candidate possessing all of the desirable aptitudes and having a fine educational record, but who refuses to work, will be of no use; so aptitude characteristics, while they are prerequisites, cannot be used as the sole determinant for achievement forecasting. *Behavioral elements* such as those listed below will definitely have to be taken into consideration.[6]

1. Personal Maturity and Stability
2. Cooperation—Interpersonal Relations
3. Communication Skills
4. Thoroughness—Dependability
5. Professional Competence
6. Job Interest and Zeal

LEVEL OF EDUCATION

As the applications in data processing tend to become more complex, the level of education required for the systems analysts and programmers increases. Their managers, in turn, will also have to satisfy certain educational requirements in order to understand and direct the effort.

Most of the scientific programmers and analysts have, for some time, been required to have at least an undergraduate degree in mathematics, the sciences, or engineering. The nature of some scientific applications has created a demand for personnel with advanced degrees.

Commercial or business programming, however, has a variety of educational requirements, depending upon specific applications to be undertaken and the policies of the particular company

---

[4]John E. Hanke, *et al.*, "Education and Training of a Business Programmer," *Journal of Data Management*, June 1965, p. 43.

[5]William A. McIntosh and George Windholz, "Evaluating DP Aptitude Techniques," *Journal of Data Management*, May 1965, p. 19.

[6]Sherwood H. Peres and Phil H. Arnold, "Identifying Programmer Behavior," *Datamation*, January 1963, p. 40.

regarding educational attainment. There are many commercial programmers who have had little or no college education and perform very well on the job. By virtue of their special experience in the business and an understanding of particular processes, they are able to work effectively within the scope of their background.

Some companies have taken the college degree requirement to extremes and have gotten to the point where practically any job that is not clerical or blue-collar must be filled by a degree-holder. The obvious result is that salary expense has increased (almost doubled in some cases) unnecessarily and in disproportion to productivity levels. In general, the degree-holder *is* a better prospect for higher level management positions and professional consulting. But, it is often wasteful to require this potential of some commercial programmers if they are otherwise capable of doing the job. In fact, an over-abundance of aggressive, high potential people at an EDP installation has been known to create turnover and morale problems because they cannot all move up fast enough.

The trend today, which should not be overlooked, is very much toward requiring at least an undergraduate degree for programming and systems work on commercial applications. A number of reasons for this trend could be stated, but probably the most significant one involves the complexity level of some of the important applications in management science. In the area of operations research, a number of applications require a background in statistics, a knowledge of linear programming, simulation and models, and other advanced techniques.

The value of data processing as a management tool is more likely to be realized faster under the direction of someone who has had the appropriate education, formal or otherwise. Another point which has to be considered is the management potential of the people in data processing. The business school graduate, hopefully, should be well versed in business theory and should know a number of new and useful management techniques. Assuming the graduate is otherwise qualified, he will probably be in a better position to manage the business than his counterpart without the education. There are also the cultural and other intellectual benefits of a college education which enter into the total picture of the individual.

In one survey, business computer programmers were asked to suggest *background subjects* for prospective programmers. Their recommendations, in the order of importance, were:[7]

1. Logic
2. Mathematics
3. Accounting
4. English and Communications Skills
5. General Business
6. Engineering
7. Natural and Applied Sciences
8. Social Sciences

The foregoing recommendations, it should be emphasized, pertain to a business programmer. Viewing the business programmer from the standpoint of promotion into systems analysis or project leadership, the top two priorities on background subjects would be:

1. English and Communications Skills
2. General Business

As time goes on, new applications will require increasingly more in the way of formal college education. The business programmer or analyst without a degree will probably not disappear for a long time, but it is safe to say that his scope of usefulness may narrow as applications get more sophisticated.

---

[7]Hanke, *et al.*, p. 41.

Operating personnel require much less in the way of formal education than analysts or programmers; but the requirements for education in many jobs is increasing, and this is true for equipment operators.

Each installation manager will, in the last analysis, have to decide exactly what educational levels he will require for specific jobs. Economic considerations will have a bearing on the ultimate decisions inasmuch as increased education means increased salary. Present and future requirements will have to be examined in order to arrive at the optimum decision. Often, the job which can be done by the high school graduate in the short run will expand and grow beyond his capabilities in the longer term.

THE VALUE OF EXPERIENCE

Perhaps one of the most unwieldy jobs of an installation manager about to hire someone is that of determining the worth of the experience of the prospective applicant. Recommendations from previous employers are frequently misleading; sometimes a good recommendation will be given by a current employer hoping that the troublesome employee will leave. As one writer put it:

> The real question the employer must face, however, is not "Does the applicant have experience in a particular area?", but rather "Has the applicant learned something of value to the employer from the experience?" Having existed or survived through a situation for a time does not mean the person has learned something of value to a prospective employer from that experience.[8]

Even if the applicant has learned something from his experience, such experience may not have had much breadth or depth. In other words, there is essentially a saturation point on experience in one area, whereby continued time spent really does not yield much more in terms of learning.

> A man who has been writing the same kind of routine for eight years is not worth significantly more than the man who has been writing similar routines for only two years.[9]

Another problem very often encountered occurs where the applicant has overstated, either directly or by inference, his experience. Statements taken from resumes might read:

"Worked on Payroll Application . . ."
"Developed Systems Design for Corporate Trust . . ."
"Knowledge of 7044 Computer . . ."
"Programmed in FORTRAN . . ."

The first statement could mean that the individual wrote one program for a payroll application. Perhaps the individual in the second example worked with three other developers. Maybe the fellow in the third statement was a console operator for two weeks. And the chap with FORTRAN experience may have written one program for a programming course in college.

Some statements are misleading by design, others are not; therefore, it is necessary to interview thoroughly the prospective applicants in order to arrive at a realistic opinion. Naturally, the interviewer will have to be knowledgeable about the field of work to be able to ask intelligent and meaningful questions and interpret the answers. Interviewing will be discussed later in this chapter.

---

[8] Ned Chapin, "Some Programmer—Employer Problems: A Report from the Field," *Computers and Automation,* August 1965, p. 14.

[9] Robert L. Partick, "The Maturing Field." *Datamation,* January 1963, p. 25.

APTITUDE TESTING

The surest way to tell whether a man can do a job is to put him in that job for a period of time and observe the results. Since it is rarely feasible to do this in practice, other methods have been developed which help the business manager to select the most likely candidates at the outset. Every student of management has discovered that one such method widely used is testing; and there are tests covering everything from hearing to emotional stability.

While tests have been praised, damned, and much debated, some tests are on their way to becoming generally accepted tools of management. However, one rarely hears of even the most enthusiastic supporters of testing insisting that final decisions be made completely on the basis of test scores.

As measurement devices, tests of all kinds have inherent error factors. The accuracy of a visual acuity test is much greater than, for example, a test to measure sociability.

Some of the better known tests include:

1. Otis Employment Test (general mental ability)
2. Moore Arithmetic Reasoning (quantitative thinking)
3. Kuder—Preference (Major interests)
4. Wonderlic Personnel Test (general problem-solving)
5. Guilford-Martin (personality)

Aside from these kinds of tests, which may be left to the personnel department, there are at least two types of tests with which data processing managers should be familiar. First is the *Machine Operator's Test* which measures aptitudes which have been found to be desirable for equipment operators. Second is a very important test called the *Programmer's Aptitude Test*, which is designed to measure aptitude characteristics found to be of importance for programming work. Most computer manufacturers have developed tests of this kind and will either test customer personnel or allow customers to use the tests.

The Programmer's Aptitude Test is widely used and has been shown to be quite reliable as a predictive tool. It has been found to be particularly reliable on extreme cases. Using an aptitude grading system from "A" to "E," the interpretations listed below are typical:

"A"—very strong indication of aptitude.
"B"—good indication of aptitude.
"C"—unreliable as an indication of potential in either direction.
"D"—good indication of low aptitude.
"E"—very strong indication of low aptitude.

The "C" case is the most difficult to evaluate. Managers who consider "C" grades as possibilities (many require "B" or better) should select only those who are known for their exceptional hard work, perseverence, drive, etc. Otherwise, this "C" candidate is considered to be too risky. In cases known to the author, wherein employers have disregarded low aptitude indications for prospective programmers, significant problems have resulted: (1) the individuals turned out to be less than satisfactory programmers, and (2) psychological difficulties arose among some of the more conscientious, but failing, programmers. Neither the company nor the man is served by attempting to make an individual into something he was "never meant to be."

Above all, remember to tell those tested that *only* programmer aptitude is being measured, *nothing more;* not intelligence, not personality, and not the potential to become company president.

Programmer's Aptitude Tests are revised every so often and, for at least one reason, it is important that managers use the latest version. That reason relates to the fact that there are at least two handbooks on the market that teach the reader how to "pass" these aptitude tests.

The handbooks with which the author is acquainted appear to be able to do this, given a man of above average intelligence. However, the author does not feel that they can produce aptitude where none exists. But, they can certainly raise the score of an otherwise marginal applicant. By using the newest version of the test, the applicant will hopefully be confronted with some different kinds of questions that *will* test his aptitude rather than his memory on how to solve a particular type of aptitude test question. A manager should consider asking the applicant whether he has used such a handbook or has recently taken the test. The prospect's responses should be considered in evaluating the test score.

Interviewing the prospective professional employee

The interview is usually the only opportunity a manager has to get to know the person he may hire prior to actually having him on the payroll. While the art of interviewing is far from perfection, there are some general guidelines that, if followed, can make the interview experience worthwhile.

Naturally, the interviewer must always remain aware that the candidate is a guest of the company. It is important that he get a good opinion of the company regardless of whether he will actually become an employee. He may someday be a customer of the company and he also may report his interview experience to others in the field.

The following discussion pertains specifically to interviewing candidates for *professional positions in EDP*. To start with, the interviewer(s) should have carefully reviewed the candidate's resumé or other summary of qualifications. This should be done in a detailed manner for two reasons: (1) resumés are often prepared with deliberation on the part of the applicant, and (2) it will guide the interviewer in structuring his questions.

At this point, an appropriate interview schedule can be set-up, arranging for various people in the EDP group to talk with the candidate for an hour or so, each. If the candidate looks strong to the manager who is hiring, these other interviewers usually provide supplemental evaluations as to technical ability, personality, etc. Naturally, the final decision rests with the manager.

There are a number of different kinds of interviewing patterns that are commonly used. Some are rather rigidly structured, whereas others are free of any particular format. One of the best ways to get an interview started is to have the prospect discuss *his interests* in pursuing a career. In this descriptive part of the interview, the interviewer will want to probe in some specific areas of both long and short term nature. Once the applicant's interests are understood, a much more productive and meaningful exchange of information is possible. Sometimes the interviewer will find that the man's interests are far removed from the job that he applied for, and in most cases it is not desirable to talk the candidate into being interested in the particular position(s) that happen to be open. At other times, the interviewer will find that the person being interviewed has no identifiable interests. Depending upon the level of the professional position that is to be filled, it is quite often of little value to undertake extensive interviewing with an individual who either has no particular interest or whose interests are significantly divergent from the requirements of the job. For example, if the company wants a software technical specialist, it will not be fruitful to pursue this subject with a man whose stated interests and desires are in the project management area. When a man expresses a strong interest, the wisest thing an interviewer can do is believe that the man knows what he is talking about.

Assuming that the applicant's interests relate reasonably well to the position that is open, the interviewer can properly pursue the man's qualifications and can attempt to make some judgment regarding his personality. As previously indicated, the resumé usually states a position objective and is a good guide to *begin* an evaluation of qualifications. The interviewer would be well advised to have the interviewee discuss an area with which he, the interviewer, is familiar.

By listening to the applicant's descriptions and explanations on particular points, it should be possible to ascertain his depth of understanding. The interviewer can induce the prospect to emphasize specific areas by stressing them with appropriate questions.

There is so much that can be said on the subject of personality that a brief discussion would fall short of being adequate by any standards. However, there is one simple piece of advice that can be offered without much discussion. Use *common business sense* in evaluating the personality of the candidate. For example, if it is felt that the position calls for a likeable fellow and the applicant is not, then, it is safe to say that he will not be more likeable after he has been hired. Similarly, if the job calls for a "ball of fire" who is fast on his feet, witty, and has a sales flair, the applicant who is quiet and withdrawn is not likely to change upon being hired for this position.

Later in the interview, after the interviewer has described the work, etc., the applicant should be asked if he has any questions. An applicant who is interested in a career will frequently ask questions concerning: the activities and responsibilities of the job; salary; policies on salary increases; opportunities for advancement; the organization structure and where he would be in it; fringe benefits; travel; and so forth. Most serious seekers of professional positions will expect to hear some specifics on these items . . . if they are too vaguely explained, it will often cause the desired applicant to reject an offer. Interviewers must be prepared to give intelligent responses on these points. For example, if for some reason the company awards an annual raise of 7 per cent for outstanding performance, the interviewee who is seriously being considered should be made aware of this fact before employment . . . instead of a year later during his termination interview . . . after he has become a truly valuable member of the organization.

Internal and external sources of personnel

A computer installation just getting started may use a combination of recently hired employees with experience and personnel transferred in from other departments. Chances are that the transferred employees will require training. On the other hand, some new installations are built entirely from employees who have been selected from other parts of their company. It may take up to two years or perhaps longer between the time a computer is ordered and the time it is delivered. It is mainly as a result of this lead time that an installation can start with inexperienced help, train them, and complete some of the applications in time for the arrival of the system.

PLACEMENT FROM WITHIN

It is a good practice to "hire from within" in the case of *inexperienced* help, providing that individuals with the required aptitudes and backgrounds are available. Some companies make it a practice to send announcements to all departments when the data processing department is seeking trainees. If the jobs open include programming trainees, everyone who desires to do so may take the Programmer's Aptitude Test, or the Machine Operator's Test, where computer operator trainees are being sought. Starting with the test results, finer screening commences.

A number of companies include the Programmer's Aptitude Test among other tests ordinarily given by the personnel department. In this way, a record of individuals with programming aptitude is available at all times.

Depending upon the size of the company, it may well be that a sufficient number of the individuals who expressed an interest for EDP work, do not have high enough aptitude levels. In this case, outside sources of personnel must be utilized. Outside recruiting of professional EDP personnel, according to several studies, typically costs from $2,000 to $3,000 per man hired considering advertising, interviewing, fees, and other costs.

EMPLOYMENT ADVERTISING

One of the simplest ways to let the public know a company is looking for data processing personnel is to place ads in newspapers and EDP trade magazines. If for some reason the company does not wish to reveal that it is looking for personnel, a *blind ad* can be used. However, the response to an ad with the company name will be greater because many people refuse to answer blind ads for obvious reasons, as well as the fact that the company name itself can be an asset in attracting applicants.

Advertising for EDP professionals in newspapers or trade magazines is done in a number of styles, as could be quickly verified by reviewing ads that currently appear in these media. Some ads have such an obvious sales pitch that the true identity of what the ad has been placed for is either nonexistent or completely overwhelmed.

In the author's opinion, the employment ad should first and foremost tell its readers something of a factual nature about the position, and, if desired, a little promotion in good taste can be appropriately included. This practice will save the company time and money in that a well conceived ad will pre-screen respondents who would otherwise answer a vaguely written ad. Further, it will help the candidate for the position more seriously evaluate whether he should spend his time investigating the position. Beyond this, one sometimes finds that good people, who really are not in the market for a job, continue to review these employment ads on a regular basis. Occasionally, these people will answer an ad that looks like "exactly the kind of position they want." Clearly, these individuals will not respond to very generalized descriptions about the job. In short, a soft-sell approach that emphasizes descriptive information is favored over the ad that is hard-sell but does not really tell its reader anything of value.

Two kinds of advertising copy are commonly used for employment ads: (1) *classified ads*, and (2) *display ads*. The classified type, which is the familiar "help wanted" ad, is widely used. It is inexpensive, as advertising goes, and can usually be placed with short notice. The display type is a more expensive ad that is very often printed in an entirely different section of the newspaper or magazine. For example, the *New York Times* Sunday Edition carries display type employment ads in the "Business and Finance" section. In general, these ads are for much higher class positions than the help wanted variety. Depending upon the particular newspaper or magazine, display ads can cost several hundred dollars for those of a modest size and thousands for big ads (four or five columns wide by five to ten inches deep). Certain smaller advertising agencies specialize in display ads; there is usually no charge to the client for these services.

In view of the expenses that can add up with even a modest personnel search, it may be advantageous to investigate the use of personnel agencies prior to initiating a massive campaign. One sometimes finds that this is the least expensive alternative since the agency fee is not paid until the desired person is employed, although this cannot be advanced as a commonly held opinion. Ads, on the other hand, are paid for regardless of whether the appropriate individual(s) is found. One final comment on employment advertising should be emphasized. Take the time and effort to produce good advertising copy. Get others to offer their opinions on it before it is placed; this will help insure that the ad means what its writer intended.

USING THE COMPANY PERSONNEL DEPARTMENT

Often, personnel departments will have contacts in the employment world and sometimes can help EDP management in finding good people. Occasionally, the personnel department receives unsolicited resumés from people looking for EDP positions. It may also be equipped, by virtue of having a Skills Inventory System, to conduct an intra-company search for personnel with skills desired by EDP.

Policies governing the role of the personnel department in the company vary. If the company has a regular department, it can save time and trouble for the data processing managers by performing the usual verifications, examinations, paperwork processing, etc. However, the personnel department should *never* be allowed to have the final authority where technical qualifications are concerned. Evaluating the level of technical competence is strictly a matter for the particular manager involved.

A number of managers find it is best to communicate and make arrangements with applicants and employment agencies directly, bypassing the personnel department until its services are needed for testing or induction processing. Unless a very unusual personnel department exists this is recommended, especially because fast action is called for in EDP where it is a job seeker's market. Evening interviewing is sometimes required.

PERSONNEL AGENCIES

There is hardly any question that personnel agencies are here to stay, but there are some questions as to exactly what some of them do for the handsome fees (10 per cent and up of one year's salary) they collect. Every service, to be sure, has good and bad practitioners, and personnel agencies have their share of bad ones, particularly where data processing personnel are involved.

Some agencies conduct interviews with the people they send out for various jobs, others work strictly by letter and telephone. Some agencies check references and personal information, others do not. The fees paid, therefore, may cover some extensive services or they may be merely a brokerage fee for getting buyers and sellers together. On the average, unless a company knows exactly what the agency will do for it, agencies can be slightly more expensive than direct hiring (most positions are "fee paid"), *where there is more than one position to be filled* (unless it is possible to get a volume discount from the agency).

Some professional people refuse to deal through agencies, as a result of having had bad experiences in the past involving carelessness. Employers have registered their share of complaints too. It would be unfair to say that all agencies operate in a similar fashion; each therefore must be evaluated individually. Agencies specializing in EDP personnel are usually geared to provide better service.

PERSONNEL CONSULTANTS

Personnel consultants may be an adjunct of a management consulting firm or may be established independently. Their purpose is the same however, and that is to provide individual attention to their clients, especially in conducting *confidential searches* on higher level positions.

These staffing consultants can be of assistance in determining the kinds and quantities of people required and in advising management regarding organizational methods. If the consultant knows his business, he can be quite useful in insuring that the data processing organization gets started off properly personnel-wise.

As one might expect, these custom-tailored consulting services often are very expensive in terms of the initial outlay of money (15 per cent to 25 per cent of annual salary); over the long run, however, it may be the least expensive means.

Ordinarily, a competent data processing manager ought to be able to handle the staffing and organization on his own, unless a new, or a particularly large or complex installation is involved. He and his associates should also be able to use their contacts in the field to good advantage, in this regard.

Deciding on pay scales

Someone once said that computing will come of age when it comes to the realization that two $8,000 a year programmers produce considerably less than one $16,000 a year programmer. Clearly this is not true of all situations, but the message in this statement will certainly ring clear to many data processing managers. Simply put, the point is that a bona fide, expert performer in data processing is bound to cost more than someone who plods along at an average pace; but, the thing to consider is whether the difference in pay is reflected in increased performance. In a number of cases, it has been found that the difference in pay yields a performance improvement which more than offsets that difference in pay.

One study of data processing personnel shows an average annual turnover rate of 18 per cent.[10] In recent times turnover has been quoted in the 20 per cent to 30 per cent range. Certain industries, especially those that do not usually employ many professionals of any kind, have experienced turnover in the 50 per cent plus area. In view of the current shortage of qualified data processing personnel and the high growth rate of computerization (around 20 per cent), the personnel turnover picture is likely to become more critical.

The *cost* of turnover includes items such as: hiring costs, training, and on-the-job familiarization with the new practices. Quite a few installations have learned that it is often more economical to grant competitive salary increases, rather than lose a good man and have to find his replacement on the open market. More and more businesses have found that the equivalent replacement frequently must be paid the same salary that the man who has left will be getting on his new job.

Considering the break-in costs and the unknown capabilities of the new hire, careful attention must be paid to the matter of salary levels.

MARKET SALARY LEVELS

The most straightforward way to determine whether a given set of salary ranges is competitive is to find out what the market calls for in each job category.

At least one publisher produces a comprehensive handbook on data processing salary levels which is revised annually. The title of the handbook is *Salary Administration for Data Processing Personnel*,[11] by Philip H. Weber.

The magazine, *Business Automation*, has made a practice of publishing an annual data processing salary survey in one or two of its summer editions.

Major metropolitan newspapers carry numerous ads of both employers and personnel agencies. In many cases these ads show salaries or ranges for various EDP positions. *The New York Times* Sunday edition, for example, carries many ads in its "Business and Finance" section and also in the "Help Wanted" columns (the help wanted ads are not usually included for circulation outside the New York metropolitan area).

Using the sources of salary information mentioned, there is hardly an excuse for a manager not knowing market levels. Clearly, learning competitive salaries only after having had some valued employees leave for better remuneration indicates a weakness in management practices.

To arrive at a salary figure for a specific man in a given position, factors such as those listed below[12] are of major importance:

1. *Responsibility*—Is he responsible for a $10,000 or a $10,000,000 project. Does he manage a $75,000 a year installation or a $75,000,000 operation?
2. *Record of Accomplishment*—What are his outstanding demonstrated abilities?
3. *Experience and Know-how*—What does he know about EDP, its applications, management, the company, etc?

---

[10]Jay Mettler, "Profile: Computer Personnel Characteristics—1964," *Business Automation*, April, 1964, p. 30.

[11]Available from: The Business Press Division, Business Publications International, 288 Park Avenue West, Elmhurst, Illinois.

[12]Except for being related to the company chairman or president.

4. *Education*—Does he have a B.S., B.A., M.B.A., M.S., or Ph.D, and in what fields and perhaps from what college?
5. *Geographic Area*—What are the going rates of pay in a particular city or metropolitan area?
6. *Industry Type*—Aerospace has higher salary bases than, for example, insurance.
7. *Business Size*—As a general rule, larger companies pay more than smaller ones. However, EDP personnel requirements are often more stringent in a large company.

It is these factors that make it difficult to use most of the salary studies mentioned earlier. For example, a number of studies show that data processing managers (responsible for all computing in the company) earn in the $10,000 to $20,000 a year category as average figures. Without an indication as to company size, as some studies are, these numbers do not mean much. In fact, the author's knowledge of the salary range, although titles may be different, is literally from $8,000 to $80,000 for this kind of position.

Systems analyst and programmer salaries have less of a difference percentage-wise, but the numbers are important. The author's knowledge of the range for professional technical positions is $5,000 to $35,000, the high end being largely consulting activities. Yet, a popular business magazine says that average systems and programming salary in 1968 was in the range from $6,000 to $9,000. Such information can mislead the uninformed. Consider, for example, that in 1968 the average starting salary was over $11,000 for a man with a B.S. and an M.B.A. who had no business experience whatsoever.

The point of the foregoing discussion is to show that while published salary ranges and averages are useful in a general way, the specifics on any of the seven items outlined previously can change the numbers dramatically. It should also be pointed out that identical job titles often bear little relationship to actual activities and responsibilities in different companies.

Naturally, the law of supply and demand for particular skills introduces important differences in salary levels. For skilled EDP professionals, it is now a "seller's market." Most skills in EDP have a demand that far exceeds supply . . . it has been this way since the early 1960's and will no doubt remain so for at least a decade. Demand, in recent times, has been the heaviest for professionals with three to seven years of experience. Experts in systems programming and telecommunications systems have shown the greatest percentage increase in salary in recent times. Operations research personnel salaries are also growing rapidly. At least two personnel placement companies have been publishing EDP salary data on an annual basis. Both relate salary to years of experience by type of position: Source EDP, Inc. (Chicago, New York and other major cities) publishes a "Computer Salary Survey" that gives data and discussion by *size* of installation; Albert & Nellissen, Inc. (New York City) publishes a "Wage/Experience Survey" that illustrates trends in EDP salary changes together with brief commentary.

These kinds of sources for salary data, plus those mentioned earlier, are of considerable value, so long as the seven criteria outlined previously are taken into consideration.

INTERNAL RESTRICTIONS AND LIMITATIONS

Intra-company salary policies have often clashed with the status of competitive data processing salary levels. In some companies, an entirely new compensation policy, covering data processing exclusively, has had to be developed due to the nature of the market.

Few factors are as important to the employee as the amount of money he is paid. The sensitivity of the problems in this area is well known, and data processing management has definitely had more than its share of money grievances. Good people are in short supply and demand is high, and this means increased salaries; to overlook this fact and attempt to make independent pay determination could be ruinous.

Some companies have discarded outdated guidelines and have decided that it is in their best interest to meet competitive salary levels. With still other companies, the "battle" continues as they try to retain employees by every other means besides competitive pay scales.

All kinds of rationalizations can be heard in connection with holding data processing salaries to a reasonable level. One argument is that the demand will be met with increased supply. Naturally, if this should happen (and it could take ten years), the data processing staff is unlikely to remain in place for long. The bulk of experience shows rather conclusively that companies who buck the salary trends in data processing lose their best people. Nevertheless, the matter of company policy in the area of data processing salaries must be developed by each business, taking into consideration size, ability to pay, economic conditions, and, of course, the value of the employee to the company.

SALARY INCREASES

Many companies have established practices in connection with the time between raises and pay increase percentages. Some of the increase policies work out very well for data processing; others are inadequate for these new positions. (For related discussion on increases see section "Money as a Motivator" later in this chapter.)

New employees, particularly trainees, in data processing should get an increase after satisfactorily completing a probationary period which should be from three to six months, but not longer. The amount of the increase will depend upon the evaluation by the manager as to the relative performance of the employee. Insofar as the percentage of increase goes, it is typically 10–15 per cent for apprentices who have completed their training and are performing well on the job.

After the first increase, a number of companies evaluate the employees for merit raises on an annual basis. Depending upon the basic data processing salary structure, annual considerations may be too far apart to keep pace with market conditions. For this reason, particularly for newer employees, semiannual evaluations are sometimes done. Part of the reason for adopting semiannual reviews is not that the employee may suddenly become an expert, although this has happened, but rather to compare current salaries at various performance levels to those paid elsewhere.

A salary program in data processing must be reviewed often enough to insure competitiveness. Many companies have given raises to data processing personnel just to keep their people from looking for jobs or leaving. Some of the more outstanding employees have been known to get three, perhaps more, "healthy" increases in a single year in order to stay competitive. This may sound preposterous, but weighed against the cost of replacing the individual, it is often the conclusion to retain the employee.

A number of companies have adopted a merit rating plan (part of the Hay Plan) such that *satisfactory performance* merits a cost of living increase (say 5 per cent), *commendable performance* an 8 to 10 per cent increase, and *outstanding performance* an increase of 12 per cent or higher. All such increases are annualized, meaning that they need not be given at regular time intervals. For example, if a man was rated for a 10 per cent increase he would get 5 per cent if it had been six months since his last, 15 per cent if it had been eighteen months, etc.

What a company has to do in the way of increases, of course, will depend heavily upon how its salaries compare with other salaries offered elsewhere. Clearly, every competitive position cannot be matched salary-wise and, therefore, there may be times when a good employee just simply cannot be afforded. But very careful evaluation should be done before arriving at this conclusion.

Promotions and recognition

The objective of a promotion within data processing should be to increase the effectiveness of the data processing department in achieving its goals. Although promotions are sometimes given for other reasons, the fundamental purpose should be to use the abilities of the man to the fullest extent. A promotion for a job well done may not be in order some of the time; and therefore, it may be desirable to give recognition in the form of a special award.

MAXIMIZING ON ABILITIES AND POTENTIAL

Data processing managers must be able to make determinations regarding the relative ability of their subordinates. They must also be able to recognize potential in a man for more challenging and responsible assignments.

To permit a man to work at a great deal less than his capacity for an extended period of time is to waste a resource of the business; it is much the same as wasting money, raw material, or any other asset. Furthermore, there are some individuals who do not function well if their job does not provide a sufficient, continuing challenge. So, by putting more power and capability on a job than that job really calls for, it does not necessarily follow that the job will be done properly.

A near-perfect match of employee to job can rarely be achieved for an extended time. Nevertheless, this ought to be one of the aims of the data processing managers.

For a man who has exceptional abilities in one or more functional areas, it may be that no suitable promotion possibility currently exists. Hence, consideration should be given to devising a new job, which in fact may be custom-tailored to employ fully the extraordinary capabilities of a particular individual. While it is not always possible to readily create new positions, management should remain responsive to installation requirements in order to decide whether a new position is justified.

In one installation, for example, there was an exceptionally able programmer who was officially assigned to applications programming. For some time management felt that this man potentially could do the work of two of his co-workers, but that he had attitude problems. Frequently the man produced only enough to meet the basic requirements, when, in fact, he was capable of doing twice as much. By an accidental series of events, the man was asked to work on problems involving an operating system and programming languages. He performed exceptionally well and employed his abilities to the fullest; he expended whatever extra effort was required to complete his work. Except for the physical appearance, the man became an entirely different person with regard to his job performance.

When the man was asked why he was so motivated and worked so hard, he replied, "This was a job I could get my 'teeth' into." The programmer, of course, was saying he had been given a challenge which matched his abilities. Not too long after this, the programming manager and data processing manager reviewed the needs of the installation. They came to the conclusion that there was a need for full-time effort on operating systems, languages, and standards development. A new job was created and called "systems programmer." The hero of this story was promoted to this position. He did so well in his new position in bringing about improvements that he was later promoted to data processing coordinator to further utilize his abilities.

Taking a deeper look into what took place in the series of incidents just described, one can see another principle which evolved, i.e., *management concentrated upon utilizing the strengths of a man rather than putting exhaustive efforts into trying to correct his weaknesses.*

CONFERENCES AND CONVENTIONS

Recognition frequently used on a broad basis may involve sending selected individuals to conferences or conventions. These are useful not only from the standpoint of recognition but also as a means of keeping abreast of the latest techniques, equipment, and other developments in the data processing field. Some of these events may not be directly concerned with data processing, but have a connection with either present or future EDP applications which may be considered.

An installation may be missing out on some very significant developments if it is not represented at industry gatherings; hence, plans should be made to send delegates depending upon specific needs. The idea of using these meetings as forms of recognition, then, may be thought of as an auxiliary benefit.

In general, the delegates returning from conventions or conferences should be asked to write a short report or give a presentation to their groups and management on the significant technical highlights of the meeting.

Establishing Incentives

Many things constitute incentives in the total working relationship. Some are well recognized and used, such as money and position. Other incentives are less obvious. Certain individuals are motivated to excel when they are placed in a competitive environment, others respond to frequent praise, some individuals are stimulated if they are made to feel very important.

It is not the purpose here to delve into these matters in great detail but rather to mention them in passing because of their importance. However, there are at least two areas in data processing *operations* where more formal incentive systems have been used successfully. The first is a piecework incentive system for keypunch and proofmachine (used in banking) operators, whereby the employee is paid on the basis of production. In this system, either straight or differential piecework schemes can be used. The second kind of incentive system provides a paid vacation day for each month in which an operator exceeds a predetermined production quota. Under this plan, the employees are permitted to save their "incentive days" up to five days. Otherwise, they can take specific days with the permission of their managers.

Another incentive systems, of sorts, has been tried with some success on computer operators. In this case, each computer system had a three man team on each shift. These teams compete with each other with the objective of *highest percentage computer utilization*. The monthly prize is "first place" among the teams and some token recognition by the EDP manager. A number of benefits were realized:

1. Fewer mistakes were made.
2. Set-up and tear-down time was reduced.
3. Team leaders either changed or had replaced unsatisfactory operators.

There is much to be done in the way of incentive plans for data processing that will certainly challenge the imagination of EDP operations managers. Remember, however, that *quality control* must be built into these plans to cover poor work, rework, and rejects.

Career Development

Data processing specialists, like many other professionals, have a normal interest in moving ahead in their careers. For the most part, the tangible evidence of moving ahead is a promotion, notwithstanding salary increases.

Some companies have been moving so quickly in data processing that attention to the matter of career development has been haphazard, to say the least. As the "computer age" starts to mature a bit, career paths may begin to follow a general pattern. In the meantime, data processing managers will be faced with the problem of what to do with the man who wants to get ahead, unless they take steps to insure that the installation has a career development plan.

One of the factors to keep in mind is that not everyone wants to become a manager. Therefore, for these individuals, the idea of being a boss someday is not really a valid motivating force.

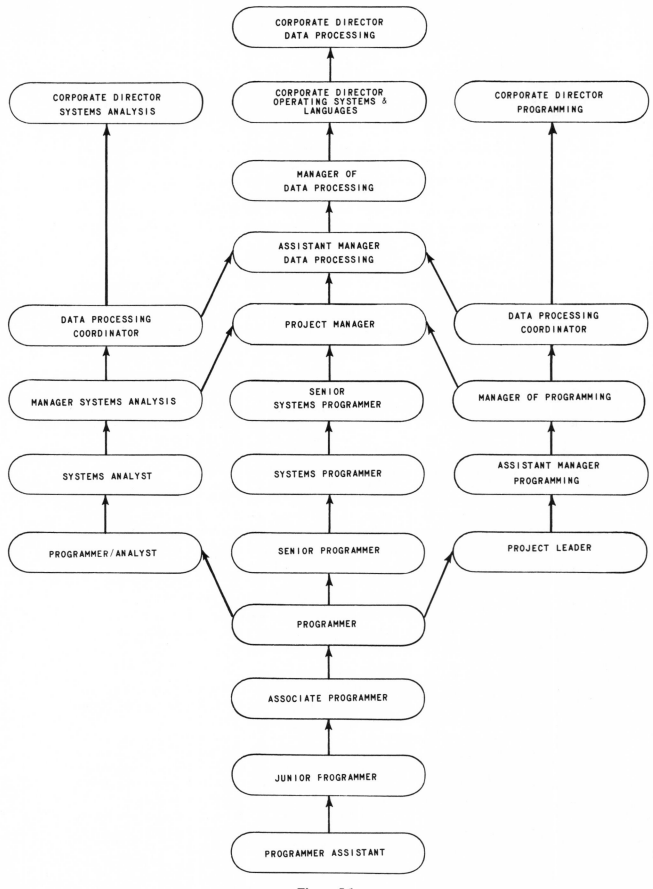

Figure 5.1
Management Oriented Programmer
Career Advancement

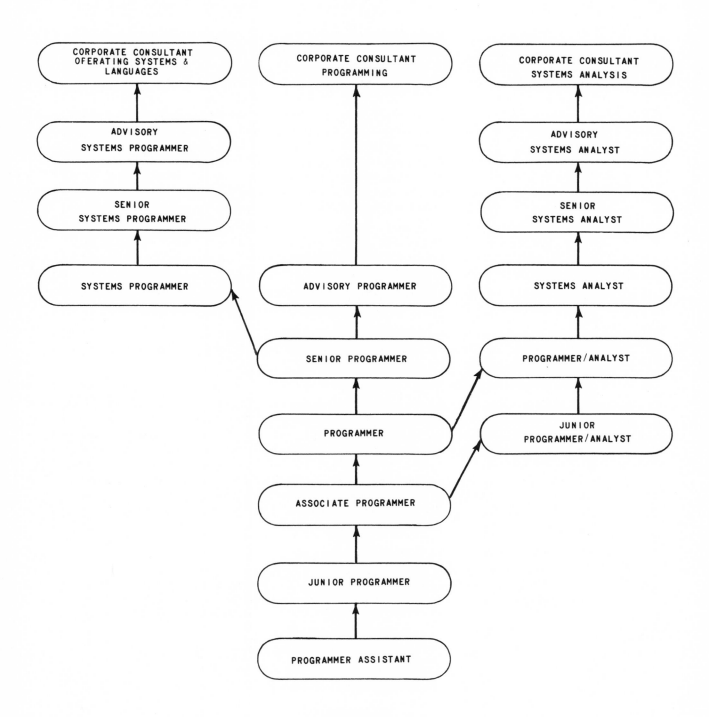

Figure 5.2
Technically Oriented Programmer
Career Advancement

Basically, a realistic career program for data processing personnel would be comprised of two paths for career growth: (1) toward management, (2) toward technical advancement.

Many of the positions in data processing, to be sure, are mainly technical; and as one might expect, individuals who will ultimately become managers will have to possess a reasonable degree of technical competence.

The following two diagrams which show possible career growth for programmers, illustrate some of the possibilities for advancement. The first diagram, Figure 5.1, is oriented toward management development, whereas the second, Figure 5.2, is for technical development. The two ladders shown for career development are by no means all inclusive. Possibilities for advancement will vary greatly depending on company needs, size, the nature of the business, etc. Not shown in the charts are promotions out of data processing work, altogether. For certain individuals, out-of-department promotions may even have been the original intention of management.

> By study and looking ahead, the data processing manager can be ready to move with management. He also will get a better understanding of what's important in his own installation and its current contribution to the organization. His profit can come in many ways, such as:
>
> 1. *Professional pride.* Not edible but more important to most of us than we're likely to admit.
> 2. *Advancement.* It helps to be the person who can understand management's problems and can help solve them.
> 3. *Crossing over into management.* Knowing how to use computers can be a real asset to a person's position in internal competition, and to a company's position in staying ahead of competition.[13]

Professionalism in the field

There are a number of factors which are characteristics of a profession. Rather than undertake a debate on whether data processing is a profession,[14] the time could be better spent by discussing *professionalism* as it pertains to data processing. The aims and standards of data processing have been the concern of several data processing organizations, and also the USA Standards Institute.

The Data Processing Management Association (DPMA), the Association for Systems Management (formerly the Systems and Procedures Association), and the Association for Computing Machinery (ACM) have all been concerned with the ideals and philosophy of data processing as a profession.

DPMA's Certification Program

> To date, there is only one vehicle for qualification purposes and that is the certification program offered by DPMA. The fact that its Certificate in Data Processing may not be entirely to everyone's liking and could be improved upon does not alter the fact that it is the only measuring stick now available to quality men in the data processing field.[15]

As of 1968, the awarding of certification was based upon four specific factors:

1. Prescribed course of academic study.
2. Three years direct experience in data processing.
3. Character qualifications.
4. Passing the examination.

---

[13]William Worthington, "Management Use of Computers," *Journal of Data Management*, June 1963, p. 31.
[14]Robert P. Rich, "Is Computing a Profession," *Computers and Automation*, August 1965, pp· 22–25.
[15]Charles H. Johnson, "A Systems Auditor Is Qualified," *Business Automation*, June 1963, p. 39.

Candidates for the 1968 certification examination had to attain passing scores in each of four general categories:

1. Automatic Data Processing Equipment
2. Computer Programming and Software Systems
3. Data Processing Systems and Management
4. Quantitative Methods—Accounting, Mathematics, and Statistics

The DPMA has given the CDP examination once a year since 1962 and publishes a brochure (available from The Data Processing Management Association, Park Ridge, Illinois), which describes the certification requirements and includes a study guide to the examination.

ACM's Guidelines for Professional Conduct in Information Processing[16]

Introduction

This set of guidelines was adopted by the Council of the Association for Computing Machinery on November 11, 1966 in the spirit of providing a guide to the members of the Association. In the years to come this set of guidelines is expected to evolve into an effective means of preserving a high level of ethical conduct. In the meantime it is planned that ACM members will use these guidelines in their own professional lives. They are urged to refer ethical problems to the proper ACM authorities as specified in the Constitution and Bylaws to receive further guidance and in turn assist in the evolution of the set of guidelines.

Preamble

The professional person, to uphold and advance the honor, dignity and effectiveness of the profession in the arts and sciences of information processing, and in keeping with high standards of competence and ethical conduct: Will be honest, forthright and impartial; will serve with loyalty his employer, clients and the public; will strive to increase the competence and prestige of the profession; will use his special knowledge and skill for the advancement of human welfare.

1. Relations with the Public

1.1 An ACM member will have proper regard for the health, privacy, safety and general welfare of the public in the performance of his professional duties.

1.2 He will endeavor to extend public knowledge, understanding and appreciation of computing machines and information processing and achievements in their application, and will oppose any untrue, inaccurate or exaggerated statement or claims.

1.3 He will express an opinion on a subject within his competence only when it is founded on adequate knowledge and honest conviction, and will properly qualify himself when expressing an opinion outside of his professional field.

1.4 He will preface any partisan statement, criticisms or arguments that he may issue concerning information processing by clearly indicating on whose behalf they are made.

2. Relations with Employers and Clients

2.1 An ACM member will act in professional matters as a faithful agent or trustee for each employer or client and will not disclose private information belonging to any present or former employer or client without his consent.

---

[16]Copyright © 1968, Association for Computing Machinery, Inc., (*Communications of the ACM*, February 1968, p. 135).

2.2   He will indicate to his employer or client the consequences to be expected if his professional judgment is over-ruled.

2.3   He will undertake only those professional assignments for which he is qualified and which the state of the art supports.

2.4   He is responsible to his employer or client to meet specifications to which he is committed in tasks he performs and products he produces, and to design and develop systems that adequately perform their function and satisfy his employer's or client's operational needs.

3.   *Relations with Other Professionals*

3.1   An ACM member will take care that credit for work is given to those to whom credit is properly due.

3.2   He will endeavor to provide opportunity and encouragement for the professional development and advancement of professionals or those aspiring to become professionals with whom he comes in contact.

3.3   He will not injure maliciously the professional reputation or practice of another person and will conduct professional competition on a high plane. If he has proof that another person has been unethical, illegal or unfair in his professional practice concerning information processing, he should so advise the proper authority.

3.4   He will cooperate in advancing information processing by interchanging information and experience with other professionals and students and by contributing to public communications media and to the efforts of professional and scientific societies and schools.

ACCOUNTING CERTIFICATION

Certified Public Accountants, in increasing numbers, are required to know more and more concerning data processing, since so many accounting procedures are now and will be handled by computer. Some of the equipment manufacturers offer short courses on data processing periodically for Certified Public Accountants and accounting consultants.

It is felt that accounting certification, in order to be of practical value for businesses, will have to cover data processing. As a matter of interest, a number of accounting and auditing firms have installed their own computers which are used for regular audits, tax and other financial computing.

PROFESSIONAL ENGINEERING

With more and more engineers entering into applied computer work and the academic requirements for engineering which now often include computer courses, certainly their ability to use the computer is becoming increasingly essential. It would, therefore, not be surprising to see the examinations for Professional Engineering licenses covering data processing principles, in the near future.

Perhaps, someday, applied data processing will be among the other specialties in which licenses are awarded, e.g., electrical engineering, mechanical engineering, etc.

ENCOURAGING INDEPENDENT STUDY AND PROFESSIONALISM

Regardless of whether the engineers or accountants decide to use data processing knowledge as one of the criteria for certification, personnel in EDP should strive to improve themselves in their profession.

Many people feel that professionalism is important, mainly if their employers express an interest in activities which promote professional qualities. By encouraging and giving recognition for professional advancement, the employer is bound to get a better data processing organization as a consequence. The individuals who seek a greater professional posture in their work may be selfishly motivated. Nevertheless, the knowledge which develops in the process often stimulates the person to be more reflective about his work. He may be able to approach data processing problems with both a deeper and wider range of understanding; and as a result of exposure to new concepts, he can frequently bring better and more efficient techniques to bear on his job.

One of the ways to keep abreast of current technology and new approaches to data processing management problems is to participate in the activities of computer associations. Through participation in the meetings, seminars, and conferences offered by these organizations, a data processing installation can avail itself of ideas and innovations which others have found useful.

Another form of EDP organization called *users groups* have been formed to facilitate the interchange of management methods as well as technical information pertaining to specific computers or groups of computers. The American Management Association also sponsors a variety of data processing seminars.

At least one magazine[17] contains annually updated information regarding computer associations and users groups in one of its monthly issues.

Getting and retaining cooperation

The level of cooperation one person exhibits toward another is partly a function of the nature of the relationship between these individuals and is also often a function of psychological factors which are not directly involved, e.g., problems at home, personality traits, etc. It is not the purpose here to undertake a detailed study of psychology as it pertains to data processing personnel, but rather to illustrate some of the meaningful ways in which desirable working relationships can be developed and maintained. An understanding of psychology as it applies to business situations will undoubtedly be of great value to EDP managers.

By creating a working environment which enhances the opportunity for employees to utilize their abilities, everyone concerned benefits. This working climate does not necessarily mean that everyone works along happily. Developing the vitality and responsive attributes which are sought from employees by their managers can sometimes be engendered by encouraging a healthy dissatisfaction, which may create the impetus for the improvement and growth of the enterprise.

The role that an individual plays in molding his own goals and purposes will quite often determine the degree to which he is successful. To the extent that employees have a stake in controlling their destiny, so to speak, their involvement becomes intensified. Managers must, of course, channel these energies to appropriate causes and prevent anarchy. One could call it low-pressure leadership, consultive management, or even democratic management.

> We are just beginning to understand that free men must set their own difficult goals and be their own hard taskmasters. There is no one to tell them what to do; they must do it themselves. They must be quick to apprehend the kind of effort and performance their society needs, and they must demand that kind of effort and performance of themselves and of their fellows.[18]

Insofar as data processing is concerned, functions such as systems analysis and programming are among the most demanding jobs today. So much is new that the challenge of computerization is staggering, especially from the standpoint of sheer growth.

The managerial skills necessary to properly motivate and indeed to manage data processing personnel are in some important ways quite different, it seems, from other commonly recognized

---

[17]*Computers and Automation*, Berkely Enterprises, Newtonville, Massachusetts.
[18]John W. Gardner, *Excellence: Can We Be Equal and Excellent Too?* (New York: Harper & Row, 1961), p. 160.

qualities. For example, programmers and systems analysts are a new "breed" in terms of both qualities and quantities—there are many more now than there were a short time ago and a great deal of what they do calls for creative imagination on a production-like basis.

> No other technical innovation has changed so many human activities in so short a time. An extension to man's brainpower, it is transforming science, medicine, government, education, defense, and business. It may transform man himself.[19]

ABILITY, EFFORT, AND ENVIRONMENTAL CONSIDERATIONS

One of the first determinations a manager has to make regarding a problem of cooperation or productivity is whether the individual has the ability to do the assigned work. Another point to be considered is that if the person has the ability, does he also possess the desire to put forth the required level of effort. Some very capable people have, of course, been known to be sluggish. Supposing that the man has both the ability and sufficient desire to do the job, then other factors must be considered more closely. On many occasions, interviewing a man privately will yield some valid reasons for on-the-job performance problems. At other times, a reasonably good insight can be gained by making personal observations and soliciting the observations of others.

A classic kind of case in EDP comes to mind wherein one of the better programmers at an installation was falling behind in his work for no readily apparent reason. His manager thought that the programmer might be having personal problems or that he was dissatisfied. The man himself said that much of the delay in his work resulted from the lack of computer time for testing programs. As it turned out, the man was actually becoming involved with more things than his manager had realized. One of the key items was the amount of time the man was spending on the phone and elsewhere answering inquiries which should not have gone to him. As a result the programmer would sometimes lose a half a day or more on miscellaneous jobs.

Interruptions, it should be noted, in programming or systems work can play havoc with the output level of individuals engaged in this work. Often it is not the duration of the interruption that is critical but rather a case where a train of thought has been broken. A five minute interruption on a complicated problem can destroy hours of analysis and contemplation.

Clearly, it is impossible to completely isolate everyone, but there are a great many things which can be done to shield programmers and systems analysts from distractions. For example, consider the following for the offices:

1. Have a knowledgeable secretary direct all incoming calls (phone and in person) to the appropriate individual.
2. Keep telephone ringing at low audible level and have phone ring once only.
3. Soundproof ceilings and walls. Use industrial carpeting on floors, and use drapes to keep out street noises.
4. Consider individual or two-man offices.
5. Provide meeting rooms and classroom facilities away from the offices.

The above list shows some of the cures for weaknesses found in systems and programming offices. There are, needless to say, many other factors which will vary depending upon particular installations.

Another pair of classic EDP problems that tend to cloud a manager's ability to measure the ability and effort of programmers has to do with two factors which a programmer depends upon but that are out of his control and are likely to be out of his manager's control as well. First, if the programmer finds it impossible to get reasonable computer time to test his programs,

---

[19]Gilbert Burck, "The Boundless Age of the Computer," *Fortune*, March 1964, p. 101.

his efficiency and productivity are lowered substantially. "Reasonable" means a minimum of one short test per day—"good" is two or more per day. One installation estimated that the productivity of its programmers was in the neighborhood of 50 per cent because "turnaround time" was in the area of two days and sometimes more.

Second, the analyst or programmer who finds himself dealing with a User who either does not understand his problems or who cannot communicate them, will have to spend inordinate amounts of time in meetings, reviews, conferences, and so on. Here again, the manager must consider such factors in judging an individual's work.

SPECIAL PRIVILEGES

Programming and systems work is similar to research in some ways, in that there are times when the individual becomes mentally exhausted before the official end of the working day. There are other times when the same individual may want to continue working past the official end of the working day. Sometimes a man may want to take his lunch earlier or later than usual, take a shorter lunch, or skip it, depending upon how deeply he is involved with some work.

Some of the most creative times for data processing people are not in the office, and therefore these ideas should be captured when and wherever they occur. To attempt to "legislate" that all work must be done between nine and five o'clock is nonsense for specific kinds of jobs. Operators, for example, would have to conform to definite work rules, given the nature of this particular work. Programmers and systems analysts, on the other hand, must be given much greater flexibility. Hence, to get the greatest return to the business from certain individuals, a rather permissive approach has to be taken toward managing them. "Special privileges" such as flexible lunch periods and coffee breaks, time-off from work, variable working hours, and better than average working conditions should produce results which easily justify the variances.

Too many managers see themselves as company policemen and spend so much of their effort on it that they lose sight of what their mission is all about. A man who runs a tight ship which is not going anywhere is not really contributing to the business.

No one, however, is proposing that the manager abdicate his responsibilities and permit matters to get beyond control. Managers will generally have to operate within broad guidelines, and all that is suggested is that increased permissiveness for certain positions can possibly maximize the return to the business.

MANAGEMENT INTEREST AND KNOWLEDGE OF THE WORK

From listening to programmers talk, and observing a number of manager-programmer relationships, it would seem that a number of managers lack sufficient interest and knowledge of the work carried on by their subordinates. In this kind of environment, programmers are faced with either of two situations: (1) their managers frequently make poor decisions, or (2) the decisions are left for the programmer to make. Either way, the effectiveness and efficiency of the department turns out to be low. In addition, turnover is usually high and morale is generally low. On the whole, many such conditions are discovered by higher management and steps are taken to rectify the situation. Others, of course, persist.

In order for a manager to get the cooperation of his staff, he must almost always have a strong interest in what his people are doing. He has to know a problem when he sees one, and this requires some knowledge of the work. This does not mean that the manager must be on the backs of his men to demonstrate his interest; and it does not mean that he tells them how to do each step of their job because he has some knowledge of it.

The effective manager must know exactly the objectives his department is working toward. He must set goals before his men that present them with realistic challenges. He must also be able to accept and use good ideas from subordinates, especially when they are better than his own.

Managers in data processing must reward creativity, innovation, and hard work. They must delegate important tasks and allow for the possibility of failure; and they must share in the challenges, successes, and failures together with their men.

All of these attributes, it seems, rest upon a foundation which includes an interest in, and a knowledge of, the work involved.

Maintaining the Creative Challenge

The age of specialization has had both good and bad effects insofar as matching men to their potentials on the job. In computer programming and systems analysis, there are frequently plenty of challenging applications which call for thoughtful consideration. However, there are cases where a series of repetitively dull assignments has broken the spirit of a good worker. Programming, in particular, can degenerate rapidly after a few similar assignments at close intervals.

At times, scheduling requirements on critical projects make it impractical to experiment in an effort to determine the resourcefulness of an individual; only the best people are picked for difficult assignments in such cases. But to continue to operate in this fashion, when conditions do not require it, does not give the less experienced individual an opportunity to develop. It is only by taxing the ingenuity of the man that both he and the company will experience growth.

The important point to remember is that the manager must introduce *controls* into the plan of employee development so that progress, or the lack of it, can be ascertained. Particularly in the case of a less experienced man on a new and challenging assignment, controls must be applied such that a reasonable recovery can be made in the event of failure. Failures are bound to occur, and indeed the manager must recognize that much can be learned through failure as well as success; it is the job of the manager, therefore, to make sure that a learning process takes place.

Computer operators, as well as programmers, must be viewed with regard to job enlargement. But each person has to be considered individually. Some prefer "hum-drum" work, others would like occasional changes in job content, and a few will even give positive indications of what they would "like" to do. These signals are worth watching since productivity improvements can be substantial as a result of getting the right man, with the right motivation, on the right job.

Motivating the individual

Much has been written about the subject of motivation, and while there is no intention to cover the topic fully, it is discussed here briefly because of its importance.

The derivative of the word "motivation" is, of course, "motive" which pertains to the forces and reasons within a person which produce a reaction, given the existence of some condition. While there are over twenty[20] theories or definitions of motivation which have been postulated by psychologists, most involve the concept of *need fulfillment*.

Sometimes when people fail to live up to their expected potential, their managers frequently feel that they have erred in this judgment. Often, however, the error was not in predicting potential but rather in neglecting or misinterpreting the motivational aspects of the situation.

Motivation is elusive because it is complex and because managers tend to apply their own standards to their subordinates. So, one key to understanding motivation is to realize that motivation factors are highly individual and should be dealt with as such.

---

[20]James L. Latham, *Human Relations in Business* (Columbus: Charles E. Merril Books, Inc., 1964), pp. 133–143.

Some motive factors are:

1. Need for money or avarice.
2. Personal satisfaction.
3. Prestige.
4. Acceptance by others.
5. Ambition fulfillment.
6. Sense of obligation.
7. Strength in competitive situations.
8. Success against high odds of failure.
9. Praise.
10. Pleasing the boss.
11. Recognition.
12. Fulfilling expectations of others.
13. Security.

Many of the factors listed above are known and seem rather logical. Other motivational elements may appear to be illogical, especially some of the negative ones, e.g., destructive urge, aggression fulfillment, hatred, anger, etc.

The absence of motivation in a man often shows up as an unfulfilled need. It is this lack of fulfillment which creates the type of dissatisfaction which causes the man to look elsewhere for a new position. Employees in various industries have been studied a number of times in an effort to learn what causes the dissatisfaction leading to their decision to leave an employer. All such studies arrived at nearly identical answers. The reasons discovered (which are, in fact, unfulfilled needs) most often were:

1. Management's appreciation of the work.
2. Personal sense of achievement.
3. Recognition of accomplishments.

Salary was ranked lower than these items in all studies. This is ironic, since these particular items seem to be those which would be well within the grasp of management. In some cases it might boil down to occasionally saying to a man: "you're doing a fine job, keep up the good work."

Managers must attempt to get motivation into its proper perspective without developing an over-identification with personal problems of their men. Above all the manager should be cognizant of the dynamic nature of motivation, i.e., individuals change and so do their motives.

Money as a Motivator

Saul W. Gellerman, writing in the March 1968 issue of *Fortune*, provides important insights in his article "Motivating Men with Money." He holds the view that most salary and compensation plans do not motivate any action other than the passive one of maintaining "membership" in the company. Gellerman, in his article, is discussing motivation pertaining to the better educated and mobile executive and professional man.

He says that money can influence action, encourage extra effort, or any other type of non-routine performance. But, he claims, *it can only do this when the net gain or increment for the employee is large enough*. What "large enough" means is relative to the man's existing income, net worth, etc.

In essence, the article says that employers can only use money as a motivator when they make it worthwhile for the employee, and that this is relative to his current financial status. The secret, says Gellerman, is to give a lot of money to the right man.

INVESTIGATING SUITABILITY FOR THE WORK

Depending upon the kind of data processing job involved, individuals will display varying attitudes towards these jobs. Some positions call for a high degree of intellectual tenacity and concentration for prolonged periods, e.g., programming, systems design. Other jobs call for much attention to detail, but less mental exercise, e.g., equipment operation. Still other positions, such as project leader or data processing manager, require broader thinking with special abilities to deal with people.

There have been cases, for example, where a programmer has requested a transfer to return to being an equipment operator because he could not take the pressure of programming. Ability to work under pressure, then, is one of the characteristics to be considered in determining suitability for certain jobs. Other jobs require that the individual be a self-starter or that he define the problem and then solve it. Some individuals require a well defined plan of action with clear-cut assignments. Therefore, another characteristic of suitability would be the relative dependence or independence of outside direction.

People who are overly nervous, emotionally unstable, a little neurotic, or perhaps are easily fatigued or jump from one thing to another must, of course, avoid those jobs which require a maximum of the opposite characteristics. Desire is clearly another very important factor. Hence, the manager must weigh all of these factors in assigning work.

Considerations in assigning overtime work

Overtime work generally results from incorrectly forecasting the amount of work to be done, schedule changes, unavailable computer time for testing, or events which are beyond the control of management. The burden to meet the target dates for projects finally comes to rest upon the non-supervisory personnel who must put in extra time and effort to get a job done. Certain individuals regularly seek overtime work as a means to supplement their incomes (although many programmers are in "exempt" salary ranges), others would rather have this time to use for their own interests. But there is almost always a point beyond which people do not want to work overtime, and in fact, managers should be aware of the state and federal laws limiting overtime work, especially for women. From the standpoint of the company, overtime is usually more expensive than straight time, and as such is desirable to avoid in many instances.

A number of installations are so inept at forecasting their needs that overtime work has become a way-of-life with them. Had the managers in some of these situations stopped to analyze their overtime pay, they would have discovered that it is much less expensive to hire additional full-time help. It is also a lot easier on the other workers involved.

Needless to say, there will always be some situations in which overtime is unavoidable, but these should be exceptional cases. Where overtime is required, the manager should see that the work is distributed fairly and well in advance insofar as this is possible. It is also appropriate to see that exempt personnel are given time-off to partially relieve the burden of overtime work.

EMERGENCIES

Without a doubt there will be times when critical situations will arise when programmers and others have to be called in to work at night, or spend unscheduled overtime at the installation. The objective is to keep these occurrences to an absolute minimum by conducting the necessary testing and reviews discussed in previous chapters. However, when these emergencies arise, the manager should ascertain exactly what caused them. It is not at all uncommon to find that the equipment operator was not following instructions, that the operating procedures were not up to date, or that the programmer failed to adequately test a program after having made a change to it.

Sometimes, the remedies for the "fire-call" are short and simple. Occasionally, extensive work may be required and this may very well interfere with some other assignment. At least one installation has tried a rotation system wherein one or two programmers are to be called on one day, one or two others on another day, and so on. Certain installations have a list showing the name of each program and its author together with his home phone number. If a problem arises in a specific program, the person responsible for the program, often its author, is called. Other data processing departments have designated maintenance programmers for this purpose.

The periodic evaluation

The evaluation, which is sometimes called an appraisal or merit rating, has become commonplace in many American businesses. It is the employee's annual or semiannual review by his manager of his progress and development. Specifically, a rating form with various qualities is used to score the level of development in the qualities which are shown. Some of the qualities generally found on such forms are:

1. Initiative
2. Industry
3. Maturity
4. Cooperation
5. Communication
6. Technical Ability
7. Creativeness
8. Quality of work
9. Self-Discipline
10. Professionalism
11. Development of others

The manager is usually required to rate the employee as outstanding, very good, good, fair, or unsatisfactory. Most appraisals are designed to be used as relative measures so that employees of the same level are compared. For example, the work of a junior programmer may be outstanding compared to other junior programmers and should be rated accordingly. Clearly, the work of a junior programmer as compared with a programmer is likely to be lower.

EXPLANATION TO THE EMPLOYEE

The manager, at the time of the periodic evaluation, should explain to the employee the significance and nature of the review. An evaluation can be an opportunity for the employee to reflect upon his qualities and to discuss his progress with his manager. The appraising manager should encourage the employee to ask questions on any subject involved in the rating.

One of the primary purposes of an evaluation is to determine which employees are in line for various levels of pay increases. Another purpose of the evaluation is in connection with its use for selecting individuals for promotions.

IDENTIFICATION OF STRONG AND WEAK POINTS

Throughout the appraisal, the manager will be required to explain his ratings to the employee, particularly when a rating is below average or barely satisfactory. Time for performing an adequate evaluation, therefore, must be planned to include discussion on some of the questionable ratings.

The points on which a man is strong should be given their due consideration, and the man should be complimented and encouraged to keep up these ratings. Of particular importance are those points on which the manager feels the man is not up to potential. These should be described with concrete illustrations where possible. For the average or acceptable performer (who appears to be at this level "for life"), some managers do selective appraisals. During such appraisals, these managers neither levy criticism of any kind on the man's weaknesses, nor do they attempt to tell the man "he's not too great." Instead the appraisal turns out to be a few polite compliments . . . the idea being to avoid worrying the employee, so long as his work is satisfactory.

SUGGESTIONS FOR IMPROVEMENT

An evaluation is not complete unless the manager has thoughtfully developed a plan for the employee to realize his performance potential. Too often, the suggestions for development are hopelessly vague and of little value to the subordinate. The manager should try to prepare meaningful suggestions prior to the appraisal and try to use applicable examples in describing these suggestions.

Data processing personnel do not usually present any problems insofar as rating them on standard types of forms, although some qualities may not be relevant. The usefulness of a rating for employee improvement is only as good as the appraiser's skill and sincerity make it. Managers in data processing, just as elsewhere, have an obligation to spend the time and effort required to produce worthwhile evaluations.

: six : six : six :

EDUCATING AND TRAINING MANAGEMENT AND EDP PERSONNEL

The rapid development of computer automated systems in modern businesses has had a significant impact upon the ways in which some of those businesses are managed. Unlike a bookkeeping machine or a turret lathe, the computer can play a truly vital role as a management tool. While the obvious cost-cutting type benefits of the computer cannot be overlooked, it has become clear that successful business leaders in the future will be those who know how to fully exploit the electronic computer for *business management*.

All of the discussion on advanced business applications and computer-based management information systems has broad and far-reaching implications regarding the education of management. For only through a process involving serious study is it possible for management to grasp fully the potential of the computer as a management tool. More than just management education, it is necessary to thoroughly educate and train the technical personnel who will devise new computer uses and support the electronic data processing effort. It must be emphasized, however, that successful computerization demands much more than training.

> Considering that data processing work is highly skilled technical work requiring high intelligence, high aptitude, thorough training, creative ability, and intellectual honesty, it is not surprising that very few of those seeking to enter the field are qualified to succeed.[1]

Top management education

Top management has an obligation to learn about and vigorously investigate possible uses for computers in their company. Not only is the income statement affected by the results of data

---

[1]Walter B. Nelson, "Motto for EDP People Pickers: Quality First," *Business Automation*, November 1963, p. 38.

167

processing economies, but the entire mode of conducting the business is beginning to change through the use of computers.

> More and more frequently, advanced business systems are forcing a realignment of the corporate structure.[2]

Top executives must come into the data processing "picture" at an early stage in its development within the company. Bringing to bear their wealth of knowledge about the company, these executives can contribute heavily to the success and value of the data processing function. Of necessity, such executives will have to know something about the capabilities of computing equipment and the nature of systems design and programming. With this knowledge, they will be able to come to grips with both the potential uses and realistic limitations of electronic data processing. Chapter one examines top management's role in more detail.

The rather sudden revelation of the power to be had through use of computers by companies in various industries has had some interesting consequences.

> The systems manager, data processing manager, or whatever his title might be, has risen to unprecedented heights in the short span of less than ten years. . . . A growing number of key executives are being groomed in, and selected from, this area of the company.[3]

Focusing on the educational needs of top management, one finds that there are a number of ways in which to accomplish specific educational objectives. One of the most effective means of fulfilling part of the educational requirements for management are the executive classes and seminars conducted by computer manufacturers. Some of these programs include intensive highly concentrated sessions covering a variety of subjects designed to stimulate the imagination of the executive, ranging from the simplest applications to highly complex information systems.

Judging from the praise expressed by many executives for these manufacturer-conducted programs, many felt that their time was well spent. Sometimes, as a result of participating in such programs, the executive immediately adopts a keen awareness of the existing computer effort in his business and takes action to show it.

Admittedly, the computer manufacturer is also interested in selling his equipment, but these companies generally realize that their efforts, at the outset, must be directed toward education.

Because the executive courses are taught specifically for executives, they are more likely to develop the desired knowledge faster than other methods. In fact, many such courses are directed and limited to a certain level of executives from specific kinds of businesses.

Computer manufacturer courses, it should be noted, often emphasize the glamour of the computer to the exclusion of seriously addressing problems involved in making the "dream" come true. In recent times, however, there is a noticeable trend among hardware manufacturers to tell management about the problems since much criticism has been leveled at them for not doing this . . . and because it has become necessary for the successful marketing of equipment in the long term.

Data processing organizations, consultants, education divisions of EDP service firms, and other groups occasionally conduct executive seminars. The topics covered range from general data processing principles to in-depth studies of particular applications or problem areas. The American Management Association's list of computer management seminars is growing rapidly. Presentations by the Data Processing Management Association, the Association for Systems

---

[2]S. C. Blumenthal, "Breaking the Chain of Command," *Business Automation*, December 1964, p. 31.

[3]George R. Allen, "Executive Stature—A Challenge," *Journal of Machine Accounting*, June 1964, p. 14.

Management (formerly the Systems and Procedures Association), and others are also making significant contributions toward improving management's comprehension of problems.

Reading is another means of education. Literature of an instructional nature is available from equipment manufacturers and publishers of technical books. Here again, there is a variety of subject matter.

The EDP installation personnel at a particular company (if it has computers) can be called upon to present seminars to management on a variety of EDP topics.

It must be emphasized that even some general knowledge in the computer field becomes obsolete rather quickly. Continuing programs designed to keep executives current on new advances in the state of the art should be incorporated in the educational planning.

Middle management education

Many of the same kinds of educational programs outlined for top management also apply to middle management. However, the EDP education of middle management can readily be carried out as part of the company's management development or training program. In numerous businesses, EDP is one of a variety of subjects addressed in such programs.

Some companies have regularly scheduled one or two day courses, sponsored by the EDP department, designed to familiarize middle managers with EDP concepts and the latest information processing technology. Such courses may be planned as part of a management development program or simply offered to qualified company personnel. Certain companies conduct these courses during working hours, others run them after hours, and still others do both.

The American Management Association (AMA) offers a variety of seminars that relate EDP to specific functional areas of the business such as marketing, purchasing, personnel, and others. This education is intended for non-EDP middle and upper management in most cases. It relates EDP to the specific function to give these managers an idea of how it is computerized. AMA also conducts seminars for specific industries, such as banking, and focuses on EDP pertaining to the particular industry.

Professional societies and trade associations are also becoming increasingly more active in educational programs on EDP applications for the non-practitioner. And, EDP equipment manufacturers have maintained some degree of interest in middle management education as well.

Basic to middle management EDP training is an explanation of the difficulties in problem definition and analysis of possible areas in which the computer might be used. Since middle managers are the ones who are most intimately acquainted with detailed business procedures, it is they who will be working most closely with EDP in the majority of applications.

Some EDP managers, commenting on management education, have experienced situations wherein educational programs sometimes produce a garbled understanding which distorts management's perspective on EDP. Too often, management gets overly involved in the *how* of EDP, whereas the emphasis should properly be on the *what* . . . what information is needed to manage the business, what data is available, etc.

What gets done is the responsibility of the user or management. How it gets done is basically an EDP specialist's problem.

Installation personnel education

Education, of course, is a continuing process for all installation personnel. For this reason, management must keep up to date on the latest courses being offered by hardware manufacturers, professional organizations, and others.

To plan an educational program for EDP personnel, individual job requirements must first be defined. The question of *need to know* is the foremost criterion for developing education plans. Tasks involved in each EDP position vary from company to company, and an enumeration of these is, therefore, necessary to select appropriate instruction.

An education or training plan must also consider an individual's past performance and proficiency level. The variance between job requirements and current know-how levels will guide management in choosing the most beneficial courses and training programs.

EDP MANAGEMENT EDUCATION

A basic and sincere willingness on the part of the manager to do the best job he can does not insure success, even assuming that all else functions well. The tools which the manager brings to bear upon his job greatly affect the quality and acceptability of his performance.

Unhappily, the management aspect of the EDP effort can easily become the weakest link in the functional chain. Top management can usually be readily oriented if it desires to be, middle management presents little difficulty, and technical personnel can get adequate training. But an unfortunate gap exists insofar as *management within the installation* is concerned.

> [The] absence of the computer executive is the major weakness of most of the large corporations outside of the computer industry.[4]

One of the things which has contributed to this weakness is a weakness in education. Another is the practice of giving key data processing management positions to people who "happen to be at the right place at the right time." Politically expedient moves are sometimes made. Instead of getting the right man, some installations are apt to grab the nearest warm body. This, of course, is an ill-fated move in terms of the ultimate success and usefulness of data processing to the business. Inadequate or inferior top management education is a contributing factor in creating a poorly managed EDP function.

> . . . too many executives believe that the problem of automatic data processing is the responsibility of the controller or some similar executive. They believe he will know the questions to ask and the data to seek in order to make an effective, totally integrated information system. This, of course, is a tragic assumption on the part of the rest of the management group.[5]

The foregoing quotation may be objectionable to controllers or similar executives. The author of this book does not mean it to be, but has included it to emphasize the need to place the EDP function where it is most likely to provide the greatest benefit to the company. Whether the controller should have this function depends very much on the controller. As a general matter, the best spot for the EDP function has not turned out to be under the controller.

Whether or not the man holding the top EDP post will be successful, regardless of who he is, depends upon the capabilities of his first-line managers. Many such managers are possessed with good technical qualifications but are deficient in management skills. Giving them management training is an essential part of building executive skills. Learning exclusively by "hard knocks" may eventually work, but it is rare to find a business that can afford the serious mistakes that are made in this process of learning.

There are a variety of ways to provide management education for EDP management. Many of the management associations and computing organizations occasionally provide courses on general management techniques. Universities and schools specializing in management training are equipped to cover general management theory and practices rather fully, and management consultants can also be called upon to provide management training.

---

[4]Roger A. MacGowan, "The Corporate Computer Executive of the Future," *Journal of Data Management*, February 1964, p. 37.

[5]Arnold O. Putman, "Unified Operations Management," *Journal of Data Management*, March 1964, p. 30.

If the business is large enough to have its own management development program, managers in EDP would definitely participate in it. The technical managers must be taught how to manage.

The following list of subjects is intended to convey some idea of the kind of educational program that should be planned for managers. Background and experience of a specific individual will clearly govern the selection of subject matter appropriate for him.

- Introduction to EDP for Managers
- Fundamentals of Programming for Managers
- Operating System Concepts for Managers
- Introduction to Systems Analysis and Design
- EDP Project Management
- EDP Operations Management
- Managerial Economics
- Administrative Management
- Management Controls
- Business Organization
- Personnel Administration
- Automated Accounting for Managers
- Advanced Business Systems for Managers

PROGRAMMER EDUCATION

For the most part, programmer education consists of technical training. Such training begins with orientation courses in the basic fundamentals of EDP and specific hardware, eventually leading to courses in programming languages.

Depending upon the needs of a particular installation, the programmer would learn one or more programming languages. In some instances, it may be necessary for the programmer to learn actual machine language, i.e., the absolute instructions which the machine understands directly, without any kind of translation. "Assembler" type languages, in particular, require the programmer to have a rather intimate knowledge of the hardware.

High-level programming languages such as COBOL (Common Business Oriented Language), FORTRAN (Formula Translator), and PL/1 (Programming Language/One) are usually considered to be machine independent and do not require a detailed knowledge of machine language. However, many professionals in EDP maintain that the programmer who at least understands the hardware instructions will produce more economical and efficient programs. This author agrees.

In either case, one of the chief sources of programmer education is the equipment manufacturer. At least one manufacturer has extensive educational facilities for the education of *customer* personnel. Courses on various subjects are scheduled on a regular basis and may be attended by programmers as required by the needs of their installations. No fee or tuition is paid for these manufacturer sponsored courses as a general rule.[6]

An increasing number of private training schools have been set-up to absorb the growing demand for data processing education. However, individuals seeking jobs in data processing as programmers frequently find that experience is required. Fortunately, some employers are willing to give consideration to people who have had this training, but who lack experience. Universities and colleges offer courses in data processing, and some confer undergraduate and graduate degrees in the computing sciences. Some of these types of education are examined later in this chapter.

It should be recognized that programming requires some specific aptitudes, so that the fact

---

[6]At least two EDP hardware manufacturers give *fee courses*, but they are run by different divisions which are not directly related to equipment marketing.

that a person has been trained does not necessarily presuppose desirable aptitudes, as discussed in Chapter five.

Programmer education, with respect to specific job requirements, may be comprised of many kinds of subjects. The list below is a representative group of programmer courses.

- Introduction to EDP
- Fundamentals of Programming Languages
- Program Language(s) and Coding
- Program Design
- Data Base Management Methods and Software
- Operating System Concepts and Facilities
- Operating System Job Control Coding
- Telecommunications Concepts
- Direct Access and Input/Output Methods and Coding
- Utility Program Facilities
- Diagnostics for Programmers
- Language Conversion Methods
- Computer Automated Documentation Aids
- Documentation Methods and Standards
- Introduction to Automated Accounting
- Introduction to Management Science

SYSTEMS ANALYST EDUCATION

Unlike the study of a programming language where there are a fixed number of functional instructions to be learned, systems analysis demands a business orientation, in addition to having the prerequisite EDP education and experience.

In the terminology of data processing, the title of "systems analyst" can mean a number of things. An important function of the analyst, perhaps the main one, is that of systems design, which consists of specifying the programs required for a data processing application. To do this, he has to get the facts about business needs and analyze application requirements. Another function of the systems analyst is to conduct feasibility studies whereby the justification (or lack of it) for automating an application is established.

In connection with the systems design function, the analyst will require a knowledge of the equipment and its capabilities. He will also be in a better position to prepare realistic and workable designs if he has a knowledge of the programming language to be used.

For the feasibility studies, the analyst has to be prepared to develop economic analyses. He therefore will require education in project analysis and accounting procedures for calculations involving discounted cash flow, depreciation, taxation, return on investment, etc.

Regarding specific application areas such as inventory control, the analyst has to understand the company's inventory problem, and will be required to know about economic order point calculations, economic lot sizes, etc. Having an understanding of the business problem is, by far, the most critical factor in the analyst's and therefore the system's success.

Systems analysis usually requires aptitudes and abilities that are beyond the scope of formal training. The analyst must have the ability to visualize, integrate, plan and anticipate future business needs. He is definitely a generalist, in contrast to a programmer. The aim, therefore, of the analyst's education is not so much to develop skills as it is to equip him with information that will enable an otherwise qualified man to perform his job well. For example, some of the following subjects may be involved in the education of systems analysts.

- Introduction to EDP
- Fundamentals of Programming

- Hardware Configurations
- Operating System Fundamentals
- Direct Access and Input/output Media
- Systems Analysis and Design
- Data Base Management and Design
- Principles of Automated Accounting
- Introduction to Management Science
- Telecommunications Concepts
- Telecommunications Systems Design
- Advanced Business Systems
- Economic Analysis
- Computer Automated Design Aids for Application Systems
- Systems Simulators
- Generalized Information and File Maintenance Systems
- Linear Programming
- Probability and Statistics
- Simulation Techniques
- Inventory Management
- Optimization Methods
- Network Design
- Decision Theory

The list shown above includes some of the more general topics; naturally, where specific applications are involved, the educational needs will expand to cover such applications.

OPERATING PERSONNEL

Machine operators (also known as "console operators" if they operate computers) and other individuals who are involved with the day-to-day operation of the electronic data processing equipment must have appropriate training to perform their jobs properly. In fact such training courses must be more carefully planned and structured than those for programmers and analysts. This is because programmer/analysts are better able to learn by reading technical material than the typical machine operator. The operator is trained in class and on-the-job, rather than through self-education via reading. For the most part a training program alone must adequately equip operating personnel to do their work.

Machine operators can be trained in private schools specializing in operator training, through on-the-job and in-house methods, or by the equipment manufacturer. Like most equipment operations training, EDP operating techniques can be taught in a straightforward manner. Providing that the operators have reasonable intelligence and ability, their complete training is generally not too difficult. But some formal classroom training is a must.

More installations are finding that custom-tailored, in-house training programs for machine operators produce the best results. Installation practices and standards can be explained in specific rather than general terms. Thus, the operator can directly relate his education to actual operating conditions.

Computing hardware is becoming more sophisticated and its proper operation, in an absolute sense, requires higher quality personnel than were previously needed. Operating systems, discussed later in this book, now require that an operator, to be proficient, must be able to interpret technical information found in reference manuals.

Training programs for operators will vary from installation to installation, depending on tasks to be performed. The following list includes some of the general subject areas.

- Introduction to EDP for Operators.

- Machine Operation (Classroom and "Hands-On")
- Operating System Concepts for Operators
- Operating System Job Control for Operators
- Installation Standards and Procedures
- Selected Advanced Topics: Telecommunications, Problem Diagnosis, Trouble-Shooting for Lead Operators.

Clerical help, such as would be found in EDP reconciliation functions, usually can be easily trained, again provided that they too have reasonable intelligence and ability.

How well the operations personnel do their jobs depends on several factors: the adequacy of their training, the job documentation for operations, individual ability, and motivation. Certainly, if the operators are unable to understand and use the written operating procedures, either the documentation is poorly done or the operator may be incapable of following instructions. The former is to blame in a great many installations. It is, in fact, a problem which originates during the programming phase of the application where the run specifications (operating manual) are initially prepared.

Types of education and training

The following sections are provided to give management some idea as to the various types of EDP education that exist. Discussed here are highlights and administrative pointers for utilizing these means of education and training.

ON-THE-JOB AND IN-HOUSE TRAINING

Any position in the data processing effort will require on-the-job training to some extent. Whether this training is part of a formally recognized established program of education or simply a natural consequence of the type of work, the skills provided by on-the-job training are often unique.

With the possible exception of clerical training, most data processing positions demand a formal, classroom training program of some kind. This formalized training, in turn, is frequently linked to on-the-job training. Manufacturers of computing equipment can often provide the formal education, whereas the equipment user conducts on-the-job training at his own installation.

Formal training may be given by installation personnel or by the equipment manufacturer, either at the installation or at designated educational facilities. In addition, private schools, colleges, consultants, and data processing associations provide formalized educational programs. Regardless of where the formal education has been obtained, on-the-job training is almost always required.

On-the-job training, while it appears to be an economical method, can actually cost a great deal more than formalized training. If it is not performed properly, the wasted money related to time, effort, and data processing rework required may be substantial. It is not uncommon to find that EDP on-the-job training is, in fact, a hit and miss proposition. The chief cause of this unfortunate situation can generally be traced back to either the total absence of a training plan, or a badly prepared plan.

A number of checkpoints, such as the following, should be considered for any on-the-job instructional programs:

1. What should the trainee be taught?
2. Who should be responsible for giving the training?
3. Approximately how long should the training last?
4. What is the plan for job rotation?

5.   How will progress be determined and reported?

The answers to each of these questions, and perhaps others, should be set down on paper in outline form. In this way, a working document will be established which can be used to help manage the training program.

College and University Education

Considering EDP's growth rate and technical skills required, it is apparent that more and more college graduates will be tapped for positions in data processing. Young men and women coming from college bring, hopefully, the latest techniques of engineering, mathematics, and business to their new assignments. Many of these individuals have had at least a survey course in data processing, others may have gone on to learn computer programming. Relatively few will possess degrees in the science of information processing.

The Data Processing Management Association publishes a book that lists universities offering programs in EDP. Other EDP organizations have also compiled similar information. The number of graduates with data processing degrees and majors is sure to increase rapidly in the future. However, much remains to be done in order for the colleges and universities to supply businesses with qualified data processing professionals. With the possible exception of graduates who have majored in data processing, most other degree holders who have taken computer courses have had only a brief and rather general introduction to the subject. In other words, it may be a grievous error to assume that a college course in data processing is equivalent to its counterpart found in industry. The subjects covered, time spent, and the qualifications of the teacher will inevitably be reflected in the ability of the student to fill a position in data processing. Industrial type training imparts both a sense of urgency and immediacy, but in college (unless it is night school), students are not as likely to appreciate the imminent value of their courses. Of course, the subject of data processing is not the only one in which this situation is found to exist. All that can be said for certain is that, in the future, colleges and universities can be expected to do a much better job of educating students for this kind of work.

The standards for university courses in computer science have received much attention from the Association for Computing Machinery (ACM). Over the years, the ACM has published many excellent papers on this subject. One of the most comprehensive studies on university courses in EDP has been published in the March 1968 issue of *Communications of the ACM;* annotated bibliographies are included for each course described in the publication. Shown below is a recommended course outline, for a first collegiate course in computing, which appeared in the issue referred to above.[7]

Course B1. Introduction to Computing (2–2–3)

APPROACH: This first course in computing concentrates on the solution of computational problems through the introduction and use of an algorithmic language. A single such language should be used for most of the course so that the students may master it well enough to attack substantial problems. It may be desirable, however, to use a simple second language of quite different character for a problem or two in order to demonstrate the wide diversity of the computer languages available. Because of its elegance and novelty, SNOBOL can be used quite effectively for this purpose. In any case, it is essential that the student be aware that the computers and languages he is learning about are only particular instances of a widespread species.

---

[7]"Curriculum 68: Recommendations for Academic Programs in Computer Science," *Communications of the ACM,* March 1968, p. 170.

The notion of an algorithm should be stressed throughout the course and clearly distinguished from that of a program. The language structures should be carefully motivated and precisely defined using one or more of the formal techniques available. Every effort should be made to develop the student's ability to analyze complex problems and formulate algorithms for their solution. Numerous problems should be assigned for computer solution, beginning early in the course with several small projects to aid the student in learning to program, and should include at least one major project, possibly of the student's own choosing. Careful verification of program operation and clear program documentation should be emphasized.

CONTENT: This outline reflects an order in which the material might be presented; however, the order of presentation will be governed by the choice of languages and texts as well as individual preferences. In particular, the treatment of some of the topics listed below might be distributed throughout the course. Although not specifically listed in the following outline, programming and computer projects should constitute an important part of the content of this course.

1. *Algorithms, Programs, and Computers.* The concept and properties of algorithms. Flowcharts of algorithms and the need for precise languages to express algorithms. The concept of a program, examples of simple programs, and description of how computers execute programs. Programming languages including the description of their syntax and semantics. (10%)

2. *Basic Programming.* Constants, identifiers, variables, subscripts, operations, functions, and expressions. Declarations, substitution statements, input-output statements. conditional statements, iteration statements, and complete programs. (10%)

3. *Program Structure.* Procedures, functions, subroutine calling, and formal-actual parameter association. Statement grouping, nested structure of expressions and statements, local versus global variables, run-time representation and storage allocation. Common data, segmenting, and other structural features. (10%)

4. *Programming and Computing Systems.* Compilers, libraries, loaders, system programs. Operating systems, and other information necessary for the student to interact with the computer being used. (5%)

5. *Debugging and Verification of Programs.* Error conditions and messages, techniques of debugging, selection of test data, checking of computer output, and programming to guard against errors in data. (5%)

6. *Data Representation.* Systems of enumeration and binary codes. Representation of characters, fixed and floating-point numbers, vectors, strings, tables, matrices, arrays, and other data structures. (10%)

7. *Other Programming Topics.* Formatted input and output. Accuracy, truncation, and round-off errors. Considerations of efficiency. Other features of language(s) being considered. (10%)

8. *Organization and Characteristics of Computers.* Internal organization including input-output, memory storage, processing and control. Registers, arithmetic, instruction codes, execution of instruction, addressing, and flow of control. Speed, cost and characteristics of various operations and components. (10%)

9. *Analysis of Numerical and Nonnumerical Problems.* Applications of algorithm development and programming to the solution of a variety of problems (distributed throughout the course). (15%)

10. *Survey of Computers, Languages, Systems and Applications.* The historical development of computers, languages, and systems including recent novel applications of computers, and new developments in the computing field. (10%)

11. *Examinations.* (5%)

SCHOOLS SPECIALIZING IN DATA PROCESSING TRAINING

In literally every major city in this country today there is at least one private school devoted to the training and education of data processing personnel. Most of the training is either for programming or machine operations and is usually offered both in full-time day sessions and part-time evening classes.

Many of these schools are intended to be profit making businesses; just as any business must produce a marketable product or service, the schools must in theory produce acceptable data processing personnel. The objectives of most schooling of this type have been generally well ahead of actual results. When the schools first began to become significant, they were given their opportunity to demonstrate the value of their service. As the graduates began to get jobs, their managers were appalled at what they got. Too many of the people did not even have a trace of aptitude for the work for which they had paid to be trained. This, combined with the sometimes low quality of instruction, has created much ill-feeling toward these schools.

Federal agencies, states such as Pennsylvania, and certain trade associations have begun accreditation programs for these schools, but it will be some time before these mature sufficiently to have potent effects. An article in a popular business magazine, on this subject, included this quotation:

> . . . big companies that use the more sophisticated computer systems . . . often charge that many of the schools teach too superficially and with outmoded equipment, that they recruit unqualified students by high pressure promotion, unjustified promises, and the lowering of entrance requirements. There is also a considerable body of complaint from disgruntled students.
> . . . other observers feel that the schools are adequately filling the needs of smaller companies that use less advanced equipment.[8]

Now that the demand for data processing schooling is up, a number of schools have become more selective about whom they admit. Many claim that they will not enroll prospective students unless they can show, by means of an aptitude test, that they are capable of handling specific kinds of jobs such as programming.[9] A number of managers have been encouraged by the performance of some of the more recent graduates of these private schools; the trend, it is hoped, will continue.

One private school, The Hibbing Area Technical Institute, has a 2,160 hour EDP curriculum in four semesters which includes the following subjects:[10]

First Semester:	*Third Semester:*
Principles of Accounting I	Cost Accounting
Data Processing Mathematics	Human Relations
Introduction to Computers	Business Organization
Unit Record Equipment	Data Processing Applications
Communications English I	Introduction to Systems

Second Semester:	*Fourth Semester:*
Principles of Accounting II	Systems Development
Communications English II	Advanced Programming
Data Processing Mathematics II	Data Processing Field Project.
Computer Programming	

---

[8]"How Good are Computer Schools?", *Business Week*, October 7, 1967, p. 97.

[9]A friend of the author has proposed what he calls Miller's Law: "No one flunks an aptitude test given by these schools." We all hope the Law is proved wrong.

[10]William O. McGraw, "ADP Technical Training," *Journal of Data Management*, July 1964, p. 25.

EDUCATION BY THE EQUIPMENT MANUFACTURERS

By far, a greater number of people currently engaged in data processing work have been trained by EDP equipment manufacturers than by any other means. At least one computer manufacturer maintains extensive educational services for the use of customers in principal cities of the world. Education centers of this kind conduct courses in programming, systems design, operating techniques, and more. For the most part, the subjects covered relate to special kinds of computing equipment, and may be application oriented.

The consensus regarding the quality of manufacturer-sponsored classes has been quite favorable. The aptitudes and prior qualifications of people entering these courses can vary greatly, and the results can therefore vary. Some manufacturer courses are graded, and others are not. In most instances the grade report and certificate of completion is sent to the manager of the person attending the course. As in the case of any grading scheme, the situations (personal, business) under which the course was taken should be given due consideration before a final evaluation or determination is made. But in an absolute sense, such grades can usually be of value in determining the degree to which the student absorbed the material taught.

Equipment manufacturers sometimes teach courses on the premises of the customer, where the size of the class or special situations warrant it. There are both positive and negative factors to be considered for on-site courses:

Positive Factors

- The courses can be directed toward a specific industry or application.
- Students may be able to assist one another, since they work for the same company.
- The courses can be custom-tailored to meet specific needs.
- Student qualifications are usually known.

Negative Factors

- Normal work duties may interfere with the participation.
- Physical facilities may be inadequate.
- Environmental factors may detract from the presentation.

Training aids and materials

Training programs for EDP personnel make use of a number of special educational aids. Classroom training programs generally utilize technical reference manuals. On the other hand, student texts, programmed instruction materials, and computer assisted instruction are examples of materials that permit the student to learn on his own, at the pace best suited for him.

STUDENT TEXTS

Today, a wide assortment of EDP subjects are covered in what are called "student texts." Prior to the advent of such learning materials, the student had only the classroom and technical reference manuals. Reference manuals, with few exceptions, are meant to be used after the subject is known to the reader. They are, therefore, unsuitable for self-learning in most cases. Student texts, available from hardware manufacturers and independent publishers, have become popular as a means to bridge the gap for individuals who wish to learn on their own or to supplement formal training.

PROGRAMMED INSTRUCTION

Programmed instruction is a means of training by which the student learns by reading short explanations after which he must answer questions to test his comprehension. The correct answers to the questions are then immediately available to the student, so he will know whether he has gained an understanding.

The printed material in a programmed instruction text is arranged to facilitate the method, i.e., first an explanation, then the question(s), and finally the correct answers. Programmed instruction methods are also computer automated and will be discussed in the next section. EDP people commonly refer to non-computerized programmed instruction as "PI courses."

PI courses are available from hardware manufacturers and independent publishers and cover numerous subjects. Introductory topics and programming PI courses are widely used. Most courses are followed-up by a day or more of classroom training.

PI permits the student to advance at his own pace of comprehension. An advisor is usually assigned to answer questions or clarify sections of the reading material, but for the most part, the student works on his own. Supervised tests are sometimes given after various phases of the material. Programmed instruction has worked out well for the vast majority of students who demonstrated the appropriate aptitudes.

COMPUTER ASSISTED INSTRUCTION

Abbreviated CAI, this method employs the versatility of EDP to improve the entire learning process and, at the same time, to reduce overall education costs.

Figure 6.1 shows printed information that was produced on a telecommunications typewriter terminal linked to a distant computer. Here CAI was used to teach the student how to program, and the illustration shows part of the first lesson. Close examination of Figure 6.1 will give some indication as to how the computer and the student interact.

CAI is becoming increasingly popular for education of all kinds. As time goes on, many imaginative uses will be developed for this method of instruction.

OTHER EDUCATIONAL MATERIALS

Books and manuals covering various EDP topics are available from a number of sources. Equipment manufacturers are the most prolific producers of training aids, manuals, and other instructional literature. Such materials are usually available for customer use at little or no charge, whereas non-customers will generally have to pay the full price, particularly where a quantity of literature is needed.

A number of book publishers, such as Prentice-Hall, John Wiley, Richard D. Irwin, McGraw-Hill, and others, produce both hard and soft cover books on many topics in electronic data processing. There are more books of an introductory nature and on programming languages than on any other topic.

Occasionally, larger users of computers take it upon themselves to develop and publish training manuals and books covering either introductory or advanced subjects. In some cases these manuals or books are used to orient new data processing personnel to the standards and practices of a particular installation. Where a large installation has developed a unique programming language, for example, books or manuals must be prepared for the use of the programmers and systems analysts.

```
TUTØR1     15:36    MØN.    03/25/68

     CØPYRIGHT 1966 FØRD MØTØR CØMPANY - ENGINEERING STAFF
WELCØME TØ THE FØRD TIME SHARING SERVICE. WE WILL TRY TØ TEACH YØU
ENØUGH ABØUT THE SYSTEM IN THIS SITTING SØ THAT YØU WILL BE ABLE
TØ WRITE YØUR ØWN CØMPUTER PRØGRAMS.

BEFØRE WE CAN WRITE A PRØGRAM WE NEED TØ REVIEW THE SYMBØLS
AVAILABLE:

     [1] +
     [2] -
     [3]   /
     [4]      *
     [5]        [ ]
     [6]          ↑


AFTER THE ? BELØW TYPE THE NUMBER ØF YØUR ANSWER

WHICH ØF THE ABØVE SYMBØLS IS USED FØR ADDITIØN?1
GØØD.
WHICH SYMBØL IS USED FØR SUBTRACTIØN?2
RIGHT
WHICH SYMBØL IS USED FØR DIVISIØN?3
GØØD FØR YØU. NØW THE NEXT ØNE IS TRICKY:
WHICH SYMBØL IS USED FØR MULTIPLICATIØN?4
VERY GØØD. IF'X' WERE USED FØR MULTIPLY, IT CØULD BE CØNFUSED
WITH THE VARIABLE X. LET'S PRACTICE A LITTLE:
HØW MUCH IS 2*3?6
SURE
HØW MUCH IS 3*4+7 ?19
RIGHT YØU ARE.
HØW MUCH IS 3*[1+5]/2 ?9
GØØD
THAT LEAVES ↑ WHICH IS ØUR WAY TØ INDICATE SQUARES, CUBES,ETC.
SUCH AS X↑2 FØR 'X SQUARED' ØR X*X, Y↑3 FØR Y*Y*Y, ETC.
WE ALSØ CAN USE FUNCTIØNS SUCH AS SINE, CØSINE, ETC., AND
YØU CAN EVEN DEFINE YØUR ØWN, BUT THESE WILL BE CØVERED IN
ANØTHER LESSØN.  WE'LL USE SQR [SQUARE RØØT] IN ØUR CØMING
EXAMPLE TØ GIVE YØU THE IDEA. LET'S ASSUME YØU WANT TØ CØMPØSE
A PRØGRAM TØ CØMPUTE RADIUS VECTØRS [THE SQUARE RØØT ØF THE
SUM ØF THE SQUARES ØF THREE CØMPØNENTS.]  THIS PRØGRAM WILL
BE A SEQUENCE ØF STATEMENTS TØ TELL THE CØMPUTER WHAT TØ DØ.
DØ YØU THINK THESE STATEMENTS SHØULD BE NUMBERED:
 [1] CØNSECUTIVELY [1, 2, 3, ETC. ]
 [2] INCREMENTALLY [10, 20, 30, ETC.]
 [3] ANY SEQUENCE FØR IT DØESN'T MATTER
[TYPE NØ. ØF ANSWER]
?2
```

Figure 6.1
Computer Assisted Instruction
Used to Teach Programming
(Courtesy of Ford Motor Company)

RIGHT.
LEAVING SPACE BETWEEN NUMBERS PERMITS EASIER INSERTIØNS LATER.
FØR ØUR SAMPLE PRØGRAM, LET'S FIRST CALL FØR ØUR KNØWN
VARIABLES. WE SIMPLY TYPE:

10 INPUT X, Y, Z

10 IS SIMPLY THE FIRST STATEMENT NUMBER. X,Y, AND Z ARE
ØUR 'DATA'. NEXT WE WRITE ØUR EQUATIØN BY TYPING:

20 LET R = SQR [X↑2 + Y↑2 + Z↑2]

WHERE 20 IS THE NEXT STATEMENT NUMBER, 'LET' TELLS THE CØMPUTER
THAT AN EQUATIØN IS CØMING, AND 'R' IS ØUR UNKNØWN VARIABLE.
NØTE: UNKNØWNS MUST BE ØN THE LEFT ØF THE '=' AND KNØWNS ARE
ØN THE RIGHT. SQR IS THE SQUARE RØØT FUNCTIØN MENTIØNED
EARLIER. THE REST IS TELETYPE ALGEBRA. FRØM THIS PØINT ØN
'R' CAN BE TREATED AS A 'KNØWN' IN ØTHER EQUATIØNS. IN THIS
EXAMPLE WE'LL TELL THE CØMPUTER TØ PRINT THE VALUE ØF R
BY TYPING THE STATEMENT:

30 PRINT R

WHICH WILL CAUSE THE CØMPUTER TØ DØ JUST THAT. WE NØW ADD
AN 'END' STATEMENT AND THIS IS ØUR CØMPLETE PRØGRAM:

10 INPUT X, Y, Z
20 LET R = SQR [X↑2 + Y↑2 + Z↑2]
30 PRINT R
40 END

WHEN 'RUN' IS TYPED, THE PRØGRAM WILL CALL FØR VALUES ØF
X, Y, AND Z WITH A QUESTIØN MARK.
        [TRY IT: TYPE ANY 3 NUMBERS SEPARATED BY CØMMAS.]
?4,7,9,
  12.083   [THIS IS YØUR 'R' ØR RADIUS VECTØR.]
WELL, THE HARD PART IS ØVER AND NØW THE FUN BEGINS. BY THE
WAY YØU HAVE ANSWERED 8   CØRRECTLY ØUT ØF 8   QUESTIØNS.
IN ØRDER TØ CØNTINUE WHAT WE HAVE BEGUN, IT WILL BE NECESSARY
TØ REQUEST ANØTHER PRØGRAM FRØM ME. TØ DØ THIS,
TYPE 'ØLD' AND USE 'FØLLOW***' FØR THE PRØBLEM NAME. WHEN
THE CØMPUTER IS 'READY' TYPE 'RUN' AND I'LL MEET YØU THERE.
LAST ØNE THERE IS A HUMAN. GØØD LUCK.

TIME: 14 SECS.

Figure 6.1 (cont.)

181

CONSIDERATIONS FOR EVALUATING AND SELECTING EDP EQUIPMENT

Selecting data processing equipment is properly done after having established the criteria to be used for making this kind of decision. There are many evaluations which have to be made; some are of a tangible nature, while others are more difficult to analyze in absolute terms. For example, to compare a number of computer systems on their speed to perform the same set of instructions is rather straightforward. On the other hand, there is the matter of appraising the reputations of the EDP equipment manufacturers. Software, to be discussed in this chapter, is yet another key evaluation point.

Management also faces the problem of dissecting a manufacturer's sales pitch to assess what theoretical advantages and capabilities are attainable at what price levels. It may be that keeping up with the Joneses, whom the salesman brags about, will only cost $1,500 a month more in hardware rental. On the other hand, one sometimes finds that the Joneses spend $3,000 a month more on systems programmers and use a larger operating system with higher overhead (perhaps $2,500 a month in additional memory and storage). So, the full advantage of a $1,500 hardware feature can cost much more. While such facts are not deliberately hidden, the uninitiated can get trapped. It may be like buying a good race horse that has proven capability as a winner. Its previous owner may assume the buyer knows the overhead items: a top-flight trainer is required, a well-paid jockey, regular veterinary services, a groom, a stable, feed, work-out track, horse trailer and station wagon to get the horse to and from the race track, race entry fees, riding equipment, etc.

It is of basic importance for the data processing manager to realize that there is much more than internal speed involved in the final decision. The old and well-worn adage "you only get what you pay for" certainly seems to be true in picking computers—except that it is definitely possible to get a lot less, if the appropriate evaluation criteria are not used.

Buying problem solutions

In the process of assessing the merits of computing systems, at least one key point should be borne in mind. The computer is going to be used to solve business problems and it is the computer which is the *means* to that end. Therefore, a business may quite appropriately consider that it is *buying solutions to problems*. There is more to this seemingly innocent statement than appears at first glance, for there are a multitude of considerations involved in the process of problem solving.

One of the initial steps is that of acknowledging that there are problems to be solved and setting out to define the problems as lucidly as possible. Not only immediate problems should be considered but also those applications which are likely to evolve within five years and possibly longer. In the definition of the problem, the growth of the business must be related to specific application areas. A computer system that just barely meets current requirements probably will not be adequate to satisfy the needs in the near future. So, the decision must be made with both short and long range plans and objectives in mind. Of course, in order for computer manufacturers to be able to intelligently propose equipment and submit bids, they will need to know what the short and long range applications specifically involve. Often, EDP manufacturer representatives and applications engineers can be quite helpful in assisting the user to formulate problem definitions and in developing long range plans. Competent data processing consultants can give valuable advice and assistance too, but the final user should *not* abdicate his decision responsibility. Managers must continually strive to gain a greater in-depth understanding of the problems and technical considerations.

Equipment evaluation checkpoints

Listed below are some of the more critical aspects involved in hardware systems selection. It is felt that each of these should be carefully studied and weighed as to its value and importance. The longer term implications should generally be of primary concern in evaluating each point.

1. *Compliance with bid specifications*. Will the proposed system do the job as requested?
2. *Price-performance*. Given a specific application with specific volumes of work (10,000 accounts and 5,000 transactions), how does the cost of one system compare with another performing specific work?
3. *Throughput*. What is the time required to process a specific volume of work? Certain deadlines have to be met. Is the computer in question fast enough?
4. *Capacity for increased demand*. At what point will another type or more computers be required, expressed in suitable values, such as number of accounts or transactions? Can bigger, more powerful models be used without reprogramming?
5. *Reliability*. What has the experience been with the various types of computers, with respect to breakdown and repair time?
6. *Application programs, utility programs, diagnostic and special subroutines available*. Does the EDP equipment manufacturer give the customer access to free programs which eliminate certain programming costs?
7. *Programming language support, features, efficiency*. Briefly discussed later in this chapter.
8. *Operating system features and overhead*. What will the use of an operating system mean in terms of increased operations and programmer efficiency? How much memory and what storage devices are required? (Operating systems include control programs which automatically handle all computer functions, such as selection and loading of programs from a program library, making the transition from one job to another, and much more.) Briefly discussed later in this chapter.
9. *Maintenance costs*.
10. *Ability to add memory, input/output devices and features in the field*.
11. *Variety, speed, and cost of input/output devices available and programmed support for them*.

12. *Delivery schedules.* How soon can the needed devices be installed?
13. *Instruction repertoire and power.* How many instructions does the computer have? How do the functions they perform compare with the functions provided on another computer?
14. *Features for telecommunications and multiprogramming support.* Is the machine designed so that the concurrent running of multiple programs is feasible with appropriate devices on the system? Does the system permit the easy adaptation of telephone line type of hook-up processing?
15. *Input/output channel characteristics.* To what extent are central processor operations overlapped with channel operations?
16. *Device switching, multiprocessing, shared-file, and other advanced capabilities.* If required, can input/output devices be switched between systems or channels? Can two systems communicate with each other? Is there a feature which allows input/output devices to be used by two or more systems?
17. *Physical requirements for the computing system, such as power, floor space, air-conditioning, and floor loading.*
18. *Internal processing speeds.* How quickly can the instructions be executed? Adding two numbers together may take five milliseconds in one computer and ten on another.
19. *"Free" testing arrangements.* Does the manufacturer provide testing centers for the use of customers, or permit the system to be used at no charge for a period of time?
20. *Availability of back-up equipment.* What alternatives can be taken when the computer breaks down? Are there similar computers nearby?
21. *Guarantee or warranty.* How long is it for, and what is covered?
22. *If equipment is rented, how do contract cancellation provisions compare?*

On the less technical side, the points below may be equally as important as the others:[1]

1. *Educational facilities.*
2. *Maintenance of equipment.*
3. *Systems and programming assistance.*
4. *Conversion assistance.*
5. *Reliability of service.*
    a. Company backing.
    b. Company experience.
6. *Experience in your particular field.*

Point number three, *systems and programming assistance*, should be examined very carefully. The fact that people are supplied by the manufacturer to do programming or systems work may be completely meaningless. A number of woeful stories can be told by companies who thought they were getting a bargain when their EDP equipment suppliers included programmers as part of the deal. As it turned out, the people supplied were not really qualified programmers but were, instead, warm bodies who fulfilled the letter, but not the intent of the contract. As a result, the required work was of low quality and did not get completed on schedule.

Commitments for *completed* applications which are acceptable to the user are vastly more realistic than proposals for supplying programmers whose experience is unknown to the customer.

Providing that the manufacturer has professionally trained, experienced, and otherwise qualified consulting systems analysts, systems engineers, or applications specialists, these men can perform, by far, a greater service to the user than can programmers.

Simulation

Simulation techniques of various types have been designed to develop timing and cost esti-

---

[1]José A. Castillo-Fernandez and Enrique Rivera-Santana, "Technique for Evaluating Electronic Computers," *Data Processing*, September 1962, p. 33.

mates for computer systems. Basically, the simulation process involves modeling one computer on another. The key parameters of the computer to be simulated are set up in the computer which will run the simulation. Information regarding the input, output, and processing for particular jobs are used by the model to arrive at timing and price-performance figures.

Insofar as predicting the performance of a computer, simulation can be quite useful. As a result of job timing estimates and price performance data, which are produced *via* simulation, it is possible to rank various computers according to their predicted performance. *Price-performance* is a major criterion in the process of choosing a computer system.

Computer manufacturers and private consulting firms have developed computer system simulators which can be used either at no cost or for a fee. Two such proprietary simulators are *SCERT* and *CASE*.[2] IBM, for example, has developed a number of simulation systems. One such system is *GPSS* (General Purpose Systems Simulator). Another is *CSS* (Computer Systems Simulator). *Simscript* is yet another. There are at least several dozen simulation systems in existence, implemented on various kinds of computers.

The design of *OLRT* (On-Line, Real-Time) systems is often done with assistance of simulation methods. OLRT processing requirements are usually very time-sensitive, and simulation is one of the few ways to arrive at accurate performance characteristics.

Needless to say, not only must the simulation model be accurate, but also the job information must be carefully prepared. Simulation is most useful when the job specifications are finalized or where the jobs are actually being run.

Benchmark programs

"Benchmark programs" are used to arrive at running times for a given volume of work. This identical series of jobs is run on two or more types of computers, and the times are recorded and compared.

It is of the utmost importance that the programs chosen for the tests be truly representative of all the work being run or to be done. So, either programs which approximate the average job or programs which take a major portion of the total usage should be used.

Benchmark comparison criteria must be intelligently chosen, otherwise the indications ultimately presented may be invalid. Suppose that a given computer is required to do printing 75 per cent of the time. The fact that another computer can sort data in half the time required by the other does not lead to any reliable conclusions regarding the jobs in question, i.e., heavy printing performance.

Performance power calculations

There is, to date, no generally accepted formula which is used to rate computer performance. It is not difficult to understand why, since there are so many variables which can enter into the calculations.

One method, sometimes called *representative calculating performance*, is used to arrive at timings which can be used to compare the relative power of various computers. The performance time factor for a given computer is determined as follows:

Summation of the times to complete nine additions plus the time to complete one multiplication—divided by ten.

Each operation includes the time to assess the instructions, obtain the two operands from high-speed memory, execute the required instructions, and store the result.

There are a number of variations of instruction mixes and calculations which can be used to measure internal power.

---

[2] Systems and Computers Evaluation and Review Technique (SCERT), Comress, Incorporated, Washington, D.C.; Computer Aided System Evaluation (CASE), Computer Learning & Systems Corp., Rockville, Md.

It is interesting to note that in the late 1940's, H.R.J. Grosch, a pioneer in EDP, formulated a theory that computing power increases as the square of the cost, in a given year (hardware manufactured at the same state-of-the-art). "Grosch's Law," as it is called, is expressed as:

Computing Power = Constant (System Cost)^2

Or, to put it another way: "spending twice as much yields four times the power." Dr. Grosch's theory holds for modern equipment, according to at least one study.

Dr. Kenneth E. Knight has developed a computer power rating formula which he shows upholds Grosch's Law in a study of 225 computers introduced between 1944 and 1963. The computational model advanced by Knight is:

$$P = M(10^{12})/(t_c + t_{i/o})$$

where:

 P: power factor

 M: memory capacity

 t_c: internal speed of central processor

 $t_{i/o}$: central processor idle time waiting for input/output

Dr. Knight has developed a rather elaborate functional model-algorithm to calculate P (power factor) for any computer system. A report on his use of the model and technology curves appears in *Datamation*, September 1966.[3]

Professor Knight has also done a later study of 93 computers introduced between 1963 and 1967. His conclusion was as follows:

> In conclusion, we find that the tremendous rate of improvement in computing power for fixed cost observed between 1950 and 1962 has continued and possibly slightly accelerated from 1963 through 1966 with the introduction of third generation computers. We also find that the economies of scale predicted by Grosch's Law is supported and that today there appear to be even greater economies of scale, with larger machines providing equivalent computation at much less cost.[4]

The same article points out that the greater economies of scale, *based upon the study*, were, for K^1 constant:

- Commercial computation
    Power = K^1 (Cost)$^{3.1}$
- Scientific computation
    Power = K^1 (Cost)$^{2.5}$

Regardless of how accurate[5] the formulae and models which are developed become, it should be diligently remembered that there are almost always factors which are as important as computing power. Consider, for example, some of the 28 points outlined earlier in this chapter.

Also important, is the fact that in the 1950's it cost a user $1.38 to perform 100,000 multiplications on the IBM 704, whereas, in 1968 it costs 3.5 cents to do the same work on the IBM System/360 Model 75. Companies that are not continually evaluating and taking advantage of improved technology will soon find themselves unable to compete in the market place.

The only point which should be perfectly clear and understood is that there is a lot more to choosing computing systems than just internal power comparisons. Included among these other factors are: input/output speeds and overlapping with internal processing, operating system features and overhead, and simplicity of use.

---

[3]Kenneth E. Knight, "Changes in Computer Performance," *Datamation*, September 1966, pp. 40–54.

[4]Kenneth E. Knight, "Computer Performance 1963–1967," *Datamation*, January 1968, p. 35 (Copyrighted by F. D. Thompson Publications, Inc., Greenwich, Conn.).

[5]For interesting commentary on Dr. Knight's study and computer rating in general, see *Datamation*, May 1968, "Letters to the Editor," p. 11.

Software in the hardware selection process

Several of the 28 hardware evaluation checkpoints shown earlier in this chapter had to do with considerations involving software and ready-made application programs. Software, in particular, has become extremely important in the overall equipment evaluation process. Items referred to as software include: programming systems; operating systems; real-time monitors; input/output control systems; utility programs; sort and merge programs; information retrieval systems; and numerous other *generalized programs* (all of these are programs) that facilitate more economical use of the hardware. Application packages are not included in the author's definition of software.

In many hardware appraisals, *software is the crucial evaluation factor*. In fact, the author is familiar with several cases in which good software has compensated for hardware that was just average . . . resulting in the actual selection of "average" hardware that came with superior software. The competing hardware in some of these cases was actually superior, but its software was just average. Costs for hardware were about the same, in most of these cases.

In the early days of computing, there was very little software about which to be concerned. Today, however, there is a vast array of software that a hardware customer has access to through his equipment supplier. And there are also many companies, independent software firms, and software brokers in the business of producing and marketing a variety of software systems.

Software selection per se, is beyond the scope of this book. However, managers may find the following checklists of value in overseeing the selection process. The intent of this discussion makes it necessary to confine the explanation to a simple enumeration of key points.

PROGRAMMING SYSTEM EVALUATION

Criteria used to evaluate programming systems, such as COBOL, FORTRAN, PL/I, ALGOL, Assembler, etc., include:

- *Power* in terms of features and ease with which complex operations can be coded.
- *Object Time Efficiency* which measures the time difference during program *execution*, as related to a program written in another language, e.g., COBOL vs. Assembler.
- *Overhead* related to amount of memory used relative to code produced by another language, e.g., COBOL vs. Assembler.
- *Programming Cost* for one language compared to another for identical program requirements. Cost includes programmer and computer time for compilations and tests.
- *Compile Time* measures time required to "translate" source code into object code. Usually viewed relative to another language.
- *Documentation* as an indication as to how well the source code can be understood by programmers, and inherent or self-documenting features.
- *Diagnostic Aids* to assist programmers in debugging.
- *Ease of Learning* or training requirements.
- *Compatability* with other equipment and software, e.g., another hardware manufacturer's COBOL compiler.
- *Telecommunications System Suitablity* related to device handling, line control, error processing features, re-entrant coding capability, bit manipulation instructions, and others.
- *Data Base Management Facilities* in terms of multiple index creation, list processing, information retrieval functions, and others.
- *Availability* related to when the EDP hardware manufacturer or software house will have the language ready for use. Also, schedules for implementing various features or improvements and new language levels.
- *Reliability* related to user experience with a particular compiler, i.e., how well does it work and how many serious bugs have been experienced.

Points such as those listed above are often used to compare programming systems on a feature-by-feature basis.

OPERATING SYSTEM EVALUATION

Many criteria can be used to evaluate and compare operating systems. The evaluation points shown below are of major importance with respect to evaluating this kind of software:

- *Functional Characteristics* as related to what the system will or will not do, and to some extent how the operating system carries out certain functions.
- *Input/Output Devices Supported* and in what programming languages.
- *Data Management Methods* that may be used with specific programming languages and for specific input/output devices, such as sequential, indexed sequential, and direct access file organization methods. (See previous section.)
- *Main Storage Overhead* is the cost of main memory that must always be occupied by part of the operating system at all times during system operation.
- *System Residence Overhead* which is the cost of the input/output device, or portion of it, that is devoted to storing the complete operating system.
- *Function Speed* for specific operating system features, such as switching from one program to another during multiprogramming operations.
- *Programming Languages* supported and level or subset of language that is available.
- *Utility programs* for generalized processing functions.
- *Library Functions* pertaining to the system in cataloging, retrieval, and maintenance of programs it controls.
- *Telecommunications Devices* supported by special programs and telecommunication data management methods. Related to specific programming languages. (See previous section.)
- *Special Features* such as checkpoint and restart; file protection and security controls; job accounting routines; priority scheduling; dynamic storage allocation; device independence; input/output buffering; and many others.
- *Availability Dates* of important features, such as support of certain input/output devices, file management methods, and telecommunications special features.
- *Ease of Use* from both an operator and programmer standpoint.

The brief enumeration above gives a small indication of the many factors involved in judging an operating system. As previously mentioned, software evaluation is beyond the scope of this book. It is a matter which is replete with highly technical considerations which are the proper concern of a software specialist. The guidelines presented, therefore, are those which it was felt would assist managers in fulfilling their responsibilities in this regard.

Computer Time-Sharing Services[6]

Growth in computer time-sharing services has been phenomenal in recent years. So many companies have entered into this business that it has been virtually impossible to keep track of what new and different capabilities each is offering. It was not too long ago that one could say "scientific computing" and let it go at that. Today, however, in addition to scientific computing, services that might go under the heading of time-sharing services include: commercial computing; text editing; data bank information retrieval services; application services such as

---

[6]Usually consists of many telecommunications terminals (typewriter types, teletypes, others) linked to a powerful computer(s) wherein each user, having a terminal, shares in the processing capabilities. Even though in most systems each user gets but a "slice" of computer time every few moments, the computation takes place so rapidly that all users appear to be computing simultaneously. The transmission of data to and from the computer, however, is "buffered" so that it can take place simultaneously.

inventory control, accounts receivable, and payroll for smaller companies; administrative message switching and data collection services; and more.

Bringing up the subject of time-sharing services in connection with equipment selection is done for the reason that such services are being used more and more to supplement the ordinary "in-house" data processing capabilities. Many different kinds of computing requirements can lead to the decision to buy time-sharing services. Engineering and research people find them vitally important and much more practical than using the company's computing facilities. Financial people, project mangers, executives, and even computer programmers (as mentioned in Chapter three) are taking advantage of these services.

EDP managers need to look upon such services as part of the total problem solving capability at their command and bring them to bear where appropriate. Indeed, some larger companies have found the demand so great for time-sharing services that they have implemented the service in-house, on the company's own computers. Several have gained so much expertise in doing this that they have set up a subsidiary company and now offer the service outside the company.

Among the points management needs to consider in evaluating time-sharing services are the following:

1. *Programming languages* offered by the service. Take note of what features are and are not included, as a subset of the language may be what is actually offered.
2. *Programmed subroutines* for various functions such as: statistical and financial analysis, mathematical programming (such as linear programming code), numerical methods packages (such as for differential equations), and others.
3. *Maximum program size* per user. Expressed either in memory locations or in number of source language statement lines.
4. *Maximum number of arrays, matrices,* and amount of memory that can be used to contain them and other data.
5. *Maximum or standard peripheral device storage space* (such as disk storage) per user. Is this for program libraries, data, or both?
6. *Application packages offered* such as PERT, inventory, payroll, etc.
7. *Cost items*
    a. *Terminal rental*—usually a per month flat rate.
    b. *Usage*—may be either wall clock (from hook-up time to sign-off), or actual computer time used, or flat rate, or combination of the preceding. Note that an hour of wall clock time may represent less than a minute of computer use.
    c. *Additional charges or rates*—if capabilities beyond the maximum in points 3, 4 and above are needed.
    d. *Hook-up*—is there a flat rate connection charge each time the computer is called (by phone) to establish connection.
    e. *Transmission and related*—telephone line or toll charges, data set or acoustic coupler rental, basic telephone service flat rate.
8. *Hours "on the air,"* for example, the computer can be called from 8 a.m. to 8 p.m. Monday through Saturday. Find out what holidays it will not be operating.
9. *Contract break provisions and service guarantee* Note that system can be overloaded by too many users thereby giving slower response and perhaps otherwise downgraded service.
10. *Consulting, training, and trouble-shooting* help provided by the service.
11. *Availability,* that is, when can service commence. Note that it may depend upon delivery of telecommunications gear.

: eight : eight : eight :

DIRECTING AND CONTROLLING EDP OPERATIONS

Effectively managing a computer operation of any significant size presents many challenges that are not encountered elsewhere in the installation. Quite a few of these challenges and problems have gone unchecked for long periods of time, to the point where they have become accepted as chronic ills for which there is no cure. As a result, a high percentage of installations find that operations is not only incredibly inefficient, but also that it does not function properly despite the fact that efficiency is sacrificed.

Unabashed by what has been taking place, some EDP managers are now saying "don't worry about it," claiming that so long as management gets what it wants computing costs and efficiency do not much matter. And that is certainly one approach to the problems of operations, ableit if top management knew what computing costs the company on this basis (comparatively) they would be outraged. Whether this kind of thinking will come into vogue remains to be seen.

Management has frequently made the mistake of viewing operations apart from the context of the installation as a whole. This mistake arises from the fact that operations efficiency is closely related to practices in systems and programming. Characteristics of a system and its programs play an important role in controlling the efficiency of operations. For example, the quality of operations documentation produced by programmers is an obvious characteristic. Less obvious, but even more important are things like: (1) checkpoint and restart features that can drastically reduce the cost of rerunning jobs that failed to go to normal completion; (2) programs that help the operator reduce job set-up and take-down time by, for example, closing and rewinding tapes ahead of end-of-job processing or using plain stock paper instead of preprinted forms where practical; (3) programs that aid the operator through the use of meaningful diagnostic messages.

The operations management environment

Operations managers are typically tied up with so many day-to-day crises that very little time is spent on analyzing ways and means to eliminate them permanently. Areas that require this careful study, in order to devise realistic solutions, include:

- *Priorities* for jobs to be run.
- *Scheduling* the workload.
- *Rescheduling* work due to unanticipated critical jobs, rerunning jobs that failed to run properly the first time, and equipment and software failures.
- *Coordination* of job initiation, work-in-process, and job completion procedures.
- *Control* of data, programs, and operations documentation.
- *Operations Work Rules* covering standard procedures.
- *Training* for operators and operations support personnel.
- *Career Advancement and Pay Upgrading* plans for operations personnel to keep turnover reasonable.
- *Operator Requirements and Qualifications* to gain the competence and proficiency needed on the job.
- *Supervision of Work* of all kinds, particularly on every working shift that the computers are in use.
- *Machine Utilization* with respect to accounting for it and also improving efficiency.

Operations success in today's around-the-clock data centers does not happen by chance, but is the result of practical plans and decisive management action. Virtual chaos is assured in the absence of this kind of management action.

A practical look at operations, its people, and its problems shows the unavoidable need for rules and regulations. It is vastly different from systems and programming wherein more permissive guidelines are appropriate. Old-fashioned or hard-line management approaches *do* work for operations . . . they, of course, must be properly implemented. Discipline pertaining to work standards and procedures constitutes the main difference between good and bad EDP operations. Naturally, the non-supervisory personnel in a given situation can make a big difference, but leaving matters to their discretion has turned out to be a "chancy" proposition in the case of operations.

Operators left to their own devices are often disappointing. Equipment that should be running sits idle during 45-minute coffee breaks and hour-long phone calls. The author has witnessed this sort of thing many times with equipment worth over $300 an hour. As a result, all processing falls behind schedule with attendant complaints by dozens of people and the diminished value of information that arrives late.

Computer operations should not be permitted to jeopardize or degrade the usefulness of systems that cost many thousands of dollars to plan and program. Yet, many EDP installations face this reality daily because there has been a general failure to formalize and enforce procedures and work rules. In this chapter a number of significant points along these and other lines will be explored.

DETERMINING OPERATOR REQUIREMENTS

There is no common rule for determining precisely operator requirements, with the possible exception of card punching or similar operations. A number of factors will have to be considered to make a realistic judgment concerning the number of computer operators an installation needs. Among the factors to be considered are:

1. Number of computers to be run.
2. Computer hourly costs.
3. Numbers of shifts and working days.
4. Criticality and nature of the work-load in a particular shift.

5. Job running times.
6. Set-up and take-down time.
7. The operating system features, if one is used.
8. Operator performed functions other than computer operating.

One of the important pieces of information which must be known is the number of computers which will be running during a given work period, for example, a shift. With certain exceptions, one computer rarely takes more than two full-time operators working concurrently. One operator, again with perhaps a few exceptions, can rarely effectively operate more than two computers running concurrently. In operating, it is generally assumed that high efficiency (productive usage time/elapsed time) is desired. A possible exception to this may arise in a real-time system wherein efficiency may be much less important than reliability as in, for example, an air traffic control system.

Operator requirements should be viewed in light of computer hourly costs as well as job characteristics. For example, with a general mix of processing, a minimum of two operators should be used full-time on any equipment worth $100 an hour or more. The justification for this point of view is that it only takes a loss of three minutes or so an hour, in machine time, to pay for having the second operator on hand. While one operator is at the console the other can prepare the next job, assist in set-up and take-down, and keep the equipment operating when the lead operator is away from his post. One might reason that the second operator would be idle part of the time and that this is wasteful—to this one might cite the need for firemen who work on the same basis. That is, the operator is needed *when* he is needed, *not* when he can manage to get the time to attend to the computer. If operator idle-time is experienced in the course of realizing great improvements in efficiency—so what! Too often, one finds myopic managers in EDP who worry about such things, and forget the big picture—the overall justification in benefits to the company.

The *$100 an hour—two operator* notion is a general concept, and it does not follow that $50 always equates to one operator nor that $150 equates to three operators. In point of fact, there are many $50 systems that could easily justify two operators and only a few $150 computers that need three.

When determining the number of computer operators required, as mentioned earlier, the nature of the work becomes of great importance. Suppose that the work consists mainly of short runs, in the neighborhood of five to fifteen minutes each. The operator in this case will probably be able to operate just one computer, especially if extensive set-up is required. Where the work-load is mostly comprised of runs of an hour or more in length, the operator *may* be able to handle two such systems. Certain kinds of processing may require more than one operator, even though the runs are lengthy. The operator, for example, who has to operate a high-speed check reader is kept rather busy in just emptying and loading this device. Jobs which require much handling of card input and output often need attention every few minutes or so.

Modern computing equipment permits multiple programs to be run concurrently on the same computer. This *multiprogramming*, as it is often called, introduces further considerations about the nature of the work. Partly as a result of multiprogramming, more and more computers are using multiple printers, card readers, card punches, high-speed paper document readers, and other devices. So, while basic set-up will always have a time factor, the number of devices attached to the computer which require frequent operator intervention has now become a significant consideration.

Operating systems or monitor systems have gained wide acceptance in recent years for the medium-size computer user, whereas they were formerly only used in connection with larger computers. One of the reasons operating systems are used is to cut down the time for job-to-job transition. An operating system, for example, is typically capable of running one job after another with little operator intervention; a supervisory program has control over this and other functions at all times. Hence, the presence of an operating system on the computer may have an influence on operator requirements. Operating systems, even though they aid the operator, provide for advanced computing capabilities which may necessitate more, not fewer, operators.

Finally, the other functions required of the operator can significantly increase the requirements. For example, if the operator must physically select and transport magnetic tapes, disks, cards, or other data media to the computer area, he may very well find it difficult to keep the computer running efficiently. Some operators are expected to perform reconciliation functions as part of their jobs or to maintain extensive control sheets and operating logs. This too, tends to reduce the time the operator can spend in keeping the computer running. It is nearly always desirable to keep computer idle-time to a minimum, and this is largely a function of operator availability and, also, of careful scheduling.

OPERATOR QUALIFICATIONS

Since, in many companies, operators are selected from personnel currently employed, it might prove useful to review key points in selecting potential computer operators.

Education or the lack of it as a qualification factor for operators has not, in the author's experience, been an important consideration. Whether the man is a high school drop-out or a college drop-out may have a bearing on his potential for other jobs but is irrelevant if the man has shown that he is:

1. *Accurate*—emphasis must be on doing it right the first time.
2. *Thorough on Details*—slip-ups on little things cost plenty.
3. *Capable of Following Instructions*—there are many in today's operations environment.
4. *Conscientious about His Job*—a serious-minded person who believes in the need for work rules is highly desirable. He must be willing to take responsibility for his work.
5. *Able to Learn Simple Tasks Quickly*—and remember them exactly. People who forget as fast as they learn should be avoided.
6. *Reasonably Facile with His Hands*—dropping cards, tapes, disks, etc. wreaks havoc on efficiency. Improper handling of cards and tapes also causes serious difficulties.

If the above criteria can be met, then any other positive attributes can be considered a bonus. For example, if the man is also fast, this is a highly favorable circumstance. The operator who is fast and also accurate and thorough is a rarity—such individuals should be given extra incentives. However, the author has seen truly amazing speed exhibited by a number of operators, but unhappily every third step they completed had to be redone because it was done improperly the first time. This sort of thing costs plenty . . . so-called *fast operators* whose errors can cost hours of computer time must be advised to slow down if that is what it takes to do the job right.

OPERATOR TRAINING

Chapter six discusses operator training in some detail, and it is not the intention to repeat that material here. Instead, training in this section is viewed as it relates to sustaining the successful operation of EDP hardware.

First in importance on the matter of training is to develop a plan. This plan should outline, in detail, what the operator must know to do his job. After this outline has been prepared, the method of acquiring this knowledge can be decided.

The author has found that the most successful training programs included both classroom education and on-the-job training. The classroom training was conducted by systems programming personnel or (in larger installations) the education group within EDP. On-the-job training was accomplished by placing the trainee under the direction of a lead or senior operator.

One training approach began with a two-day orientation class after which each trainee was given to a lead operator for two days to learn *by watching*—the lead operator was given training notes so that he would make special points known to the student. Following this, one day was devoted to letting the student practice on the hardware with test programs designed to simulate actual operating experience. After this *hands-on* training, the student spent his final day in class to review the subject, hear about more advanced topics, get a "pep-talk" by the installation manager, and take a multiple choice type test. Those failing the test "washed-out" of the EDP department. Those passing the test were assigned to positions as junior operators under the direction of a lead operator. From this point their education commenced in the form of *informal* on-the-job training.

The training program above ran for six working days and began on a Monday to allow the following weekend to be used to prepare for the test. The total cost of this training was about $400 per student for a class size of from five to ten.

Smaller installations should solicit the recommendations of their equipment supplier on the matter of operator training. A number of hardware manufacturers will run in-house courses and also provide operator training at their education centers.

One installation known to the author does not have classroom training but does provide for *thorough on-the-job training* and combines this with *reading assignments* that are done partly on company time and partly on the student's own time. In this particular case the EDP manager takes a personal interest in the progress of the training program and formally assigns trainees to specific individuals for understudy.

Training is an extremely important item on the list of things explaining why operations are good or bad. All EDP operations managers should pay close attention to it, to see that it is carried out properly.

SUPERVISION OF OPERATIONS

Supervision is a subject upon which many books and articles have been written. The pointers that are applicable to all kinds of supervision apply to EDP operations. But certain points deserve emphasis with respect to running a data processing operation.

A significant number of problems in many operations centers arise from the fact that supervision simply does not exist . . . *there is none*. To begin a discussion with the good and bad points about supervision is, therefore, presuming too much. If operations in these installations ran well and efficiently, the author would be most pleased to recommend their approach—but this is not the case. In fact, most of these "supervisorless" installations have very serious and costly problems whether they are willing to acknowledge them or not. The situation is so ludicrous that operations management, in some cases, does not even know who was at work, much less what was accomplished. Particularly critical in this regard are second and third shift operations.

Many installations believe that the appointment of a lead operator constitutes supervision. This lead operator usually does all the things he did before his appointment and cannot, as a result, be expected to supervise anything but himself. Meanwhile, management incorrectly assumes that the remainder of the operators are being supervised.

For every four to eight operators on a shift, there should be a full-time supervisor. A lead operator may then be charged with the responsibility for a particular machine, in this situation. The supervisor's role is to see that the jobs are processed in an orderly manner, that work rules are adhered to, and that delays and bottlenecks are minimized. He is also the primary source for answers to technical questions and is supposed to make certain that operators learn from their mistakes.

In the absence of supervision, work is often carried out haphazardly if it is carried out at all; work rules are, in a practical sense, meaningless because there is no enforcement; *and when tie-ups or other problems occur they are left to clear-up "untouched by human hands."*

Beyond the regimen for operations supervision prescribed thus far, a supervisor of routine machine operations must himself be coached on handling the more personal aspects of his job. Motivating machine operators, for example, through encouraging, complimenting, and reward-ing high performance is exceptionally important in building a well run data center. Intelligent supervision and management innovations can also bring about an atmosphere wherein operators take pride in their work and view themselves as skilled craftsmen. Today hardly anyone cares. Operators in most installations are never presented with the incentives and management interest that could make this atmosphere a reality.

Where computers are run by unionized personnel, a whole new set of considerations can be added to what already are the makings of an intricate supervisory situation.

OPEN OR CLOSED SHOP OPERATIONS

The question of open or closed shop operations affects mainly medium-size and larger installations, and it basically involves a decision as to whether or not programmers will be per-mitted to operate the computer systems for program *testing purposes*.[1] Open shop refers to installa-tions where programmers are authorized to run equipment, whereas closed shop operations allow very little or no programmer operating. (Another meaning of the term closed shop is where all programming is done by *EDP department personnel*.)

A number of the arguments both pro and con regarding this subject are valid, but the weight of the evidence points toward the advisability of closed shop operations, i.e., programmers not *regularly* permitted to operate computers.[2]

One reason for considering the open or closed shop question early in the development of the installation is that experienced programmers may or may not know how to operate the com-puter. A prospective programmer for an open shop operation, who has had only closed shop experience, will have the liability of not knowing how to run the equipment for program testing. On the other hand, he may be accomplished at *desk debugging*.

Programmers have been known to turn down job offers principally because an installation had a closed shop policy. There have possibly been cases where the opposite has been true. For programmers who know how to debug on the machine, the computer usually saves them much time and effort. From the standpoint of operations managers, programmers tend to tie-up the equipment excessively on non-production work and they periodically cause scheduling problems because they overstay their allotted time.

Debugging a program on the computer is sometimes the fastest way for a programmer to make a program work. However, in the majority of cases, *console debugging*, as it is sometimes called, is vastly more expensive. Aside from the computer costs, the fact that a programmer is operating equipment is expensive in itself. Closed shop operations, on the other hand, generally keep the programmer at his desk doing what he was paid to do, namely, programming. (This assumes he can get reasonable turnaround from operations.) There also seems to be an overall

---

[1]If unionized operators are used, no other personnel are generally allowed to run equipment anyway, making the question academic.

[2]A closed shop policy has to be earned through good performance. If programmers can depend on operations, they will not be inclined to supplant it.

tendency for the programmer, under closed shop operations, to be more careful and accurate. However, the programmer should not be ignorant about operations problems—his systems should reflect an understanding by making the data center's work easier. Later in this chapter, methods for scheduling program testing that provide operations exposure to programmers will be examined.

From the standpoint of expense and operations control, the trend toward more closed shop operations is destined to continue. The reason for this trend is also tied to the increasing use of higher level programming languages, e.g., COBOL, FORTRAN, etc., wherein the computer becomes much less useful for debugging purposes. Closed shop installations that conduct courses to show programmers *how to debug*, using modern debugging aids, have experienced remarkable productivity improvements.

SYSTEMS PROGRAMMING

The operations management environment today has a direct relationship with systems programming that did not exist in the early days of EDP. Advances in technology have made it necessary to operate the hardware via a software interface—the computer operator and the application programmer deal directly with this software. Between them stands the systems programmer whose job is seeing that the interface (the operating system or monitor) performs properly and efficiently.

Systems programming has traditionally been more closely aligned with applications development than operations. However, the needs have changed quite a bit, to the point where routine operations are now getting much greater emphasis. For this reason, systems programming is organized as an independent department in many EDP installations. In years to come systems programming may eventually end up as a group within operations—a number of EDP managers have considered this possibility and a few have reportedly made the change.

Operations management, in the meantime, has to take steps to see that the services of systems programmers are applied to studying and implementing software that will enable high quality, efficient processing to take place. Beyond this, bugs in software have to be fixed and new features added to provide economy and convenience.

Systems programming and operations interact in still another very important way: *operations training and standards development*. Because systems programmers are the most knowledgeable individuals in the installation on equipment operations, they are usually called upon to provide training programs for operators. And since they are familiar with both operations and applications development, it is logical that they be assigned the responsibility for installation standards—especially those that pertain to both areas.

For all of these reasons and many others, the operations manager and his staff must work out methods to insure that the relationship with systems programming is constructive. Regularly scheduled meetings or briefing sessions between appropriate personnel from each group have been rewarding as means to open communication channels and work out mutually acceptable solutions to problems. Several installations have also designated a coordinator *within* operations to constantly maintain the liaison that is so badly needed.

If these steps are not taken, disharmony between systems programming and operations is inevitable. At this point, systems programming sometimes goes on its way producing impractical or unneeded software, while operations efficiency degenerates and complaints from all quarters begin to build up.

Developing schedules

For a variety of bad reasons, computer operations scheduling is frequently a major shortcoming in many installations. Some installations, including even the larger ones, do not even maintain a list of the work required each day, much less a time schedule to go with it. In far too many installations, the scheduling function is conspicuous by its absence.

It is perhaps difficult to understand how considerable amounts of important work manage to get completed on time, since scheduling is often so poor. In numerous cases the work, in fact, does *not* get completed on time.

The overall scheduling problem involves *priority decisions* and *resource allocation decisions*. Inability to arrive at these decisions on a routine basis, by definition, precludes the ability to prepare worthwhile schedules on a continuing basis.

Establishing Priorities

With the exception of a very limited number of jobs, priority cannot be permanently fixed for a long period of time. This fact introduces a number of difficulties in that priorities must be set on a short interval basis, often less than one day.

Priorities are established on the basis of the overall importance of a particular job, but this criterion does not hold for all cases. For example, payroll preempts all other work all the time. Yet, accounts receivable, which is one of those applications that brings cash into the business, sometimes competes with several other applications. In a data center that does not have much excess capacity, the successful setting of short interval priorities seeks to balance the demand for computer time in a way which tends to be reasonable and at the same time reflects the critical nature of some work.

If this balance is to benefit the installation as a whole, it must consider more than just the problem of the hour. All too frequently the matter of priorities is mishandled because it is oriented almost exclusively to the day-to-day accounting type applications. Under this arrangement it is often difficult to get new programs compiled and tested unless they have obtained a high enough priority from management. If this special treatment is required, then the EDP manager and the operations manager must expect to spend a considerable amount of their time on day-to-day priority matters and will ultimately end up as overpaid machine schedulers who are neglecting more important work.

One is always faced with the question of *what is reasonable* in connection with user service. This depends upon many factors. For instance, if a major computer in an installation has been down for an entire day, service would seem unreasonable to someone who was waiting for a five-minute job to be completed but did not know this. Assuming, however, that all needed equipment has been performing properly, it would not be reasonable to have an individual wait more than one day for a five-minute job.

On the other hand, if an individual needed five hours on the computer and only gave operations a day's notice, this might be understood to be an unreasonable request. The *running time* for a particular job, therefore, will play an important role in establishing *lead time requirements*, and also *priority*. Most computer centers have a mix of long and short jobs. The scheduling of this work load should be done such that some sort of balance is achieved. This could mean that, after the completion of a three-hour job, a number of short jobs be run before the next long job. This kind of practice will go a long way toward maintaining or improving the productivity of a much greater number of people—many of whom are likely to be anxiously awaiting the completion of five- or ten-minute jobs. Of particular significance are highly paid programming personnel whose productivity often depends upon being able to get reasonably good turnaround time on short jobs.

A careful examination of the computer time demands at an installation often shows that sandwiching small jobs between larger ones is a reasonable way to satisfy the requirements of the greatest number of people. On the other hand, many installations schedule long jobs for night processing, where possible, so that the short jobs, needed by many individuals, can be run and results used during normal working hours.

It should be clear that if sufficient machine capacity does not exist to handle the processing demand, no priority or scheduling arrangements can ever be successfully set up to operate on a regular basis. In this event good service can be reinstated either by reducing demand (discontinuing certain processing work), buying additional computing capacity, or improving the efficiency of existing operations. A number of installations that have the problem of excess demand sometimes try with the utmost of frustration to solve it by blaming their problem on low efficiency. The fundamental truth in this case is not found in the superficial statement that "things are not as good as they could be"—for this is obvious. The real question to be answered on "efficiency" is not so much whether it is high or low, but rather, can anyone implement improvements that will be effective in a short enough time span to do anyone any good.

As indicated earlier, priorities pertaining to the short interval scheduling of work depend upon circumstances that are impossible to generalize. Yesterday's events and those of the last ten minutes have a direct bearing on the assignment of priorities. To bring this point into better focus, one might consider the situation where an hour-long job has just been completed, and, due to an abnormal termination, the job has to be rerun. The individual setting priorities might properly reason that this job should be delayed until some other work is completed. However, the circumstances change considerably if the job ended abnormally due to a machine failure. In this case, the job in question will usually be put on just as soon as the equipment is in condition to permit the running of this work. One observes that the reasons for scheduling and rescheduling jobs are all-important considerations when setting priorities.

In a multiprogramming environment, priorities determine the order in which programs will be serviced by the computer. Here, a computer is handling multiple programs concurrently based upon priority. In this way, the more important jobs can gain almost complete control of the system, should they require it. Generally, on-line or real-time processing gets the highest priority rating because *response-time* is frequently a critical factor. The priorities for other jobs in the computer can be set based upon other criteria. For example, some installations give jobs of five minutes or less a higher priority than those from five to ten minutes. And, jobs from ten to fifteen minutes have a lower priority than five- to ten-minute jobs. Some operating systems recognize as many as 16 priority levels.

ALLOCATION OF RESOURCES

Through an examination of each particular job, the required computer components such as tape drives, disk drives, printers, card readers, etc., can be determined. Where possible, the run should be put on the computer which most closely matches the program requirements. While a $200 an hour system may be able to perform the same job as a $40 an hour computer, the more expensive system should be at least five times faster to justify its exclusive use. If one system takes 5 hours to complete the job, whereas a more powerful computer does it in an hour, people have a natural inclination to want their jobs run on the faster computer. In some cases, the results may be needed as soon as possible, dictating that the faster system be used.

Should an installation find that it has the situation described above, i.e., compatible systems with vastly different performance capabilities, resource allocation criteria must be skillfully chosen. For example, a process-bound (as opposed to an input/output bound) job should generally be assigned to the more powerful system. When this is not possible, the running times on the various systems should be compared. Suppose that a five- to ten-minute job on one system takes 25 to 50 minutes on another computer. In an absolute sense, the time difference (20 to 40 minutes) to the user is probably not significant, making the equipment choice relatively unimportant. But consider the situation where a one-hour job takes five hours on another system. Now a four-hour time lapse exists, and this is likely to be significant to the user. Besides this however, there is a much higher probability of machine failure during a five-hour run than on a one-hour run, with the attendant rescheduling problems and user dissatisfaction.

As a general rule, then, longer jobs, with heavy processing requirements, should be put on the more powerful systems. Conversely, shorter jobs, regardless of processing requirements, are more appropriately processed on less powerful systems. This general rule, as one might suspect, assumes that there is a sufficiently diverse demand-mix competing for available resources. If this mix or competition does not exist, then the most economical equipment—for the particular job—is chosen, so long as *acceptable turnaround time* can be achieved.

Most small- and medium-size installations have only very limited resources allocation options either by virtue of having just one computer or by having identical or nearly identical systems.

Larger installations, in particular, have adopted the practice of using *slave computers* in conjunction with larger, more expensive systems. Under this approach, the slave computers perform nearly all of the slower functions, e.g., processing cards, printing, reading paper documents, etc. The more powerful computer works almost exclusively with high-speed media such as magnetic tape, disk, etc.

When the slave computer is used for *pre-processing*, it creates magnetic tapes, disks, etc., which are later used by the larger system. In *post-processing*, the slave uses the high-speed media developed by the more powerful system as input to create printed listings, cards, etc. By adopting this method, the capabilities of the more expensive system are not wasted by performing low-speed input and output functions.

The use of slave computers is not as popular now as it has been in the past, mainly because modern hardware and software is designed to allow multiprogramming. So today, it is more customary to find "slave functions" done, via multiprogramming, on high-performance systems with multiple printers, card readers and punches, and other additional input/output devices. The slave computer advantages, in other words, are achieved by adding input/output devices to a more powerful computer main-frame and processing multiple programs on it.

Scheduling Methods

The scheduling problem in a computer center is not unlike that which is found in an industrial job shop. Computer operations, as in the job shop, can often be characterized as having a number of somewhat different programs (jobs) to be run in a given day. More often than not, the job requirements for computer operations are known well in advance; many of the same jobs are run day after day. From time to time, new production programs will be added while some others may be dropped. Occasionally, jobs are changed as a result of changing needs.

Operations managers sometimes complain that they are constantly involved in turmoil resulting from unreasonable demands for computer time and an ever increasing influx of *rush jobs*, but are unable to adequately defend their position because they cannot account for every minute of computer time *in advance*.

At the very least, a schedule or timetable of work, displayed in easily understood terms, can can be used to show the *planned computer usage*. In this way, the operations manager can say with reasonable confidence *if and when* special and nonscheduled jobs can be done. Questions which concern the priority of scheduled or nonscheduled work can also be discussed and answered intelligently.

Schedules are widely used for the purpose of determining whether work is proceeding at the expected or specified rate. As a means of control, therefore, a timetable of events is an essential

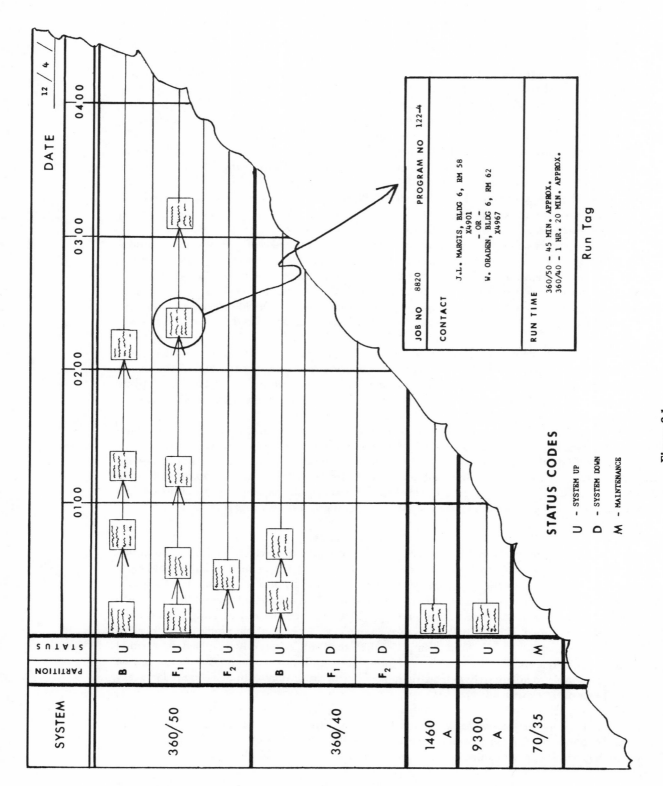

Figure 8.1
Scheduling Board with Magnetic Run Tags

200

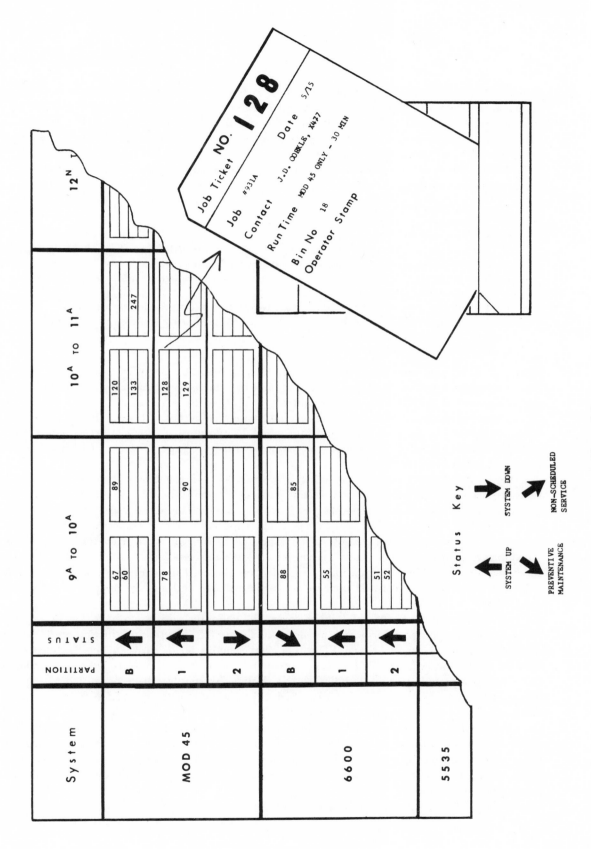

Figure 8.2
Scheduling Board with
Card Inserts

201

tool for managerial decisions. A properly devised scheduling system will show out-of-control situations at a glance. Steps to correct whatever problems may exist can be taken quickly, very often before they would have otherwise become critical. Alternatives to problem situations can also be intelligently reviewed with a good grasp of the overall picture—by having working schedules on-hand to facilitate rapid analysis.

What, then, must the planner know in order to arrive at a schedule? The list below shows the principal ingredients:

1. Job identification.
2. Running time (average, peak).
3. Relative priority (latest status).
4. How often job is run (continuously 10 hours a day Monday through Friday, twice a day, daily, weekly on Fridays, biweekly on Mondays, last day of the month, etc.).
5. The latest time at which the job *must* be complete (consider mainly when reports and other output must be sent out.).
6. List of job steps and input data upon which this run immediately depends.
7. Needed incoming data which is *not* directly controlled by the computer is shown with arrival times (average, latest, average or peak frequency).
8. Hardware required to process the job.

With the above information about each run, the scheduler can begin to lay out a timetable. Those jobs which have the highest priority should be scheduled so that they are completed as far in advance of their deadlines as possible.

Many installations use a magnetic or chalk type display board on which small magnetic pieces of various kinds are used to indicate schedule information. For example, Figure 8.1 is a 24-hour schedule employing *magnetic run tags* containing a paper insert on which indicative information has been recorded.

Figure 8.2 shows a similar scheduling board, except that this board has slots in which *job cards* are placed for each time period. In this particular system, the shift supervisor removes the cards just before a given time period begins. They then become his authorization to carry out the work identified by an *operations control number*. The supervisor or his assistant uses the job card to obtain the necessary data and other items needed to run the work from the *control section*. The job card stays with the job until it is completed—at some installations running time, operator identification, and other information is recorded on the card as work progresses. Eventually these cards are keypunched and used for *job cost distribution* and also for operations *control and analysis reports*.

Schedules running *beyond* the 24-hour period shown on the scheduling boards in Figures 8.1 and 8.2 are recorded on a form such as shown in Figure 8.3. Routine production work can be scheduled-in on a permanent basis. The time that remains open can then be scheduled on a "first-come first-serve" basis—of course, emergencies and higher priority jobs can make it necessary to supersede previously scheduled work, but this should not be permitted to happen often. The individual who had originally scheduled the time must be notified as soon as possible and a good alternate time arranged—which may necessitate other schedule adjustments.

Some individuals find it to their advantage to use strips of paper to represent each run, where the length of the strip is scaled to the running time. By having time frames blocked-out on a piece of paper, the strips can be moved into position and changed as required. When a suitable schedule has been developed by this method, the result can be displayed on a semi-permanent bar-chart.

It should be recognized that consideration must be given to the *equipment maintenance time*,

TIME ON	JOB NO.	CONTACT - PHONE (Date Entered)	TIME ON	JOB NO.	CONTACT - PHONE (Date Entered)
		System	360/30-A		
		RESERVED TIME for	9 /18 /6		
9:00A			3:00P		
9:15A			3:15P		
9:30A			3:30P		
9:45A			3:45P		
10:00A			4:00P		
10:15A			4:15P		
10:30A			4:30P		
10:45A			4:45P		
11:00A			5:00P		
11:15A			5:15P		
11:30A			5:30P		

Figure 8.3
Computer Time Reservation Log

whether it be preventive or nonscheduled. There may also be, as indicated, overriding priorities in handling the scheduled work. For example, critical work may preempt less critical jobs in the case where the computer has been down.

SCHEDULING PROGRAMMER JOBS

Program compilation and testing is another matter that must be appropriately dealt with in the course of computer scheduling activities. Some installations follow the practice of having programmers submit tests on the expectation that the computer center will carry out the work whenever time becomes available. All too often, this method causes much frustration and inefficiency among programmers because time does not become available in a reasonable period . . . and jobs sometimes wait for several days or more before it does. To cure this, some installations simply permit programmers to schedule time as needed. This practice has been successful in some centers and meaningless in others because program testing was often preempted by higher priority jobs.

Several installations with which the author is acquainted successfully managed to avoid or solve this problem by implementing a different approach. Very simply, the method provided an "iron-clad" guarantee of machine time for programmers at three time periods during the day—the only exception was when the computers to be used were down during a time period, in which case there was no reimbursement.

The time periods were signed-over to the programming manager to use as he saw fit. At one data center the designated times (plus or minus 15 minutes) were 8:00 AM to 9:30 AM, 12:00 noon to 1:00 PM, and 3:00 PM to 4:00 PM. The programming manager at the installation allocated the time by simply letting the programmers sign-up on a bulletin board schedule in the programming department. Each programmer could schedule up to 15 minutes during any one of the three time periods—if more time was needed, the programmer could use more if others did not require it. Otherwise the programming manager worked out priorities.

If the computers were found to be idle during any of the three time periods, the operations department phoned the programming department to determine whether they should proceed with regular production work.

In these installations, programmers were permitted in the machine room to look at and otherwise attend to their jobs. At times other than the three time periods, programmers were not permitted in the computer room. It did look inefficient to have programmers hanging around the computer. But the practical fact of the matter was that they did get a great deal accomplished, learned much in the process, got a good feeling for how their job would be handled when it went into production, and as a result, developed an awareness that led them to build-in features for operator convenience and improved operations efficiency.

One installation, with a number of compatible computers, allocated one computer from 8 AM to 3 PM exclusively for program compilation and debugging. These remote shots (programmer not attending) were limited to half an hour or less and were run as received. The time from 3 PM to 8 PM could be scheduled (either remote or hands-on) by programmers for longer jobs.

Most programmers preferred to have the operator run the jobs, giving him assistance as needed, although they had the option to operate the computer themselves if they desired to do so. Besides the daytime test shots, programmers in these installations also submitted compilations and tests for overnight processing.

Regardless of what features are incorporated in the schedules, it is important to remember that scheduling methods must be experimented with to ascertain what buffer time must be allowed for variances. So, it is likely that the first schedule will not be the one finally employed. Some trial and error analysis will be needed.

Work rules

Work rules in an EDP operations center are of fundamental importance to the proper execution of production activities. They are necessary to insure that jobs are carried out in an efficient and orderly manner. As would be expected, such rules are instituted for very practical reasons and must be vigorously enforced.

Each installation must evaluate its own processing requirements to arrive at work rules pertaining to specific application types. However, basic regulations for machine operators and support or clerical personnel can be established for most installations.

Operator Work Rules

Rules pertaining to the activities of computer operators cover their responsibilities in the machine room and those directly connected with machine utilization. First among the basic regulations are those pertaining to the general appearance of the computer area. A well-run data center usually looks boring. A messy machine room is an almost certain indication of careless work habits, and for some strange reason many installations have taken only sporadic action to eliminate this condition. For the uninitiated, it is perhaps easy to assume that personnel would be concerned enough to maintain the machine area in a neat and orderly fashion. As a practical matter, one finds that good housekeeping does not come naturally to many people, thereby making it necessary to establish certain standard practices. Common rules in this area cover:

1. Proper storage of paper, cards, tapes, disk-packs, and other supplies.
2. Proper placement of jobs waiting to be run.

3. Collecting and returning job information and data to the control section after job completion.
4. Regulations on cleanliness in connection with eating and refreshments in the work area.
5. Regulations regarding smoking and the use of ashtrays.
6. Operating practices covering the appearance of equipment and the computer area in general.

Other operator work rules pertain directly to the handling of *work-in-process*. A number of specific rules could be present at a particular data center, and as a general rule they cover items relating to:

1. Accurately recording computer time and logging-in jobs.
2. Specifying the appropriate error code when a machine problem arises.
3. Standard actions to be taken on operating system or input/output control system messages or indicator lights.
4. Emergency procedures.
5. Procedures for job initiation and job completion activities.
6. Recording control information if required, during processing.
7. Care of tapes, disk-packs, cards, and other data media.
8. Care and cleaning of tape drives, paper document readers, and other devices.
9. Console procedures in the event of a machine failure or software malfunction.
10. Placement of identification stickers on data media.
11. Security measures covering file protection, security of printed information and lock-up of confidential data cabinets.

Standards pertaining to the execution of operations activities are considerably easier to establish than enforce. *Enforce* in this context means constant checking and surveillance. Arguments can be advanced that this should not be necessary. But the brutal fact, in many installations, is that rules are given lip-service in the absence of enforcement that entails penalties for offenders.

Penalties take a variety of forms, depending on the installation and particular regulations. In one data center, for example, insurance rates and the local fire department's inspection report on the machine area necessitated a "no smoking" rule in the computer room. Signs were posted and personnel were told—the rule was *not* obeyed. Personnel were then told about the insurance rates, the inspection report, and the importance of the matter was explained—the rule was obeyed for only one day. Next a memorandum was posted on the bulletin board and circulated among operations personnel. Its contents read something like this: *first offense*—verbal warning, *second offense*—written warning and a week off without pay, *third offense*—immediate termination. The net result—*smoking in the computer room ceased*.

Numerous other examples of rules and penalties could be discussed. The point is, however, that reasonable work rules must often be backed-up with appropriate penalties applicable to all personnel involved. Trying to handle these matters on a highly selective, individual basis brings cries of favoritism, etc. from employees—whether justified or not—which work to the detriment of the total operations team.

SUPPORT PERSONNEL WORK RULES

The bulk of the concepts that were discussed for operators apply equally well to support personnel. These individuals perform functions such as controlling incoming jobs, reconcilement of data, storage and gathering of data and programs for jobs, and maintaining data libraries and user contact.

Procedures in the support area generally cover standards relating to the recording of control information, external identification practices, controlling access to data libraries, assembling job information, care of data media, dispatching jobs, forms control, security of proprietary information, and others depending on specific functions performed.

EQUIPMENT AND DATA MEDIA CARE

Operators at most computer installations are responsible for a limited amount of equipment care. Tape drives, for example, require cleaning after six to eight hours of regular use, and a number of installations do it every four hours. Paper document devices, such as those used to read bank checks, require vacuum cleaning and other maintenance attention every few hours of continous use to keep them in good working order. Many installations have devices to scrape and clean magnetic tapes, and some have certification equipment to test tapes for bad spots that affect the reading and writing of data. A tape librarian or an assistant is usually responsible for this.

All of this care of equipment and data media is designed to maintain or improve the productivity of computer operations . . . if it is not done properly and as specified, overall effectiveness declines . . . there are no exceptions.

The author has seen numerous instances wherein the absence of proper care has resulted in serious losses in efficiency. One case comes to mind in which computers with paper document readers attached were rejecting an abnormally high percentage of documents. The rejects had to be keypunched and entered by a special program. Not only were keypunching costs increasing, but the job was delayed to the point where operators and other personnel had to work overtime regularly to finish the job. Aside from the frustration associated with this set of circumstances, the costs were around $5,000 a month more than they should have been. The whole problem was solved by applying 45 man-minutes of work each day to proper cleaning and other maintenance duties.

Recalling the series of events leading to the solution of this problem, here is what happened. The operators were first trained on how to properly care for the equipment. They were given detailed explanations on the devices and then were asked to try it while the instructor watched. In the next few weeks things improved a little, but the problem did not look as though it was going to be solved.

As it turned out some operators were following the rules as specified during instruction, most were not. All of them, it was shown, knew what had to be done, when it had to be done, and how. They simply were neglectful. To cure this, a *sign-off sheet* was put on a clip-board and attached to the side of the document reader at eye-level. Each service time-period was shown and the operator on duty was asked to sign his name and time of day, on the appropriate line, each time he cleaned the device. This very simple remedy brought immediate results and the equipment problem was solved. Apparently, these operators "got the message" when they knew their performance was going to be checked. None of them was inclined to falsify the sign-off sheet, for that was grounds for dismissal.

It is interesting to note that there were a few days, sometime later, during which the sign-off sheet was not posted for some reason. In this period, most of the operators returned immediately to their old, neglectful habits.

Sign-off sheets are successfully used in many installations, although they are not always attached to the machine, for such duties as tape cleaning, job-logging, power-off procedures, close-down procedures, and other activities. They are sometimes designed with a checklist to help remind the responsible individual of the required functions.

Coordination of work flow

Evaluating critical points in computer centers often leads to the conclusion that service provided could be enhanced substantially by establishing better coordination *between the user and operations group*. This means that the user should not have to concern himself with the mechanics of getting a job through the center, but that he can call upon a *coordinator* to expedite work, take care of special arrangements, follow-up on the progress of work, and look out for the user's interests in general. By having a "service representative" of this kind, two major benefits can be gained: (1) A user finds it easier and more effective to deal with a coordinator, (2) operators and other production personnel can concentrate on doing a better job in their specialty areas. The alternative generally amounts to a state-of-affairs wherein the operators and other production personnel try to fill the "coordinator role"—they do this badly because they cannot give it much attention and, in addition, find that their production work suffers because they are unable to devote the appropriate level of effort to it. Keeping today's expensive and high-performance hardware working at peak efficiency is a full-time job for an operator. It demands his careful attention, concentration, and a high degree of skill. *Diluting this in any way reduces productivity.*[3]

MAKING THE COORDINATOR FUNCTION WORK

Coordination can be somewhat difficult to make effective for several reasons. For one thing, the coordinator will typically have authority that is quite limited. He has no authority over the user, of course, and he has a very limited amount of power to bring to bear on operations activities per se.

A coordinator's effectiveness depends upon:

1. How seriously the operations manager views the coordinator function.
2. How well the operations manager has impressed the importance of coordination upon operators and support personnel.
3. A dedication on the part of operations personnel to see that the user's wants and needs are satisfied.
4. The coordinator's ability to deal effectively with a variety of personality types.

Cooperation is an essential ingredient in making the coordinator function perform as desired by operations management. Managers and supervisors at the data center must have attitudes that permit the coordinator to interact and partially direct certain activities even though the coordinator is not endowed with absolute power to do so.

The coordinator, as an individual, must have a definite orientation toward *customer service* type of work. He has to be able to accept the fact that his importance arises from his ability to effectively handle problems that exist through no fault of his own.

Establishing a coordinator function does not mean that it would begin to act effectively right away. This is one of those activities that requires some experimentation to learn how it can be made to work in a specific installation. Each installation will have different kinds of people participating, along with unique problems that pertain to the application jobs as well as general company practices.

COORDINATOR DUTIES AND RESPONSIBILITIES

Data center coordinators can concern themselves with any activity that the installation engages in to get a job completed to a customer's satisfaction. In the course of a day, a coordinator is likely to be in contact with every other group or department in the operations center. For exam-

---

[3]If managers want to vary tasks, job rotation is the answer in this case—not job enlargement.

DATA CENTER OPERATIONS FUNCTIONS

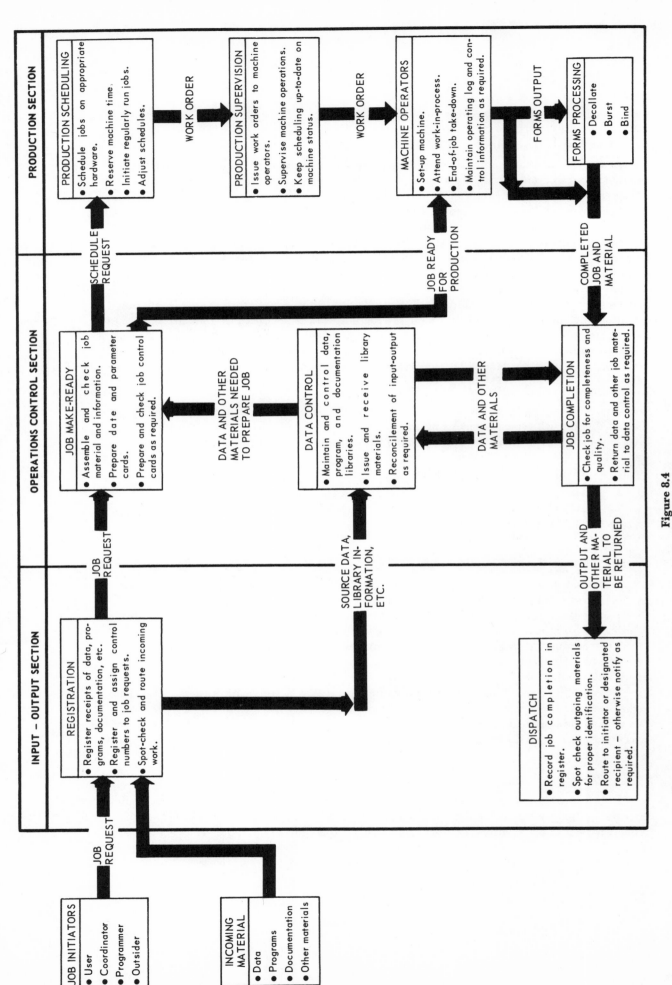

Figure 8.4
Data Center Operations
Work-Flow Diagram

COMPUTER CENTER
WORK REQUEST AND JOB CONTROL FORMAT

DATE/TIME SUBMITTED _____ SHEET ____

DATE/TIME WANTED _____ OF ____

REQUESTOR WILL FILL IN ALL BLOCKS THAT APPLY. ENTER NO. OF PROBLEMS IN SPACE PROVIDED.

PUNCH	1–3	ACCESSION NUMBER	11	12–14	15	16	CO.	LOCATION	ACCOUNT	ORDER NUMBER		40
X	/ / K	0016928				J O B	'					'

	41	REQUESTOR NAME (DO NOT USE PERIODS)	56	57	BLDG. NO.	60	REQUESTOR ADDRESS BUILDING – ROOM NO.	68	69–71	72	73–78	79,80
				'				'	,	C		

PUNCH	1, 2	REQUESTOR TO SPECIFY RERUN REASON BELOW (DO NOT PUNCH)	15	16–22	FOR OPERATIONS USE ONLY	28–39	40
X	/ /			' R E R U N =		' , M S G L E V E L = 1	
						72	79,80

PUNCH	1, 2	JOB STEP NAME	11	12–15	16	17–21	PROCEDURE NAME	22		29	30–36	ESTIMATED MINUTES	40
X	/ /			E X E C		P R O C = K				, T I M E = (		'

NUMBER OF PROBLEMS

EST. SECONDS 43

) 72 79,80

OPERATIONS LOG

K P	KEY PUNCH		START TIME	STOP TIME	ELAPSED MIN.	OPER. STAMP	SHIFT	VERIFY		START TIME	STOP TIME	ELAPSED MIN.	OPER. STAMP	SHIFT
COMPUTER	MACHINE	START	STOP	MINUTES	SHIFT	TYPE	TAPES	PRT	PCH	PROBLEM	OP	DATE	MACHINE	START	STOP	MINUTES	SHIFT	TYPE	TAPES	PRT	PCH	PROBLEM	OP	DATE

PUNCHED AND FILL IN ADDITIONAL INSTRUCTIONS IF USE SINGLE PART FORM ATTACHED SHEETS.

PUNCH	1, 2		11	16	
	/ /				
					72 79,80

PUNCH	1, 2		11	16	
	/ /				

	RUN NO.	VOL	OP CD	SYS UNIT AREA	OPER #	DATE MO. DAY	TIMES SET-UP	START	END	TAKE DOWN	ERR CD	SERIAL NO.	RERUN METER START	STOP	

JOB TICKET and WORK ORDER

RUN # _____ VOL. _____

OP. CD. _____ SYS # _____

OPER. # _____ Ctl # [ ]

INPUT REC'D. _____

D.C. CLERK _____

USE TIME CLOCK

SET-UP _____

START _____

END _____

TAKE DOWN _____

ERR. C.D. _____ SER # _____

RERUN METER START _____ STOP _____

Figure 8.5
Job Request Forms

JOB #	RUN #	HRS. MIN. EST. TIME	PROG./USER NAME	PROG. #	EXT.	FL.	P/D	JOB NAME	LOG #

NYRCC 360 JOB REQUEST

Volume #	Volume Ser.	Label	T r k	D e n s	In	Out	Wk	L b l d	Source	Retention	Disposition

SPECIAL INSTRUCTIONS:

LINES OUTPUT _____

CARDS OUT: ☐ YES ☐ NO

TROUBLE CONTACT _____

PHONE _____

OPERATOR COMMENTS:

Figure 8.5 (cont.)

ple, he will have to deal with machine schedulers, the job set-up group, data control personnel, the data librarian, shift supervisors in charge of machine operation, operators, personnel in the keypunching group, and others.

The coordinator is likely to be in contact with systems programmers and application programmers, in the course of diagnosing systems problems. Troubleshooting activities of all kinds bring a coordinator into contact with various user personnel as well as those at the installation.

Basically, the coordinator's principal responsibility is to see that the user(s) to which he is assigned gets the best possible service from the data center, consistent with demands placed on the installation by other users. Clearly, the coordinator will find it impossible to bring about user satisfaction on a regular basis if adequate computer capacity does not exist or if the installation is poorly managed. Too often the coordinator is bypassed by user and EDP management, resulting in the degradation and ineffectiveness of the coordination function. To avoid this, the coordinator must be given the authority to do his job and must be taken seriously by both sides, otherwise he merely adds to the confusion. If the coordinator is simply to be "window dressing," the best thing to do is not have this function at all.

Operations control

Controlling EDP operations is a subject of many facets . . . far too many to describe in detail here. However, a number of the management controls highlighted in this section are ones wherein significant problems have been experienced. The typical areas of control include: keeping track of jobs entering and leaving the center and monitoring work-in-process, checking the results of the processing for accuracy at various points between the time a job starts and ends, and maintaining production records that can be used to analyze and solve hardware and software problems.

Figure 8.4 shows how work flows through the data center from inception to completion. At each point along the way, control functions of various kinds are performed. Some of these are explored in the following sections and elsewhere in this chapter.

Job Initiation

Jobs can be initiated in a number of ways. Medium-size and larger installations often use job request forms of the type shown in Figure 8.5. Some request forms contain information that the computer operator will need to set-up the job and also provide spaces for *time-stamping*. Other request forms are used simply for identification and control purposes and are accompanied by a *run sheet* or a *run book* that contains operator instructions.

Regardless of what kind of job initiation form is used, it is necessary to maintain some kind of control on work entering the data center, even if it is only a sequential *job number*. Figure 8.6 shows forms used to log-in jobs as they arrive. The basic type of control sheet in Figure 8.7 is attached to run instructions and stays with the job until it has been completed.

Work-In-Process

After a job has been registered and the contents of the specifications briefly reviewed, the job request goes to the person or group that is responsible for making up the job, i.e., gathering the data, programs, and other information that may be needed to carry out the work. The job make-up function directs the work to the appropriate starting point, which in some cases may be the *data control group*, to be discussed later in this chapter. Assuming data control has completed its part of the job and that the data media and program information are assembled, the job moves on to the machine room where the computer operator takes over. When the job is put on the computer, the operator, in many installations, enters various information on a *console log* or *system log* such as those shown in Figures 8.8 and 8.9.

Control Number	Time Received	Customer	Type of Work	Special Instructions	Due Out

Figure 8.6
Operations Work Register

The system log is used for *control purposes* and *performance analysis* as well as for distributing the charges for computer time. On EDP systems using an operating system, job accounting data can be automatically recorded (using the computer's timer) without having the operator write anything. However, unless the automatic job accounting methods are rather elaborate, it is still a good idea to maintain some kind of log. Of particular importance is its information regarding hardware failures, reruns, idle-time, machine set-up time, operator identification, and comments.

Installations that have done away with most of the customary logging procedures, by electing to have an operating system take over certain of these functions, are supplementing operating system information by other means. A number of operations centers, for example, are now using small tape recorders or dictating machines to make it easy for operators to provide exception information. Equipment repair engineers and software specialists have found that operators will describe problem incidents in good detail, using the recorder, thus permitting better diagnoses to be made. Operators also use these recorders to leave trouble messages or job information for operators who will come in on the next shift; and the servicemen do likewise. Some installations prepare typewritten reports from selected information that has been recorded.

Job log information, regardless of where it appears, can be analyzed and statistics can be developed which may indicate problems, especially when the statistics are compared to past performance records.

One of the problems which arises in the use of handwritten logs is that some of the information is recorded inaccurately and does not describe pertinent details. There are various time-stamping and card punching devices which can be of value for accurate time record keeping. But, the manager in charge has to enforce whatever logging system is used in order for it to be of value—this is the weakness which must be dealt with most often.

COMPUTER OPERATIONS CENTER

JOB CONTROL SHEET

Job Control #

Customer_____

Type of Service_____

Work Received_____ _____
                    Date   Time
Received From_____

Record of Work Flow

Section	Processing Time		Time in * 10th of Hours	Cost *
	Start	Finish		
			.	
			.	
			.	
			.	
			.	
			.	
			.	
			.	
			.	
			.	
			.	
			.	
			.	
			.	
			.	
			.	
			.	

*To be completed by Costing Section

Figure 8.7
Operations Control Sheet

COMPUTER USAGE LOG

Date _____ COLS. 1–6

Shift _____ COL. 7

COLS. 8–12 MACHINE CODE					COLS. 13–14 OPERATION CODE	COLS. 15–19 RUN #	COLS. 20–39 RUN NAME	COLS. 40–41 SET-UP	COLS. 42–45 TIME IN	COLS. 46–49 TIME OUT	COLS. 50–53 ELAPSED	COMMENTS	OPER. INITIALS
30	40	Tp	Dk	Oth									

OPERATION CODE

Running
01 Production (Include Set-Up)
02 Idle
03 Demonstration
04 Loan
09 Other

Programming
10 Assembly
11 Test
19 Other

Rerun
20 Data Error
21 Key Punch Error
22 Tabulating Error
23 Clerical Error
24 Operator Error
25 Program Error
26 System Error
29 Other

Maintenance
90 Scheduled Maintenance
91 Unscheduled Maintenance
92 Machine Down Time
99 Other

MACHINE CODE
0 – Not Used
1 – Used
1/O – Enter Number Used

Figure 8.8
Console Log Sheet

214

System Utilization Log

	1	2		3		7						
				YR	MONTH	DAY		YEAR	DAY OF YEAR		WORK DAY	
SYSTEM			DATE									PAGE _____ OF _____

PROGRAM OR RUN IDENT	OP	SET UP START	PROCESS START	PROCESS STOP	METER STOP	NO. OF DR.	APPLICATION OR PROJECT NO.	*	RUN COMMENTS	OPERATOR'S LAST NAME
8 9 10 11 12 13	14 15	16 17 18 19	20 21 22 23	24 25 26 27	28 29 30 31	32 33	35 36 37 38 39	40	41 42 43 44 45 46 47 48 49 50 51 52 53 54 55 56 57 58 59 60 61 62	

Reprinted by permission from MANAGEMENT PLANNING GUIDE FOR A MANUAL OF DATA PROCESSING STANDARDS, © *by International Business Machines Corporation.*

Figure 8.9
System Utilization Log

JOB COMPLETION

When the job being processed has been completed, and at certain steps during the course of running a job, the operator is responsible for carrying out *end-of-job* or take-down functions. Among these are:

- Making the appropriate entries in the operating log.
- Removing file protection rings from newly created magnetic tapes.
- Applying the standard sticker-type label to the proper reels of tape, disks, etc.
- Placing covers on tape reels, disks, etc.
- Properly marking punched card output and printed output with date, job number, and other information.
- Seeing that the run sheet is completed properly and that the job moves on to the next step, and that data, programs, output, etc., are properly returned to the control group or job completion group.

Jobs, other than program tests, that fail to come to completion in the normal manner, for any reason, should be brought to the attention of the floor supervisor. Abnormal job ending may indicate hardware malfunctioning, an application program bug, a software bug, an error on input or output media, or improper operating procedures. It is important for management in the machine room to know what condition caused the problem on production jobs in order to maintain good user service, to avert additional problems, and to render recovery assistance, if indicated.

SYSTEM CONTROLS AND AUDITING WORK-IN-PROCESS

The need for controls in data processing cannot be emphasized enough, since so many of the hardships which have arisen in application processing have resulted from inadequate control.

BATCH NO. ____

DATE ___/___/___

RECEIPT INFORMATION

	TIME RECEIVED	NO. OF REELS
1. Paper Tape Reels:		
1st Group		
2nd Group		
3rd Group		
Last Group		
TOTAL REELS		
2. Correction Cards		
3. RIDE Input Cards		

PRE-PROCESS

JOB NO.	RUN NO.	RUN NAME	MACH.	PROCESS START	PROCESS END	RECORD COUNT	OPER. NO.	COMMENTS
	010	Corrections	360					
	020	RIDE List	1400			N/A		
	030	Paper to Mag	360			N/A		
	040	Accepted Orders	360			N/A		
	045	List Unedit Trans.	360			N/A		
4622	050	RIDE Report	1400			N/A		
	080	Edit Transactions	360					
	090	Linno Report	1400			N/A		
	095	Reseq. Linno	1400			N/A		
	100	Corr.Card List	1400			N/A		

POST-PROCESS

JOB NO.	RUN NO.	INPUT FILE/RUN NAME	COUNT	PROCESS MACH.	PROCESS START	PROCESS END	OUTPUT FILE/RUN NAME	COUNT	COMMENTS
	030	Spec.Handling		360			Spec.Handling List		

Figure 8.10 — Application Control Sheet for Operations

Code	Description	Value	Control/Report
140 & 141	Std.Billing Ctl.	360	Bill Ctl.Debits Bill Ctl.Credits TOTAL BILL CTL.
150	Edited Trans.	360	New Unbill.Ship. Written Summaries Written Unbilled TOTAL MERGED
165	Bal.Fwd.Sum.(Prior) STD Unbill.Ship. *	1400	Bal.Fwd.Summ.Read New Unbill.Read
170	TOTAL MERGED Std.Bill Control	360	New Unbill.B/F New Unbill.To Date Old Bal.Fwd.Read Bill Ctl.Read
180	List Unbill.Pages	1400	N/A

4623

* - Reduce count by 2 errors.

Code	Description	Value	Report
010	Invoices Credits Broker	360	Invoices Credits Broker
030	Reason for Hold	360	Hold Report
050	Shortages	360	Shortage List
070	O/O Errors	360	Error Report
080	O/O Inquiry	360	Inquiry Report

4624

Code	Description	Value
100	Stat.Amt.This Mo. $ Stat.Amt.Last Mo. $ TOTAL STAT. $	360

GRAND TOTAL NIFS $

4625

SUPERVISOR REMARKS:

SHIFT SUPERVISOR SIGNATURE

Figure 8.10
Application Control
Sheet for Operations

Input, output, and processing controls are, for the most part, built into a program at the time it is designed and written. However, it is sometimes an operations control function for the operator to validate certain controls during actual program running.

A control may be maintained on the dollar value of all transactions entering the system. When the transactions are processed, the dollar amount accumulated by each job is checked-back to the original amount. Another kind of control may be what is called a *hash-total*, which is an accumulation of figures such as account numbers, part numbers, etc. The hash-total, verified at each stage of processing, gives reasonable assurance that nothing has been lost. In magnetic tape and disk processing, a count of the records is often kept with the data and is automatically checked by the program.

Whether information is recorded on cards, tape, disk, or other media, there are a number of kinds of identification controls which can be associated with it; for example, a unique number, description, date of creation, the sequence number for multiple sets of information, retention period, totals of various kinds, and other control specifications. It must be emphasized that even the best system of controls is worthless unless steps are taken to see that they are checked and validated.

Figure 8.10 is an example of an *application control sheet* that was designed to audit the processing of a particular series of jobs. The operator (actually an assistant to the lead operator) fills in the required information which in this example includes start-end times, record counts, and dollar control information.

Control figures made available by the system can be recorded either by hand, as in Figure 8.10, or in the form of a computer produced document. If the computer is equipped with a typewriter console, control information may be logged on such a device where it can be referred to readily. During runs or job steps which last an hour or more, it is a good idea to provide audit and control information, periodically throughout the job.

The computer can be used to perform a great deal of control-checking, and other verification if it has been programmed to do so. Action taken by the operator, when an error is indicated, depends upon the specific circumstances. If, however, the operator fails to respond properly or inadvertently ignores error indications, the value of the controls is lost. Therefore, it is not only important to have appropriate controls but, also, to strive to make the responsible individuals alert in doing their part in the overall control function.

As part of a professionally designed system, one finds provisions to audit the operations in phases, whereby errors can be isolated quickly. Many installations have formulated standard practices which are incorporated into most jobs, e.g., record counts, self-checking identification numbers, ledger group dollar totals, and others. Checkpoint and restart capabilities, that permit a job to be started-up at some logical breaking point in case an in-process stoppage occurs, are highly desirable for longer runs. Pointers on good audit practices for the control and detection of *fraudulent* practices are given in Appendix B.

DOWNTIME RECOVERY PROCEDURES

When it is necessary to adopt alternate procedures as a result of the primary EDP system being partially or completely inoperative, it is of the utmost importance to make certain that everyone involved knows exactly what is required of him. In certain computer systems it is possible to switch to another computer or to use other devices in order to capture incoming information. Some computers can be programmed to perform the switching automatically, others require manual intervention by the operator to effect a switchover.

The use of standby equipment is likely to be an infrequent occurrence, and for that reason the procedures involved in recovery and restarting or alternate equipment switching must be practiced from time to time. Some installations make a practice of checking their auxiliary equipment every day. They also conduct periodic review sessions on emergency procedures so that they will not be forgotten.

Information control

Information control, in the context of a computer operations center, is concerned with controlling and monitoring the accuracy and completeness of information processing, controlling the use of data media, managing and controlling the access to information contained in data libraries, maintaining job processing instructions and other documentation, and the security of programs and data.

The set of activities in which the information control group engages differs quite a bit from installation to installation. In one data center this function includes everything short of actually operating equipment. In another installation it can simply comprise a group of people with adding machines who develop input control figures on incoming data sources. This is especially true in businesses that have massive paper-work handling steps prior to computer processing. For these reasons and others, an information control department can be quite large or quite small. Some installations have no information control group at all—the absence of this function, as a formal group, goes a long way toward explaining why many of these centers have operations which are constantly troublesome. In these cases, the function is performed badly if it is performed at all because it has been left to machine operators or general clerks who have not been organized to carry it out properly.

It should be emphasized that the information control function is extremely critical to the sustained well-being of the company's vital data.

DATA CONTROL

Data control in some installations is the name given to all activities which fall under the general heading of information control. This function relates to EDP operations in a way that is similar to the way quality control relates to a manufacturing process. In most cases more effective control is usually experienced when operations and data control are separate functions. Many installations have set these up as separate functions, and each reports to the manager of EDP operations. However, in some installations such as banks, brokerage houses, and insurance companies, data control is often a completely independent department reporting to the manager of data processing or to a similar individual. Some of the responsibilities typically associated with the data control group or department are:

1. External input controls.
2. Internal data controls.
3. Output data controls.
4. Records management.

External controls should be designed to insure that the work entering the data processing department is accurate and meets the standards which have been set-up as part of the system. For example, documents representing transactions may have a batch total slip associated with them. After these documents have been converted into machine readable data and have been processed by the computer, data control runs down the error if the total amount of transactions accumulated by the computer is not the same as the amount on the batch total slip. Another external control function is that of checking to ascertain whether the required information has been provided on the original document.

Internal controls are those which are provided for within the framework of the systems design and often must be recorded and examined by the individual responsible for an application or a period of running time. Internal controls are sometimes referred to as *run-to-run controls*, i.e., they are figures which are developed and checked in successive runs. In this way an audit trail is maintained whereby the point or origin of an error can be quickly detected.

Output controls are those which, as the name implies, often concern data leaving the data center and which are frequently in printed form. In the case of a transaction journal, for example, the total amount of transactions within each classification may be checked against the figures which were developed from the initiating source documents. Spot-checking and auditing of non-financial output also helps to insure its accuracy.

Records management involves the retrieval and storage of data used by the system, regardless of the medium upon which the information is stored. The librarian function, mentioned previously, is included within the data control group and is chiefly concerned with records management. Controlling the flow of information from the library (and into the library) is certainly one of the most important aspects of this work. As information enters and leaves the library, it must be given an external identification and classified as to its destination or origin.

In general, the data control manager will be responsible for carrying out the control specifications which have been developed in the original applications design. He will also recommend and employ additional controls as the need for them becomes evident. Depending upon the size of the EDP installation and the type of applications processed, the control department may perform a variety of functions. Some of the additional installation support activities *may* include operation scheduling, equipment performance analysis, coordination between departments, and others.

Media Library Control

Input and output media, programs, and various kinds of run documentation should be stored in a room constructed so that it has high resistance to fire, water damage, and dust. The temperature and humidity are also controlled in many such libraries. There are specially designed filing facilities for magnetic tapes, disks and cards in the storage room or library. Since some of the vital records of the business are likely to be stored in the library, it is advisable to appoint an individual to be responsible for it.

A number of medium-size and larger installations have designated that a librarian control the access to information which is contained in the library. Among the duties normally assigned to the librarian are: dispatching data media to operators, maintaining the inventory of data processing supplies, labeling media with external identification, and preparing EDP equipment usage reports.

Installations which do not fully utilize the librarian approach generally permit the operators to remove and replace data in the library. The problems encountered in the course of operating in this manner are, in many ways, similar to those sometimes found in a public library. A few of the common problems involve:

1. Misfiled data.
2. Data removed and not returned.
3. Incorrect data taken.
4. Important information destroyed.
5. Improper external identification.

It is of the utmost importance that all reasonable safeguards be employed to insure that vital company records are not destroyed. Some installations have constructed expensive safe storage rooms but, ironically, expose the data to destruction by not controlling access to it.

The data librarian function also includes, in many installations, the responsibility for maintaining supply records, keeping error statistics on magnetic tape and other media by times used and vendor classification, maintaining a list of retention dates by reel number and releasing available tapes for use, seeing that vital data media are stored in a safe deposit box or at the company's location for vital record storage, and cleaning and recertifying magnetic tapes.

The librarian in some installations is also responsible for ordering data processing supplies. This individual maintains an adequate inventory of preprinted forms, stock forms, cards, disk packs, printer ribbons, and other supplies. Where preprinted forms are involved, no more than six months' supply should be ordered at any one time because such forms are subject to change as a result of new processing requirements, and also because they take up a large amount of storage space. The volume discounts that are available on preprinted forms sometimes tempt people to order too much and, as a result, they find that when changes are necessitated, the savings through volume discount have been "wiped-out" because forms have to be discarded. Magnetic tapes present a few of the same problems except that in this case there are other considerations. If an unknown vendor's tapes are being bought, it is a good idea to buy only a limited number of tapes to find out how well they work. If the results are satisfactory, then it may be desirable to take advantage of a volume discount. In addition, prices on certain kinds of data processing supplies are coming down, and it is not prudent to maintain a great deal of stock which is overpriced.

The most frequently encountered problem in the supply area is that the need has not been properly forecasted. Computer centers with this problem are always in danger of running out of one sort of supply or another and often do. Another major problem area in EDP operations is that some individuals buy supplies on price and price alone. They fail to recognize the importance of having high quality supplies in connection with computer operations. One sometimes finds that installations have bought inferior tapes at only a slight discount and have ended up having to pay many times more when those tapes fail to perform properly—necessitating rerunning of jobs and the expense and inconvenience that arises in having to do so. The same is true for forms, cards, disk packs, printer ribbons, and all other supplies that affect computer operations directly. A $2 price break on a reel of tape that turns out to be inferior may end up costing the computer center thousands of dollars in lost computer time; good tapes may be contaminated, and a great deal of inconvenience is visited upon users as well as operations personnel. Simply put, *be suspicious of cheaply priced supplies—be sure to test them thoroughly prior to regular use.*

JOB DOCUMENTATION

Manuals specifying the operating requirements of a particular computer run can also be considered as elements under the general heading of controls. Since it is necessary for an operator to follow definitive instructions in order to produce desired results, a *run book* containing operator instructions is required for reference purposes when running the job and especially in case some error arises in processing. A run book, the contents of which are discussed briefly in Chapter three, which has not been properly prepared is likely to be of little value in any kind of emergency.

It is often the responsibility of the operations control group to see that this documentation is kept up to date with the latest changes arising from program modifications or new procedures pertaining to the job. When operating changes are made, the documentation outlining the new procedures must become part of the run book. *Out-of-date information as well as the lack of it is a source of a potential operations problem.*

It is of significant importance to maintain the usefulness of run documentation by seeing that its preparation follows standard practices and procedures. What happens occasionally is that, after the job has become operational, changes are sloppily done, if they are done at all. As mentioned earlier in this chapter, operations management is in some installations responsible for approving or disapproving the quality and workability of the run information.

To have the ability to recover from a serious fire or other disaster, *documentation control procedures*, in many installations, call for microfilming the latest version of system and program documentation and storing the microfilm in a safe place. Microfilm or duplicate copies should be kept outside the city in which the data center is located. A bank safe-deposit box or the corporation's record storage facility is appropriate.

ON-LINE CONTROLS

Many of the controls found in an on-line program are the same as their counterparts in off-line or batch processing jobs. However, since there is a greater possibility for introducing errors into this system in an on-line environment, additional controls are always provided. Many of these systems require the use of telephone lines for the transmission of data; and there is the possibility that interference or noise on the telephone lines may alter the data between the time it is sent and received.

Data center responsibilities for on-line procedures vary depending on the nature of the application involved. In some cases the operations center is responsible for maintaining error statistics and generally monitoring the operations by checking certain indications periodically. These indications might simply be a printout on the console typewriter of traffic information, malfunction data, and other information used to track or verify the correctness of processing.

Most of the controls to be used in an on-line operation are the responsibility of the systems designer, but it is operations that carries out the control function on a day-to-day basis. In order to help eliminate some of the problems which can arise in an on-line environment, there are a number of control features which may be instituted by the systems designer:

1. If a printing terminal is used to transmit and receive during the same transaction, identifying information, such as account number, should be reprinted in the response message.
2. Self-checking identification numbers may be utilized.
3. A combination of two identification characteristics may be used. (For example, account number and day of birth.)
4. All transactions and messages should be logged on a magnetic tape or disk for restart or reference purposes and to be used in off-line updating runs.
5. The time-stamping or sequential numbering of each transaction is a common control method used in on-line systems.

In short, the role that operations plays in controlling on-line computer operations is frequently dictated by the characteristics of the systems design. However, the operations department then has the responsibility for seeing that these and other control features are properly implemented after the job goes into regular production.

OTHER OPERATIONS CONTROL ACTIVITIES

The operations department gets involved in many control activities which directly relate to the effectiveness of computer center operations. One such activity entails the review and approval of operations documentation that is submitted by the systems and programming staff and is to be used by operators for the regular running of the job that goes with it. This kind of control may or may not be a formally established activity, but it is one that is quite important and is often carried out by data center managers. In some installations this approval or disapproval is left solely to the discretion of these managers and is not subject to review. What this means is that the operations manager either approves the documentation or rejects it and specifies the reasons why—in which case the programming and systems group reworks it to the satisfaction of operations management.

Security in the data center is also the responsibility of operations management. In this regard some installations have set up sign-in and sign-out procedures for non-operations personnel who find it necessary to be in the data center. These individuals wear visitors badges throughout their stay. Operations personnel wear specially prepared badges that contain their photographs. Many operations centers today simply post a sign on the door that reads *authorized personnel only*. This constitutes little if any security in that almost anyone can enter and leave the room unnoticed and unquestioned.

The security of *proprietary and confidential information* is also a control function of operations management. It is their responsibility, for example, to see that when the payroll is running only authorized persons witness the event. In fact, in some cases the computer room is locked during certain confidential runs like payroll, and all data concerning the particular application is locked when it enters the machine room and locked when it leaves.

Time usage reporting is another control function and within this general category performance analysis is often done. This kind of control gives operations management the ability to learn whether equipment is performing satisfactorily and whether productive time relates favorably to idle-time or set-up time. Through studying control or performance type reports, managers can initiate courses of action to improve or correct problem situations.

Unauthorized use of data center equipment and facilities is also a potential problem for operations managers. There are known cases of dishonesty in connection with this. Published information on these cases of dishonesty reveals that operators were selling time to outsiders and pocketing the cash. The practice persisted in some cases for quite a long time and usually took place on second or third shift operations. In a number of these cases, operators worked with no supervision and were virtually free to do whatever they wished. Job accounting procedures and general installation controls were so poor in these cases that computer usage could be charged to rerunning of jobs or machine failure, when in fact it was being sold illegally. The auditing function, discussed later in this chapter, can be planned to detect these and other cases of defalcation.

Operations employing an operating system

The use of operating systems has become widespread as a result of advances in computing technology in recent years. Operating systems or monitor systems, as they are sometimes called, are used to increase the effectiveness or utilization of computer resources. Among the common functions that an operating system will perform, if properly instructed, are:

1. Selection and assignment of input and output devices.
2. Selection and loading of programs from a system resident library.
3. Handling the steps necessary to accomplish job-to-job transition in a stacked job environment.
4. Controlling the allocation of memory space.
5. Controlling concurrent operation of multiple programs.
6. Providing all input and output functions.
7. Handling telecommunications devices.
8. Protecting data from being inadvertently destroyed as a result of an operator or program error.

These capabilities, on the one hand, have eased the clerical burden that was formerly associated with equipment operations but have, in the process, introduced a series of other considerations. The operator, like the programmer, must in many cases deal with the operating systems as an *interface* between him and the hardware. As one might suspect, some means of communication must exist in order to have this happen.

A computer operator interacts in a number of ways and in some cases is taking instructions from the operating system. One reason for this is to reduce errors and set-up time in preparing a job for processing on the hardware. The extent to which these benefits are realized depends heavily upon the ability of the operator to understand what the operating system is doing and to be able to, as a result, direct it when unusual conditions arise. For example, a typical operating system will frequently ask questions of the operator, who in turn must be able to interpret the questions and give the appropriate response. Usually, the operator has a number of choices in responding to the operating system.

The philosophy behind an operating system controlled computer is an excellent and workable one, provided that the operator is able to deal with it effectively. Some operating systems are so complex that to run the hardware properly with them would take several full-time "near geniuses." The typical operator however, has no such qualifications and ought not to be required to have them. It is important then, to realize that all operating systems are not the same, nor are they even approximately similar in operating characteristics. An operating system may be an extremely complex and powerful piece of software having many advanced capabilities and many options within it. This introduces the compound problem of selecting from among the choices, and this is not always a simple process. Smaller less sophisticated operating systems, conversely, do not do nearly as much as the more powerful ones and, as a result, are easier to use. In all but the very simplest of operating systems, there are a great many messages that the operator might be required to understand or interpret sometime in the course of running a job. Not all of these come up frequently, but when they do it is important that the operator be able to deal with the situation. A large part of the communication to an operating system takes place through the use of control cards or *job control cards*, as they are called in some systems. The arrangement of these cards and the information contained on them can be quite complex, particularly in the case of a large operating system. It is therefore desirable that the operator not be involved on a regular basis with preparing and arranging these cards. This activity should be carried out by the information control function. Once again, as mentioned earlier, the fact that a *job control language* now exists on the system usually means that the operator will concern himself with it at one time or another.

The extent to which an operator has been trained or has trained himself to deal with minor problems arising through job control card errors or job control language usage will, in many cases, determine whether a job will go on and be processed or has been returned to the control section or person submitting the job in order to get corrective action. It is quite beneficial to have an operator who is able to unscramble things, just a bit, in order to get the job run. However, he should not be expected to do this as a regular activity.

Some operations departments are responsible for restarting or reinitializing a job that has failed to run to completion during processing as a result of a non-application program error. In these cases, it may be necessary for the operator or operations control group to prepare special instructions to the operating system to permit restarting of the job. In addition, personnel in operations find themselves dealing more and more with the systems programming personnel who are setting-up operating procedures and new features for software, providing special purpose programs, and debugging or trouble-shooting software malfunctions. The operations department in many instances is involved with systems programming on these kinds of projects and offers diagnostic explanations. The data center may also specify certain software that it needs to do a better, more effective job.

Operating systems is indeed a subject upon which a great deal of discussion could be provided. Chapter seven offers a short discussion on evaluating such software. It is, however, inappropriate to examine this subject in great detail because so many of the topics contain a number of involved technical questions and considerations. Aside from this, many features and capabilities must be analyzed relevant to the unique problems of a particular installation. Some installations are better equipped than others, as a result of having highly qualified operations personnel, to carry out a successful operation employing a sophisticated operating system. By the same token, installations that are not endowed with the blessing of a highly capable staff often fall into a somewhat different category because they tend to use smaller systems and less complex software. The important point to remember, in managing operations that are concerned with operating systems, is that the computer operator must concentrate more of his attention on the brain work associated with using them and that this has various implications regarding operator qualifications in terms of both level of intelligence and training.

Anticipating auditor exceptions

The audit of computer operations could easily be taken up as an individual chapter or as the subject of an entire book, because auditing encompasses many topics. However, it is the intention here simply to mention a few important points in this regard.

Whether the auditors are internal, or are from a firm retained by the board of directors, all are responsible for checking into the EDP department at one time or another. Now that auditors are becoming more familiar with computing equipment, they can be expected to help correct, by way of their reports to management, a myriad of poor EDP practices. Just to provide some idea as to their areas of interest, the list below shows some major points of concern:

1. Organization of the EDP Department
2. Methods and Procedures Standards
3. Data and Operations Control
4. Programming Documentation
5. Security
6. Physical Plant

On the organization of the EDP department, most auditors agree that it should be separate from those departments it serves. They also, in some companies, prefer to see data control, operations, and programming and systems as separate functions, i.e., one is not subordinate to another.

Regarding standards, the auditors will look for run book information to follow an acceptable standard format; standard symbols; a standards and technical bulletin manual; programming controls; program change and production authorization forms in use; good systems and program testing procedures; and many others.

In connection with data and operations control, the auditors will want to see work schedules; security measures for data and documentation; proper identification of all media and documentation; program change procedures; illustrative diagrams for systems and programs; and more.

Program documentation practices which have been adopted, such as comments in programs and labeling conventions, may concern the auditor. He will look for complete files on every program in use, including authorizations for program changes. The auditor may also be interested in the efficiency of the programming effort and the security and safekeeping of proprietary information and vital data.

Many installations, in an effort to detect unauthorized use of company EDP facilities and information, have a formally established relationship with the internal auditor whereby he conducts routine and surprise audits of processing. He will check that standard operating procedures are being used. In addition, he may have his own set of production programs, some of which he will check against those at the data center. If they are not identical or produce different results with the same data, he undertakes an investigation. Especially for financial applications, the auditor may also have special audit programs (written by him personally or by a non-company programmer) that are run during his audit to provide checks of various kinds. Computer related embezzlement, which is being reported in the news more and more frequently, is certainly another forceful reason to involve the auditor deeply in EDP practices and procedures. Recommendations concerning *fraud control* appear in appendix B.

The physical facilities may come under the scrutiny of the auditor in terms of floor plans and environmental factors such as temperature, humidity, and lighting. Further, the physical storage for data and general appearance of the installation will be of interest to him.

In general, the auditor may usually concern himself with anything which may prove detrimental to the business. He can be a valuable source of knowledge on EDP controls and can often be influential in changing company management's ideas about practices and policies concerning the EDP function.

COST ESTIMATING, ANALYSIS, AND CONTROL FOR EDP

This chapter briefly introduces the subject of EDP cost and related management controls. Decision areas on these financial matters relate to salary considerations, equipment financing, budget preparation, job costing, physical plant, and numerous other activities with financial implications.

Cost information is, of course, essential to EDP management in terms of those control and planning functions which are basically internal to the department. But financial documentation and reporting is also indisputably a common means of communication—the fact that cost reduction and profit improvement data are well understood by top management is of vital importance. When proposals and results can be explained and sold in these financial terms, the advantages make it imperative to do so.

Project costs

One of the important financial activities of managers in data processing is that of estimating or forecasting costs for projects under consideration. Project estimating is not, nor should it be expected to be, a totally scientific endeavor. But it does start with an understanding of the problem, after which experience and basic guidelines are used to develop time and cost estimates.

In setting out to develop a cost plan for a project, there are generally a number of classifications into which costs can be distributed. The elements listed below are those research and developmental expenses which can be considered as *nonrecurring* for a given EDP project:

- Project Management
- Feasibility Study
- Initial Recruitment
- Personnel Training
- Systems Design
- Programming
- Physical Plant

- Pilot and Parallel Tests
- Conversion

Each of the above items could be further refined into separate cost factors. For example, *programming* can involve these costs: specification reviews; flow charting; block diagramming; coding; card punching; desk checking; computer tests and debugging; documentation; and rework.

Obviously, the breakdown of activities can be carried to extremes, wherein the whole purpose of cost forecasting gets lost among the details.

The other type of costs which are involved in the data processing function are what can be termed *recurring costs*. They include:

1. Rental, leasing, pro rata purchase cost of equipment
2. Operating overhead
3. Supplies, forms, cards, etc.
4. Salaries for maintenance programmers
5. Salaries for operators
6. Clerical salaries
7. Operating management salaries
8. Hiring and training costs as a result of turnover.

Figure 9.1 shows a worksheet that has been designed to guide the planner in specifying a project estimate for various nonrecurring and recurring expenses. The data that go into the preparation of this worksheet are developed as a result of studying the details of the project under consideration. Estimating methods discussed elsewhere in this book are used to calculate some of the costs involved. Typically, this kind of worksheet is just one of several key documents in a *cost vs. benefit analysis*. One also finds descriptive information, schedules, and justification data supplied as part of the complete analysis report.

Economic analysis

In the process of economic analysis, it is the ultimate goal to distribute financial and other resources among alternative uses to maximize the return to the company. It should be borne in mind that: "Analysis is no substitute for imagination."[1] Regardless of how profound and well formulated an analysis may be, if the alternatives have not been skillfully chosen, the outcome may be relatively poor.

Very often, data processing economics involves the spending of money to directly reduce costs or to perhaps increase revenue. The analysis, then, will involve a study which may include the following:

1. Projected old system costs compared with new system projected costs.
2. Payback period.
3. Return on investment.

In addition, a number of *alternative proposals* may have to be compared.

The so-called nonrecurring costs or start-up costs should usually be spread over a period of three years or longer. Capital expenditures, such as equipment purchase costs, should also be spread over time to provide a fair and accurate analysis.

ECONOMIC EVALUATION METHODS

A number of approaches may be pursued in economic analysis, depending upon the nature of the project or company practices:

---

[1]Neil E. Harlan, *et al.*, *Managerial Economics* (Homewood: Richard D. Irwin, Inc., 1965), p. 5.

DATA PROCESSING COST ANALYSIS WORKSHEET

JOB DESCRIPTION—		REFERENCE—	
PREPARED BY— DATE		APPROVED BY— DATE	

NONRECURRING EXPENSE ITEMS	HOURS	COST	RECURRING EXPENSE ITEMS	AVERAGE HOURS/DAY	COST
SYSTEMS ANALYSIS			**PERSONNEL**		
1. PROBLEM DEFINITION............			1. EQUIPMENT OPERATORS.........		
2. FEASIBILITY STUDY.............			2. CARD PUNCH OPERATORS........		
3. REQUIREMENTS REVIEWS.........			3. CLERICAL....................		
4. SYSTEMS DESIGN...............			4. MAINTENANCE PROGRAMMERS....		
5. CHANGES & REWORK.............			5.		
TOTALS			TOTALS		
PROGRAMMING			**SUPPLIES**		
1. REQUIREMENTS REVIEWS.........			1. FORMS.....................		
2. BLOCK DIAGRAMMING............			2. CARDS.....................		
3. CODING......................			3.		
4. TESTING & DEBUGGING..........			TOTALS		
5. CHANGES & REWORK.............			**EQUIPMENT**		
TOTALS			1. COMPUTER SYSTEMS...........		
EQUIPMENT USAGE			2. PUNCHED CARD EQUIPMENT......		
1. PROGRAM TESTING..............			3. FORMS MACHINES.............		
2. CARD PUNCHING................			4.		
3. CONVERSION..................			TOTALS		
4.			**OVERHEAD**		
TOTALS			1. NORMAL CHARGE..............		
SUPPLIES			2.		
1. DATA MEDIA USED IN OPERATIONS..			TOTALS		
2. MEDIA USED IN TEST & CONVERSION			**GRAND TOTAL**		
3. CONTROL PANELS & WIRES........					
4.					
TOTALS					
OTHER EXPENSES			**REMARKS—**		
1. MANAGEMENT..................					
2. CLERICAL....................					
3. TRAVEL.....................					
4. LODGING & MEALS..............					
5.					
TOTALS					
OVERHEAD					
1. NORMAL CHARGE..............					
2.					
TOTALS					
GRAND TOTAL					

Figure 9.1
Data Processing Cost
Analysis Worksheet

229

1. *Payoff Period Test.* This method, very simply, is a determination of how long it will take to recover the amount invested to achieve a cost savings or profit improvement. Payoff Period Tests fail to examine the rate of return beyond the recovery period. Although such methods may be useful for "screening" purposes, they are generally considered insufficient to measure investment worth.
2. *Average Rate of Return Method.* The life of the system is generally reflected in this method of investment analysis, although it ignores the time value of money and time patterns of cash flow. For example, spending a dollar today for a 10 per cent return tomorrow is not the same as getting a 10 per cent return nine months later. Yet most Average Rate of Return Methods fail to distinguish between them.

Other methods include: the MAPI (Machinery and Allied Products Institute) System, the Minimum Cost Method, the Year-to-Year Book Approach, and the Discounted Cash Flow Method.

The *Discounted Cash Flow Method* (DCF), which takes into consideration the time value of money, has received much attention and use in recent years. Since a majority of projects involved in data processing are ones wherein the total life is more than one year, this method is appropriate, although relatively complex. Of all the basic methods in use, DCF comes the closest to reality. DCF provides a single figure that reflects *payback period, rate of return, and the time value of money.* It has one minor shortcoming in that the time value of money (interest rate) remains fixed for a given analysis.

Despite the importance of economic analysis, it is beyond the scope of this book to explore the matter more fully. Suffice it to say, however, that it is not a substitute for managerial judgment. Appraising the less tangible benefits of a proposed system is just one such area that calls for judgment.

It should also be well recognized that the economic evaluation and other efforts involved (to make the decision on whether to undertake a project) can be quite costly in themselves; not every project deserves the same kind of scrutiny.

EVALUATING PROPOSAL ECONOMICS

Economic studies in EDP can deceive managers who fail to look behind the resultant numbers. The arithmetic by which an answer was obtained can be 100 per cent correct, but inaccurate data entering into the calculations can, of course, lead to completely incorrect decisions.

Before accepting the conclusion of any economic analysis, management is advised to probe into the basis for *cost data*, in particular. Cost data that are subject to the greatest inaccuracy are those pertaining to: (1) developing the new system (systems analysis and programming), and (2) manpower to support the system when it goes into operation.

In the case of development costs, management should look for some criterion by which their validity can be judged. The experience of other installations (as well as that within the company) can provide initial guidelines. Be careful, however, not to do too much scaling-down. For example, the systems and programming costs to produce a New York State payroll system are not a function of number of employees. Assuming indentical calculations, a system to pay 500 employees costs as much as one to pay 5,000.

Manpower to support the system when it goes into operation is sometimes underestimated for several reasons. The main reasons are simple oversight and over-optimism about the *scope of exceptions* the system will handle automatically. Another reason is that the business requirements are assumed to be static, whereas, in reality, the system will have to conform to a more dynamic environment.

Support manpower includes: (1) systems analyst and programmer effort to maintain and sustain system operation,[2] (2) operator and clerical personnel within EDP, and (3) personnel expense within the user organization associated with the system.

Aside from cost data, per se, the forecasts of various kinds that go into the calculations deserve scrutiny. Forecasts of business growth, for example, usually have a direct correlation to the volume of data that the system must handle. Such forecasts have important implications pertaining to hardware capacity, manpower to support the system, and perhaps office space and machine room facilities.

Budgeting

A budget is a quantitative expression of a plan. Budgets should be viewed in this way to help insure that management will keep an open mind for opportunities to increase profits and effectiveness. Changes in plans are frequently accompanied by budget changes. However, too many managers see the budget, not the plan, as the controlling factor. And it is this kind of thinking that leads to poor decision-making processes in EDP.

When budgets are used to justify, deny, or delay projects, managerial decision responsibility is supplanted. This misapplication of the budget concept permits the real issues and the plan to be swept aside with the common expression, "it's not in my budget."

It is also helpful to recognize that the budget is not an authorization to spend specified amounts of money on particular items. It is management that authorizes spending. Budgets, on the other hand, should be used as part of a financial control system.

There are a number of practices followed in budgeting. Among them are *ask* budgeting, *tell* budgeting, and *variable* budgeting. Ask budgeting basically involves the department manager requesting a specific amount of money, whereas in tell budgeting the manager is allocated a specified amount by his company. Under either of these two schemes, it is generally rather difficult to make changes to meet unforeseen demands.

Under a tell budget there is often a tendency to spend all money allocated, when it is not really necessary. In ask budgeting, overstatements of needs are often made in anticipation of cutbacks. Much gamesmanship is involved in these two approaches. There are also a number of other weaknesses in these two methods, not the least of which is rigidity.

Variable budgeting, it is felt, provides the *responsiveness* to changing times and needs which is a vital attribute, particularly in a competitive market. The factor of variability need not make this kind of budget sloppy. In fact, there is a real opportunity to see that the required funds get to the places where they will do the most good. Of course, the dynamic nature of budgets places a continuing responsibility for project selection and the allocation of funds on management— where it belongs. The responsibilities and challenges, however, are not always attended with the blessings of some managers, as there are risks involved.

Any kind of budget should originate from *plans* which reflect anticipated financial needs. Budget performance, then, is a comparison between forecasted and actual needs. If the plans change either from additions, deletions or alterations, the budgeted amounts may also be expected to change. Clearly, the more the manager knows about the future, the less changes there are likely to be.

Figures 9.2 and 9.3 are other examples of forms that are used to record budget data. Managers will periodically receive comparison reports that show variances between the planned and actual expenditures.

---

[2]It is difficult to estimate what this cost will be. To a large extent it depends on the particular type of system and the quality of its "construction." A figure of from 10 per cent to 25 per cent (per year) of the system's original cost seems reasonable.

CONSOLIDATED BUDGET FORECAST
DEPARTMENTAL INCOME & EXPENSE
DATA PROCESSING

PREPARED BY—	DATE	FOR THE YEAR ENDING—	REVIEWED BY—

ITEM	MONTH											
	1	2	3	4	5	6	7	8	9	10	11	12
INCOME												
1. SALE OF EQUIPMENT TIME....												
2. APPLICATION SERVICES												
3. CONSULTING												
4. PROGRAMMING..............												
5.												
TOTALS												
EXPENSES												
SALARIES												
1. SYSTEMS ANALYSTS.........												
2. PROGRAMMING												
3. OPERATIONS...............												
4. DATA CONTROL.............												
5. MANAGEMENT..............												
6. OVERTIME.................												
7. FRINGE BENEFITS...........												
8.												
TOTALS												
EQUIPMENT												
1. OPERATIONS												
2. DATA CONTROL												
3.												
TOTALS												
SUPPLIES												
1. FORMS & CARDS												
2. TAPES & DISKS												
3.												
TOTALS												
PHYSICAL PLANT												
1. RENT....................												
2. MAINTENANCE.............												
3. LIGHT & HEAT.............												
4.												
TOTALS												
OTHER												
NET TOTALS												

ANNUAL	1ST QUARTER	2ND QUARTER	3RD QUARTER	4TH QUARTER
INCOME				
EXPENSE				
NET				

Figure 9.2
Consolidated Budget Forecast Form

Cost control

As a by-product of budget performance information, there may be specific areas indicated where the actual expenses were considerably more than those anticipated. Where changes in plans have been made, the differences can usually be readily explained; however, in other cases the manager may want to investigate the reasons for the variations. For example, overtime wages which run far in excess of the expected amount are not an uncommon occurrence in programming and EDP operations. As part of the cost control program, therefore, the reasons for the excesses must be determined.

In one case, the operations department overtime for a particular period was well above any normal variance. Some investigation revealed that one piece of equipment was failing to operate correctly which necessitated rerunning a number of jobs. Immediate action was taken to have the appropriate repairs performed.

Unusual increases in the volume of work have also been the cause of extra overtime. Another case in operations revealed that input data was poorly prepared and controlled, so that the computer program had to be restarted much too often. The trouble was traced to the card punching section where it was learned that a number of inexperienced operators were producing the poor quality input data. Still further investigation yielded the fact that employee turnover had been high as a result of low salaries, and that it was impossible to attract experienced help at the salaries offered.

In another situation involving increased overtime and travel expenses for programmers, it was discovered that most of the computer testing had to be done at night because the computer was used for production during the day. A study of the scheduling requirements for the production work led to the rearrangement of production work which permitted testing during regular working hours.

Cost Controls Related to Management Action

Cost controls are, of course, directly connected with other kinds of management controls. The relationship between various kinds of controls must be carefully examined by managers prior to instituting a particular control. In one case known to the author, for example, an EDP manager was rated on machine utilization, i.e., the hours "clocked" on the computer (meter time) as compared with idle time. Failing to convince his manager that this was an inadequate measure of efficiency, the EDP manager simply had extra useless work processed on the computer to make his rating look good. This added computer time was accompanied by larger computer and personnel expenses that were reflected in budget overruns. Controls that "backfire" in this way are not uncommon where superfical management exists.

Short-sightedness of a different kind caused another cost-cutting scheme to backfire. In this case a data center processed numerous poorly programmed, small jobs of dubious value to the company. Together they represented a big drag on computer operations efficiency. By some mysterious process, the manager reasoned that by simply cutting or holding computer costs, efficiency would automatically rise and marginal applications would be dropped because of the increased difficulty in obtaining needed computer time. The end result was disastrous. Efficiency did not improve but instead declined. Marginal application representatives along with other users clamored vociferously for processing time and kept the EDP manager constantly harassed on this matter. After some period of time, not immediately, the manager in desperation reevaluated his method of control and found it lacking in at least two respects. He concluded that his "hold-the-line" policy on computer costs would work only if:

1. It was accompanied by a definitive plan to improve EDP operations efficiency. A series of steps had to be spelled out.

DATA PROCESSING DEP'T.

BUDGET WORKSHEET 19 ___

PEOPLE { Exempt / Non-Exempt / Total

		JAN	FEB	MAR	TOTAL FIRST QTR.	APR	MAY	JUN
003	SALARIES							
004	Overtime							
007	Special Severance Payments							
046	Military Allowance							
050	Layoff Allowance							
055	Termination Allowance							
060	Employee Plans Expense							
065	Pay in Lieu of Vacation - Exempt							
066	Pay in Lieu of Vacation - Non-Exempt							
090	Employee Payroll Taxes							
	RELATED EXPENSE							
131	Printing, Stationery and Office Supplies							
133	Books, Pamphlets and Periodicals							
134	Office Postage							
171	Telephone - Long Distance & Private Line							
172	Telephone - Local							
173	Telegraph and Teletype							
217	Maint. and Repair - Bldgs. & Corp. Equip.							
218	Alterations & Rearrangements - Bldg. & Equip.							
240	New Hire Moving Expense - Taxable							
241	Housing Program Costs - Trsfd Empls - Taxable							
242	Taxable Moving Expenses - Trsfd Employees							
249	Non-Taxable Moving Exp-Trsfd Empls & New Hires							
414	Conferences and Conventions							
415	Business Meals							
416	Entertainment							
418	Traveling - Domestic							
419	Traveling - Foreign							
451	Rent - Space							
453	Rent - Office Machines							
480	Not Otherwise Classified							
483	Attorneys, Consultants & Advisory Services							
484	Clerical Agency Fees							
490	Contributions and Donations							
491	Professional Memberships							
493	Overtime Allowances							
541	Trfd. Costs — UCC - EDP Services							
543	Share of Other Departments							
651	Time Sharing Services							
655	D/P Supplies - Paper & Cards							
656	D/P Supplies - Mag. Tape & Disk							
657	Sup. Rent - Owned Equip. (Dep'n.)							
658	Maintenance - D/P Equip.							
659	Air Conditioning							
660	Operating Power							
661	Extra Shift Lighting							
663	Special Maintenance							
664	Purchased Serv. Bureau Computer Time							
700	Recruiting							
901	Office Equipment							
979	Receipts and Credits - General							
	ALL OTHER EXPENSE							
	TOTAL EXPENSE							
995	Expense Transferred to Others							
	NET EXPENSE							

Figure 9.3

EDP Budget Worksheet

(Courtesy of Union Carbide Corporation)

Unit _____

TOTAL SECOND QTR.		JUL	AUG	SEP	TOTAL THIRD QTR.	OCT	NOV	DEC	TOTAL FOURTH QTR.		TOTAL YEAR
	003									003	
	004									004	
	007									007	
	046									046	
	050									050	
	055									055	
	060									060	
	065									065	
	066									066	
	090									090	
	131									131	
	133									133	
	134									134	
	171									171	
	172									172	
	173									173	
	217									217	
	218									218	
	240									240	
	241									241	
	242									242	
	249									249	
	414									414	
	415									415	
	416									416	
	418									418	
	419									419	
	451									451	
	453									453	
	480									480	
	483									483	
	484									484	
	490									490	
	491									491	
	493									493	
	541									541	
	543									543	
	651									651	
	655									655	
	656									656	
	657									657	
	658									658	
	659									659	
	660									660	
	661									661	
	663									663	
	664									664	
	700									700	
	901									901	
	979									979	
	995									995	

Figure 9.3 (cont.)

2.   Applications of marginal or no value had to be selected individually and removed from the processing work-load.

Naturally, these courses of actions involved much more work than the simple policy statement; however, in this case, the policy would not have produced the desired result without them.

COST REDUCTION

It is impossible to propose a set of steps for a cost control program which will encompass every situation that may appear to need rectification. There is also the consideration of work improvement programs wherein costs, which may not be out of control, can be reduced, or better ways to do the job can be developed. Some of the questions which may be considered concerning the work are:

1.   Why is it needed?
2.   What purpose does it serve?
3.   At what time should it be done?
4.   Where is the best place to do it?
5.   Who can do it best?

In reviewing the various aspects of a process or job for cost reduction, the following items may be involved in the development of a new method:

1.   Extract unnecessary details.
2.   Consolidate details where feasible.
3.   Reorganize work for improved sequence.
4.   Simplify work if practical.
5.   Seek the advice of others.

Many work improvements and cost reductions can usually be made, provided that the employees and especially their managers are given time for this activity. An illustration of why time must be allocated to this end may become more clear in the actual case described below.

One of the senior programmers at a medium-size computer installation had heard about a new sorting routine which was supposed to reduce computer sorting on magnetic tapes by as much as 50 per cent. For over four months he had wanted to look into this matter a little further, but never seemed to have the time. In a three-week period which followed he, for some reason, did not have much regular work to do. During this time he took it upon himself to modify the new tape sort for the needs of his computer center. Some time later the sort was thoroughly tested and put into regular use. The net result: a $500 per week saving of computer time!

Hardware purchase, rental, and leasing considerations

One financial decision that most EDP managers face from time to time involves the several alternative approaches to financing hardware:

- *Outright purchase* of new equipment.
- *Rental* from the original equipment manufacturer.
- *Leasing* from a leasing company or bank, including "purchase and lease-back" agreements.

PURCHASE AND RENTAL

Most hardware manufacturers provide the option to either purchase or rent by the month. If the equipment is rented, there is usually a minimum charge (often based on 176 hours of usage per month) that must be paid regardless of whether the minimum usage is attained. Beyond this minimum, additional usage is offered at a rate that is generally much lower than the minimum use rate. Some hardware rental agreements provide an option to buy at a reduced price in the future.

Rental agreements, as a rule, can be cancelled on 30 or 60 day notice. The charges for service and preventive maintenance are usually included in the basic rental price.

Outright purchase, on the other hand, requires that the buyer sign a contract or maintenance agreement to cover parts, service, and preventive maintenance. Such contracts usually state a specific daily time period during which service will be rendered without additional charge. Should the equipment require service at a time other than that specified, a service call charge is made—although parts are covered in the contract regardless of when they are used.

Purchase prices for computers are typically 45 to 50 times the minimum monthly rental charge. Naturally, a purchased machine can be used 24 hours a day, 7 days a week without having to be concerned about "extra use charges" that would mount up on a rented computer.

Even though less than 25 per cent of all computers are bought outright, it is interesting to note that more than 50 per cent of the computers used by the federal government are purchased. Banks and other financial institutions also have more of a tendency to purchase relative to other industry groups. However, the growth of leasing companies in recent times is resulting in more outright purchases, but such purchases are not being made by the final user.

LEASING

Leasing has become a major factor in the computer industry because it has been able to undercut normal rental prices and offer certain advantages found in rental and also in purchase. Leasing is midway between outright purchases and rental from the original equipment manufacturer. As such, it has attracted a substantial number of users that want these advantages. Leasing contracts are quite varied and frequently negotiated on specified points covering situations unique to a particular installation. Lawyers are always required to check the terms of most leasing agreements.

A leasing contract may have provisions covering price and price differentials; extra use charges; service; cancellation of the lease; upgrading and downgrading of the hardware configuration with particular features specified; and others. One contract with which the author is familiar, for example, provided that the price for the first two years would be equal to the original manufacturer's rental. After two years, the rate would drop by 20 per cent. This particular agreement included service and had a 90 day cancellation notice requirement.

It should be noted that original equipment manufacturers will provide free systems assistance, consultation, training, software support, etc. to the *first user* of new equipment, but have not been anxious to do so for subsequent leasees or owners. At this writing, manufacturers are offering services to non-original users dealing with such leasing companies and used equipment companies.

HARDWARE FINANCING DECISION POINTS

Economic analysis to determine whether it is most advantageous to purchase, rent, or lease, can best be made by using the *Discounted Cash Flow* method, mentioned previously. However, the validity of the conclusion reached depends on a reasonably accurate assessment of a number of factors:

1. *Costs.* Rental, purchase, leasing, maintenance and service. Market conditions will affect these costs. For example, there has been a tendency for purchase prices to decrease and rental to increase—because hardware manufacturers need cash.
2. *Useful Life.* This time period is governed by tax regulations on depreciation. Computers always have a useful life that is much longer than that used for depreciation purposes. But, obsolete hardware (in light of current technology) is more expensive to operate for a given volume of processing.

3. *Utilization*. Projected hours of computer usage for regular and extra use. Note that extra use is obtained at a lower rental cost.
4. *Capacity*. The point at which additional computing power or another computer must be added may play an important role in deciding on financing as well as selecting a particular computer. This relates to the terms of a lease and also to the economics involved in possibly being *locked into* a purchased machine.
5. *Salvage Value*. This can be the "going price" for a particular piece of used hardware in the open market, or the trade-in allowance guaranteed by a particular manufacturer. Demand is greatest for computers that were, at one time, the most popular models—because there is a larger, more receptive market.[3] Obscure machines, on the other hand, have substantially lower prices by proportion, even though they are just as good or even better than popular models.
6. *Alternate Uses of Capital and Interest Rates*. These considerations must be analyzed for a particular business in a particular economic climate.

It should be clear that the financing analysis interacts with the computer selection process as explained in Chapter seven, *Considerations for Evaluating and Selecting EDP Equipment*. The selection process is the first step that is intended to isolate the workable possibilities for equipment. Deciding on a method of financing is the second step.

---

[3]Used equipment brokers deal primarily in the most popular, general purpose machines. Programmers, programs, and backup are more plentiful for this equipment.

: ten : ten : ten :

MANAGEMENT STATES ITS PROBLEM

A number of surveys and studies have been conducted to determine the effectiveness of electronic data processing. The work which has been done in this area has also brought out the principal management problems involved in the EDP effort.

Ultimately, in practically any computer management survey, the general conclusions drawn are remarkably similar. As will be seen shortly in reviewing several important and representative studies, the words used to describe certain symptoms may be somewhat different, but many of the problems and perhaps their solutions are apparently universal.

The author of this book has also conducted interviews with EDP executives and managers concerning major problems. The results will be described toward the end of this chapter. Now, however, the findings of others will be presented.

Computer effectiveness studies

As this book goes into production, the results of yet another computer effectiveness study are being reported. The conclusions of this study match those examined later in this section. *Business Week*, which has for a number of years covered such studies, offers this summary:

> According to the results of a survey of 36 top companies in 13 industries released this week by McKinsey & Co., "From a profit standpoint . . . computer efforts in all but a few exceptional companies are in real, if often unacknowledged, trouble." One startling statistic: Several of the companies polled have computer budgets approaching $100-million a year.
>
> McKinsey's answers to the problem are similar to the conclusions contained in a report it issued in 1963 and one issued in 1966 by Booz, Allen & Hamilton:
>
> —Operating management and top executives must become involved in computer applications.

239

—Computer men should familiarize themselves with the broadest spectrum of the company's activities.[1]

A study team of a large consulting firm spent a year conducting in-depth interviews with managers responsible for various phases of their firm's computer effort. In the 189 interviews which took place in 33 manufacturing companies, the following conclusions and observations were made.

A major problem for management, according to the survey, is planning most effectively for future computer applications.[2]
Coordination of applications planning—the determination what additional activities of the firm will be computerized, what existing computer activities will be improved and how this is to be accomplished and in what sequence—is a major area of concentration for most companies.[3]

Based upon the observations made so far, it is clear that management is becoming more involved with problems of intermediate and long range planning for computerization. Consider this statement in connection with long range planning activities: "All of the 33 firms have either generally defined an ultimate total system concept for their business or are in the process of doing so."[4]

Notice that the plans for developing the total system most probably have not been worked out—only the concept. Perhaps it may sound superficial to say, but the real planning and effort truly *follows* the basic conceptualization phase. Most of these companies are probably five to ten years away from seeing their concepts in action. In fact, this author seriously doubts that they have indeed "generally defined an ultimate total system concept" . . . whatever that is.

"The study team found that a major reason for aggresive computer application was to beat the competition."[5] Top executives in this study were eager to express their feeling that the companies which can use computing most effectively are the ones that will survive. They have realized that, in a large measure, the computer will be used more and more for solving complex management problems as opposed to general accounting functions.

Another interesting finding of the Booz, Allen report revealed that: "In the 33 firms, 23 had assigned the key computer management positions to men with significant experience in their firm's operations."[6]

Simply explained, someone high in the management ranks of these 23 companies realized that the more knowledge the EDP managers had about the company, the better suited their computer applications could be made. The men who actually designed the systems and took on the more technical challenges were no doubt computer specialists. But it was the man who was intimately familiar with the company who *defined* the most important *requirements* of the systems.

A later study,[7] also conducted by Booz, Allen, & Hamilton, reported that, in a study of 108 leading manufacturing companies, only 11 did not have a top computer executive at the corporate level. Annual sales of the companies surveyed ranged from below $50 million to over $10 billion. As a point of interest, this same survey showed that total computing costs averaged 0.56 per cent of sales and had a range of 0.02 per cent to 3.4 per cent. Companies with more than

---

[1]*Business Week*, June 15, 1968, p. 87.
[2]Booz, Allen, & Hamilton (staff), "Computer Usage in the Manufacturing Industry," *Business Automation*, October 1966, p. 53.
[3]*Ibid.*, p. 56.
[4]*Ibid.*, p. 57.
[5]*Ibid.*, p. 54.
[6]*Ibid.*, p. 56.
[7]Neal J. Dean, "The Computer Comes of Age," *Harvard Business Review*, January-February 1968, pp. 83–91.

10 years experience with computers averaged 0.65 per cent of sales. Manufacturers of industrial products spend significantly more on computing (as a percentage of sales) than consumer product firms, according to this survey.

One of the key features of a previously quoted survey was the ranking of the 33 companies on computer effectiveness in areas such as finance, marketing, etc. Significantly, it was learned that: "All but two of the firms surveyed employ a regular evaluation audit, usually on an annual basis. The two not making regular audits were rated 29th and 31st in usage effectiveness."[8] The evaluation audits, as they were called, probably had these three objectives: (1) review performance against plans, (2) seek out and formulate cures for problems, and (3) set new goals. Such audits serve as control devices to keep the effort moving on the right track. However, it is felt that the annual type of audit possibly was more of a grand finale to a series of reviews—perhaps made at intervals of a month or so.

A study performed in 1964 included a survey of 300 top executives who were responsible for the administration of computer centered data processing functions within their firms. Essentially, the questions asked dealt with the profitability or lack of it in computerized operations in these companies. In those cases where business was not too pleased with profitability performance, the executives gave these reasons, in the order of importance:

> Company organization, systems and procedures not studied properly before installation.
> Too much EDP equipment for tasks desired.
> Not enough implementation, by management, of EDP system after installation. [Implementation means proper analytical use of the system.]
> Persons at key points of information system not trained to analyze and act on management reports produced by EDP.
> Equipment oversold by manufacturer as to job that could be accomplished properly.[9]

In the same survey, its author finally states what he feels are some of the chief points in successful computerization. Mr. Kornblum summarizes:

> If one can draw any over-riding conclusion from this entire survey it would seem to be this: A user's resultant profitability when applying EDP is a consequence of his knowledge of his own operations; awareness of present and future information handling needs; corporate ingenuity in tackling specific business problems; and degree of conversance with competing EDP manufacturer's lines.[10]

This survey shows that the business enterprise must be thoroughly understood and that the methods and requirements for various application areas must be analyzed in detail. In addition, the planner must have a good grasp of the future goals or objectives of the company in order to integrate the computer effort in such a way that the requirements of the *future* are receiving due consideration *today*. Mr. Kornblum also touches upon the factor of ingenuity as a prerequisite to success; certainly, the creativity or inventiveness of the staff of one installation as compared with another, is very often immediately evident. This study also indicated that either the wrong computer, or one which was too large or too small, was being used at some of the companies who indicated their discontent. Management, therefore, must see that its EDP staff is capable in the area of hardware evaluation.

Next, one of the most well known computer studies will be discussed. The McKinsey Report,

---

[8]Booz, Allen, & Hamilton (staff), p. 57.
[9]Richard D. Kornblum, "Profit or Loss—EDP Users Survey," *Business Automation*, September 1964, p. 31.
[10]*Ibid.*, p. 32.

as it is called by some people, was designed to determine whether computer operations were paying off for manufacturing industries. Completed by the staff of a consulting firm, the study revealed the foremost factor determining the difference between successful and relatively non-successful computer installations. Gilbert Burck has written the following synopsis of the now famous McKinsey Report.

> By no means have all installations to date been unqualified blessings. In a study of more than 300 installations in twenty-seven major manufacturing companies more than a year ago, McKinsey & Co., the management consultant, found that eighteen of the companies weren't earning enough on computers to cover their investment . . . Overselling was not the problem, though doubtless there was some. The main reason for the trouble seems to be that management, particularly top management, did not give enough study and thought to the potential of computers.
>
> The success stories help explain the failures, and why there are steadily fewer failures. Almost invariably the companies that made the machines pay off put computer operations decisions in the hands of senior managers.[11]

The findings of this study tie in closely with the findings expressed in other reports. Specifically, the most significant factor in determining the success of EDP is the direct involvement and support of top management. Clearly, such support would be manifested in a number of ways, not the least of which is gaining an understanding of the computer and its dynamic uses.

EDP executive ground rules

Business Week, reporting on computing in the world of finance, had the following information in the area of advice to computer executives in banking . . . although the concepts apply elsewhere.

> Charles A. Agemian, an executive vice-president of New York's Chase Manhattan Bank, is a banker with a puckish sense of humor—and some well-aimed barbs for bankers who trip over their computers. Agemian has come up with six laws on "the power of prudent thinking as applied to banking automation." In them, Agemian sounds a warning for banks that rush headlong into the computer race. The warning is simple enough: "A computer may be perfect image-wise, but is it economically feasible?"
>
> Here are Agemian's six laws:
>
> "*He who hesitates is sometimes saved.*" The first computers weren't completely suited to commercial use, Agemian reasons, "and trying to automate with an unsuitable tool is not an activity fraught with success." The problem holds today. "Smaller banks are growing, and are just getting to the point that they could get computer oriented. They should make sure they're not getting into this just to have a computer."
>
> "*Think small and carry a big staff.*" Here Agemian cites two facts of computer life. Chase discovered, he says, that "a small computer was conceptually and electronically no different than a big computer." Similarly, "a small complex clerical operation was structurally no more difficult to automate than a large complex clerical operation—but it is considerably less risky to try."
>
> "*Automation doesn't cut red tape—it perforates it.*" Agemian calls this his "most profound law of prudent thinking." The main thing to remember, he says, is that automation "must be seen in perspective: it's not an end, it's an improvement."
>
> "*One way to make the new automated system cost more than the old is to pioneer the wrong thing.*" Here says Agemian you run into the problem that "too many computer users are still falling in love with the hardware and software: that is, with the fastest tape

---

[11]Gilbert Burck, "The Boundless Age of the Computer (Part One of a Series)," *Fortune*, March 1964, p. 108.

speeds and the jazziest programming language. Microseconds are given more importance than methods, and Cobol (the common computer language) is running a close second to motherhood." Agemian argues: "I believe in pioneering, but I'll pioneer better operating procedures and better management information systems: not better machines and programming languages."

"*Those who lean too far into the future will fall flat on their faces.*" The "negative moral here," says Agemian, "is to beware of sophistication for its own sake. The problem automation planners have is foreseeing when in the future technical achievement and economic feasibility will coincide."

"*My blue sky is not your blue sky.*" Agemian cautions bankers that what is right for one bank isn't necessarily right for another. "You've got to do good stiff research before you move. Don't be too anxious to jump. Don't be overwhelmed by your computer."[12]

Environmental factors

Other EDP executives have cited additional hurdles that must be overcome in order to successfully bring about an operational system. As indicated in Figure 10.1, in many cases 50 per cent or more of the total problem has little to do with EDP per se. Yet, if ignored or handled improperly, these factors can, and very often do, result in systems that are what one might call "technical successes but commercial failures."

One point in illustrating the total problem as shown in Figure 10.1, is to convey the idea that the end product, a successful operational system, must penetrate the layers of indifference, misunderstanding, confusion, and so forth. Tactics employed to do this are varied and sometimes devious. For example, these environmental problems can be dealt with prior to getting into any serious development work, or while it is ongoing, or even after it has been completed. Approaches to solving these problems can be straightforward, full of chicanery, or some of both. Timing, of course, is of paramount importance. The magnitude of these "external forces" varies greatly from company to company . . . in fact, such forces are not always impediments but, instead, might be supportive. Regardless of what these forces ultimately prove to be, it is prudent to initially assume that they are nonsupportive until the contrary is evidenced. And, by all means, one must be sure that an *appraisal* of these items is made at the outset and that a *strategy is developed* for dealing with them. If this is not done, then only 50 per cent of the complete problem may get solved. At 50 per cent, or even 90 per cent for that matter, the application system in EDP turns out to be a flop. Weakness in computer automated applications cannot be remedied by the same kind of magic that keeps some non-computer systems running . . . that is, by unstructured and undefined human interaction.

Management interviews

A series of interviews conducted by the author of this book elicited about the same conclusions as those found in the studies just reviewed. The interviews which are about to be described included several vice-presidents and other managers responsible for various EDP functions. Each individual was either totally responsible for the computer effort in his business or it was a major part of his responsibility.

Rather than unnecessarily complicating the interviews, one simple question was used: "*Please describe the three most important problems and challenges you face as a manager in data processing, considering the long term prospects in this area.*" Below are some of the responses which seem to be typical of not only this sample, but of the vast majority of responses an interviewer would find to such a question.

---

[12]"Banks Open a New Window," *Business Week*, October 17, 1964, p. 156.

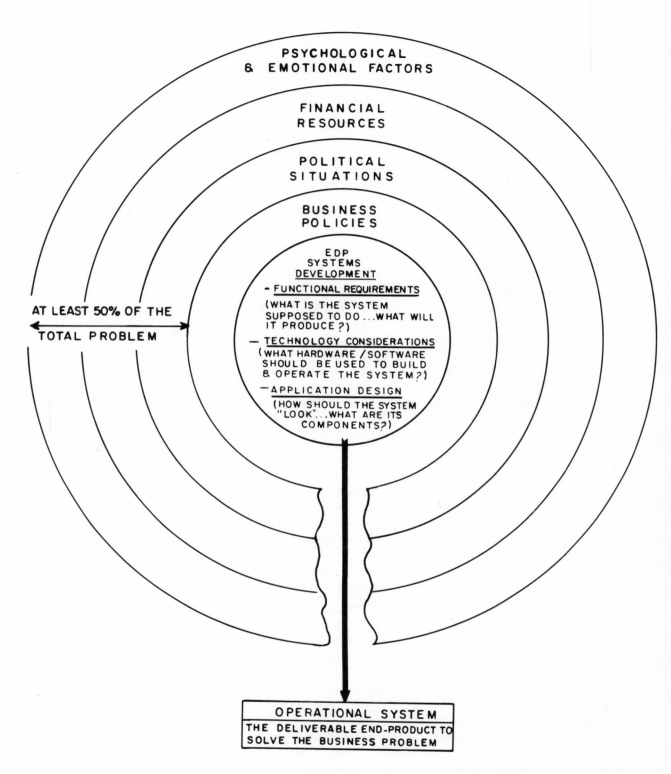

Figure 10.1
Environmental Realities in
Producing an Operational System

One vice-president stated his answer to the question with these three items:

1. Developing new computer applications to improve the management and operation of the business. Planning the information system to cut down the guesswork in decision making. A great creative challenge exists in extending the power of the computer beyond routine accounting functions.
2. Developing the skills within the data processing section to take on new and more creative work.
3. Standardization of routine methods and procedures to see that the right information gets to the right people at the right time.

The EDP manager of a medium-size installation gave the following response to the question:

1. Uninformed top management as to the nature of EDP. The problem may clear up in ten years or so as the more knowledgeable men assume these top posts in the company.
2. Obtaining and keeping qualified and competent data processing personnel.
3. Profitability analysis and justification criteria for new applications.

A programming manager in a larger installation felt that the following three problems were of fundamental importance to him:

1. Planning applications so as to mesh with future needs and advanced techniques.
2. Developing personnel in terms of abilities, experience, and education.
3. Coordination between internal EDP departments [systems programming, operations, etc.] and also between data processing and user departments are key problems.

The computer operations manager in a medium-size installation put his feelings this way:

1. Converting data processing work to newer systems which will handle it more efficiently.
2. Reorganization of management for better control and communications—both upward and downward.
3. Dealing with personnel needs, especially in maintaining incentives and developing people for advanced positions.

Another individual whose primary responsibility is in the area of operations and data control responded by stating the three points below:

1. Selling management on the need for revising policies regarding personnel, salaries, and qualifications.
2. Planning for the acquisitions for new and improved computers.
3. Clean up and standardize controls and documentation.

In expressing his thoughts on the interview question, one corporate officer who is totally responsible for the data processing effort put it this way:

1. The control of the testing and documentation of programs is a major problem. The systems cannot get off the ground if the programs have not been thoroughly tested.
2. Maintaining adequate supervision and staffs. An effort has to be made to pay people what they are worth to the company and to take into consideration competitive salaries being offered.
3. Much education is required to give other departmental managers a good grasp of computer power and limitations.

Another data processing manager gave these answers:

1. Reorganizing the department to get rid of inefficient methods which were introduced by ill-planned systems.
2. Management must focus more of its attention upon planning for advanced applications, especially some of the exotic ones.

3. Trying to keep data processing personnel trained to take advantage of advanced techniques is a significant problem.

A rather interesting response to the question by a programming manager was:

1. Education
2. Education
3. Education

This manager said that the root of most every problem in the data processing department could be traced to inadequate, insufficient, or improper *education*. This was particularly critical, he said, in relation to the involvement of top management.

A vice-president in charge of EDP felt that the points shown below were of primary importance to him:

1. A major problem is reorganizing the data processing staff to deal more effectively with the problems. And to at the same time fill data processing management positions with good people.
2. The rapid growth of computing in the company has also compounded the problem of maintaining control of the activities of each area. Also, the growth has made it increasingly difficult to keep up with technical changes and educational requirements to implement new systems.
3. Preparing plans for the future management systems—five years away. Analyzing current work and needs of the future in terms of systems and physical facilities is another key factor.

One high-level, corporate computer executive, who had a long list of major problems in his desk, selected the following:

1. Developing and/or obtaining top-notch, all around professional managers to take charge of important projects.
2. Building worthwhile systems for the administration and control of EDP projects.
3. Getting someone who is knowledgeable and has the authority to speak for the user . . . someone on the user's staff who will properly coordinate user participation.
4. Much frustration could be eliminated and overall effectiveness could be greatly improved if computer operations ran smoothly. Many challenges exist in this function alone.

A final comment

Many of the so-called problems brought out during this survey were in reality not problems, but symptoms of problems. It is not particularly exciting to find that quite a few of the managers tended to have the same troubles, inasmuch as other surveys have tended to describe such problems in a similar fashion. Furthermore, while this sampling shows a remarkable agreement on the chief problems, some of the respondents may not have been entirely frank. That is, they either were not aware of the fundamental problems or chose not to reveal them. Nevertheless, a great deal can be learned through the careful examination of the answers.

In analyzing the statements, it very definitely appears as though the challenges which face professional managers in the EDP field will not be solved in an orderly way unless some fundamental principles are understood and applied. Upon a more detailed review of these problems it was concluded that far too many managers did not fully grasp the *management* role they were supposed to play in the computer effort. There is strong evidence to suggest that some key managers did not know some of the essential concepts of management. In fact, some of the managers reporting to certain key corporate executives indicated that their bosses never took time to coach them on managing.

Certainly, it is felt that amidst all the problems which have been described in all of the surveys, stands one basic problem which greatly affects the others. The problem is that too many managers do not know what management is all about—and it is not difficult to observe the manifestations of this unhappy situation in the EDP field.

Offering what is felt to be an appropriate conclusion to this chapter, the vice-chairman of an Ohio bank has made the following remarks in connection with the subject of senior management and the automation revolution.

> Unfortunately management is still reacting to things which happened in the past and not to things as they are currently happening . . . These differences [in computer effectiveness] show up in four areas: First, in the quality of leadership that corporate executives provide; secondly, in the planning and control tools that management has built into the computer system programs; third, in the role of operating management; and fourth, in the caliber of the computer system's staff.[13]

---

[13]C. Gordon Jelliffe, "The Need for 'Third Generation' Management Skills," *Bankers Monthly Magazine,* June 15, 1966, p. 34.

EDP Management
Bookshelf Selections

Accounting & the Computer. American Institute of Certified Public Accountants, Inc., New York, 1966, 356 pp.

> *This book is comprised of 26 selected articles from The Journal of Accountancy and Management Services. While the book offers subject treatment in fairly broad prospective, its coverage is excellent. A number of topics deal directly with EDP management considerations: feasibility studies, financial analysis, systems planning, and others.*

Brandon, Dick H., *Management Standards for Data Processing.* D. Van Nostrand Company, Inc., Princeton, New Jersey, 1963, 404pp.

> *Practical guidelines and illustrations are well presented in the area of EDP standards. Although written a number of years ago, most basic concepts and practices discussed still apply and remain of vital importance to the success of EDP installations.*

Computer Management Series: Reprints from Harvard Business Review. Harvard Business Review, Boston, 1967, 137pp.

> *A series of sixteen articles that have appeared in HBR from 1962 up to 1968, of which about a third are of vital importance in connection with managing the EDP function. The remainder deal with application topics and introductory type subject matter. Certain of these articles are definitely required reading for professional EDP managers.*

Controlling the Computer—Management of EDP Problems. American Management Association, Inc., New York, 1967, 64pp.

> *Fourteen separate articles are published in this little booklet. Some pertain to the management of EDP while others deal with its application. Intended more for a layman than a practitioner, the collection is worthwhile reading for both.*

Dearden, John and F. Warren McFarlan, *Management Information Systems: Text and Cases.* Richard D. Irwin, Inc., Homewood, Illinois, 1966, 427pp.

Three distinct sections are provided. The first is 60 pages and deals with management problems of computer information systems. Second, 61 pages discuss PERT, simulation, and information retrieval. The remainder contains 25 "true-to-life" cases that are intended for student analysis. This textbook presupposes that the reader has had an introduction to computing.

Greenwood, Frank and Erwin M. Danzinger, *Computer Systems Analysis: Problems of Education, Selection, and Training.* American Management Association, Inc., New York, 1967, 40pp.

The authors hit the highlights of the topics addressed in this short booklet. Almost half of it is devoted to three appendices, all of which should be of interest to managers. Particularly helpful to installations that are looking for information on systems analyst education.

Horn, Jack, *Computer and Data Processing Dictionary and Guide.* Prentice-Hall, Inc., Englewood Cliffs, New Jersey, 1966, 200pp.

Besides a dictionary that is nicely done, the author provides seven appendices covering diverse topics including systems and programming conventions, names of computer manufacturers, and other industry information.

Lecht, Charles Philip, *The Management of Computer Programming Projects.* American Management Association, Inc., New York, 1967, 224pp.

Details formalized management planning and controls for each phase of a systems development project, from inception through implementation. Acceptance procedures, documentation requirements, and administrative controls are discussed. Many checklists are included as part of this author's structured approach. Of particular value for major projects.

Management Control of Electronic Data Processing. IBM Corporation, White Plains, New York, Manual No. F20–0006, 33pp.

This concise manual was written by Price Waterhouse and Company for IBM. It is written from the vantage point of a CPA's viewing EDP and touches on numerous key management points concerning controls.

Management Information Series: Reprints from Harvard Business Review. Harvard Business Review Reprint Service, Boston, 1967, 119pp.

A series of fourteen articles that have appeared in HBR from 1962 up to 1968. Half of these articles also appear in the Computer Management Series (see the third entry in this bibliography). The remaining seven articles are concerned with applications and other subjects.

Management Planning Guide for Manual of Data Processing Standards. IBM Corporation, White Plains, New York, Manual No. C20–1670, 62pp.

The title of this manufacturer manual is exactly right. A very useful reference, it is packed with a variety of topics. Originally published in the United Kingdom, the translation into American EDP practices has improved its readability.

Miller, Robert W., *Schedule, Cost and Profit Control with PERT.* McGraw-Hill Book Co., New York, 1963, 227pp.

Offers good explanations and coverage on the topic.

Nelson, E. A., *Management Handbook for the Estimation of Computer Programming Costs.* U. S. Department of Commerce—Clearinghouse for Federal Scientific and Technical Information, Springfield, Virginia, Publication No. AD648750, 141pp. (Prepared by Systems Development Corporation in performance of contract with U. S. Air Force Systems Command.)

The Handbook should prove worthwhile as a source of reference information and ideas on planning, organizing and managing the systems development process. A project cycle is viewed as having six distinct activities, each of which is explained together with the factors that impact cost estimates.

Organizing the Data Processing Installation. IBM Corporation, White Plains, New York, Manual No. C20–1622, 62pp.

Two-thirds of this reference booklet contains EDP job descriptions that are for positions that arise in a functional type EDP organization. Information presented is quite useful. Intended to stimulate ideas on EDP organization and management, it should be used for this purpose.

APPENDIX A

Job Descriptions for
Selected EDP Management
and Professional Positions

**Descriptions cover these titles and
alternate titles**

JOB TITLE

Manager of Data Processing

ALTERNATE TITLES

Data Processing Manager, Manager of Information Systems, Director of Management Information Systems, Vice-President—Data Systems, others.

SUMMARY

- Plans, administers, and controls all data processing activities of the company.
- Responsible for providing professional services for feasibility studies, systems analysis and design, hardware and software selection, programming, data center operations.
- Interprets and applies company policies and objectives across all data processing activities.

DUTIES AND RESPONSIBILITIES

The Manager of Data Processing is responsible for all data processing activities at his installation (or in his company). Managing subordinates, reporting to upper management on data processing affairs, and dealing with personnel, administrative, and operations problems are among his duties. This position calls for departmental policy making, financial planning and control activities, equipment selection, and overall organization and planning for departmental functions and needs.

He has overall responsibility for evaluating new technological advances, developing more efficient methods, and developing managerial and technical talent in the staffs. Equipment and personnel evaluations and the control of the various activities under him are included among his responsibilities. He is the chief contact between data processing and those outside the department; in this liaison function he is required to review requests for new applications and determine priorities and the relative merit of proposed computer usage.

He must maintain highly competent staffs to meet the established needs of the business, hire and fire personnel as may be deemed necessary, and administer and formulate salary and personnel requirements as they pertain to his department.

Among the Manager's other responsibilities are seeing that company policy is carried out or complied with, forecasting personnel and financial needs of all activities under him, and keeping abreast of developments that affect the functions performed in each reporting department.

ORGANIZATIONAL RELATIONSHIPS

- *Reports to:* Vice-President—Information Systems, President, Vice-President—Administration, Vice-President—Operations, or other high-level officer
- *Manages:* Manager of Systems Analysis, Manager of Programming, Manager of Data Center Operations, Manager of Systems Programming, Project Managers, Manager of Data Control, Coordinator of Data Processing, Assistant Manager of Data Processing

JOB TITLE

Assistant Manager of Data Processing

ALTERNATE TITLES

Development Control Manager, Technical Assistant, Administrative Assistant.

SUMMARY

- Carries out activities as designated by the Manager of Data Processing and *may* be responsible for Manager's duties in his absence.
- Participates, as the Manager's representative, in analyzing proposals, evaluating systems and programming methods, time and cost estimating, and trouble-shooting installation problems.
- Responsible for performance measurement and reporting, budgetary control, personnel recruitment programs, and long range plans.
- May be in charge of the EDP department's general administrative services.

DUTIES AND RESPONSIBILITIES

The Assistant Manager of Data Processing carries out the functions which have been delegated to him by the Manager. These may include special studies required by the department, investigating new equipment and techniques, and controlling activities in the department according to the instructions of the Manager. He may review application requirements which have been prepared by the systems analysis group, devise methods and procedures improvements, and suggest and implement standards in systems analysis, programming, and operations.

At the direction of the Manager, the Assistant may coordinate activities between various departments. He may also have the responsibility for understanding detailed technical matters regarding equipment, programming, systems analysis. He may administer the budget, perform cost analyses, and present written and verbal reports on technical and administrative subjects.

As required by the Manager of Data Processing, the Assistant Manager may carry out or give assistance in performing certain of the Manager's duties.

ORGANIZATIONAL RELATIONSHIPS

- *Reports to:* Manager of Data Processing
- *Manages:* Depends on particular installation. May supervise all departments within EDP either regularly, or only in the absence of the Manager of Data Processing, or may have no supervisory responsibilities.

JOB TITLE

Coordinator of Data Processing

ALTERNATIVE JOB TITLES

Coordinator Information Systems Services, Data Processing Coordinator, Project Coordinator.

SUMMARY

- Participates in various application project activities, as an advisor and consultant, including systems definition and functional requirements, design, hardware and software selection, evaluating techniques and standards, multi-system interfacing and implementation plans.
- User contact for pulling together data processing resources to see that good service is provided and maintained.
- Trouble-shooter on organizational and technical problems—recommends practices and policies to improve overall service and to remedy specific user–installation problems.

DUTIES AND RESPONSIBILITIES

The Data Processing Coordinator is responsible for seeing that the activities of various departments are smoothly and coherently related (or synchronized). He must insure that specific requirements are met, and that certain projects are expedited to meet target dates. He also functions as an auditor for the entire installation in order to detect problems in management and operations control. His duties include the development and maintenance of standards, the continual improvement of methods and procedures, and the creative analysis of any data processing effort.

He may carry out such duties as may be required by the Manager of Data Processing dealing with areas such as physical planning, equipment evaluation, operating system and language evaluations, and operations control. One of his responsibilities is to see that communications both to and from management are clear and timely. Internal training programs, technical bulletin publication, and other educational programs may be within the scope of his job.

ORGANIZATIONAL RELATIONSHIPS

- *Reports to:* Manager of Data Processing
- *Manages:* In some installations the Coordinator may have the systems programming function and would have systems programmers on his staff.

JOB TITLE

Manager of Data Center Operations

ALTERNATE TITLES

Data Center Manager, Computer Operations Manager, Manager of System Operations and Control.

SUMMARY

- Directly responsible for the optimum utilization (consistent with user needs and priorities) of all computing and associated hardware, maintaining satisfactory service, preparation of production schedules, maintenance of operating logs, hardware and data media performance and usage evaluations and recommendations, and distributing data center costs.
- Accountable for the organization and proper execution of control functions, including: input-output validation, accuracy and quality checks on work performed, security and maintenance of data and program libraries. Establishes and enforces standard practices and procedures for data center functions.
- Reviews and approves (or rejects) operations documentation and recommends systems features to enhance operations effectiveness.
- Specifies physical plant requirements; maintains inventory of data processing supplies; responsible for equipment and data media care and maintenance; trouble-shoots operations center problems.

DUTIES AND RESPONSIBILITIES

The manager of Data Center Operations is responsible for planning, organizing, and controlling the activities within his department. He assigns and schedules such tasks as may be required under the general direction of the Manager of Data Processing. In this capacity, the Manager of Data Center Operations is responsible for reviewing the performance of his men and seeing that installation policies, standards, and documentation requirements have been complied with.

He is responsible for evaluating the performance of his personnel for salary increases and promotion. The training requirements within his group are specified by him, and he may recommend that individuals be hired for his department or removed from it.

The allocation of computing resources and preparation of schedules is carried out under his direction. The Manager is responsible for distribution of machine charges, the analysis of operating statistics to improve utilization, and setting up systems and procedures to insure smooth and orderly production operations. He participates in all decision-making activities relative to hardware selection and is consulted on software considerations.

Working closely with other departments in connection with data and operations control considerations, he may suggest modifications or prepare control specifications for any application or program in the installation. Further, he may assist in the establishment of documentation practices and standards, particularly where they affect operations directly. He is responsible for the maintenance of all operating libraries in the computer center including data media, programs, and documentation records—he is responsible for the security and safety of the libraries and controlling their use.

Among his other duties are seeing that controls on incoming data and output information are verified, validated, and recorded appropriately, and that such information and data is sent to the proper individuals or location. Maintaining the inventory of forms, tapes, disks, and other supplies used in operations is another of the Manager's responsibilities.

ORGANIZATIONAL RELATIONSHIPS

- *Reports to:* Manager of Data Processing
- *Manages:* Supervisors of Operations, Data Control and Libraries, Scheduling, Forms Processing, and Operations Coordination.

JOB TITLE

Manager of Systems Analysis

ALTERNATE JOB TITLES

Manager of Systems Engineering, Systems Design Manager, Manager of Information Systems Planning, Supervisor of Systems Analysis.

SUMMARY

- Directly responsible for activities carried out in connection with feasibility studies, recommending courses of action for systems under consideration, investigating potential new uses for computers in the company, and the preparation of work plans for systems development.
- Directs professional systems analysis staff in functions including problem definition, systems analysis and design, documentation, forms design, preparing program specifications, and design innovations to improve or extend capabilities of existing systems.
- Defines the sub-system breakdown, tasks, and scope of systems to be developed.

DUTIES AND RESPONSIBILITIES

The Manager of Systems Analysis is responsible for the planning and control of activities within his department. He assigns and schedules such tasks as may be required under the general direction of the Manager of Data Processing. In his capacity, the Manager of Systems Analysis is responsible for reviewing the efforts of his men and seeing that installation policies, standards and documentation requirements are complied with.

He is responsible for evaluating the performance of his personnel for salary increases and promotion. The training requirements are specified by him and he has the duty to keep the staff at the most highly skilled level to meet the needs of the installation. He may recommend that individuals be hired for his department or removed from it.

In the performance of system design work, cost analysis, feasibility studies, and designating equipment needs, the Manager of Systems Analysis has the final responsibility for the work prepared by his department. He may also suggest systems and operating changes as various needs may require. Among his duties are management reporting, and policy making as it pertains to his own department. In general he may be looked to for technical and analytical guidance in identifying and solving problems within the functional limits of his department. He has the responsibility to seek out new and improved techniques and other developments for the benefit of the installation as a whole and for his own area.

Organizational Relationships

- *Reports to:* Manager of Data Processing
- *Manages:* Senior Systems Analysts, Systems Analysts, Associate Systems Analysts, Junior Systems Analysts, Forms Design Specialists, and Supervisors.

Job Title

Manager of Programming

Alternate Titles

Programming Manager, Manager of Applications Programming, Supervisor of Programming.

Summary

- Carries direct responsibility for work performed under his direction, including review and acceptance (or rejection) of program specifications, preparing time and cost estimates for programming, participating in hardware and software evaluations, and advising management on programming and related matters.
- Defines and directs professional programming staff functions in developing program logic, coding, testing and debugging, documentation and implementation of the system of programs.
- May initiate and direct system performance appraisals. Recommends, develops, and enforces standard techniques; in charge of maintaining or improving existing programs.

Duties and Responsibilities

The Manager of Programming is responsible for the planning and control of activities within his department. He assigns and schedules programming tasks as may be required under the general direction of the Manager of Data Processing. In this capacity, the Manager of Programming is responsible for the efforts of his men and seeing that installation policies, standards, and documentation requirements are complied with. He is responsible for evaluating the performance of his personnel for salary increases and promotions. The training requirements are specified by him and he has the duty to keep the staff at the highest level of skill to meet the needs of the installation. He may recommend that individuals be hired for his department or removed from it.

In the performance of programming, documentation, and other activities, the Manager of Programming has the final responsibility for the work prepared by his department. He will also be called upon to review system designs and evaluate equipment and programming systems. The development of time and cost estimates, project scheduling and organization, and periodic reports to management are among his duties. Logic reviews and program evaluations are performed by him or his delegates. He is responsible for coordinating the efforts of his group and seeking improved methods for programming and for the installation as a whole. The Manager may set standards and develop certain policies as they pertain to his own department.

ORGANIZATIONAL RELATIONSHIPS

- *Reports to:* Manager of Data Processing
- *Manages:* Senior Programmers, Programmers, Associate Programmers, Junior Programmers, Programmer Trainees, Technical Writers, and Supervisors.

JOB TITLE

Manager of Systems Programming

ALTERNATE TITLES

Software Systems Manager, Software Programming Manager, Systems Programming Manager

SUMMARY

- Primary responsibilities involve the evaluation, modification, development, and implementation of software systems (operating systems, languages, utility programs, generalized input-output control systems, information retrieval access methods, etc.).
- Directs efforts of the professional systems programming staff in carrying out hardware-software studies, standards development activities, technical and management education programs, and application system design quality appraisals.
- Assists operations center staff via developing and implementing software to improve utilization effectiveness. Advises applications development on best approaches to systems design relative to software capabilities and hardware features. Trouble-shoots problems in software-hardware areas.

DUTIES AND RESPONSIBILITIES

The Manager of Systems Programming is responsible for the planning and control of activities within his department. He assigns and schedules such tasks as may be required under the general direction of the Manager of Data Processing. This individual is responsible for reviewing the efforts of the systems programming staff and seeing that installation policies, standards, and documentation requirements are adhered to.

He is responsible for evaluating the performance of his personnel for salary increases and promotion. Training requirements are specified by him and he has the duty to keep the staff at a level of skill which, at minimum, meets installation needs. He may recommend that individuals be hired for his department or removed from it.

In the performance of activities associated with systems programming, the Manager has the final responsibility for providing the installation with the appropriate software and coordinating hardware vendor relationships as they pertain to operating systems, languages, and other general purpose software. The Manager of Systems Programming is responsible for investigating new or improved software that is announced by hardware manufacturers as well as independent software firms. This individual is also responsible for providing in-house training programs for systems development and operations personnel and advising the installation on other matters pertaining to education. In addition he and his staff are expected to work closely with other EDP department groups on problems involving hardware and software.

Among his duties are management reporting and policy making as it pertains to his own department. In general he may be looked to for technical and analytical guidance in identifying and solving problems within the functional limits of his department.

ORGANIZATIONAL RELATIONSHIPS

- *Reports to :* Manager of Data Processing
- *Manages :* Systems Programmers, Senior Systems Programmers, Hardware-Software Consultants, Training Specialist, Standards Analysts.

JOB TITLE

Project Manager

ALTERNATE JOB TITLES

Project Director, Program Manager, Configuration Manager, Project Administrator

SUMMARY

- Usually considered to be in full charge of and responsible for a major application system development effort (sometimes for a group of smaller projects that have common characteristics).
- Plans, organizes, and directs the efforts of a professional staff (and sometimes user representatives) in all activities required to produce a working system, such as determining system functional requirements, systems specifications preparation, work plans, time and cost estimating, systems design and programming, implementation, and certain follow-up efforts.
- Key contact with user and EDP upper management for the project. Coordinates and generally is responsible for bringing appropriate resources (inside and outside of the company) to bear as needed.

DUTIES AND RESPONSIBILITIES

A Project Manager is responsible for the planning, administration, and control of all activities required to produce a working system. Managing subordinates, reporting to EDP and user management on data processing affairs, and bringing together resources needed to carry out the project are among his duties. This individual is also responsible for the organization of his staff, preparing time and cost estimates, and conducting technical reviews of application analysis and design, software, and hardware. He is also charged to see that installation standards and policies are carried out properly.

Operating under general managerial direction, this individual's attention is generally focused upon a major project for which he assembles whatever talent is needed to carry it out.

He is responsible for evaluating the performance of his personnel for salary increases and promotion. Training requirements are specified by him and he is obligated to maintain a highly skilled professional staff consistent with the needs of the project. He may recommend that individuals be hired for his project team or removed from it.

In conducting the project, he is responsible for the quality and results obtained in functions which include systems analysis and design, economic evaluations, programming, and conversion and implementation. A project manager may, in the course of developing a system, be responsible for the selection of outside contractors and administering contracts.

ORGANIZATIONAL RELATIONSHIPS

- *Reports to :* Manager of Data Processing.
- *Manages;* Group Leaders, Systems Consultants, Senior Programmer/Analysts, Programmer/Analysts, Hardware-Software Specialists, User Personnel assigned to the project.

JOB TITLE

Group Leader

ALTERNATE JOB TITLES

Project Leader, Senior Project Analyst, Project Planner, Lead Analyst.

SUMMARY

- Usually responsible for a sub-system within a major project or a smaller system development project. Participates in project definition activities; recommends and proposes ways and means to carry out the project; prepares economic appraisals, work plans, and schedules within area of responsibility.
- Organizes and directs the functional efforts of the professional staff on sub-system development work that includes system studies, systems design, hardware-software recommendations, programming, system testing, and implementation.
- Works to see that sub-system interfacing and coordinated planning come about on the project as a whole. Responsible for maintaining good working relationships with user staff that relates to the sub-system. Frequently is a heavy, if not major, contributor to the sub-system design.

DUTIES AND RESPONSIBILITIES

A Group Leader is responsible for the planning and control of efforts carried out in connection with a small project or sub-system. He works under the general direction of the Project Manager on his assignments and is considered to be technically proficient in systems analysis and design. This individual participates in the definition of application functional requirements, interviewing and fact-finding with the user, and conducting technical evaluations on applied systems and software and hardware. He is an active contributor in systems analysis and design efforts.

An advisor to the Project Manager, a Group Leader engages in considerations affecting the total project, especially on approaches to interfacing sub-systems and developing common data bases or data banks.

He is responsible for preparing work plans and proposals, and reports to project and user management on schedules and progress. A Group Leader directs the functional efforts of a small professional staff and participates in performance appraisals for these individuals.

ORGANIZATIONAL RELATIONSHIPS

- *Reports to:* Project Manager or to functional department manager such as Manager of Systems Analysis.
- *Manages:* Senior Programmer/Analysts, Systems Consultants, Programmer/Analysts, Programmer Assistants, Technical Writers. In most cases this is *functional supervision*—the Project Manager has *administrative* as well as overall functional responsibility.

JOB TITLE

Systems Consultant

ALTERNATE TITLES

Data Processing Consultant, Project Consultant, Information Systems Consultant

SUMMARY

- Provides assistance and recommendations to Project Manager(s) and installation management on certain specialized topics pertaining to applied systems, such as telecommunications techniques and network design, methods of industrial operations research, mathematical programming, information retrieval systems techniques, advanced programming methods, and others.

- Reviews proposed applications development plans, evaluates system design approaches, conducts hardware-software comparative evaluations, and may be a general trouble-shooter.
- May act as general consultant in studying and recommending action on a wide variety of EDP areas, such as project management controls and organization, data center procedures and methods, project time and cost estimates, economic evaluations, performance audits and others.

DUTIES AND RESPONSIBILITIES

A Systems Consultant works under the direction of a Project Manager or, in some cases, a Group Leader. His responsibilities are, to a great extent, determined by the nature of the job that has been assigned to him. In general he is usually expected to maintain a high degree of proficiency in at least one specialty area and to expose himself reasonably well to other advanced systems and programming state-of-the-art developments.

In some cases the Systems Consultant will be called upon to participate in, or even spear-head, development work in a narrowly defined area that requires exceptional creativity or innovation. At other times, he may work a broader spectrum that includes application system design reviews, economic appraisals, time and cost estimating, work planning, hardware-software comparative analysis, and project administration problems.

ORGANIZATIONAL RELATIONSHIPS

- *Reports to:* Project Manager or Group Leader (functionally) or to functional department manager such as Manager of Systems Analysis.
- *Manages:* On rare occasions, members of the technical staff—otherwise no one.

JOB TITLE

Senior Programmer/Analyst

ALTERNATE TITLES

Senior Project Engineer, Lead Programmer/Analyst, Project Analyst

SUMMARY

- Responsible for analyzing job requirements, preparing specifications, evaluating hardware-software, and preparing time and cost estimates for systems development work. *May* function as a programmer and participates in programming activities in certain stages of the project.
- Designs systems and *may* oversee the efforts of a small group of junior staff members on application development work. Carries out technical reviews of systems as designated by installation management and may act as a trouble-shooter for a variety of systems problems.
- May be assigned as totally responsible for a small project, or for a sub-system in a some-what larger project. Considered to be a member of the technical staff on a large project with heavy technical emphasis.

DUTIES AND RESPONSIBILITIES

A Senior Programmer/Analyst is the mainstay of a computer development project in that he carries most of the first-line, analytical and technical responsibility for the majority of project phases. He has to keep up to date on technological developments in systems and programming.

A technical expert, he is expected to keep detailed design considerations in focus and to counsel and develop less experienced members of the technical staff. As advanced diagnosticians, Senior Programmer/Analysts spend part of their time solving other people's tough technical problems in connection with systems design and programming. They participate and often play a major role in nearly all important project and sub-system considerations, evaluations, etc.

Senior Programmer/Analysts are called upon to program, not only to stay on top of the techniques, but also to tackle complex or tricky programs, e.g., trying a new language, time dependent programs for scanners and telecommunications, modifications to software, others.

ORGANIZATIONAL RELATIONSHIPS

- *Reports to:* Project Manager or Group Leader (functionally) or to functional department manager such as Manager of Systems and Programming.
- *Manages:* Functional supervision, guidance, or on-the-job training responsibility (depending on particular set of circumstance at the installation) for Programmer/Analysts, Associate Programmers, Programmer Assistants.

APPENDIX B

- **Pre-Installation Checklist**
- **Specimen Activities for Critical Path Method**
- **Physical Planning Considerations**
- **Fraud Control Checklist**

Pre-installation checklist

I. ORGANIZE THE EDP DEPARTMENT

    A. Establish top management advisory board

    B. Appoint managers

        1. Data processing

        2. Systems analysis

        3. Programming

        4. Operations

        5. Data control

        6. Project leaders

    C. Select systems analysts and programmers

    D. Design organization chart

II. EDUCATIONAL REQUIREMENTS

    A. Develop timetable for courses

262

        1. Executive and advisory board orientation
        2. Seminars for department heads
        3. Systems analysts and programmer courses
        4. Equipment operators
    B. Obtain appropriate instructional materials, texts, and manuals

III. APPLICATION SELECTION AND GENERAL SYSTEMS DESIGN

    A. Establish preliminary schedule of events
    B. Decide on applications by phase and assign priorities
    C. Define the problem and application requirements
        1. Analyze source information and conduct interviews
        2. Determine report requirements
        3. Layout master files
        4. Develop timetables for due-in and due-out reports and data
        5. Review existing operations and manpower for possible changes
        6. Arrive at personnel requirements for department using new system
    D. Prepare general application flow charts
    E. Review changes to existing system and get agreement to modifications
    F. Determine general plan for implementation
        1. Detailed systems design completion target dates
        2. Programming target completion dates
    G. Design computer configuration required
    H. Plan visits to other EDP installations

IV. DETAILED SYSTEMS DESIGN AND PROGRAMMING

    A. Prepare detailed application flow charts
    B. Develop forms designs
    C. Conduct application review with interested parties
    D. Freeze specifications
    E. Prepare programmer portfolio for each program in application
        1. Description of program
        2. Input and output layouts
        3. Logic and processing requirements
    F. Establish basic programming and documentation standards
        1. Symbols for flow charts and block diagrams
        2. Labeling conventions for programs
    G. Decide and specify languages, input/output control system, and operating system to be used.
    H. Assign programming work
        1. Detailed block diagram
        2. Logic Reviews
        3. Coding
        4. Set-up job control cards for operating system
        5. Testing and revision
    I. Design run controls
        1. Audit trail diagram
        2. Halt system and console messages standardized and documented
        3. Define control procedures
        4. Develop operating log
    J. Define assembly and compilation procedures
    K. Set up run and file numbering schemes

L. Plan tape and disk backup, retention system
M. Appoint specialists for sort, merge, utility programs, and operating system
N. Review and finalize equipment specifications and supplies requirements
O. Prepare programming and testing progress chart
P. Review savings and cost analysis
Q. Review detailed pre-installation preliminary schedule of events and make adjustments
R. Verify program test results

V. PHYSICAL PLANNING AND SITE PREPARATION

A. Prepare physical planning progress chart
B. Determine space requirements
C. Determine power and air conditioning requirements
D. Design machine room
E. Determine cable requirements
F. Plan floor layout
G. Plan for room construction
H. Obtain contractor
I. Review physical plans with the EDP equipment manufacturer

VI. TEST SESSION PREPARATION AND PROCEDURES

A. Establish test procedures
B. Book test time on test computer
C. Enforce desk checking practices
D. Prepare and check control cards, etc.
E. Test data preparation
F. Maintain utility program decks

VII. ESTABLISHMENT OF CONVERSION PROCEDURES

A. Establish installation time schedule
B. Analyze equipment and personnel requirements
C. Finalize equipment and personnel requirements
D. Establish procedures and controls for:
    1. Auxiliary operations
    2. Library operations
    3. Console operations
    4. Machine room operations
E. Set up data conversion system and procedures

VIII. SECURE FIRM COMMITMENT ON SYSTEM DELIVERY DATE

IX. MACHINE ROOM LAYOUT FINALIZED AND CABLE ORDER APPROVAL

X. SELECTION AND TRAINING OF OPERATING PERSONNEL

A. The following personnel must be selected:
    1. Console operators
    2. Auxiliary equipment operators
    3. Librarian
    4. Clerks
    5. Others
B. Provide training for all operating personnel
C. Prepare console operator's checksheet
D. Establish emergency procedures and teach to operators

XI. APPLICATION PROGRAMS TESTED INDIVIDUALLY AND READY FOR PARALLEL OR PILOT RUNS

    A. Schedule conversion operations
    B. Place physical labels on tapes, disks, etc.
    C. Complete tape and disk initialization
    D. Perform board wiring
    E. Finalize sorts, merges
    F. Prepare final run books
    G. Confirm system compatibility and workability
    H. Integrate parallel or pilot operations
    I. Prepare audit control sheets

Specimen activities for critical path method[1]

APPOINT MANAGERS

EDP manager
Programming supervisor
Operations supervisor
Phys. plan manager
Staff services manager

TRAIN PROGRAMMERS

Assess number required
Advertise
Aptitude test
Interview
Select
Wait for them to come
Company training
IBM course booking
Wait for IBM course
IBM training
Do simple program
Obtain manuals
Obtain coding sheets

TRAIN OPERATORS

Assess number required
Advertise
Interview
Select
Wait for them to come
Company training
Practical work
Write operators' rules
Print rules
Design operating forms
Print forms
Draft operating schedule
Approve schedule
Publish schedule

TRAIN SUPPORT GROUP

Assess number required
Advertise
Interview
Select
Wait for them to come
Company training
Practical work
Write support manual
Print manual
Design forms
Print forms

PUNCH/VERIFIER OPERATORS

Assess number required
Advertise
Aptitude test
Interview
Select
Wait for them to come
Arrange IBM training
Wait for training
IBM training
Practical work
Practice on punching forms

ORDER EDP HARDWARE

Write order
Check RSDP will not delay
Confirm configuration
Check loading
Check daily schedule
Confirm order
Enter frozen zone
Arrange transport
Wait for data processor
Install

---

[1]Reprinted by permission from *Management Planning Guide for a Manual of Data Processing Standards.* © by International Business Machines Corporation.

Customer takeover

IBM CUSTOMER ENGINEER

Discuss requirement
IBM train engineer

AUXILIARY MACHINES

Assess keypunch
Assess sorting
Assess collating
Assess interpreting
Assess tabulating
Assess bursting
Assess dispatching
Choose machines
Order machines
Wait for machines
Check machines ready
Arrange maintainance

STATIONERY & FORMS

Decide standard sizes
Design stationery
Choose supplier
Order
Wait for stationery
Check arrival

CONSOLE PRINTER

Assess requirement
Check size
Choose supplier
Order
Wait
Check arrival

OPERATORS SUNDRIES

Order panels
Order panel masks
Order wires
Order wiring tools
Order carriage tapes
Order carriage tape punch

TESTING

Locate test machine
Book time
Wait for test
Testing
Design test forms
Print
Design halt report
Print

BUILDING

Select building or site
Management approval
Planning permission

MACHINE CONFIGURATION

Assess final configuration
Assess takeover configuration

IBM PHYSICAL PLANNING

Contact IBM Phys. Planner
Wait for him to come
Draw up plans
Approve plans
Management approve
Assess electrical requirement
Assess air conditioning
Assess floor loading
Assess accessibility
    — passages
    — lifts
    — scaffold
Building
Structural alterations
Floor loading
Raised floor
Partitions
Air conditioning   Design
Water supply   Approve
Sound proofng   Choose
Adequate electrical supply   contractor
    — reliability   Organize
    — stabilizers   work
    — converter   Wait for start
    — transformer   Start work
    — earth wire   Check
Temp. and humidity recorders   progress
Fire protection
Telephones
Furniture and trollies
Tape racking
Stationery racking

ORGANIZE PROGRAMMING

Decide applications
Assign priorities
Decide target dates
Rough plan for application
Decide programs required
Assign jobs to programmers
Prepare job specifications
Approve

Freeze job specifications
Decide programming standards
Choose programming languages
Assess additional training
Book training
Wait for training
Training
Simple problem
Appoint specialists
   Testing
   Utilities
   Sort and Merge
   IOCS and oper. sys.
Set up tape and DASD format register
Set up card format register
Set up program no. register
Obtain writeups
Obtain program decks

MASTER FILES

Design layouts
Assess volumes
Register layouts
Assess programs required
Assign programmers
Define programs etc. (normal program list)
Design, create master forms
Approve
Print
Check arrival
Fill in forms
Trial punching
Trial with program
Prelist
Check output
Create master files
Check correct
Design update forms
Print
Start using update procedure
Trial punching

Trial with program
Check output
Update master

CONVERSION PROBLEMS

Assess compatibility for parallel running
Assess programs required
Organize programming
Check data
Start conversion programs

MANAGEMENT INFORMATION

Arrange appreciation course
Book course
Wait for course
Attend course
Arrange visit to other installations
Article in house magazine
Management inform staff
Assess new job requirements
Assess changes to jobs
Change documentation
Print documentation

RELATIONS WITH AUDITORS

Initial meeting
Approve method of approach
Approve plan for application
Approve controls
Prepare test packs
Approve test packs
Check output

PARALLEL RUNNING ON TEST MACHINE

Select staff
Set up group
Train
Check ready
Check current work up to date
Program compatibility test
Parallel run
Check output

Physical planning considerations[2]

	Higher-Level Management	Systems Analysts	Electronics Engineer	Air Conditioning Engineer	Architect	Electrical Engineer	Building Maintenance	Power Company Engineer	Computer Manufacturer Representative	Punched Card Supervisor
Location of computer, general	X	X			X		X			
Allocation of space, changeover problem	X	X					X			
Floor loading		X			X		X		X	
Getting equipment into building		X					X		X	
Floor area		X			X		X			
Volume of room		X		X	X		X			
Air conditioning										
Location of temperature and humidity controls			X	X			X		X	
Air inputs and outlets			X	X	X		X		X	
Which areas to air condition	X	X		X	X					
Fire protection	X	X	X	X	X	X	X	X	X	
Equipment layout		X	X	X					X	
Layout of cable trenches		X			X	X	X		X	
Determining cable lengths		X	X						X	
Voltage variations		X				X	X	X	X	
Vibration, location to reduce	X	X	X		X		X		X	
Dust in computer room			X	X					X	
Floor material					X				X	
Future expansion of equipment	X	X	X	X	X	X	X	X	X	
Possible shifting of equipment		X	X	X	X		X		X	
Location of personnel, general	X	X			X		X			
Programmers and systems analysts		X			X		X			
Operators		X			X		X			
Supervisor of installation		X			X		X			
Secretary-receptionist		X			X		X			
Maintenance		X			X		X		X	
Location of tape storage vault	X	X		X	X		X		X	
Location of temporary tape storage	X	X		X	X		X		X	
Location of maintenance area	X	X			X		X		X	
Location of punched card equipment	X	X								X
Location of punched card storage	X	X			X		X			X
Location of paper storage, for printer	X	X			X		X			X
Location of transaction recorders	X	X					X			
Location of typewriters	X	X								

[2]Canning, Richard G., *Installing Electronic Data Processing Systems* (New York: John Wiley & Sons, Inc., 1957), 193 pp.

CHECKLIST OF CONTROLS TO MAKE IT DIFFICULT TO COMMIT FRAUD WITH THE HELP OF THE COMPUTER

1. Changes in master memory records such as payroll, inventory, and control accounts should be handled by personnel other than those doing the day-to-day transactions. For example, information regarding personnel joining or leaving the company should be transmitted by personnel department representatives rather than a foreman or timekeeper.

2. Changes to master records, where possible, should be made on a serially prenumbered, registered-at-the-point-of-issue document, and again recorded at the data processing department, including necessary authorization for the change and proper check for such authorization.

3. Personnel checking and recording receipt and distribution of input, output, and moves between program and machine steps, should work independently of computer operating personnel. Furthermore, computer programming personnel should have nothing to do with the operation of the computer, except for strictly controlled time to debug and test programs.

4. Master records in data processing should be controlled by suitable batch totals, so that control accounts are maintained independently of the computer for each type of master data. For instance, in payroll, control accounts should be maintained for each type of deduction.

5. Clear records should be kept of file maintenance updating, if possible, notifying point of issue to confirm updating, keeping the original notifications on file in data processing to back up all changes made.

6. There should be a periodic printout of master data for checking source data.

7. The control group in data processing should have records of movement of data as follows:

   a. Receipt from source
   b. Issued to operations (computer)
   c. Returned from operations (computer)
   d. Returned to source
   e. Output records and reports received from operations (computer)
   f. Distribution of output records and reports.

8. The records control group in data processing should have input controls as follows:

   a. Document count
   b. Control totals for hours, rates, dollars, units, quantities, serial numbers etc.
   c. Batch controls, including document counts and control totals
   d. Batch summary controls, daily or weekly or other cycle
   e. System summary totals, to control variety of document batches involving total system such as a payroll, for instance.

9. The records control group in data processing should have output controls:

   a. Columnar totals
   b. Hash totals, like totals of the order numbers in a batch, to determine that data is included
   c. Record counts corresponding to the number of records involved in a transaction or an account balance, or total system balance
   d. Cross footings to check columnar totals
   e. Limit checks, causing computer to reject listings of any data not within programmed limits
   f. Check points during processing to provide means of locating errors quickly, or making it unnecessary to rerun an entire program when an error is discovered

g. Zero balance, to prove accuracy of computations within a known total

h. Parity check. A method manufactured into the computer to assign an identification "bit" or mark by the computer to compare to preceding item of information to make sure that proper sequence of data is maintained.

10. There should be pre-authorization of all computer usage (especially overtime), including operating instructions, programs to be used, tape reference files to be drawn from library, and planned start and stop time of run.

11. Computer operators should maintain operating logs, including estimate vs actual run time, and explanation of stoppage or interruption of run.

12. No operator should be allowed to enter the computer room and operate the computer alone. A second operator should be present and both should initial the operating log.

13. A register of errors should be maintained, including computer printout of error, action taken, and record of manual intervention. If possible, a printout record of all manual intervention.

14. Control totals should be checked by control staff, not by operators. For double check have the computer build up and check its own controls against input data. No output should leave data processing without passing through the records control group.

15. Magnetic tapes should be in a library, with someone official responsible.

a. Maintain a written record of each tape reel with history of its use, including contents, periodic updating, run numbers, number of passes. Of course, this should include the reference label and other information which positively identifies the reel

b. Link tape usage with pre-authorization of computer usage, so no tape can be issued without proper pre-authorization

c. Planning and programming staffs should not have access to any tapes used for processing. If necessary, copies may be provided but never let them use the original

d. Use a trailer label with control totals of major items on the tape updated during processing. Records control group should maintain similar controls for comparison

e. Do not allow any reference tape, or master tape, to be overwritten during an amending or updating process. A new tape, up-dated, should be written, the old tape becoming the sire, the new the son, and so on, maintaining a generation identification

f. For master tapes of unusual importance, like a customer list, keep the supporting documents, and a copy of the tape in a different location for security.

16. Programs should include: (1) a register of all changes, showing dates, reference to specific program and cross reference to other programs which might be affected by the change. (2) No changes or new programs should be allowed in actual operation until they have been tested and properly authorized by the head of the data processing department.

---

[3]Reprinted from *Modern Office Procedures* (September 1968), © 1968 by Industrial Publishing Company, Division of Pittway Corporation.

Fraud control checklist[3]

INDEX